Created by Lee Carroll Wentker

The Dividend Times, LLC
ISBN-13: 978-0692523056
ISBN-10: 0692523057

Table of Contents

In loving memory of my father Lawrence Wentker and my brother, Lawrence Christopher Wentker; I wish they were here to see this. I know they would be proud.

I would also like to dedicate this book to my mother, Jeanne Wentker, for being my mom. My brother, Jason Keith Wentker, for not laughing at me when I told him I was writing a book and to my special lady, Carol Linda Leipzig, who has cheered me along and willingly sacrificed so much of our little "we time" we have together.

I Love You All!

Disclaimer

I'm really excited to bring you this new twist on an old approach to securities investing. Quite honestly, with all the investment advice floating around out there, I was quite surprised to discover that a method similar to mine wasn't already available.

Before you start exploring this new and exciting investment technique, I have to give you the customary, *"Use at your own risk. This technique utilizes leverage. Although the use of leverage can greatly increase your returns they can have the opposite effect if you are on the losing end of an investment. Author is not responsible for any losses incurred using the techniques outlined in this book or any add-ons associated with this product. We are merely introducing an investment technique that works in conjunction with your own tolerance for picking investments and in no way, shape, or form offer any financial advice in which investments you should invest in nor how you should invest in them."*

I am a "buy and hold" advocate, however, for the purpose of this book, and since I am presenting snap shots of time regarding particular securities, I may use "buy and sell" terminology to put emphasis on the returns you may notice when the "Divi-X" System strategy is used.

About The Author

First off, I am not an author. A little background about me and what qualifies me to write this book. I won't bore you with the mundane, such as, where I was born, or my humble beginnings. Instead, I thought I would jump ahead a few years to what makes my experience relevant and save all that other stuff for another book.

I started my first business on a shoestring budget when I was twenty years old, back in 1990. It was a television and VCR sales and repair business that quickly expanded into air conditioners, microwaves, camcorders, fax machines (a device that transmitted images through phone lines for those of you too young to remember) and basically anything else that was profitable at the time. Long story short, after three years and three locations, my business partners and I parted ways after differences of opinion on the company's long-term prospects.

After leaving the sales and repair business, I went to work for a major national bank for several years while looking for my next foray into entrepreneurship. I had been putting money in the market since I was sixteen years old (mostly mutual funds), but now, I started giving a long hard look at investing for a living. Having always been fascinated with the subject and having a rudimentary knowledge of it to the extent that I was confident in picking my own mutual funds, I was seriously determined to know the ins and outs of it. So much so, that there came a realization that I was suffering from analysis paralysis; the act of planning so much that the right time to move almost never came.

Growing depressed and disgusted with myself over my own inability to act while working at a very good paying job that I had absolutely no interest in, I finally threw caution to the wind and decided then and there to purchase the next piece of real estate that I find that made good sense to me on paper. It was a mere few days later that I found myself putting a down payment on a duplex that was fully occupied in a low income neighborhood. Over the years, that investment became quite an adventure for all the wrong reasons. High turnover, theft, vandalism, horrible tenants... basically every horror story you have ever heard about being a landlord, this property was where all the stories originated. I do, however, have to take part of the blame for that. As my investment career progressed, this property received less and less of my attention.

Nonetheless, despite all the negative aspects surrounding that wild ride, it provided the catalyst that proved more valuable than the property several times over. It gave me the confidence to go out and make my next deal, then another and yet another which became more and more successful than the last. However, that wasn't enough for me. My goal from the beginning was to become a successful investor, not a successful landlord so I had to expand outside of my comfort zone once again. I knew the big, potential returns were in business so that's where I aimed my sites next.

Now before you remind me that I had already owned a VCR Repair business when I was twenty, I want to point out to you that there is a huge difference between investing blood, sweat and tears to build your baby; and taking an unemotional, objective look at a business model and building that out. At least it was for me. The most notable is your level of commitment. I micro-managed every little detail of that business. If something didn't go right, I took it personally. Everything had to be done exactly a certain way, mine. Twelve to eighteen hour days were the norm, not the exception. Did I mention I had business partners? What a pain! To this day, I have nothing but fond feelings for them, but we just had different goals.

Investing in a business model is quite different; if you can keep your ego out of it, of course. You don't have to reinvent the wheel with an investment model. You just have to make sure a, b, and c gets done. Then repeat it, over and over. Taking emotion out of the equation allows you to a.) not fall in love with a bad idea, b.) play it strictly by the numbers and c.) get out of dodge when the numbers don't add up before you lose too much.

After evaluating several businesses that were up for sale, I concluded that I would get a little more familiar with the Vending Business. I saw an ad by a private owner for three locations for sale and felt it was the perfect opportunity to learn the business on a small scale, with a minimum investment of time and money, and learn at my own pace. Once I felt competent enough, I started looking for my next acquisition, which didn't take long. I found a business owner with thirty-six locations who was forced to sell under the terms of his pending divorce.

The business took on a life of its own almost immediately. I eventually made one more large acquisition and several smaller acquisitions, all while marketing my existing business and still maintaining my rental properties. It wasn't long before I had over a hundred locations, and it wasn't long after that, I started losing interest in the business. I sold off several locations to people who were where I started a few years earlier. Soon after that, the economy tanked, I got divorced, and my mother came down with dementia. That pretty much decided for me, what I would do with the business next. And here we are.

Introduction

What You Want To Know Up Front

This is not a crash course or an advanced course on securities investment or the use of margin. This book assumes you already have a sufficient knowledge that gives you the confidence to pick and manage your own portfolio, even if it is only a handful of mutual funds. The Dividend Times or the "Divi-X" system is a powerful tool to aid you in capitalizing on what you already know.

The Dividend Times offers you the simple option of very little involvement or if you are a very hands-on type of person, like me, you will definitely want to take advantage of all the information provided to you in this book which can greatly enhance your potential returns over the long-term.

By the time you complete this book, and unlike a lot of the other books out there that require you to buy this or attend that; you will have all the information needed to implement the strategies outlined in this book with no further interaction from me. In the back of the book, there are easy to use forms to help you along as well as a free offer and a discounted offer to make use of this system even easier. Even though the concept of this method is very simple and straightforward, repeating the process over and over can be quite cumbersome. So, as promised, no further assistance will be required from me after you have learned the techniques in this book but for simplification reasons alone, it would be well worth it to look at the paired materials that marry to it and the special offers available to you just for purchasing this book.

'The Dividend Times' system (from here on out to be referred to as the "Divi-X" system) that I developed is so simple I could have written the entire concept in one chapter; but that by itself would probably not be that impressive and wouldn't show you the true value of this system. All of the pages in this book are meant to examine, support, and show you the tremendous possibilities that the "Divi-X" system has.

You will be shown a lot of charts. So many, I may be accused of putting them in just to fill pages. I urge you to use them. These charts will show you the behavior of securities in many different scenarios. I promise they have a lot to offer.

To be completely honest with you, I had serious reservations about even publishing and marketing the "Divi-X" System Workbook for fear of being ridiculed by industry experts because of the systems simplicity. The workbook itself, I was going to finish, if only for my own use, but I kept plugging away at the book, determined to put it out there for one very simple reason. I kept replaying in my mind the possibilities if I had something like this when I started putting my money into the market. I started investing when I was sixteen years old. Had I come across a system like this when I was younger, I would have felt like I had found the holy grail of investing and scared at the same time, praying that I would use the system wisely.

When I got started in the market, and now that I think about it, even today, the prevailing wisdom was to work your butt off and sock away ten percent of your income for the long-term. Don't get me wrong, that's great advice and I would recommend it to anybody but I'm just too curious to leave it at that. From there, the natural progression is to answer "what do I invest my ten percent into?"

I don't want to get off topic here. This book isn't meant to answer that question for you. I did have some modest success in where I did invest my ten percent. It provided me the seed money to invest in things outside of the securities market. If I had a system like this when I got started, I can only imagine the possibilities. I could have quit my corporate job sooner. Maybe I could've gotten an earlier start in my real estate investments or taken my business further, faster? Or maybe even a different path altogether. Maybe, in some way, it could possibly do the same for you. Good luck, good learning, and may all of your investments take off like a rocket.

Before we get started, I cannot stress enough, that even though the content of this book goes into great detail of the ins and outs of 'The "Divi-X" System,' I want you to keep in mind that this system is unbelievably simple. To offer an analogy, there is plenty of material for those that like to work on their car but the system is designed for those who just like to drive it.

THE MAJOR UNDERLYING, AND MOST SIGNIFICANT, PRINCIPAL BEHIND THE "DIVI-X" SYSTEM IS TO EARN INCOME WHILE YOUR INVESTMENTS PAY FOR THEMSELVES. TO MAXIMIZE YIELD ON YOUR INVESTMENT DOLLARS REGARDLESS OF THE DIRECTION OF THE MARKET AND HOPEFULLY, IN THE LONG-TERM, WALK AWAY WITH A NICE PROFIT WHEN YOU CASH OUT.

Other Than Share Price and Dividend History, All Data in This Book Has Been Compiled Exclusively by:

'The "Divi-X" System Workbook.'

Chapter 1
Introducing "The Dividend Times"
aka The "Divi-X" System

What Exactly Is the "Divi-X" System?

There are numerous books out there that tout their "set it and forget it" dividend investment method and I'm not here to dispute any of them; but "The Dividend Times" or the "Divi-X" system is the ultimate "set it and forget it" investment system that actually helps you pay for your investments. While there truly is no such thing as "set it and forget it" in the investment world, I guess it would be more accurate to say that the "Divi-X" system is any other conventional dividend investment method, times'd. Is that even a word? According to my word processor's "add to dictionary" feature it is.

The "Divi-X" System is a method that incorporates the use of leverage and dividends designed to amplify returns on investment securities that you would otherwise not benefit from if you were to use cash only. This is not a "winning stock-picking strategy" guide and learning the system counts on you knowing the difference between a good investment and a bad one. Or at the very least, know when you're in a good one or a bad one.

If you are a bit hazy on the subject, I suggest you prepare yourself more before attempting the use of leverage. There is a wealth of information out there to aid you in learning more about investment fundamentals. If you do not know where to begin, go to www.Amazon.com and begin searching the term "Warren Buffett fundamentals." This would be a good place to start.

Whether you use just the techniques outlined in this book, or if you opt to take advantage of the power and ease of the "Divi-X" System Workbook (a sister companion to this book), I think you'll find the results very appetizing if your stock picks don't cry foul.

Who Would Benefit From This System?

The obvious answer is everyone, but not everyone feels comfortable with the concept of using leverage. Maybe you've never used it before or got badly burned in the past. One of the many benefits of using the "Divi-X" system is that you can start with baby steps until you build up your tolerance and comfort level. For those of you that have used leverage before or are currently utilizing a leverage strategy in your investment portfolio, you may find this as a wonderful alternative to your current method.

This system provides an effortless approach to maximizing your 'Cash Appreciation' return. Get used to the emphasis on the term 'Cash Appreciation.' We'll mention total returns from time to time, but the true goal is to maximize the actual returns on the amount of cash that comes out of your pocket.

Why I Developed This System

I'm a bit of a spreadsheet geek, so basically anything that has a unit of measure I run it through a spreadsheet. Pulling on my past experience of investing outside of the securities market, I knew that this technique had tremendous potential and at the time I wasn't even remotely thinking about developing it into a system to be marketed to anyone else.

I started punching some numbers into a spreadsheet to see how many shares I could buy using the dividends to finance my purchase. It was a convenient little tool, so I saved it for the next time I would purchase another security. The more I tinkered with it, the more I realized how much potential it had.

Like I always do, I decided that I wanted it to do more so I started asking myself questions about what mattered to me as an investor. What would happen if interest rates went up? What if I wanted to put some money in my pocket while I'm holding my stocks? How much leverage am I comfortable with? How much leverage is too much?

By the time I finished answering all of my questions, I had developed a workbook with literally thousands of equations and to this day, I'm still adding bells and whistles to enhance its usefulness.

I mentioned in the previous section how I came up with the concept of the "Divi-X" system, but it was the years of experience that I have built on over the past that allowed me to know what questions, as an investor, to ask in the first place.

I've made a decent living using leverage to acquire assets over the years; bank financing, owner financing, equity lines, etc., but I never actually took advantage of margin made available to me through my brokerage accounts. I'm sure it was always there to use, but I was so busy with my investments outside of the securities market, it never even dawned on me to use it.

Fast forward a few years later, after one of the biggest economic collapses in recent memory, I witnessed the bottom fall out of all of my real estate holdings; there were massive layoffs among many of my business clients and basically, to make a long story short, I found myself starting all over again.

Taking what few dollars I had left, I decided to focus on the stock market until I built up enough equity to invest in whatever new venture might come my way. That's actually how I got started in investing before. The reason I changed my focus to the stock market is life had dealt me a hand that restricted my time away from home and quite honestly, I wasn't quite sure I wanted to do the whole landlord/business owner thing again.

Taking the time to explore the margin option available to me through my brokerage account, I knew this would be a huge boost in getting me back on track faster (wherever that track may lead) than the first time around. I also started applying the techniques I used in other asset investing to securities investing.

Using leverage (margin and leverage will be used interchangeably throughout this book) to invest in securities is nothing new; fortunes are made and lost every day using leverage in and out of the stock market. You probably hear more horror stories than success stories which would account for a lot of reluctance of some people to use leverage. I personally love leverage. Always have and likely always will. When used properly, it is one of the most powerful wealth creation tools in the world.

Let me give you an example relating to a situation that has affected a lot of us after the recent housing bubble. It used to be the norm that if you purchased a home, the bank would require at least twenty percent down of the purchase price. That twenty percent provided the bank with a cushion should you be foreclosed on. It was a fairly cushy cushion as well. What was the likelihood that a home could lose over twenty percent of its value practically overnight? Especially, in a market where prices keep going up?

For whatever reason, and there are several books on the subject, banks started to relax their terms. You no longer needed twenty percent down. In some cases, you didn't need any money down at all. Houses were selling left and right driving prices through the roof.

It was unsustainable and eventually, the inevitable happened, the housing bubble burst. Millions (myself included) saw their property values plummet. Some (myself included) saw their property values tank in excess of over fifty percent! Millions lost their homes in foreclosure. Many, if they were lucky (if you can even call it luck), were able to reach an agreement with their bank and arrange a short sale. A short sale is where the lienholder agrees to release the lien so the property may be sold for less than what is owed, but doesn't necessarily release the debtor from the balance shortfall.

As the problem progressed, people stuck in these "underwater" loans just started walking away from their homes. The houses weren't worth anywhere near what was still owed on them. I couldn't recall a more depressing time in our country's history during my lifetime. I use to drive around with a partner and we would play a sad little game called, "There's a new 'Out of Business' sign." Every week, we would drive the same route and the first one to spot a new 'Out of Business' sign... well, let's just say, there were no winners.

When the banks relaxed their terms, I didn't relax mine. I continued to put twenty percent down on all of my properties. It just made good investment sense to not use one hundred percent leverage on anything (unless it could be flipped right away). Although, I wasn't exempt from the housing catastrophe, twenty percent down and years of mortgage payments allowed me to walk away with cash in my pocket when my divorce forced me to sell. Personally, I would have loved to keep those properties. The rents were still coming in. I envy the lucky buyers that bought them from me.

Leverage is a powerful tool, and just like you wouldn't use a hammer to fix everything, leverage is not a one size fits all proposition, so for your own sake, use it but use it wisely.

Cash Is "The" True King

Despite the name of this investment system, cash is the true king. The "Divi-X" System was developed by me as a self-help tool that evolved quickly. I built this system with the single goal of an investor being able to maximize their Cash Appreciation return over the long-term using leverage efficiently, conservatively, and effectively.

That does not mean that an investor with a shorter time horizon cannot benefit from the "Divi-X" System. The charts included in this book will give any investor an idea of how they could benefit from this system in the short or the long-term. As long as the security you purchased is above your purchase price when you sell, you'll automatically benefit from the "Divi-X" System. I know that sounds simplistic, after all, no one invests in a stock with hopes it will go down, unless you're a shorter, but that's not what this system is about.

Isn't Leverage Risky?

You're darn right it is! But so is investing in the stock market. So it seems you are a bit of a risk taker already. If your journey of wealth creation has taken you down a similar path to mine, I'm sure you've heard many infomercials and read several books telling you that real estate has been one of the best wealth creators of all time. I'm not here to dispute that. My real estate holdings had afforded me many a fine meal, but I couldn't have done it without leverage. Even the gurus that tout no money down; how do you think it's paid for? Leverage, of course. Like I said, I'm not here to dispute real estate as one of the best wealth creators of all time, as well as growing a business, but I don't believe either is made any more easier if not for the use of leverage. That being said, I would have to say that leverage is "the" greatest wealth creator of all time.

Why Would I Use the "Divi-X" Method of Leverage? I've Been Using Leverage for Years Without the "Divi-X" System

If you're happy with your current system, great! I'm not here to talk you into or out of anything. You may have a better system than mine but haven't written your own book about it yet. When you do write it, I'll probably buy it. I don't know everything and I am always looking for better ways. But let's face it. If you've read this far, you likely already bought the book so you might as well read it.

In the many pages that follow, you'll find that the "Divi-X" System offers a clearly calculated, easily measured, results oriented approach to maximizing your investment returns while taking a sensible approach to risk. You can be as conservative or aggressive as you are comfortable with.

The honest truth is that most of the examples you'll see in this book would have benefited you with or without the "Divi-X" system anyway, but to what extent? And, since I'm being completely honest, pertaining to the examples in this book, you may have made more money by blindly throwing borrowed money at these investments than using the cool, calculated approach offered to you by using the "Divi-X" system but hindsight makes geniuses of us all.

So, back to your original question, why would you use the "Divi-X" method of leverage? If I had written this book back in 2009, most of you wouldn't be asking that question. Some of you wouldn't even consider buying this book because the market probably just wiped out almost everything you owned and the last thing you wanted to see was anything market related. It would've certainly wiped out everything I had owned if not for the prudent use of leverage. You've heard the saying, "live by the sword; die by the sword?" It could just as easily apply to leverage as well.

Do you recall in the previous section, where I explained the use of twenty percent down on all of my properties even when not required? I acquired all of those properties with the use of, and only because of leverage. I was forced to sell those properties at the worst possible time, because of a divorce. Had I gone in all leverage on those properties, I could've easily been amongst those that had to short sell or just walk away.

If I had been all in the market back in 2009, being fully leveraged could have possibly bankrupted me. I'm sure for many, it did. Had myself and millions of others took a measured approach to using leverage in the market, exactly the type of measured approach that the "Divi-X" system provides, we all could have sat back, waited it through, maybe added to our positions using more leverage and imagine how well we would all be doing now. But... like I said, hindsight makes geniuses of us all.

Bringing you the "Divi-X" system is a very rewarding and exciting opportunity for me and hopefully, for you as well. I certainly don't want to burst my own bubble. However, just like hindsight seems to make geniuses of us all, some of us refuse to learn from history, even though it keeps repeating itself. As I'm writing this today, many respected Wall Street talking heads (that I seldom listen to) are predicting a crash as bad, or far worse than, that which happened in 2008. They're probably right. It's not unprecedented. It's happened more than once and will likely happen again. I would even go so far as to say, it's less a prediction and more like common sense. I'm going to change tones now as we move into the next chapter. I have no intention of making this a doom and gloom book.

Call from Your Broker

Real quick, I'm going to paint you a hypothetical. Mr. Smith and Mr. Jones both have a brokerage account at XYZ Securities. Mr. Smith invests using the "Div-X" system and Mr. Jones who is more an "all or nothing" type of guy, does not. The market takes a turn for the worse and both Mr. Smith and Mr. Jones get a call from their broker.

First, Mr. Jones:
> **XYZ Securities: Mr. Jones?**
> **Mr. Jones: Yes?**
> **XYZ Securities: Mr. Jones, we're sorry to inform you that your margin account has exceeded its threshold. You have to deposit more money or we'll be forced to liquidate your holdings to cover the short-fall.**

Now, Mr. Smith:
> **XYZ Securities: Mr. Jones?**
> **Mr. Smith: No, this is Mr. Smith.**
> **XYZ Securities: Sorry Mr. Smith, wrong number.**

Just a light-hearted look at a possible outcome (although, not so light-hearted for Mr. Jones). There are many scenarios using the "Divi-X" system that could also prompt a call from your broker under certain circumstances, but least likely if used responsibly.

Another very good reason for using the "Divi-X" system is accountability. A normal situation, not involving the "Divi-X" system, is to buy on margin and hope for the best. Unless you have your own system in place, there is no allocation, no accounting for interest expense or returns related to the actual margin expense. In fact, once you purchase at least two securities on margin, your interest expense and outstanding margin balance is pooled, not differentiating one investment from another. The more securities you purchase on margin, the harder it is to keep track of. We dive into this deeper in a later chapter. I think you'll be shocked at the conclusion.

The "Divi-X" system is a treasure trove of functionality and accountability. Once a position is initiated, the only input needed from you is share price updates and the seldom dividend and interest rate changes.

In the back of this book, there are user forms which are not as fun and easy to use as the full version of the "Divi-X" System Workbook, but they get the job done. Also, in the back of the book is an offer for a "Lite" version of the "Divi-X" System Workbook free to download. We'll call it, "Divi-X" Lite. It provides everything you need to make investment decisions using the "Divi-X" system but it does not offer detailed tracking as the full version does.

Also, in the back of the book, is a special offer should you decide to make the plunge and purchase the full version of the "Divi-X" System Workbook. This offer is exclusive to owners of this book.

"Divi-X" System Workbook: The "Divi-X" Systems Workbook allows you to view sixteen different investment alternatives at once using our "Multiplier Pick" feature.

Chapter 2
Dow 30: The Last Five Years

The Dow Thirty (With and Without the "Divi-X" System)

I thought we would dive right in. Following is a five year history of The Dow Industrial components. I chose the Dow 30 for two very specific reasons. One is that everyone is pretty much familiar with the stocks in the Dow 30. Reason number two is that anyone can cherry-pick stock selections to sell their latest investment technique, I won't. I'm using a broad approach and showing you both the good and the bad so you may make an informed decision on whether or not this method is right for you.

All illustrations are intended to show you actual data results using our system, "The Dividend Times" System hereinafter referred to as the "Divi-X" system, and the results of not using our system. It is important to note that all Dow components are modeled after the economy took it's turn for the worse in 2008 so most of the stocks illustrated here are higher than in 2008 and will show positive gains using our method and not using our method. Regardless, the results are impressive. IN ALL OF THE EXAMPLES BELOW, THE RETURNS INDICATED DO NOT INCLUDE REINVESTED DIVIDENDS. ALL INVESTMENTS REPRESENTED HERE AND THROUGHOUT THIS BOOK, UNLESS OTHERWISE NOTED, USE A PURCHASE OF ONE HUNDRED SHARES. THE BALANCES INDICATED IN THE CHARTS ARE RETURNS BASED ON ACTUAL CASH INVESTED, 'NOT' TOTAL SHAREHOLDER VALUE.

> ***"Divi-X" System Workbook:*** Purchasing the "Divi-X" Systems Workbook makes this whole process ridiculously simple. My workbook literally makes this as easy as one, two. You don't even need the three. In addition to the procedures outlined in this book, the workbook includes a multitude of additional info, charts and analytical information to let you know where you are and to keep you on track of your goal constantly.

The next few pages will show the five year results of every stock in the Dow that paid dividends within the period of June 2009 till May 2014 or May 2010 till April 2015 (before Apple was added and AT&T was removed).

What the Lines on the Charts Mean

Multiplier Return – the projected share price with dividends. This line does not take into account future dividend increases.

Expected Return – this is a consistent trajectory of your anticipated or expected rate of return. Throughout this book, it defaults at an annual 9% unless otherwise indicated. If you were to own 'The "Divi-X" System Workbook,' this value would be entered by you.

Actual Return or "Divi-X" Return – before actual data is entered, it is also a projection. As actual data replaces projected data, it gives you a snapshot of your total actual returns based on your actual cash investment. Share price appreciation/depreciation, dividends paid less margin interest.

Without "Divi-X" or Equal Cash Unleveraged – this is the same as "Divi-X" Return less all leveraged shares and additional dividends from leveraged shares with no margin interest since this is a pure cash scenario.

Rule of 72 – this is a feature only available in 'The "Divi-X" System Workbook.' It is only included here because it serves a useful visual aid to see how much sooner your investment doubles using the "Divi-X" system.

What the Rest Means

Yield – The dividend yield of the stock at the time of purchase.

MultiPick – An abbreviation for "Multiplier Pick" which you'll notice referenced in this book considerably.

Div Amt – The actual dividend payout per share at the time of purchase.

Freq - How often the Div Amt is paid out.

Levered – This is the amount of purchase used on margin based on factors such as, "Multiplier Pick," "PmtPerc," etc. This will all be explained later.

"PmtPerc" – This is the percentage paid every month on the outstanding margin loan that is associated with the particular investment. Normally, this is to be determined by the user.

Return $ - This is the actual dollar return from your "Cash on Cash" investment using the "Divi-X" System. In other words, the actual dollar amount that 'your' actual cash out of pocket, minus leverage and margin interest, would have returned you at the different one thru five year intervals.

Ttl Return % - This is the total 'share value' return on leverage plus cash out of pocket less margin interest. This number is not nearly as important as the '"Divi-X" Rtrn' section.

"Divi-X" Rtrn or Actual Return - This is the actual return on cash invested using the "Divi-X" system. The primary focus in this book will be to constantly compare these returns with "Without "Divi-X.""

Without "Divi-X" or Equal Cash Unleveraged – This is the return on the dollar amount that includes dividends on actual cash invested had you not used the "Divi-X" system. It differs from the **Ttl Return%** because it does not include margin interest. **Without "Divi-X"** and **Equal Cash Unleveraged** are used interchangeably.

Now, onto our first stock in the Dow:

| AXP | American Express | Purchase @ 24.64 share | Yield 2.92% |

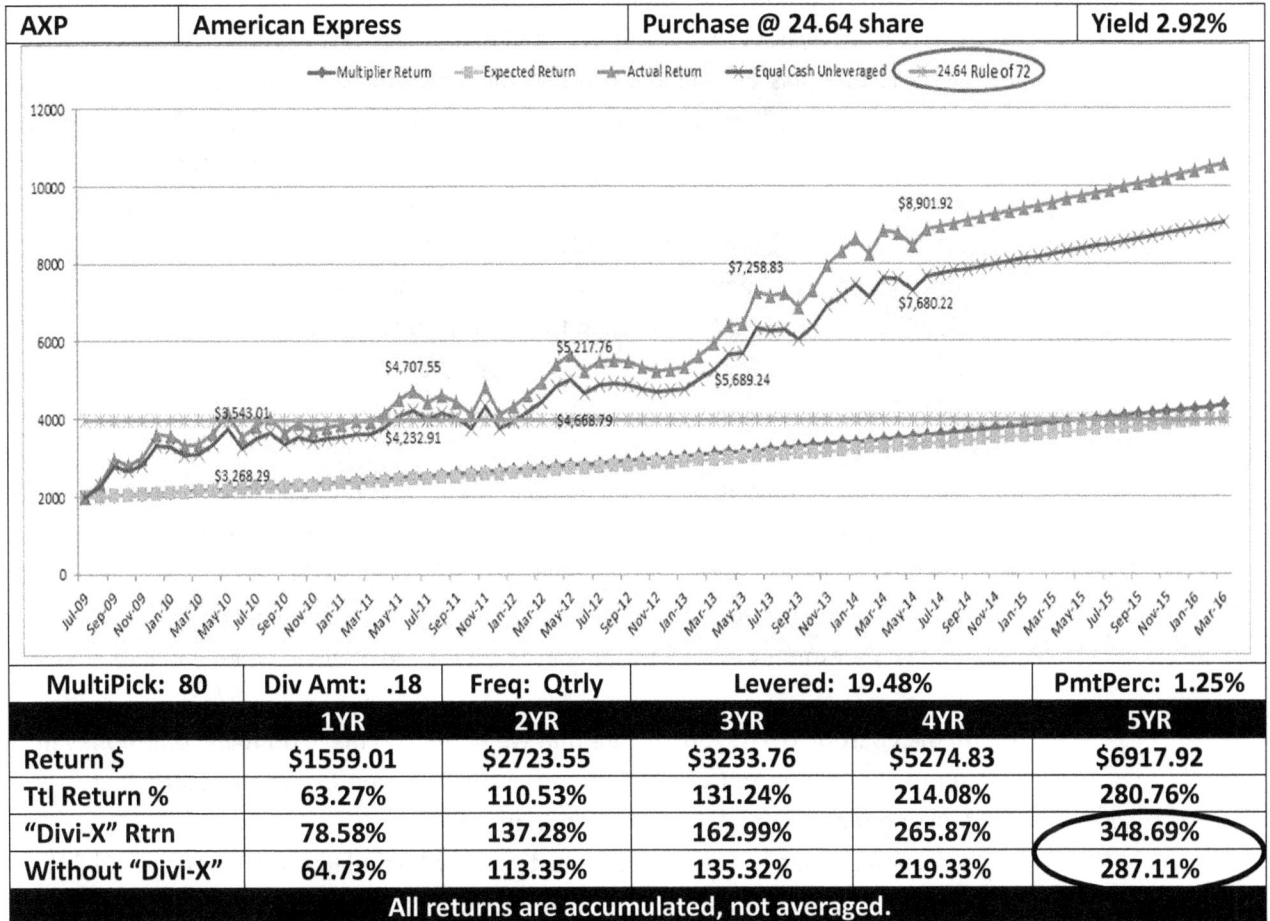

Legend: Multiplier Return — Expected Return — Actual Return — Equal Cash Unleveraged — 24.64 Rule of 72

Chart data labels: $8,901.92; $7,258.83; $7,680.22; $5,217.76; $4,707.55; $5,689.24; $3,543.01; $4,668.79; $3,268.29; $4,232.91

MultiPick: 80	Div Amt: .18	Freq: Qtrly	Levered: 19.48%		PmtPerc: 1.25%
	1YR	2YR	3YR	4YR	5YR
Return $	$1559.01	$2723.55	$3233.76	$5274.83	$6917.92
Ttl Return %	63.27%	110.53%	131.24%	214.08%	280.76%
"Divi-X" Rtrn	78.58%	137.28%	162.99%	265.87%	348.69%
Without "Divi-X"	64.73%	113.35%	135.32%	219.33%	287.11%
All returns are accumulated, not averaged.					

A few things to note about this chart:

1. Expected Return – This is an arbitrary number I entered (9% in this case). You would enter this number if you purchase the workbook. As you can see in this instance, the returns have exceeded my expectations from the very beginning.

2. Without "Divi-X" (Equal Cash Unleveraged) – This line represents the actual return you would have experienced if you purchased this stock using the "same cash amount" that you would have used in the "Divi-X" System. The "same cash amount" is in quotes because it is important to note that this is actual dollars invested by you out of your pocket that would have also been used in the "Divi-X" System, NOT the total purchase price of the stock.

   a. Using the chart above, this transaction consisted of 100 shares purchased using the "Divi-X" System. Using the same cash amount without the "Divi-X" System would have netted you only 80.52 shares.

3. Actual Return – uses the "Divi-X" System. Right away, you can see that the "Divi-X" System far outperformed my expected return rate as well as the returns generated Without "Divi-X" (Equal Cash Unleveraged).

   a. The "Divi-X" System results are net of all margin interest expenses.

   b. As more time passes, you'll notice that the difference between the Actual Return and the Without "Divi-X" (Equal Cash Unleveraged) returns widen. This difference is highly attributed to the continued increase in the stock's value, the continued decrease in the outstanding margin balance associated with this purchase (I'll explain this later), and higher dividends paid on more shares.

   c. At the end of five years, "Divi-X" System returns are an impressive $1221.70 ($8,901.92 - $7,680.22) more than the returns Without "Divi-X" (Equal Cash Unleveraged). A very pleasing 61.58% more than the returns without using the "Divi-X" system.

4. Rule of 72 –

   a. The number before 'Rule of 72' circled in the legend tells you how long it would take to double your money based on the stocks yield when you purchased it.

   b. The flat line in the chart shows you where your returns will have doubled your money. In the example above, the 'Rule of 72' in the legend indicates you would double your money in 24.64 years based on the stocks yield when you purchased it.

   c. In the chart below it, you can see that we hope to achieve doubling our money in approximately six and a half years represented by our 'Expected Return' line crossing the 'Rule of 72' line around March 2016.

   d. Also, you can see by the line representing your 'Actual Return', using the "Divi-X" System, you would have doubled your money around April 2010, about ten months after you purchased the stock; not the 24.64 years indicated by the Rule of 72.

   e. You will also notice that without using the "Divi-X" System, it would have taken you approximately **one full year later to double your money than had you used the "Divi-X" System**, indicated by the "Equal Cash Unleveraged" line.

   f. The "Rule of 72" function is included in the "Divi-X" System Workbook but you can easily calculate it on your own. The formula is:

72	divided by Yield %	= Time to double your money
72	divided by 2.92%	= 24.64 years

BA	Boeing Co.		Purchase @ 48.88 share	Yield 3.47%

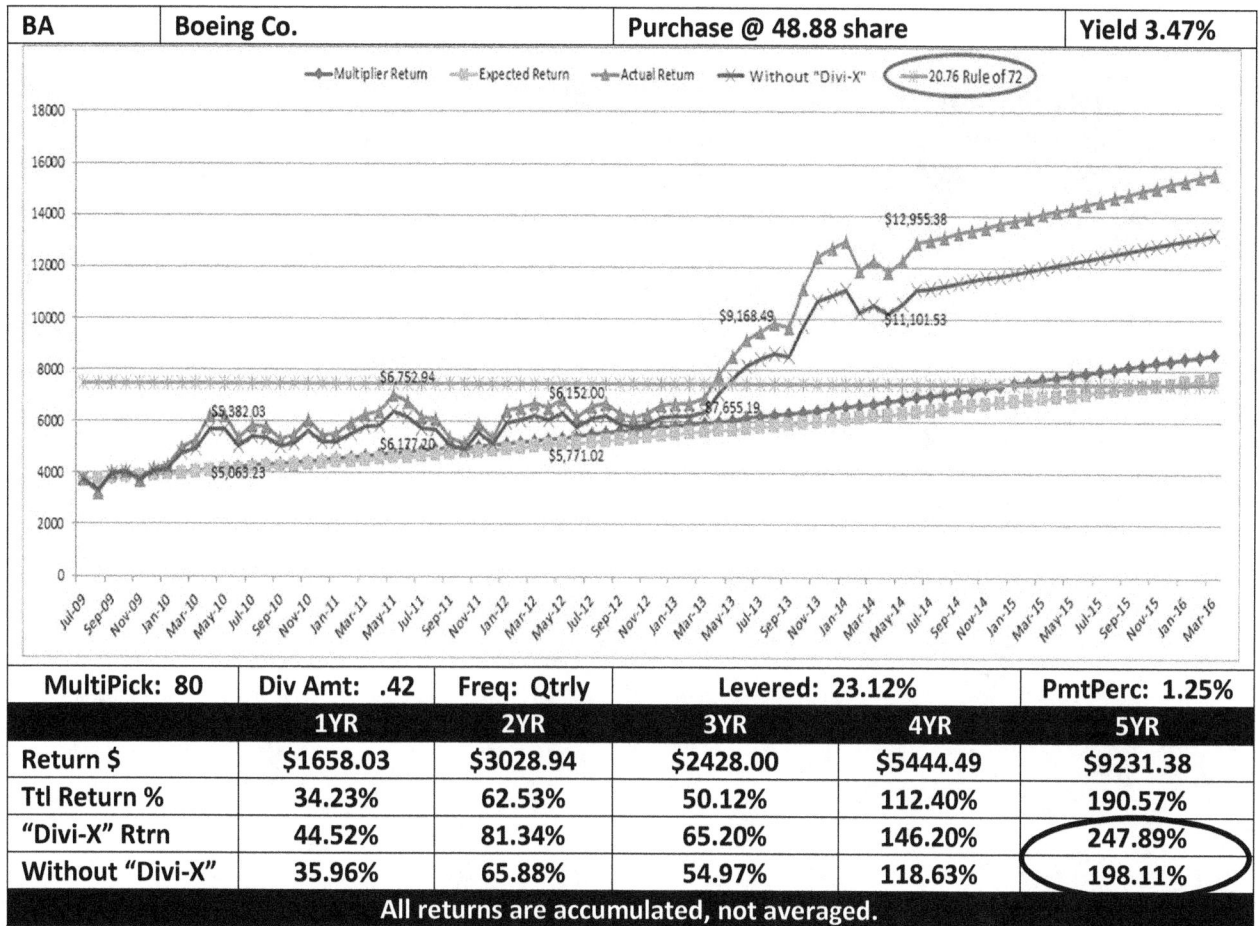

MultiPick: 80	Div Amt: .42	Freq: Qtrly	Levered: 23.12%		PmtPerc: 1.25%
	1YR	2YR	3YR	4YR	5YR
Return $	$1658.03	$3028.94	$2428.00	$5444.49	$9231.38
Ttl Return %	34.23%	62.53%	50.12%	112.40%	190.57%
"Divi-X" Rtrn	44.52%	81.34%	65.20%	146.20%	247.89%
Without "Divi-X"	35.96%	65.88%	54.97%	118.63%	198.11%
All returns are accumulated, not averaged.					

A few things to note about this chart:

1. I again used a 9% Expected Return Rate. If this were my actual expected return rate, I would have been very pleased with this stocks performance almost immediately and throughout the duration of the five year period my smile would have gotten bigger along with my returns.

2. Notice that the cash value took a modest dip immediately after the purchase date, but once it recovered, it never revisited its lows.

3. After the initial dip, notice that the "Divi-X" system (Actual) returns (except for the initial dip and Nov. '09), always surpassed my expected 9% return rate and the Without "Divi-X" rate, ever widening as more time passed.

4. Even though the stock was always in the green (except for the initial dip), it wasn't until May of 2013 when the cash value really popped. Almost a full four years after purchasing the stock.

5. The faster the growth rate, the more the "Divi-X" System will outpace Without "Divi-X".

6. And lastly, the increased return of the "Divi-X" system over the Without "Divi-X" was a very satisfying 49.78%, or $1853.85 more.

"Divi-X" System Workbook: Notice that in the unused data portion circled in the graph on the next page, that the trend lines continue to go up. In the "Divi-X" System Workbook, every time the share price rises, "Divi-X" automatically sets the bar higher. For example, when you enter a 9% expected return rate and your goal is exceeded, "Divi-X" continues to add a 9% expected return rate on top of that.

CAT	Caterpillar		Purchase @ 33.65 share		Yield 4.99%

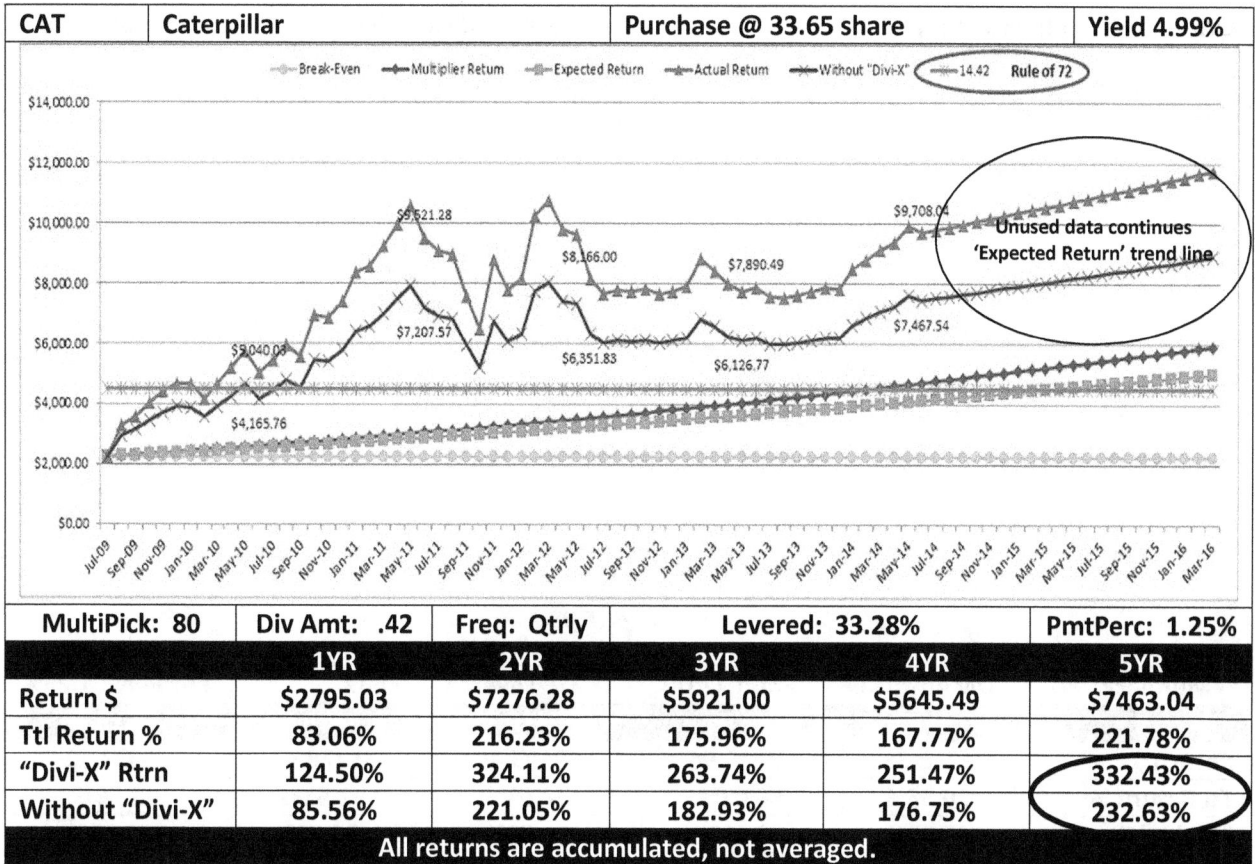

Legend: Break-Even — Multiplier Return — Expected Return — Actual Return — Without "Divi-X" — 14.42 Rule of 72

Chart values: $9,521.28 · $8,166.00 · $7,890.49 · $9,708.0 · $7,207.57 · $6,351.83 · $6,126.77 · $7,467.54 · $5,040.03 · $4,165.76

Unused data continues 'Expected Return' trend line

MultiPick: 80	Div Amt: .42	Freq: Qtrly	Levered: 33.28%		PmtPerc: 1.25%
	1YR	**2YR**	**3YR**	**4YR**	**5YR**
Return $	$2795.03	$7276.28	$5921.00	$5645.49	$7463.04
Ttl Return %	83.06%	216.23%	175.96%	167.77%	221.78%
"Divi-X" Rtrn	124.50%	324.11%	263.74%	251.47%	332.43%
Without "Divi-X"	85.56%	221.05%	182.93%	176.75%	232.63%
All returns are accumulated, not averaged.					

A few things to note about this chart:

1. I again used a 9% Expected Return Rate.
2. Reality Check: Notice that even though the "Divi-X" Systems results spiked considerably more than the Without "Divi-X" results, they also dropped further on the dips, significantly further from the period of March 2011 to around November 2011.
3. The wider the performance gap between Actual Return and Without "Divi-X", the more violent the balance swings will be on your Actual Return in the event of large price swings. That's great when the stock price is moving up. Not so great when it's going south.
4. Fortunately, all ended well and "Divi-X" System results returned a hefty 99.8% higher return than the Without "Divi-X" results did, or $2240.50 more over five years.

CSCO Cisco Systems, Inc. Paid no dividends during our time window and would not work.

CVX	Chevron Corporation	Purchase @ $68.06 Share	Yield: 4.00%

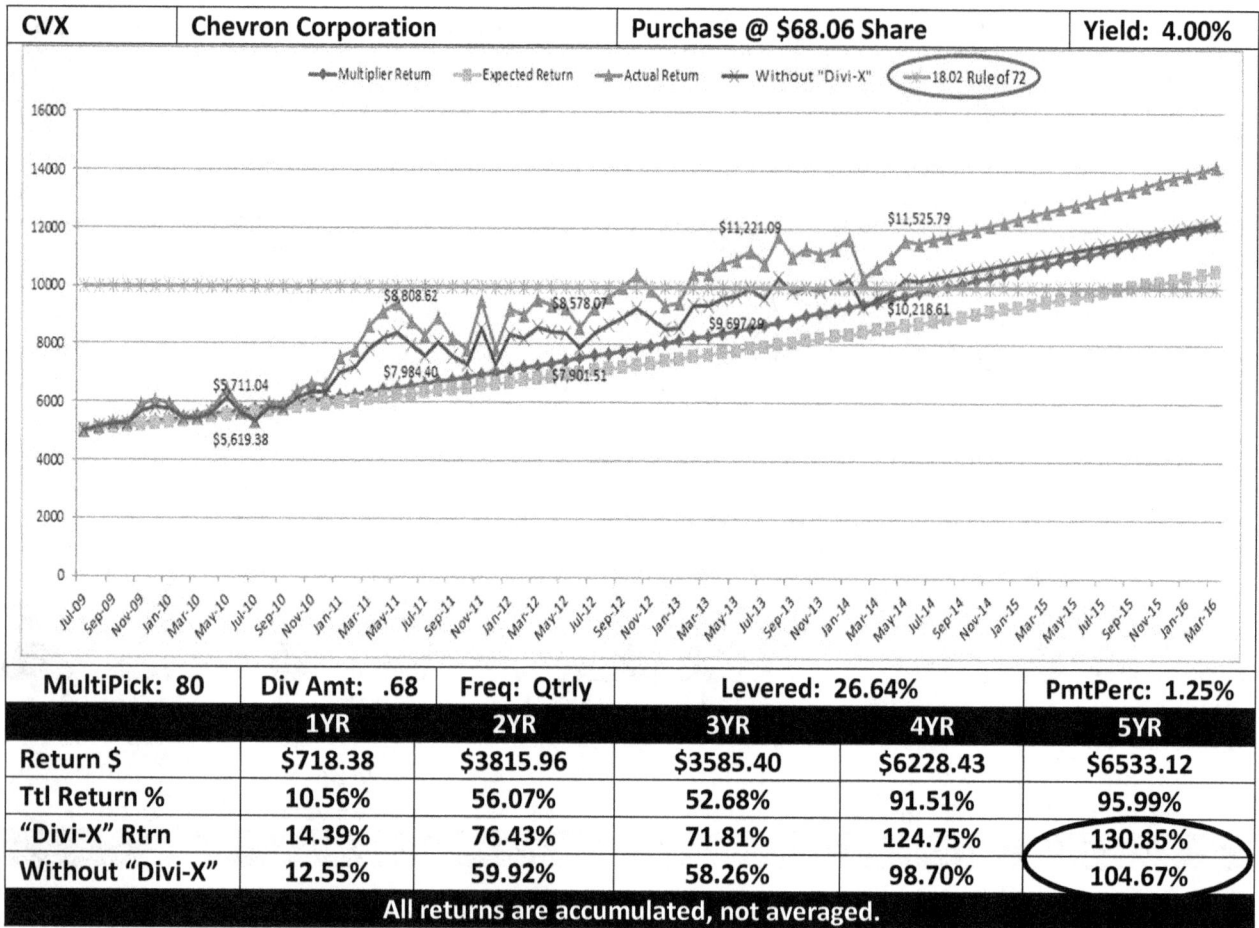

Legend: Multiplier Return, Expected Return, Actual Return, Without "Divi-X", 18.02 Rule of 72

Data labels on chart: $5,711.04, $5,619.38, $8,808.62, $7,984.40, $7,901.51, $8,578.07, $9,697.09, $11,221.09, $10,218.61, $11,525.79

MultiPick: 80	Div Amt: .68	Freq: Qtrly	Levered: 26.64%		PmtPerc: 1.25%
	1YR	**2YR**	**3YR**	**4YR**	**5YR**
Return $	$718.38	$3815.96	$3585.40	$6228.43	$6533.12
Ttl Return %	10.56%	56.07%	52.68%	91.51%	95.99%
"Divi-X" Rtrn	14.39%	76.43%	71.81%	124.75%	130.85%
Without "Divi-X"	12.55%	59.92%	58.26%	98.70%	104.67%
All returns are accumulated, not averaged.					

A few things to note about this chart:

1. I again used a 9% Expected Return Rate.
2. As mentioned earlier, but adding a little more detail now, the better performance delivered by the 'Actual Return' over the 'Without "Divi-X" Return, as will be the case in many of our examples, was the result of:
    a. Higher dividends resulting from the additional shares we purchased on leverage. In this case, 26.64 extra shares that we purchased on leverage.
        i. For future reference, since all of our examples deal with 100 share lots, the levered % listed is equal to the amount of shares purchased on leverage. If a stock is 10% levered, that's 10 shares on leverage. 20% levered, 20 shares and so on.
    b. Share price appreciation on the extra 26.64 levered shares.
    c. Less the margin interest paid on the 26.64 levered shares.
3. Using "Divi-X" would have doubled your cash investment about ten months sooner than 'Without "Divi-X."
4. "Divi-X" System outpaced Without "Divi-X" by 26.18%, or $1307.18

DD	E I Dupont De Nemours and Co	Purchase @ $24.97 share	Yield: 6.57%

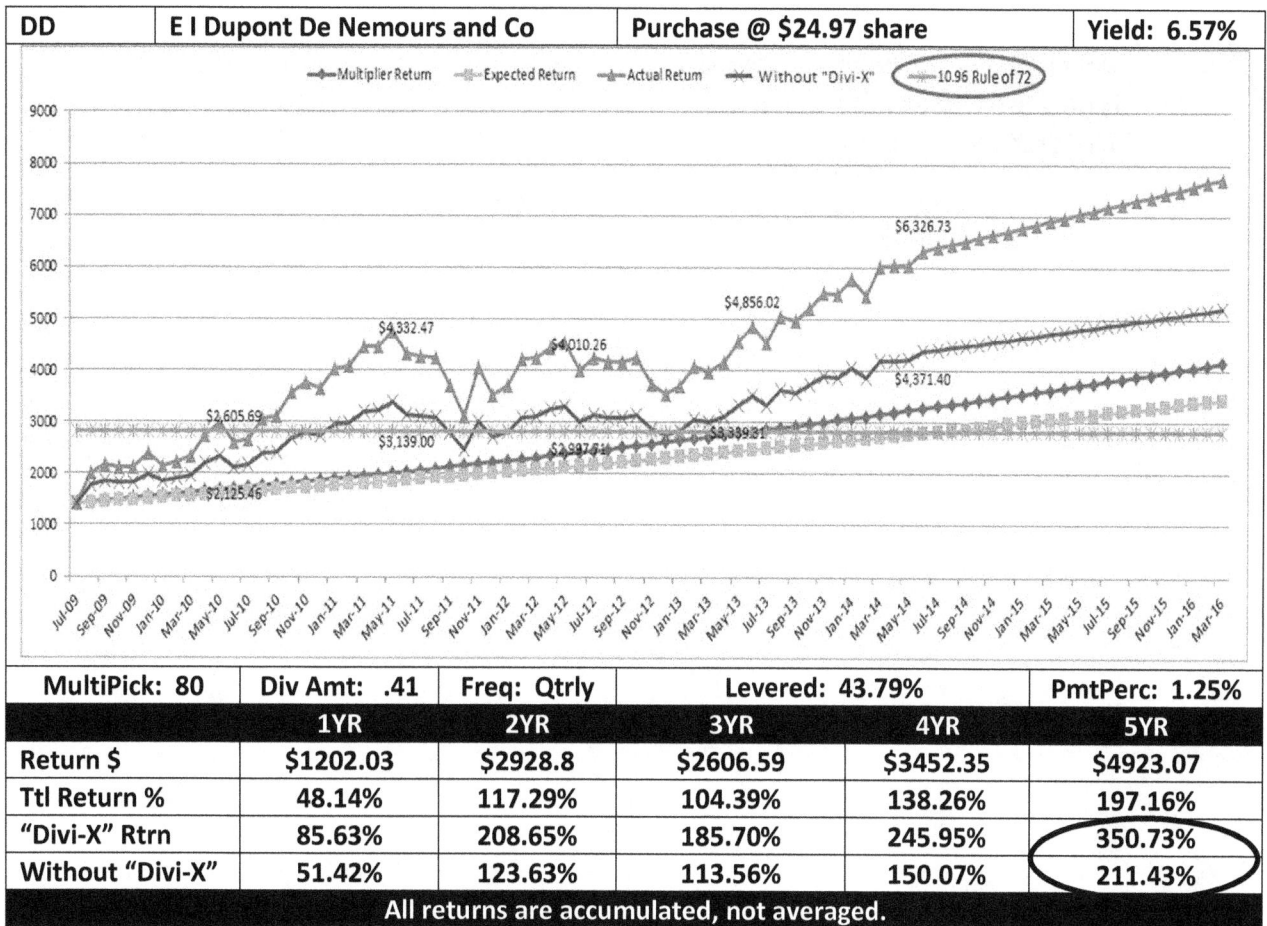

MultiPick: 80	Div Amt: .41	Freq: Qtrly	Levered: 43.79%		PmtPerc: 1.25%
	1YR	**2YR**	**3YR**	**4YR**	**5YR**
Return $	$1202.03	$2928.8	$2606.59	$3452.35	$4923.07
Ttl Return %	48.14%	117.29%	104.39%	138.26%	197.16%
"Divi-X" Rtrn	85.63%	208.65%	185.70%	245.95%	350.73%
Without "Divi-X"	51.42%	123.63%	113.56%	150.07%	211.43%
All returns are accumulated, not averaged.					

A few things to note about this chart:

1. I again used a 9% Expected Return Rate.
2. You'll notice that almost right out of the gate, the "Divi-X" System (Actual Return) was well on its way to taking a commanding lead over the Without "Divi-X" returns. Here's why:
   a. The higher dividend yield allowed us to buy considerably more shares (remember, levered at 43.79% buys an extra 43.79 shares).
   b. The smaller cash outlay enabled the appreciation on a greater number of levered shares to significantly enhance our 'Cash Appreciation' return.
3. Now is a good time to point out that high yield investing alone is a very risky strategy. Coupled with leverage makes it significantly more risky. I personally do invest in high yield securities using the "Divi-X" System and I'll show you examples of actual investments later in this book but its not meant to be considered as an endorsement and I'll refer you back to the disclaimer in the beginning of this book.
4. "Divi-X" System wins again pulling in a 139.3% gain over Unleveraged Cash Return (Without "Divi-X"), or $1955.33.

"Divi-X" System Workbook: The reason the Without "Divi-X" return is higher than the "Ttl Return%" is because it does not include margin interest but you'll notice in many cases that both the "Ttl Return%" and the Without "Divi-X" returns are lower than the "Divi-X" system returns.

GE	General Electric		Purchase @ 12.10 share		Yield: 3.31%

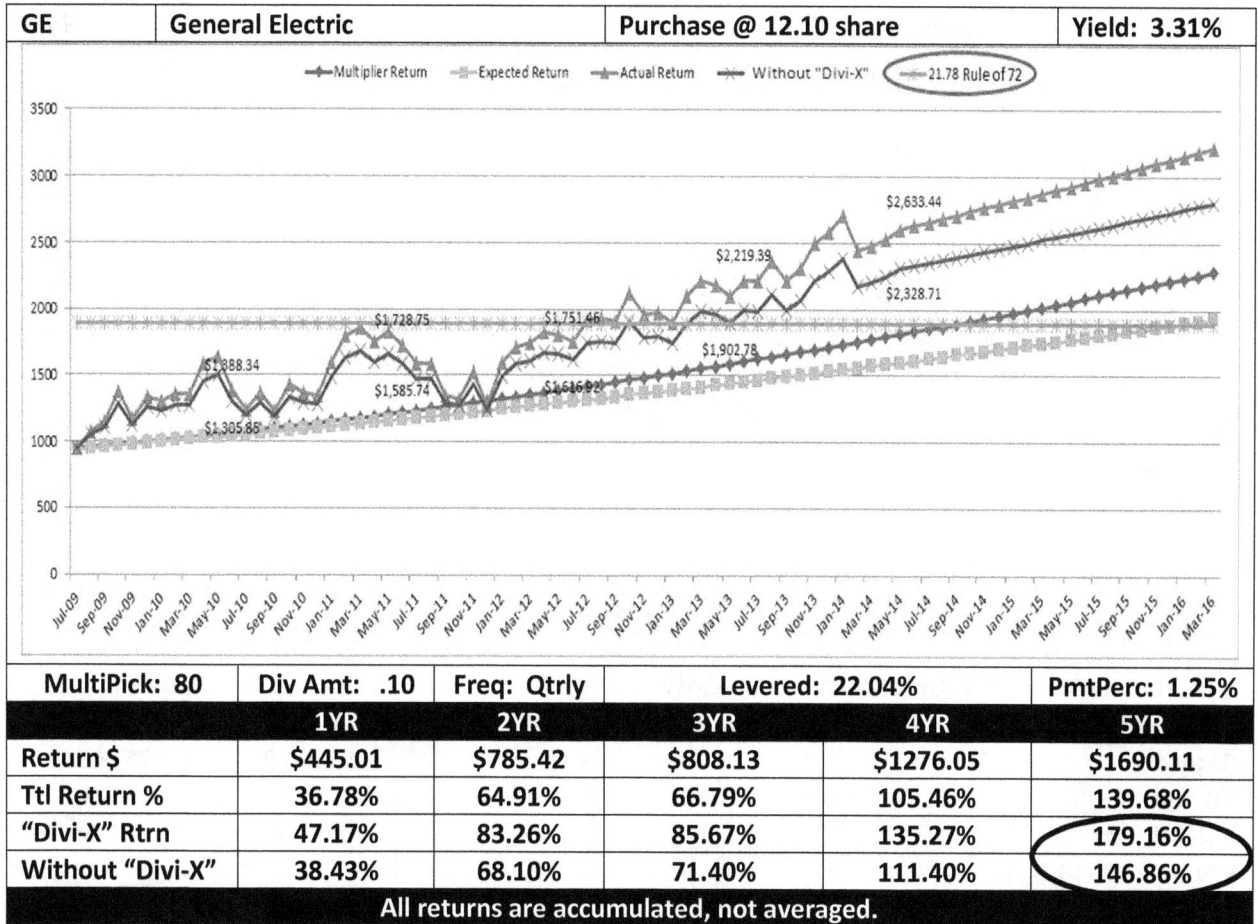

MultiPick: 80	Div Amt: .10	Freq: Qtrly	Levered: 22.04%		PmtPerc: 1.25%
	1YR	2YR	3YR	4YR	5YR
Return $	$445.01	$785.42	$808.13	$1276.05	$1690.11
Ttl Return %	36.78%	64.91%	66.79%	105.46%	139.68%
"Divi-X" Rtrn	47.17%	83.26%	85.67%	135.27%	179.16%
Without "Divi-X"	38.43%	68.10%	71.40%	111.40%	146.86%
All returns are accumulated, not averaged.					

A few things to note about this chart:

1. I only used an 8% Expected Return Rate this time. The low stock price and small dividend (even though a pleasing 3.31%), along with the large market cap of GE; I just didn't anticipate aggressive growth from them.

2. Because of the reasons mentioned in #1, "Divi-X" System only managed a 32.3% edge over the 'Without "Divi-X" Return, or $304.73.

We're only up to **(GE)**, but by now you have already seen a variety of scenarios (high price/yield, low price/yield) and return results and so far they have all had positive outcomes. Hopefully, you like what you have seen so far and there is still plenty more to show you, even the not so positive outcomes. I mentioned earlier that I did not cherry-pick stocks just to make my system look good and that's why I just went with the Dow 30. The irony is, that I'll have to cherry-pick the poor outcomes to show you the potential pitfalls associated with using the "Divi-X" system.

It is essential that you understand that this is not a magic formula. It will not make a bad security pick suddenly good. Ultimately, the responsibility and due diligence falls on you.

GS	Goldman Sachs Group, Inc.	Purchase @ $146.74 share	Yield: 0.95%

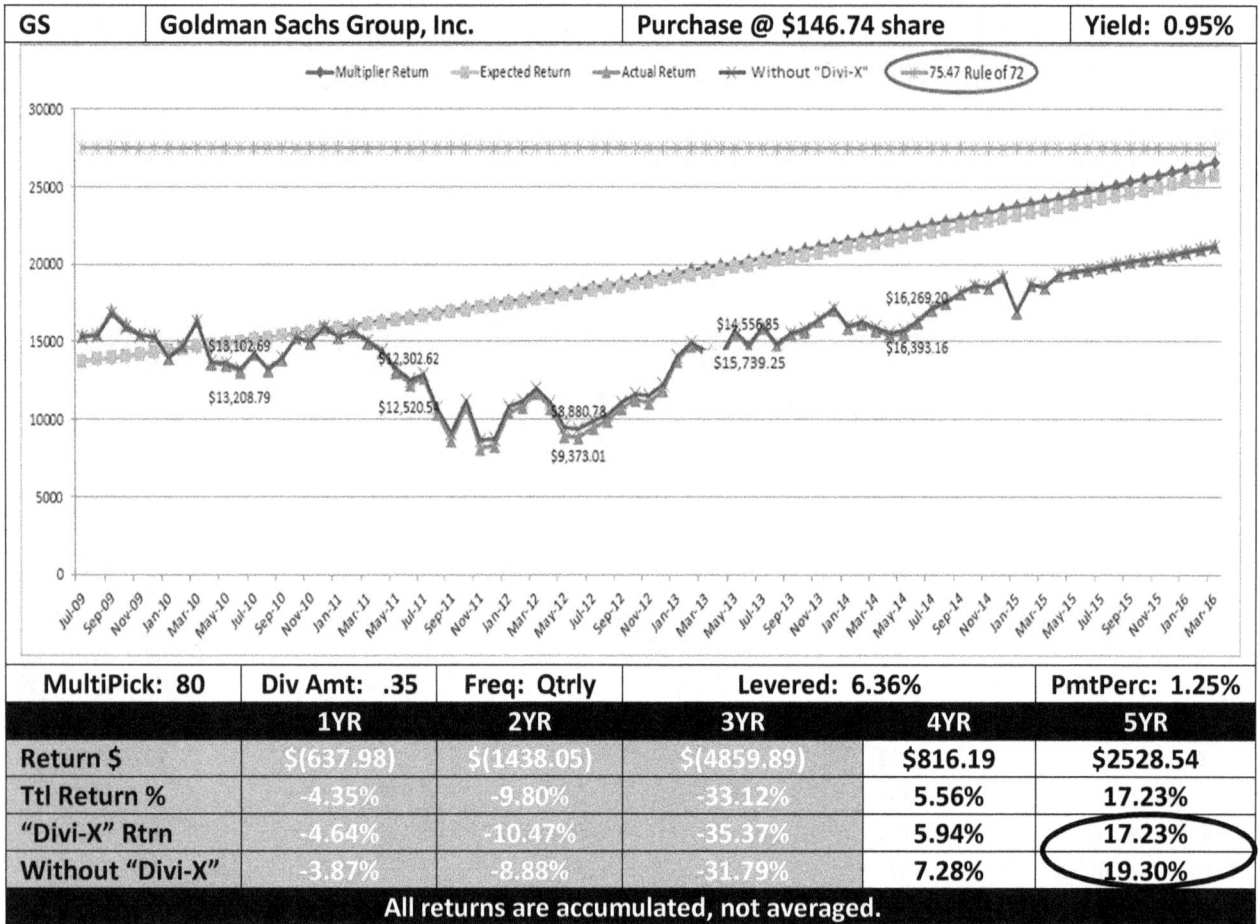

Multiplier Return — Expected Return — Actual Return — Without "Divi-X" — 75.47 Rule of 72

Data labels visible on chart: $13,102.69, $13,208.79, $12,302.62, $12,520.5, $9,373.01, $8,880.78, $15,739.25, $14,556.85, $16,269.20, $16,393.16

MultiPick: 80	Div Amt: .35	Freq: Qtrly	Levered: 6.36%		PmtPerc: 1.25%
	1YR	2YR	3YR	4YR	5YR
Return $	$(637.98)	$(1438.05)	$(4859.89)	$816.19	$2528.54
Ttl Return %	-4.35%	-9.80%	-33.12%	5.56%	17.23%
"Divi-X" Rtrn	-4.64%	-10.47%	-35.37%	5.94%	17.23%
Without "Divi-X"	-3.87%	-8.88%	-31.79%	7.28%	19.30%
All returns are accumulated, not averaged.					

A few things to note about this chart:

1. I like this chart. It illustrates so much. The not so pleasant outcomes I just mentioned in the previous example? Believe it or not, this is not one of them, unless you were to sell this stock on any of the dips between August 2011 and July 2012.

2. Up until now, it was pretty obvious which dollar amount in the charts represented the 'Actual Returns' and the 'Without "Divi-X"' Returns, but now, because the lines are so close together I have to point out that the dollar amount above always represents 'Actual Returns' ("Divi-X" System Returns) and the dollar amount below always represents the 'Without "Divi-X"' Returns.

   a. The return lines hug each other very closely throughout the entire 5 year investment period, that is because the very small dividend yield only allowed us to invest in a very small number of extra shares (6.36 shares to be exact). In this case, I wouldn't exactly say that was a bad thing since 'Without "Divi-X" did manage to eke out "Divi-X" by a miniscule 2.07%, or .41% a year on average.

   b. Despite how closely both returns mirrored each other, if you look closely at the dollar amounts, the differences are rather large in years three and four. That's because, even though we only purchased 6.36 shares on leverage, the shares were rather expensive at $146.74 each when they were purchased.

3. As I'm writing this now (04/24/15), Goldman Sachs just closed at 197.99. So, nine months after this chart's time window, your investment would be worth just over $3200.00 more, but "Divi-X" would continue to trail the Without "Divi-X" Return by a very small margin.

4. I used 9% again for the Expected Return Rate. You can see it failed miserably. If we waited till 04/24/15 (as I'm writing this), it still failed to meet my expectations but rallied a bit to make it… not as bad.

5. Despite the disappointing returns from this stock, it did end up in positive territory at the end to average 3.86% a year (3.45% a year with "Divi-X" System). Even though "Divi-X" trailed the 'Without "Divi-X" return for the entire period, it had no material, negative impact on this investment.

HD	Home Depot	Purchase @ $23.61 share		Yield: 3.81%

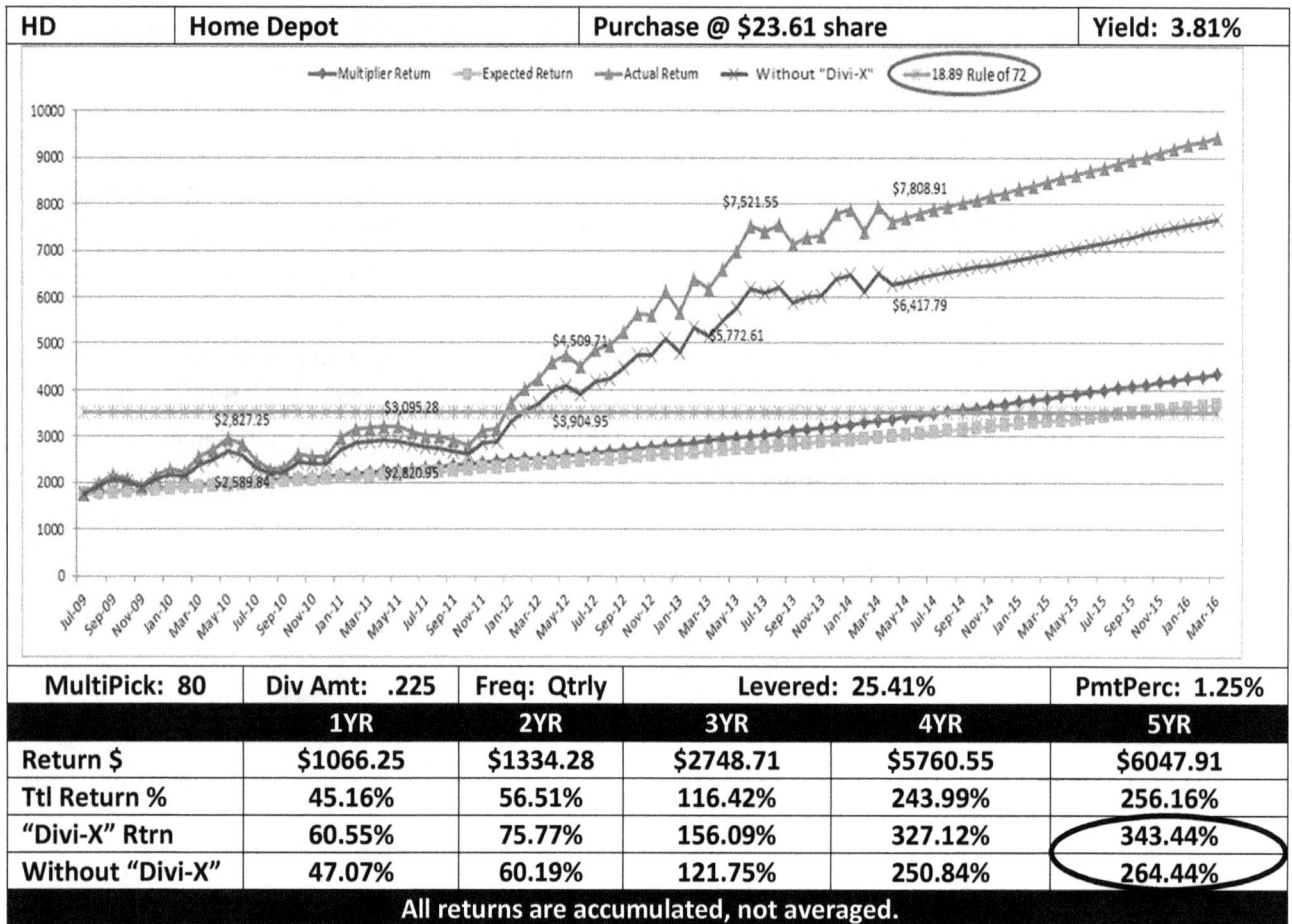

MultiPick: 80	Div Amt: .225	Freq: Qtrly	Levered: 25.41%		PmtPerc: 1.25%
	1YR	**2YR**	**3YR**	**4YR**	**5YR**
Return $	$1066.25	$1334.28	$2748.71	$5760.55	$6047.91
Ttl Return %	45.16%	56.51%	116.42%	243.99%	256.16%
"Divi-X" Rtrn	60.55%	75.77%	156.09%	327.12%	343.44%
Without "Divi-X"	47.07%	60.19%	121.75%	250.84%	264.44%
All returns are accumulated, not averaged.					

A few things to note about this chart:

1. Used the 9% Expected Return Rate
2. We levered at 25.41%, or 25.41 shares of our shares.
3. "Divi-X" System consistently outperformed my Expected Return Rate as did the 'Without "Divi-X".
4. Are you noticing a consistent theme here? The longer you hold, the better your returns and even greater with the "Divi-X" System.
5. After 5 years, Home Depot in conjunction with the "Divi-X" System outpaced 'Without "Divi-X" by 79.0%, or $1391.12.

MMM	3M Co		Purchase @ $59.37 share		Yield: 3.44%

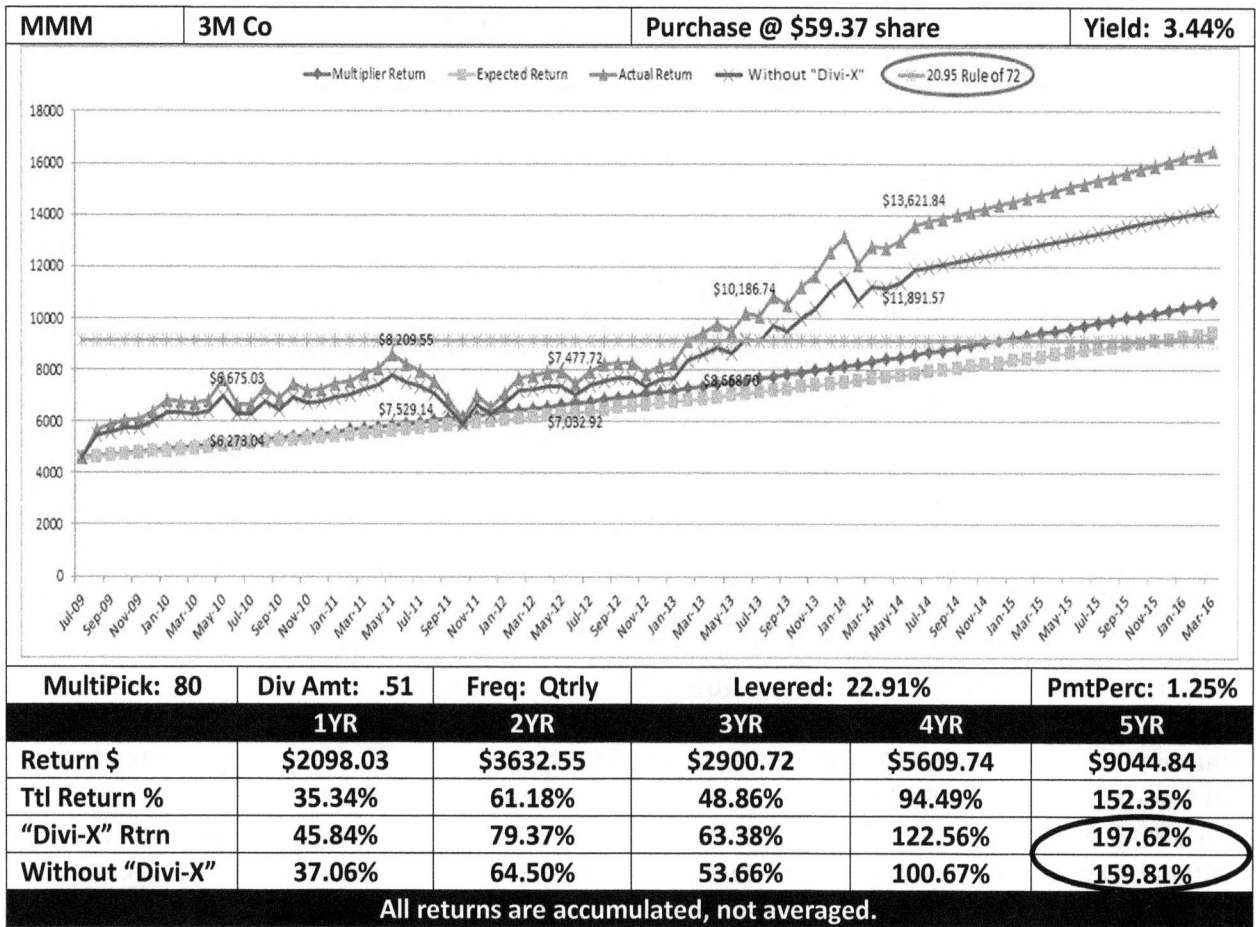

MultiPick: 80	Div Amt: .51	Freq: Qtrly	Levered: 22.91%		PmtPerc: 1.25%
	1YR	**2YR**	**3YR**	**4YR**	**5YR**
Return $	$2098.03	$3632.55	$2900.72	$5609.74	$9044.84
Ttl Return %	35.34%	61.18%	48.86%	94.49%	152.35%
"Divi-X" Rtrn	45.84%	79.37%	63.38%	122.56%	197.62%
Without "Divi-X"	37.06%	64.50%	53.66%	100.67%	159.81%
All returns are accumulated, not averaged.					

A few things to note about this chart:

1. From now on, unless otherwise noted, all investments have an expected return rate of 9%.
2. We levered at 22.91%, or 22.91 of our shares.
3. "Divi-X" consistently stayed ahead in the game. The pullback to the 'Expected Return' line back in Oct – Nov 2011 essentially reset the clock putting all return scenarios at about even (with "Divi-X" system holding a slight lead). However, as in the months prior, "Divi-X" system continued to take its place in the lead for the remainder of our five years.
4. Five year tally? "Divi-X" taking the gold once again with a 37.81% lead over 'Without "Divi-X", or $1730.27.

T	AT&T		Purchase @ $24.04 share		Yield: 6.82%

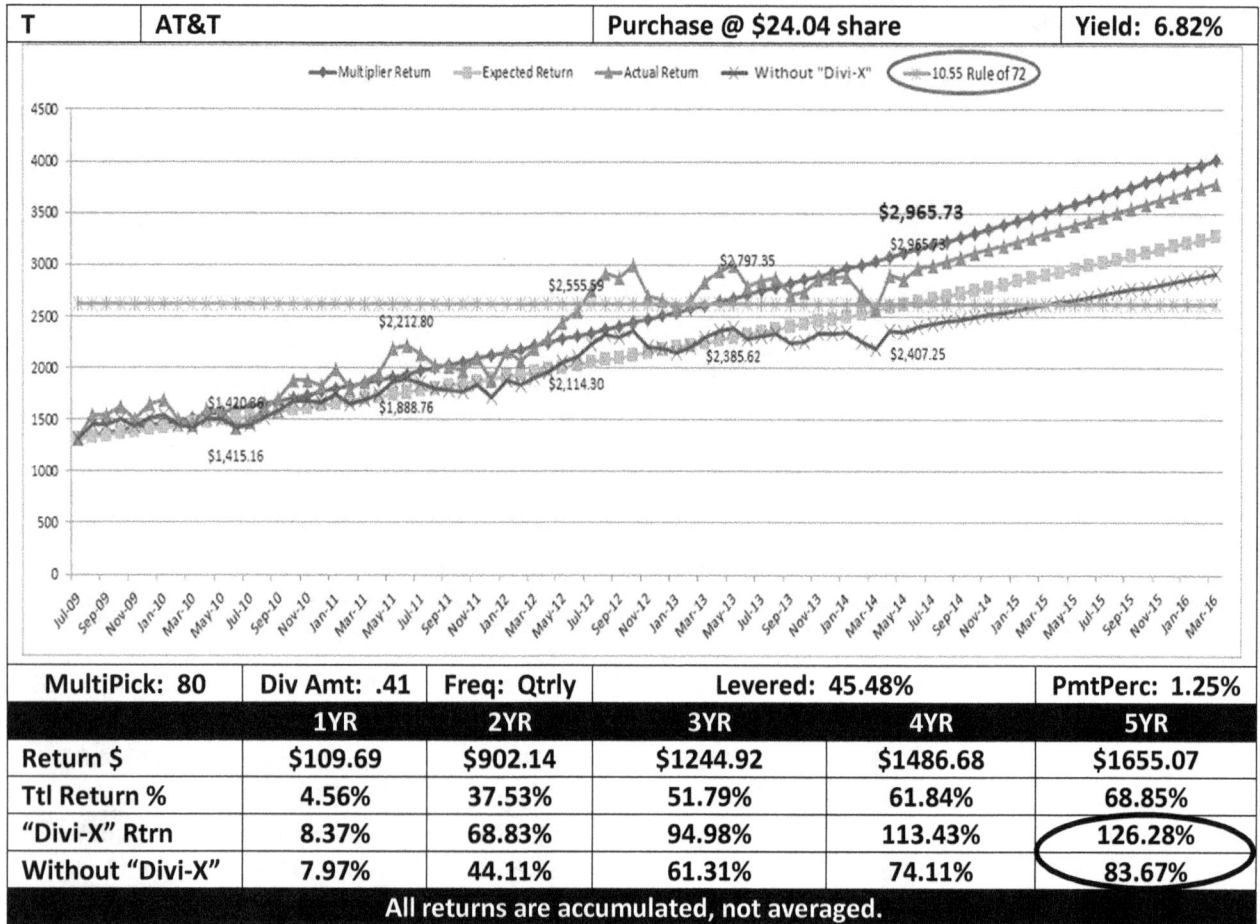

Legend: Multiplier Return · Expected Return · Actual Return · Without "Divi-X" · 10.55 Rule of 72

Chart annotations: $2,965.73, $2,965.73, $2,797.35, $2,555.59, $2,385.62, $2,407.25, $2,212.80, $2,114.30, $1,888.76, $1,420.68, $1,415.16

MultiPick: 80	Div Amt: .41	Freq: Qtrly	Levered: 45.48%		PmtPerc: 1.25%
	1YR	**2YR**	**3YR**	**4YR**	**5YR**
Return $	$109.69	$902.14	$1244.92	$1486.68	$1655.07
Ttl Return %	4.56%	37.53%	51.79%	61.84%	68.85%
"Divi-X" Rtrn	8.37%	68.83%	94.98%	113.43%	126.28%
Without "Divi-X"	7.97%	44.11%	61.31%	74.11%	83.67%
All returns are accumulated, not averaged.					

A few things to note about this chart:

1. We levered at 45.48%, or 45.48 of our shares.
2. The most noticeable thing that jumps out at me on this one is that, had it not been for "Divi-X" system we would not have even made our expected 9% return rate.
3. Also, once "Divi-X" system crossed the "Rule of 72" (doubled your money) it pretty much stayed there; 'Without "Divi-X" didn't cross that territory once (remember the trailing tail at the end is unused projected data).
4. In summary, "Divi-X" finishes the winner with a 42.61% margin, or $558.48.

INTC	Intel Corporation	Purchase @ $32.08 share	Yield: 1.96%

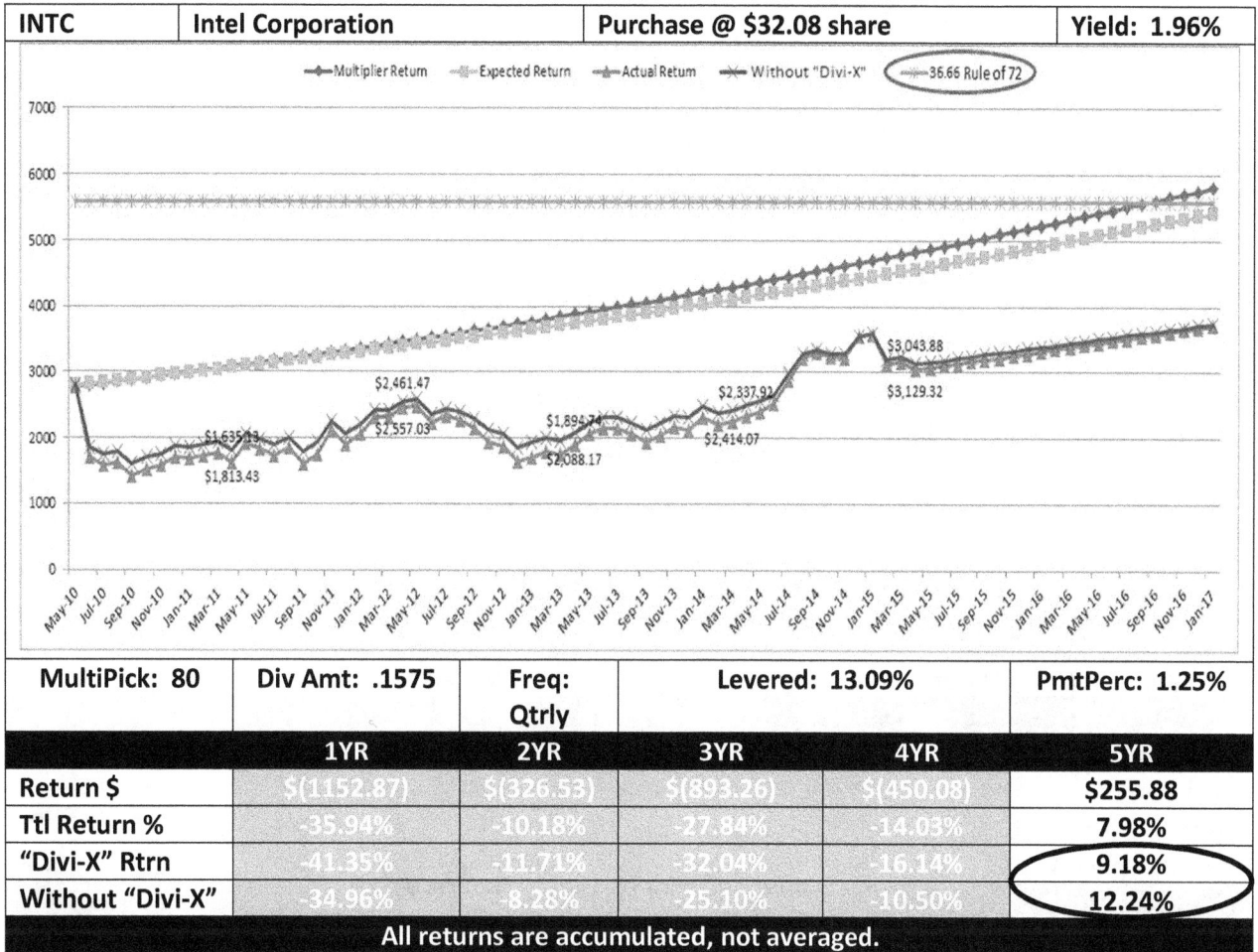

MultiPick: 80	Div Amt: .1575	Freq: Qtrly	Levered: 13.09%		PmtPerc: 1.25%

	1YR	2YR	3YR	4YR	5YR
Return $	$(1152.87)	$(326.53)	$(893.26)	$(450.08)	$255.88
Ttl Return %	-35.94%	-10.18%	-27.84%	-14.03%	7.98%
"Divi-X" Rtrn	-41.35%	-11.71%	-32.04%	-16.14%	9.18%
Without "Divi-X"	-34.96%	-8.28%	-25.10%	-10.50%	12.24%
All returns are accumulated, not averaged.					

A few things to note about this chart:

1. Ouch! We shot ourselves in the foot on this one. Had we waited at least two more months before we jumped into this one, we would've come out much better. Oh well, it's going to happen from time to time.

2. Fortunately, we were only levered at 13.09%, so most of the pain was felt whether or not you used the "Divi-X" system.

3. All in all, it did finish in the green after five years. "Divi-X" system had to yield the floor on this one as it lagged by 3.06%, or a five year average of 0.61%.

XOM	Exxon Mobile Corporation	Purchase @ $71.05 share	Yield: 2.36%

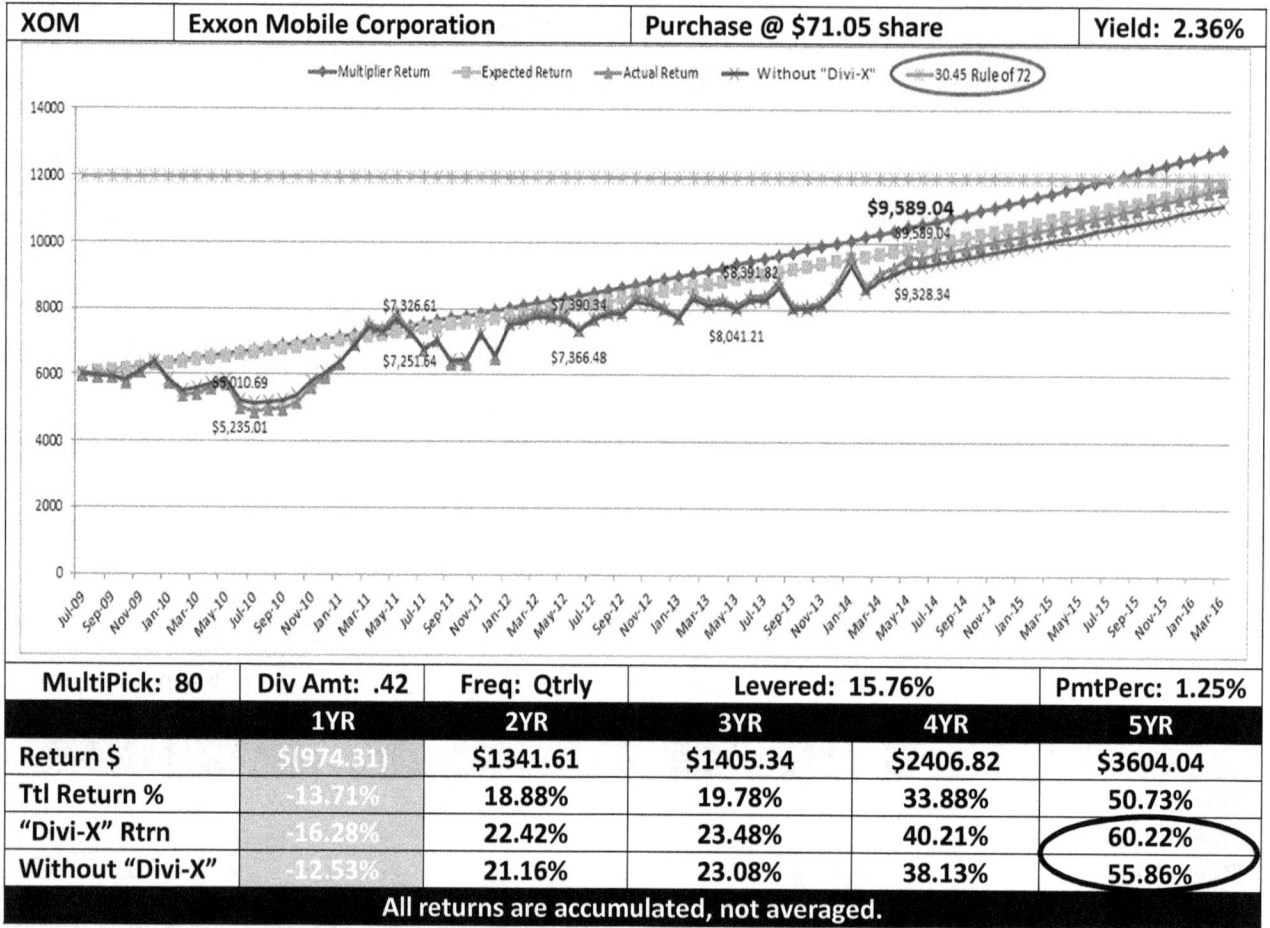

MultiPick: 80	Div Amt: .42	Freq: Qtrly	Levered: 15.76%		PmtPerc: 1.25%
	1YR	2YR	3YR	4YR	5YR
Return $	$(974.31)	$1341.61	$1405.34	$2406.82	$3604.04
Ttl Return %	-13.71%	18.88%	19.78%	33.88%	50.73%
"Divi-X" Rtrn	-16.28%	22.42%	23.48%	40.21%	60.22%
Without "Divi-X"	-12.53%	21.16%	23.08%	38.13%	55.86%
All returns are accumulated, not averaged.					

A few things to note about this chart:

1. We levered at 15.76%, or 15.76 shares.
2. This thing didn't start to turn positive until about December 2010. In the long run, "Divi-X" ultimately prevailed, but had I made this purchase, I'm certain that in Year 1 I would have kicked myself and thanked the stars above that I only levered in at 15.76%.
3. In this stock and all the others where the 'Actual Return' and the 'Without "Divi-X" returns run so closely together, it's easy to ask, "Why even bother?" Unfortunately, that's a luxury only hindsight can answer and in this case, "Divi-X" did get the better return.
4. When all was said and done, we averaged just over 12% a year (60.22% / 5YR's).

IBM	International Business Machines Corp.	Purchase @ $129.99 share	Yield: 2.00%

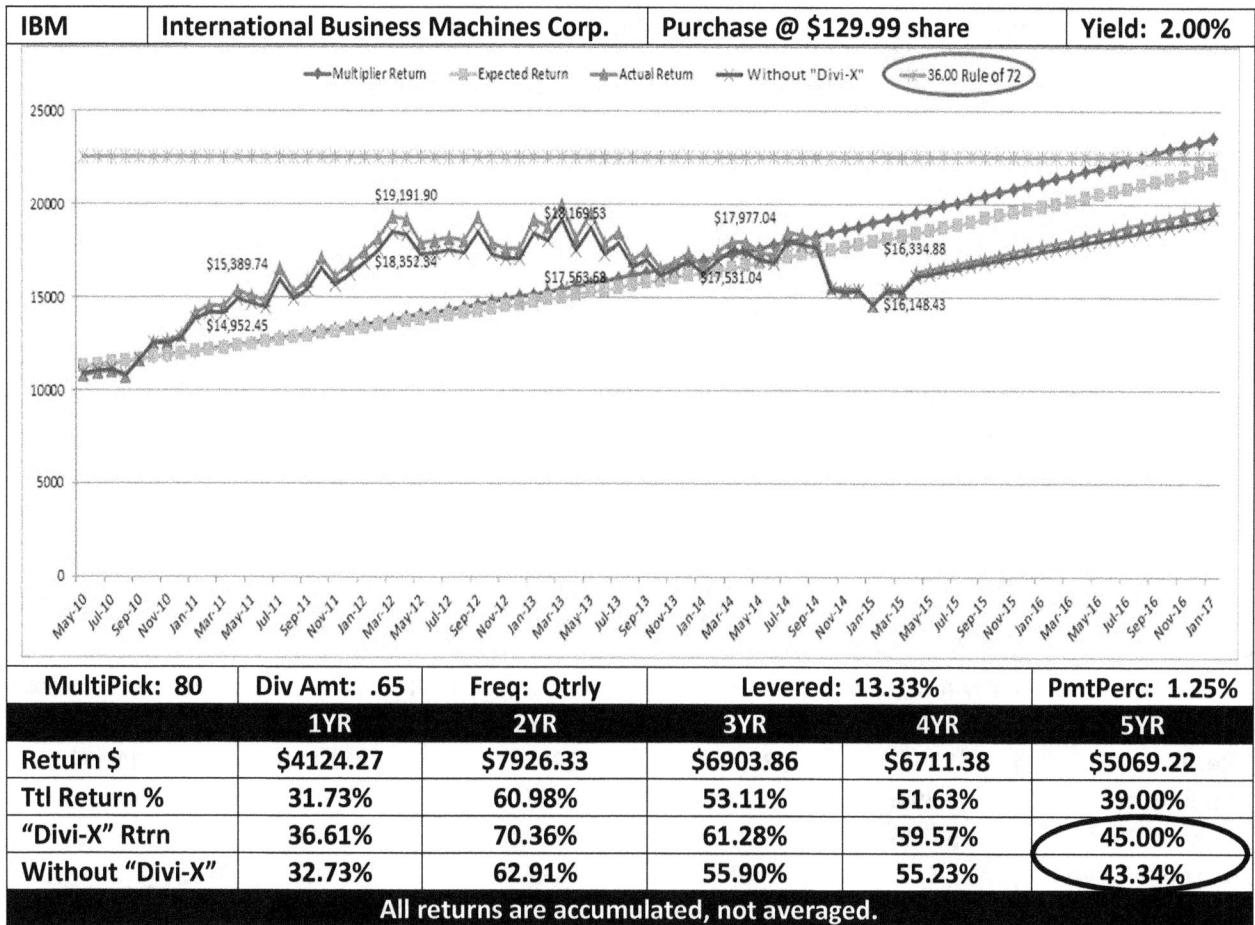

Legend: Multiplier Return — Expected Return — Actual Return — Without "Divi-X" — 36.00 Rule of 72

Data labels visible on chart: $19,191.90, $18,169.53, $17,977.04, $15,389.74, $18,352.34, $17,563.68, $17,531.04, $16,334.88, $14,952.45, $16,148.43

MultiPick: 80	Div Amt: .65	Freq: Qtrly	Levered: 13.33%		PmtPerc: 1.25%
	1YR	2YR	3YR	4YR	5YR
Return $	$4124.27	$7926.33	$6903.86	$6711.38	$5069.22
Ttl Return %	31.73%	60.98%	53.11%	51.63%	39.00%
"Divi-X" Rtrn	36.61%	70.36%	61.28%	59.57%	45.00%
Without "Divi-X"	32.73%	62.91%	55.90%	55.23%	43.34%
All returns are accumulated, not averaged.					

A few things to note about this chart:

1. We levered at 13.33%, or 13.33 shares.

2. Looks like you would've made all your money in the first couple of years on this one. Unfortunately, hindsight didn't tell you what was going to happen in the next three years. Still… better with "Divi-X" than without.

3. Just like Exxon in the previous chart, leverage didn't really help or hurt us on this. If you decide that the "Divi-X" System is right for you, don't automatically discount these low-yield, low-levered stocks. Later on, you'll see a couple instances of how even this can payoff very nicely in the long-term.

4. Even though "Divi-X" didn't contribute much to the overall five year returns, it still netted you an extra $186.45.

JNJ	Johnson & Johnson		Purchase @ $ 64.30 share		Yield: 3.36%

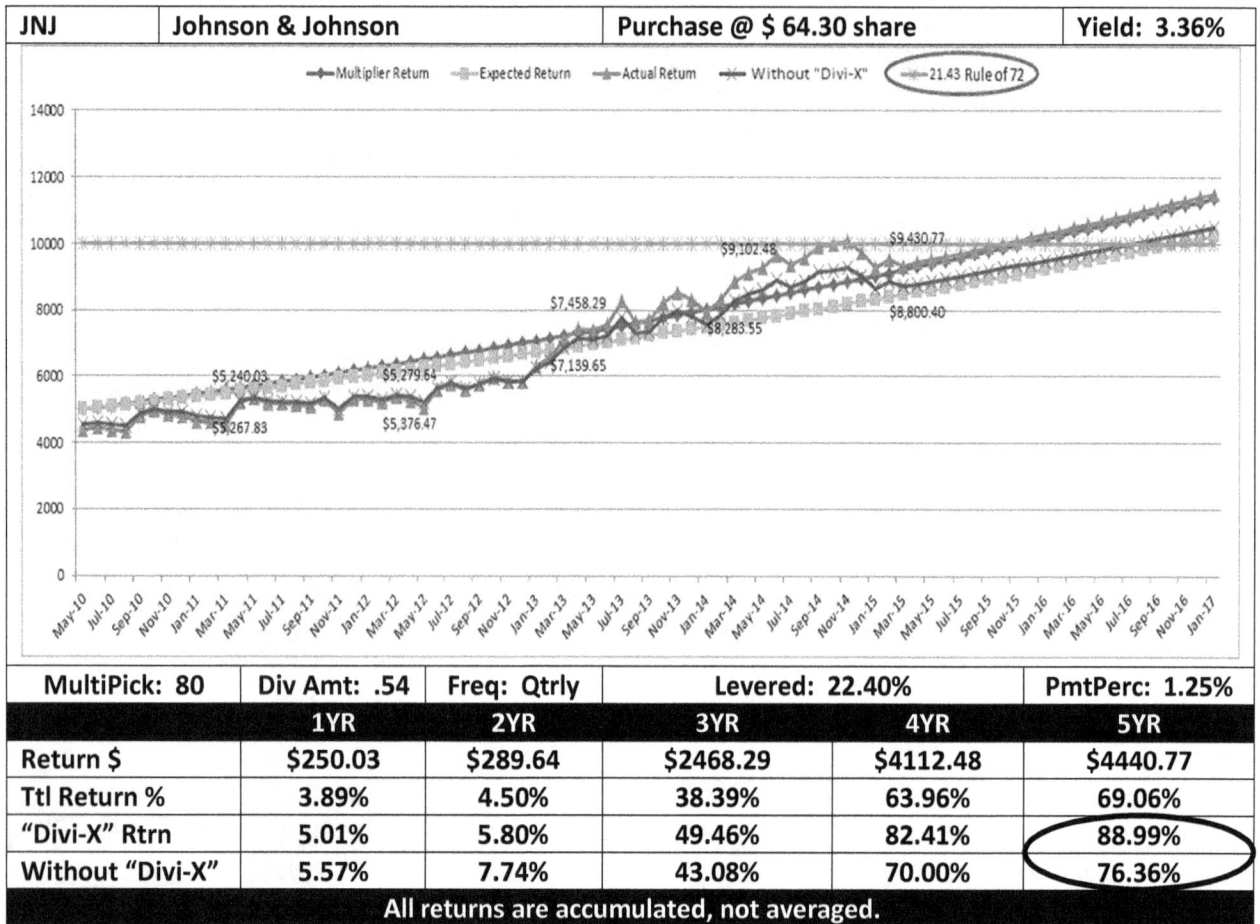

Legend: Multiplier Return — Expected Return — Actual Return — Without "Divi-X" — 21.43 Rule of 72

Chart data points: $5,240.03, $5,267.83, $5,279.64, $5,376.47, $7,458.29, $7,139.65, $9,102.48, $8,283.55, $9,430.77, $8,800.40

MultiPick: 80	Div Amt: .54	Freq: Qtrly	Levered: 22.40%		PmtPerc: 1.25%
	1YR	**2YR**	**3YR**	**4YR**	**5YR**
Return $	$250.03	$289.64	$2468.29	$4112.48	$4440.77
Ttl Return %	3.89%	4.50%	38.39%	63.96%	69.06%
"Divi-X" Rtrn	5.01%	5.80%	49.46%	82.41%	88.99%
Without "Divi-X"	5.57%	7.74%	43.08%	70.00%	76.36%
All returns are accumulated, not averaged.					

A few things to note about this chart:

1. We levered at 22.40%, or 22.40 shares.
2. **Not bad.** I don't believe at any time you would have questioned yourself on whether you should have purchased this or not.
   a. It pretty much stayed within a decent range of our 'Expected Return' rate
   b. The only time within the five years your money had doubled was with the "Divi-X" system around January 2015.
3. In the end, "Divi-X" bought you a nice weekend getaway with $630.37, or an extra 12.63% more than 'Without "Divi-X."

JPM	JPMorgan Chase & Co.	Purchase @ $ 44.94 share	Yield: 0.45%

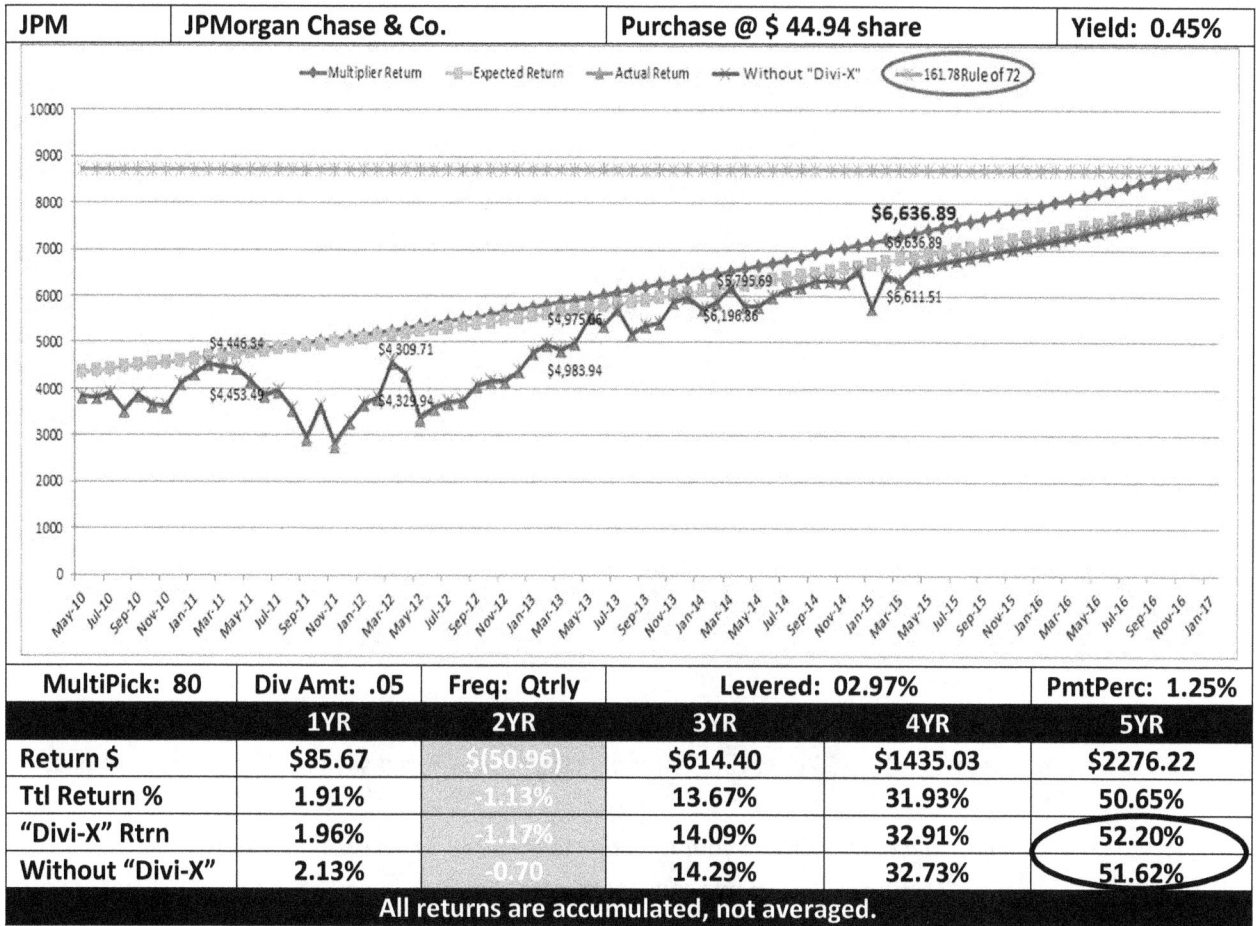

MultiPick: 80	Div Amt: .05	Freq: Qtrly	Levered: 02.97%		PmtPerc: 1.25%
	1YR	**2YR**	**3YR**	**4YR**	**5YR**
Return $	$85.67	$(50.96)	$614.40	$1435.03	$2276.22
Ttl Return %	1.91%	-1.13%	13.67%	31.93%	50.65%
"Divi-X" Rtrn	1.96%	-1.17%	14.09%	32.91%	52.20%
Without "Divi-X"	2.13%	-0.70	14.29%	32.73%	51.62%
All returns are accumulated, not averaged.					

A few things to note about this chart:

1. We only levered at 2.97%, or 2.97 shares.
2. "Divi-X" only managed to leverage us just under three shares. After five long years, we only got an extra $25.38. In this particular instance, I would not need hindsight to help me decide if this is worth it or not. Later on, you'll see a scenario where we use a "Multiplier Pick" (MultiPick) of 100 for this stock, and even then it only purchased 3.71 sharesIs there any scenario, without speculating on price, that this stock could be worth my while? The only thing I can think of is if I used all the leverage this stock's dividend could afford me. The only way I can do that is to increase the "Multiplier Pick." **This is a crucial element of the "Divi-X" System. Immediately following this example, I explain the significance of "Multiplier Pick" and its sister "DIV Multiplier" which are the same thing, but not. Please familiarize yourself with 'The Difference between "Multiplier Pick" & "DIV Multiplier" and then come back to this point.**
   a. If you are using the worksheets provided to you in the back of this book, trying to pinpoint the maximum "Multiplier Pick" you can use when the yield is so small could be a rather large waste of time.

b. If you download the free excel spreadsheet (details in back of book), it'll save you a lot of time.

c. If you purchase the full "Divi-X" System Workbook (details in back of book), it will take you no time at all, a quick precursory glance and then choose.

3. Now that you have read up on the differences between "Multiplier Pick" and "DIV Multiplier, you should have a good understanding of what the "Multiplier Pick" is all about and when I say that for this stock we could go with a "Multiplier Pick" of 155 you should know what I mean. If we were to use a "Multiplier Pick" of 155 in this example, it would have allowed us to purchase a total of 5.76 leveraged shares. Here's the breakdown:

Monthly Dividend Total = .0167 (Qtrly Div of $.05/ 3 months)

x 100 shares

= $1.67 a month

X Multiplier Pick of 155 = $258.85

/ Share Price of $44.94

= 5.76 Shares, or levered at 5.76%

I'll spare you another chart for now. After five years, the extra leverage would have only earned us just under $50 over the 'Without "Divi-X" return. I'd say I'm going to have to pass on this one.

a. Invest according to your own risk tolerance, but I personally opt for a higher "Multiplier Pick" when the stocks yield is so low, if I invest in it at all. If I were to invest in a stock with such a small yield, it would have to be because of a high degree of confidence that the share price will increase.

"Divi-X" System Workbook: The Rule of 72.
Now that you understand what the Rule of 72 is and see how poorly this particular stock did to meet the Rule of 72, go back and review how well the others did.

The Difference between "Multiplier Pick" & "DIV Multiplier"

If you were a user of the "Divi-X" System Workbook, which I hope you will be, you would become familiar with the "Leverage Projection Worksheet." All the charts shown in this book are the result of the simple variable entries that you would enter on it. Below is what it looks like.

Ticker	Stock Price		No. Shares	Purch Date	End Date	DIV Pmt	Multiplier Start	Rtrn Rate?	% Levered
PFE	$ 16.7200		100	04/30/10	A-10	$ 0.1800	20	9.00%	28.71%

									Rule 72	16.72
	Multiplier Pick	DIV Per/Year	Monthly DIV	Pmt Perc	Margin Rate	Multiplier Step	Mth DIV Ttl	Based on DIV	16.72
	80	4	$ 0.0600	1.25%	7.75%	5	$ 6.00	On Est Rtrn	4.90
								On Act Rtrn	1.88

DIV Multiplier	Cash Out Of Pocket	Leverage Amt	Ttl Share Value	#Shares Purch by Leverage	DIV Yield	Min Pmt	Principal	Margin Interest	Net DIV Cash	Monthly Net Div Cash (1yr)	Monthly Net Div Cash (5yr)	Yield Less Margin Int	Yield Less Marg Int (1YR)	Yield Less Marg Int (5YR)	Leverage Ratio
20	$ 1,552.00	$ 120.00	$ 1,672.00	7.18	4.31%	$ 1.50	$ 0.73	$ 0.78	$ 4.50	$ 5.26	$ 8.28	3.48%	4.07%	6.41%	
25	$ 1,522.00	$ 150.00	$ 1,672.00	8.97	4.31%	$ 1.88	$ 0.91	$ 0.97	$ 4.13	$ 4.91	$ 8.02	3.25%	3.87%	6.32%	
30	$ 1,492.00	$ 180.00	$ 1,672.00	10.77	4.31%	$ 2.25	$ 1.09	$ 1.16	$ 3.75	$ 4.56	$ 7.76	3.02%	3.67%	6.24%	
35	$ 1,462.00	$ 210.00	$ 1,672.00	12.56	4.31%	$ 2.63	$ 1.27	$ 1.36	$ 3.38	$ 4.21	$ 7.50	2.77%	3.46%	6.15%	
40	$ 1,432.00	$ 240.00	$ 1,672.00	14.35	4.31%	$ 3.00	$ 1.45	$ 1.55	$ 3.00	$ 3.86	$ 7.24	2.51%	3.25%	6.06%	
45	$ 1,402.00	$ 270.00	$ 1,672.00	16.15	4.31%	$ 3.38	$ 1.63	$ 1.74	$ 2.63	$ 3.51	$ 6.97	2.25%	3.00%	5.97%	
50	$ 1,372.00	$ 300.00	$ 1,672.00	17.94	4.31%	$ 3.75	$ 1.81	$ 1.94	$ 2.25	$ 3.16	$ 6.71	1.97%	2.76%	5.87%	
55	$ 1,342.00	$ 330.00	$ 1,672.00	19.74	4.31%	$ 4.13	$ 1.99	$ 2.13	$ 1.88	$ 2.81	$ 6.45	1.68%	2.51%	5.77%	1
60	$ 1,312.00	$ 360.00	$ 1,672.00	21.53	4.31%	$ 4.50	$ 2.18	$ 2.33	$ 1.50	$ 2.46	$ 6.19	1.37%	2.25%	5.66%	2
65	$ 1,282.00	$ 390.00	$ 1,672.00	23.33	4.31%	$ 4.88	$ 2.36	$ 2.52	$ 1.13	$ 2.11	$ 5.92	1.05%	1.97%	5.54%	23
70	$ 1,252.00	$ 420.00	$ 1,672.00	25.12	4.31%	$ 5.25	$ 2.54	$ 2.71	$ 0.75	$ 1.76	$ 5.66	0.72%	1.68%	5.43%	25.
75	$ 1,222.00	$ 450.00	$ 1,672.00	26.91	4.31%	$ 5.63	$ 2.72	$ 2.91	$ 0.38	$ 1.40	$ 5.40	0.37%	1.38%	5.30%	26.9
80	$ 1,192.00	$ 480.00	$ 1,672.00	28.71	4.31%	$ 6.00	$ 2.90	$ 3.10	$ -	$ 1.05	$ 5.14	0.00%	1.06%	5.17%	28.7
85	$ 1,162.00	$ 510.00	$ 1,672.00	30.50	4.31%	$ 6.38	$ 3.08	$ 3.29	$ (0.38)	$ 0.70	$ 4.87	-0.39%	0.73%	5.03%	30.50
90	$ 1,132.00	$ 540.00	$ 1,672.00	32.30	4.31%	$ 6.75	$ 3.26	$ 3.49	$ (0.75)	$ 0.35	$ 4.61	-0.80%	0.37%	4.89%	32.30
95	$ 1,102.00	$ 570.00	$ 1,672.00	34.09	4.31%	$ 7.13	$ 3.44	$ 3.68	$ (1.13)	$ 0.00	$ 4.35	-1.23%	0.00%	4.74%	34.09
100	$ 1,072.00	$ 600.00	$ 1,672.00	35.89	4.31%	$ 7.50	$ 3.63	$ 3.88	$ (1.50)	$ (0.35)	$ 4.09	-1.68%	-0.39%	4.58%	35.89

Fig. 2.1

For the time being, I want you to focus primarily on the three circled fields above; the "Multiplier Pick," the "Mthly DIV Ttl" and the "DIV Multiplier," fields.

The "Multiplier Pick" is the number of times the "Mthly DIV Ttl" (Monthly Dividend Total) has been multiplied to arrive at the amount of leverage we will borrow.

The "DIV Multiplier" (Monthly Dividend Total x Multiplier Pick = "DIV Multiplier" or the Dividend Multiplier) shows you the anticipated results of your "Multiplier Pick" and the additional info you filled in at the top of the "Leverage Projection Worksheet" (Share Price, No. Shares, DIV Pmt, etc.).

In the example above, the user chose to multiply the "Mthly DIV Ttl" by eighty times. This gave the total amount borrowed to be $480 ($6 x 80 = $480). Had the user chose a "Multiplier Pick" of 50, the total amount borrowed would have been $300 ($6 x 50 = $300).

For the purpose of the "Divi-X" system, regardless of company's dividend payout frequency, "Divi-X" will always break it down as a monthly dividend amount, or "Mthly DIV Ttl."

MCD	McDonald's Corporation	Purchase @ 70.59 share	Yield: 3.12%

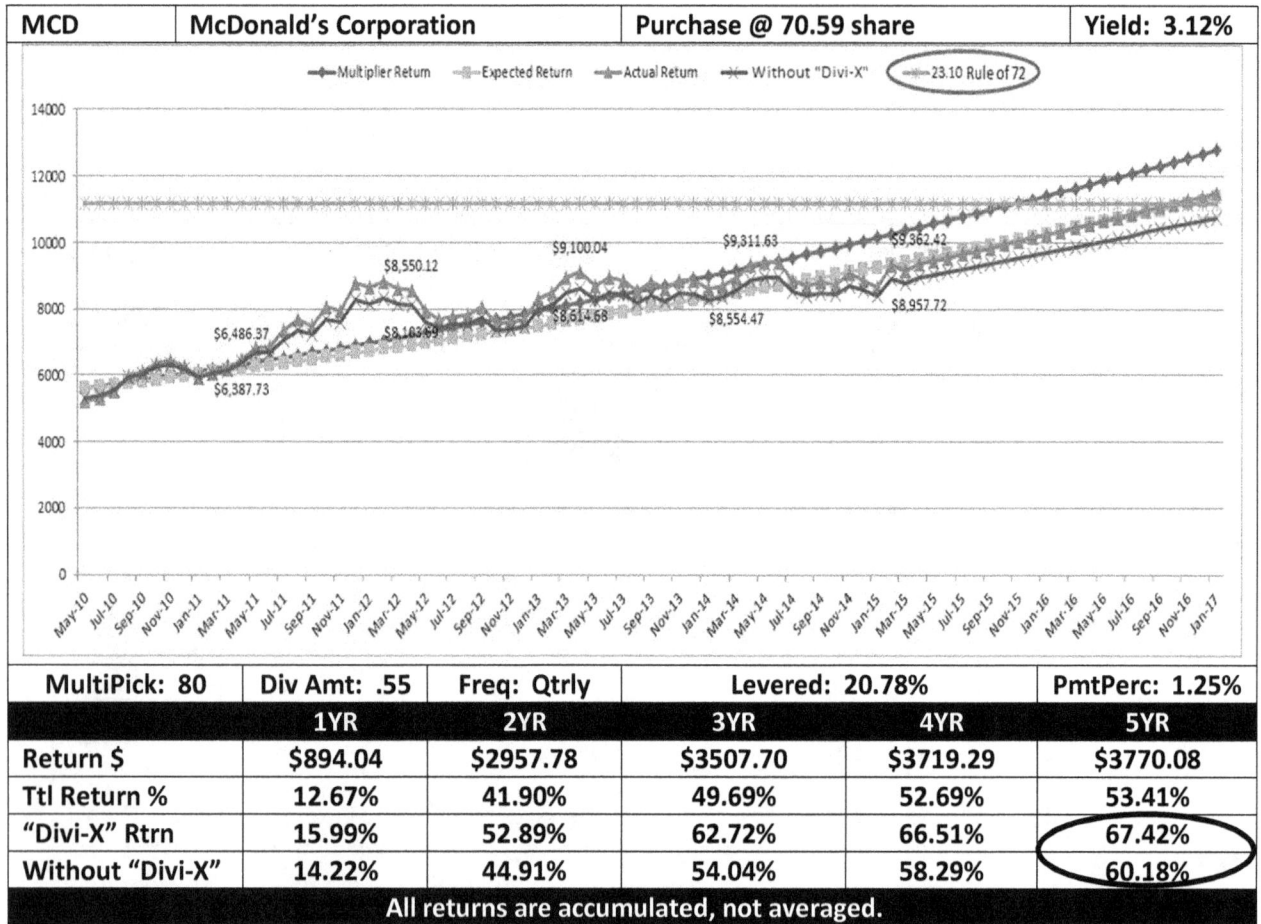

Multiplier Return — Expected Return — Actual Return — Without "Divi-X" — 23.10 Rule of 72

$6,486.37 $6,387.73 $8,183.69 $8,550.12 $8,614.68 $9,100.04 $8,554.47 $9,311.63 $8,957.72 $9,362.42

MultiPick: 80	Div Amt: .55	Freq: Qtrly	Levered: 20.78%		PmtPerc: 1.25%
	1YR	2YR	3YR	4YR	5YR
Return $	$894.04	$2957.78	$3507.70	$3719.29	$3770.08
Ttl Return %	12.67%	41.90%	49.69%	52.69%	53.41%
"Divi-X" Rtrn	15.99%	52.89%	62.72%	66.51%	67.42%
Without "Divi-X"	14.22%	44.91%	54.04%	58.29%	60.18%
All returns are accumulated, not averaged.					

A few things to note about this chart:

1. We levered at 20.78%, or 20.78 shares.
2. **Not very exciting. The "Divi-X" System wins again.**
3. I ran a few numbers on this one. At no time, under any circumstance, would this stock have doubled your money.
4. This stock could have been maxed out at a "Multiplier Pick" of 150 and still covered margin interest. That would have yielded a "Divi-X" Rtrn of 77.79%. A full ten percent better than the "Multiplier Pick" of 80 and 17.61% more than had you not used "Divi-X."
5. Both "Divi-X" and 'Without "Divi-X" managed to pretty much hug the 'Expected Return' but when all was said and done, "Divi-X" crossed the finish line more in line with the 'Expected Return.'

MRK	Merck & Co Inc	Purchase @ $ 35.46 share	Yield: 4.29%

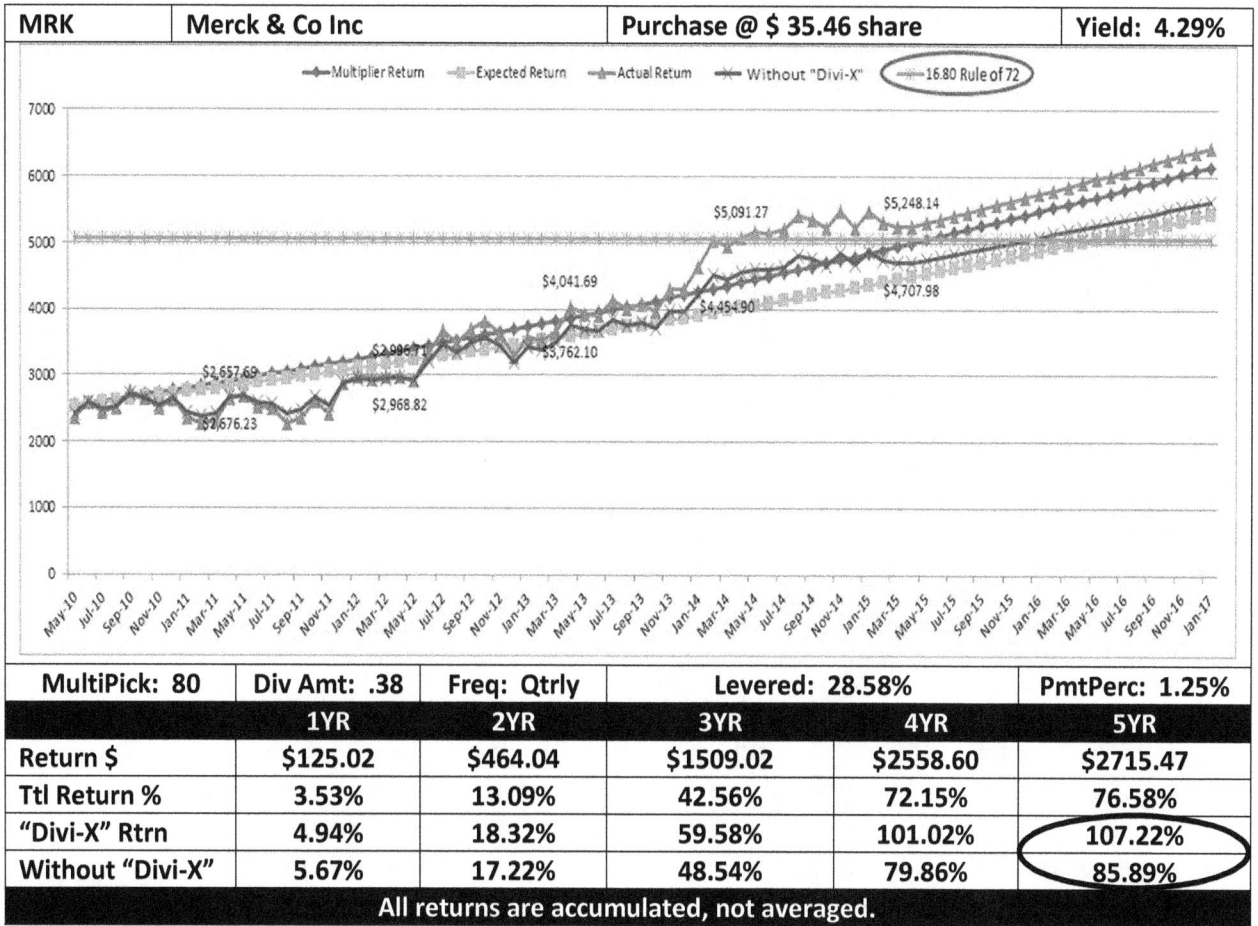

MultiPick: 80	Div Amt: .38	Freq: Qtrly	Levered: 28.58%		PmtPerc: 1.25%
	1YR	2YR	3YR	4YR	5YR
Return $	$125.02	$464.04	$1509.02	$2558.60	$2715.47
Ttl Return %	3.53%	13.09%	42.56%	72.15%	76.58%
"Divi-X" Rtrn	4.94%	18.32%	59.58%	101.02%	107.22%
Without "Divi-X"	5.67%	17.22%	48.54%	79.86%	85.89%
All returns are accumulated, not averaged.					

A few things to note about this chart:

1. We levered at 28.58%, or 28.58 shares.
2. A very nice performance with and without "Divi-X" but nicer with.
3. Notice that using "Divi-X" would have doubled your money just short of year four and appreciated slightly more thereafter.
4. Current trend, indicated by the unused data after year five, would give you a degree of confidence that eventually 'Without "Divi-X" would double your money, but at no time during our target window.
5. "Divi-X" outperformed again with a very respectable 21.33% lead over just cash 'Without "Divi-X."

MSFT	Microsoft Corporation	Purchase @ $ 30.96 share	Yield: 1.68%

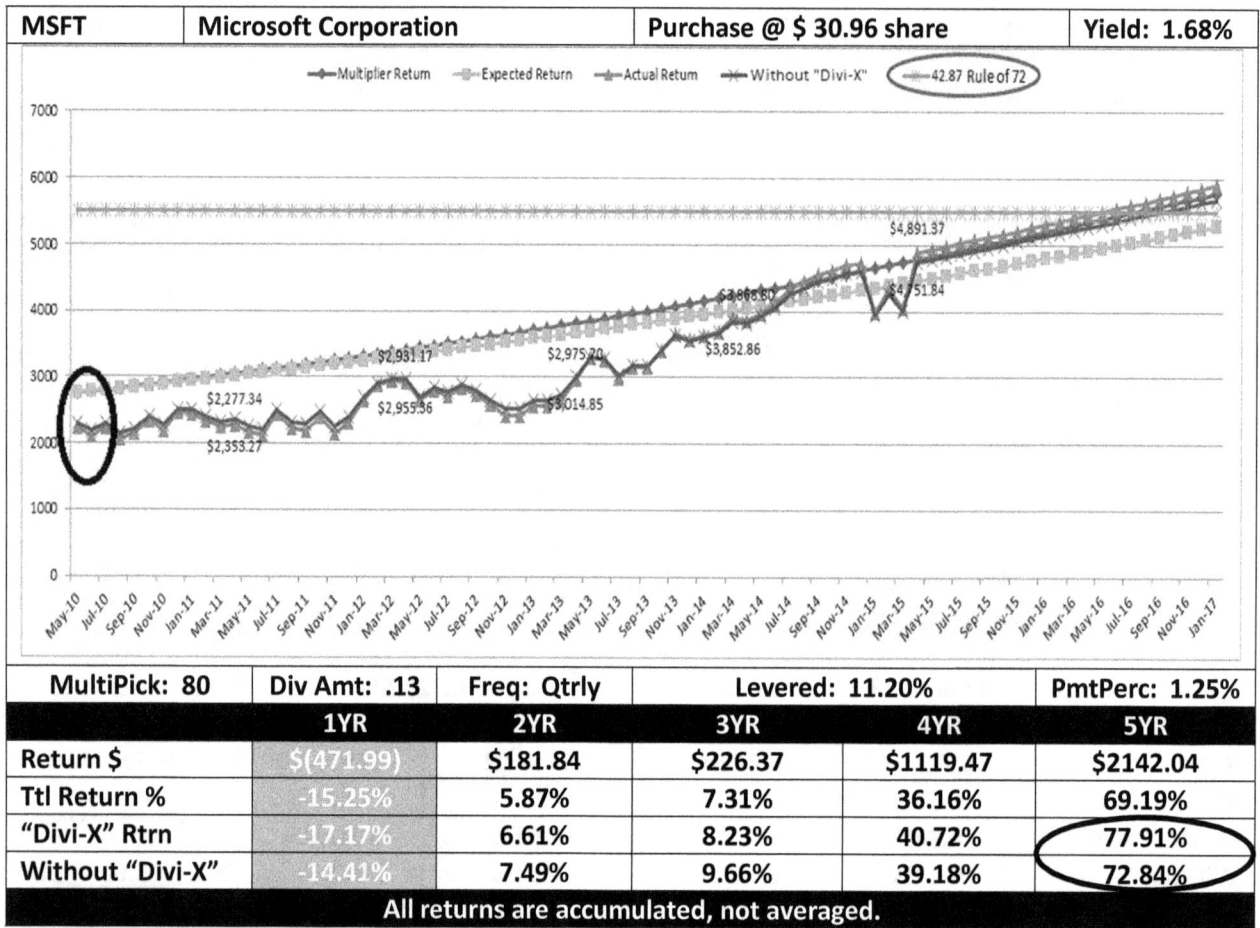

MultiPick: 80		Div Amt: .13	Freq: Qtrly	Levered: 11.20%		PmtPerc: 1.25%
	1YR	**2YR**	**3YR**	**4YR**	**5YR**	
Return $	$(471.99)	$181.84	$226.37	$1119.47	$2142.04	
Ttl Return %	-15.25%	5.87%	7.31%	36.16%	69.19%	
"Divi-X" Rtrn	-17.17%	6.61%	8.23%	40.72%	77.91%	
Without "Divi-X"	-14.41%	7.49%	9.66%	39.18%	72.84%	
All returns are accumulated, not averaged.						

A few things to note about this chart:

1. We levered at 11.20%, or 11.20 shares.

2. If the thought hasn't crossed your mind already, I would like to point out the disparity between the 'Expected Return' and the 'Actual/Without "Divi-X" Returns' at the very beginning of the time window (highlighted by the circle above). Often you'll see the 'Actual/Without "Divi-X" Returns' immediately surpassing or lagging the 'Expected Return' even though all points start out at exactly the same spot. The cause for this is the result of a noticeable share price increase or decrease almost immediately after purchasing the security. In the case above, MSFT's share price declined by $5.16 immediately after our hypothetical purchase.

3. We win again. Yayyy! It was a race till the end. "Divi-X" trailed 'Without "Divi-X" almost the entire time but managed to cross the finish line in first place with just over a 5% better return.

NKE	Nike Inc		Purchase @ $ 38.95 share		Yield: 1.39%

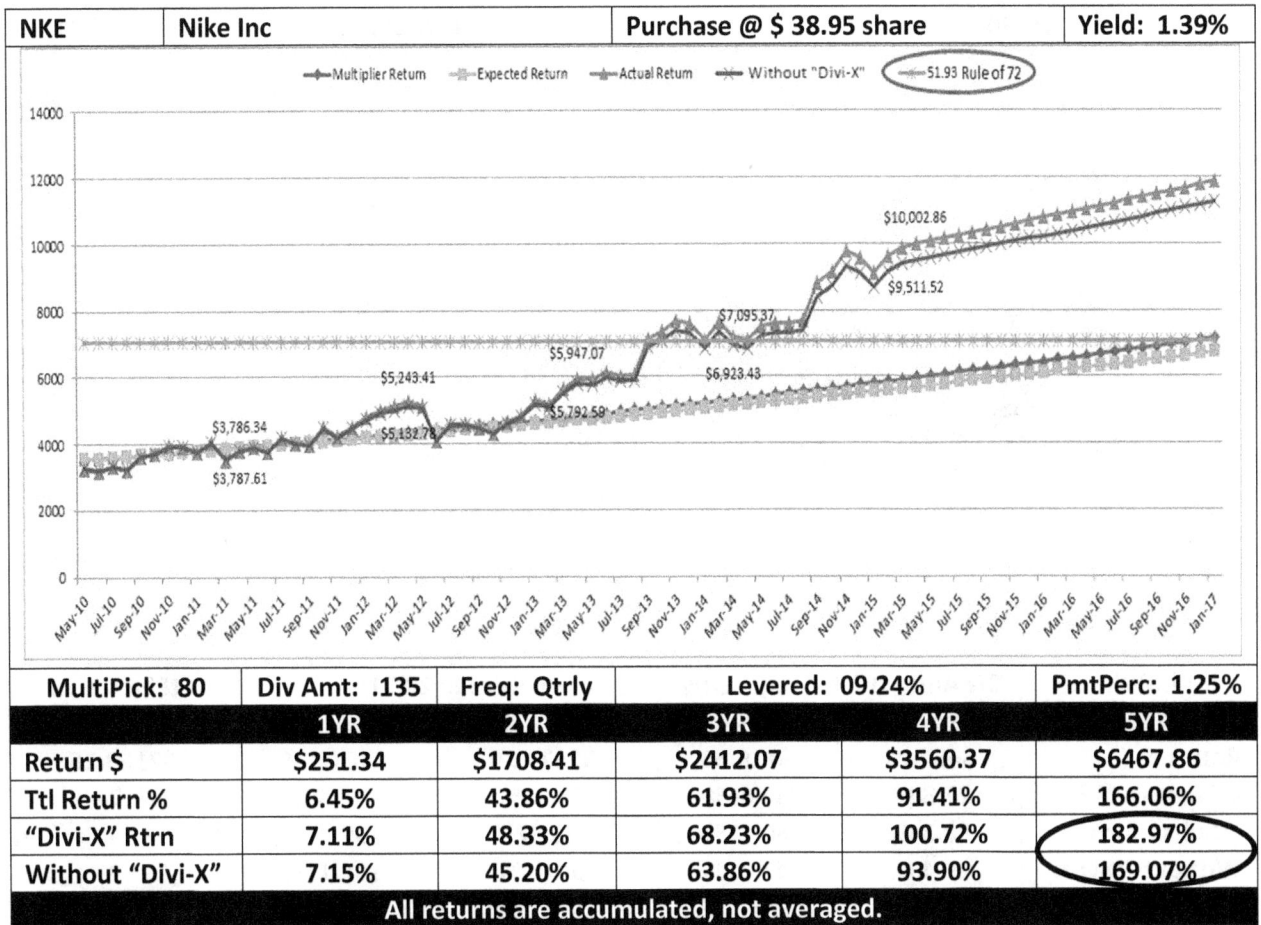

Chart legend: Multiplier Return, Expected Return, Actual Return, Without "Divi-X", 51.93 Rule of 72

Data labels on chart: $3,786.34, $3,787.61, $5,243.41, $5,132.78, $5,792.59, $5,947.07, $6,923.43, $7,095.37, $10,002.86, $9,511.52

MultiPick: 80	Div Amt: .135	Freq: Qtrly	Levered: 09.24%		PmtPerc: 1.25%
	1YR	**2YR**	**3YR**	**4YR**	**5YR**
Return $	$251.34	$1708.41	$2412.07	$3560.37	$6467.86
Ttl Return %	6.45%	43.86%	61.93%	91.41%	166.06%
"Divi-X" Rtrn	7.11%	48.33%	68.23%	100.72%	182.97%
Without "Divi-X"	7.15%	45.20%	63.86%	93.90%	169.07%
All returns are accumulated, not averaged.					

A few things to note about this chart:

1. We levered at 9.24%, or 9.24 shares.
2. Both scenarios pulled in stellar performances, but do I need to say it again? "Divi-X" wins again. A 13.9% lead using only 9.24% leverage.
3. Later in the book, we'll be revisiting these stocks in various situations, but just to point out now, if we used maximum leverage (dividends fully cover just the margin interest), we would have the following:
   a. A "Multiplier Pick" of 154 (later in the book, I actually have guidelines on when to use a "Multiplier Pick" higher than 100, so in fact, you'll discover that the returns noted below in "**c.**" would have indeed been the 'Actual Return' based on the "Divi-X" suggested guidelines)
   b. Leverage at 17.79%, or 17.79 shares. Very conservative.
   c. A return of 198.84%. Almost sixteen percent more than our "Multiplier Pick" of 80; almost thirty percent better than no "Divi-X" at all.
4. This is a great example of how even a little leverage can go a long way.

PFE	Pfizer Inc		Purchase @ $ 16.72 share		Yield: 4.31%

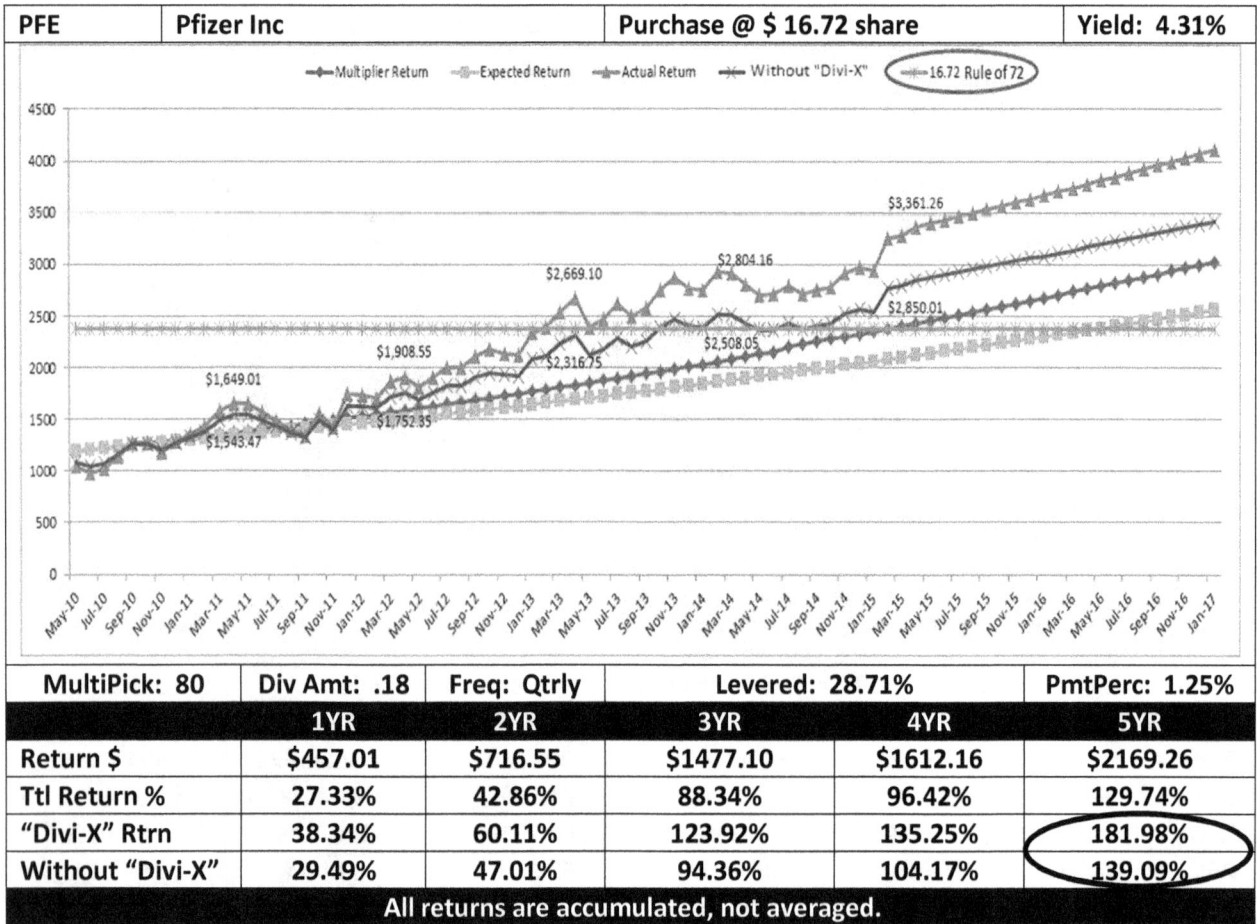

MultiPick: 80	Div Amt: .18	Freq: Qtrly	Levered: 28.71%		PmtPerc: 1.25%
	1YR	**2YR**	**3YR**	**4YR**	**5YR**
Return $	$457.01	$716.55	$1477.10	$1612.16	$2169.26
Ttl Return %	27.33%	42.86%	88.34%	96.42%	129.74%
"Divi-X" Rtrn	38.34%	60.11%	123.92%	135.25%	181.98%
Without "Divi-X"	29.49%	47.01%	94.36%	104.17%	139.09%
All returns are accumulated, not averaged.					

A few things to note about this chart:

1. We levered at 28.71%, or 28.71 shares.
2. Simply beautiful.
    a. Always trending up
    b. At or above the 'Expected Return' the whole time
    c. Very nice dividend
    d. Cash doubled in a couple of years (nine months later Without "Divi-X")
    e. Cash almost tripled after five years
3. Oh! And "Divi-X" wins again with a 42.89% thrashing on top of 'Without "Divi-X"'s very impressive 139.09% return for a total of 181.98%.

PG	Procter & Gamble & Co	Purchase @ $ 62.16 share		Yield: 3.10%

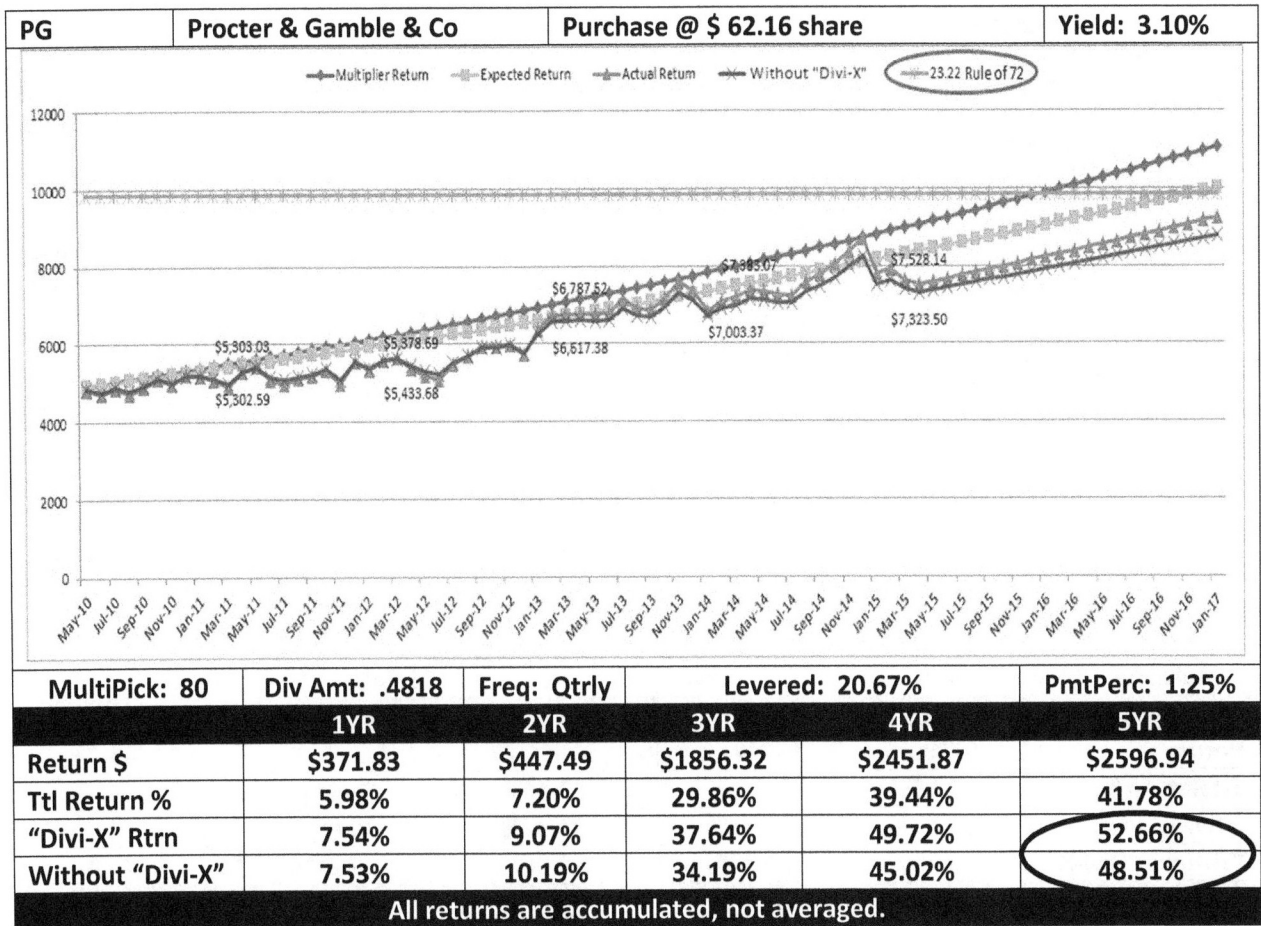

Legend: Multiplier Return — Expected Return — Actual Return — Without "Divi-X" — 23.22 Rule of 72

Data labels on chart: $5,303.03 $5,302.59 $5,378.69 $5,433.68 $6,787.52 $6,617.38 $7,385.07 $7,003.37 $7,528.14 $7,323.50

MultiPick: 80	Div Amt: .4818	Freq: Qtrly	Levered: 20.67%		PmtPerc: 1.25%
	1YR	**2YR**	**3YR**	**4YR**	**5YR**
Return $	$371.83	$447.49	$1856.32	$2451.87	$2596.94
Ttl Return %	5.98%	7.20%	29.86%	39.44%	41.78%
"Divi-X" Rtrn	7.54%	9.07%	37.64%	49.72%	52.66%
Without "Divi-X"	7.53%	10.19%	34.19%	45.02%	48.51%
All returns are accumulated, not averaged.					

A few things to note about this chart:

1. We levered at 20.67%, or 20.67 shares.
2. Eh. I'll take it. They're all not going to be PFE's (Pfizer's).
3. Had we maxed out leverage, we would have a "Multiplier Pick" of 150. That would have purchased us 38.75 shares, or levered 38.75% of the total share price. That would have added another 5.93% to our 52.66% return.
4. Looking at the long-term trend of this one, it always hugged or slightly trailed our 'Expected Return' except for a couple times that only "Divi-X" managed to pass it before pulling back again. If you were to pull a 5 year history on a security and noticed a trend like this one, you would have to give serious thought as to whether or not to invest in this one when so many others have performed so much better. But on the flip side, consistently maintaining an approximate 8% - 9% return year after year is nothing to dismiss too lightly (past performance is no indication of future performance).

KO	The Coca-Cola Co	Purchase @ $ 26.72 share	Yield: 3.29%

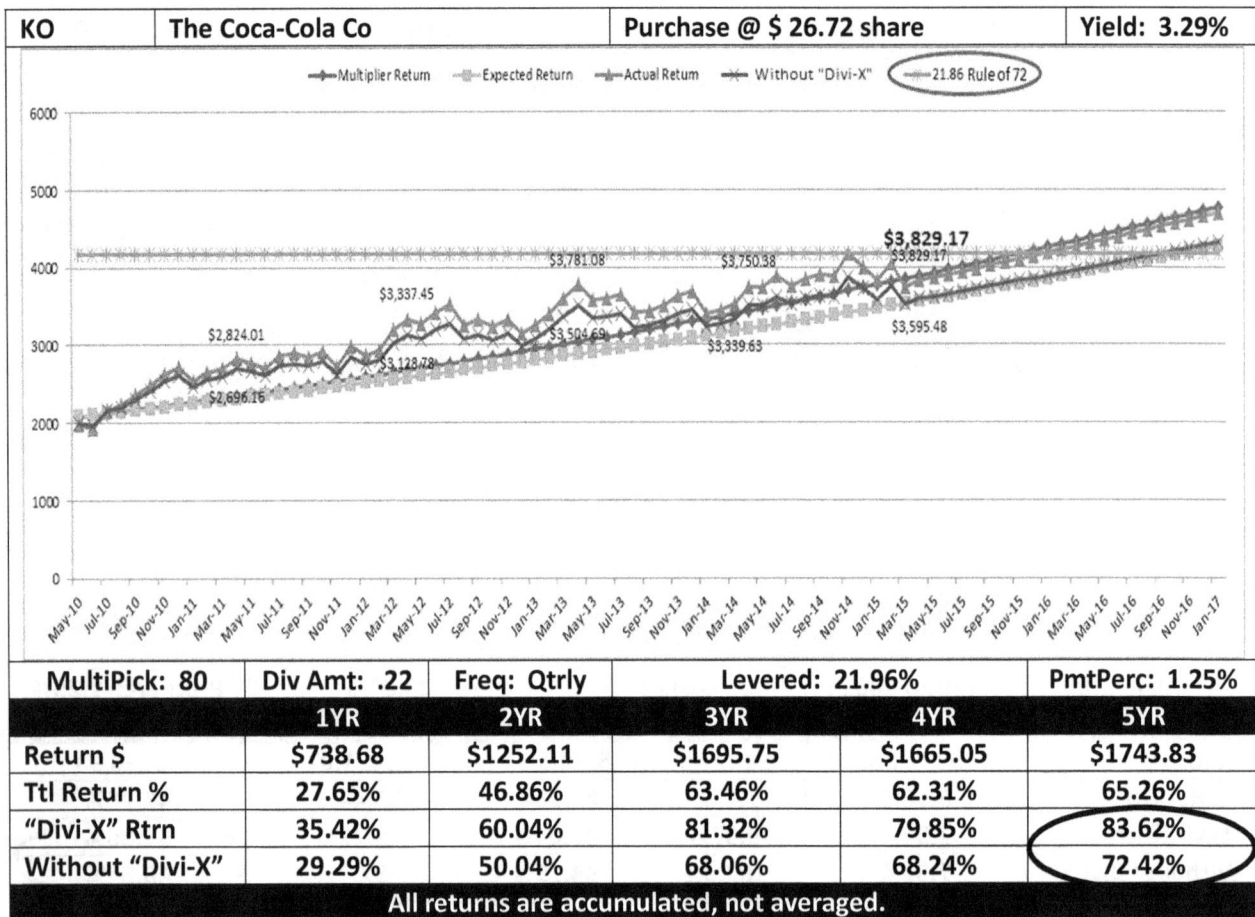

MultiPick: 80	Div Amt: .22	Freq: Qtrly	Levered: 21.96%		PmtPerc: 1.25%
	1YR	**2YR**	**3YR**	**4YR**	**5YR**
Return $	$738.68	$1252.11	$1695.75	$1665.05	$1743.83
Ttl Return %	27.65%	46.86%	63.46%	62.31%	65.26%
"Divi-X" Rtrn	35.42%	60.04%	81.32%	79.85%	83.62%
Without "Divi-X"	29.29%	50.04%	68.06%	68.24%	72.42%
All returns are accumulated, not averaged.					

A few things to note about this chart:

1. We levered at 21.96%, or 21.96 shares.
2. Whenever you get results at or above your 'Expected Return' level, you have to be happy or you should have expected more.
3. Notice in Nov-14, we doubled our money using the "Divi-X" system. It retreated slightly afterward, but still a nice morale boost. At no time during the five years would you have doubled your money Without "Divi-X."
4. Still champion… "Divi-X," with an 11.20% margin over 'Without "Divi-X".

TRV	Travelers Companies Inc	Purchase @ $ 50.74 share	Yield: 2.84%

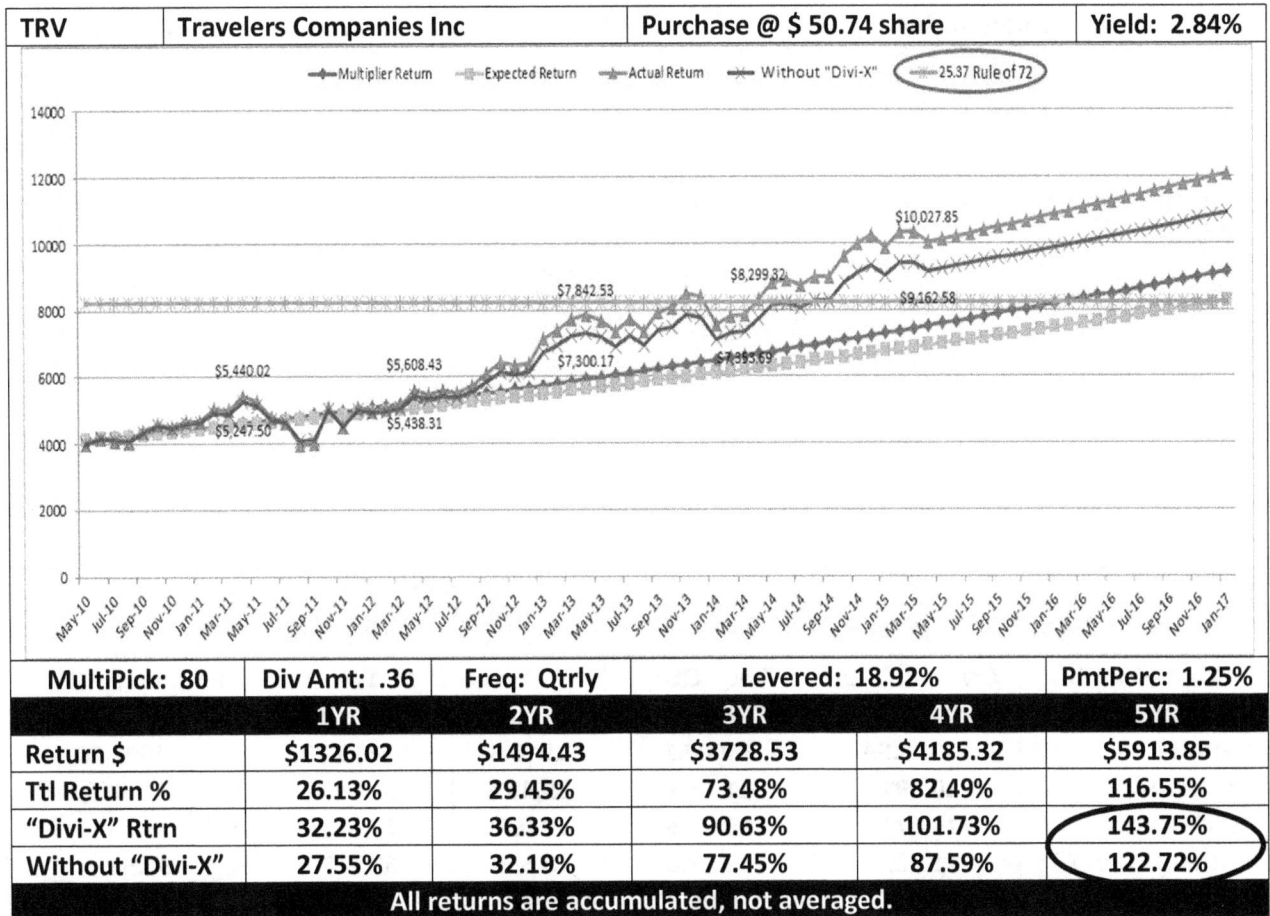

Legend: Multiplier Return — Expected Return — Actual Return — Without "Divi-X" — 25.37 Rule of 72

Values shown on chart: $5,440.02, $5,247.50, $5,608.43, $5,438.31, $7,842.53, $7,300.17, $7,395.69, $8,299.32, $9,162.58, $10,027.85

MultiPick: 80	Div Amt: .36	Freq: Qtrly	Levered: 18.92%		PmtPerc: 1.25%
	1YR	2YR	3YR	4YR	5YR
Return $	$1326.02	$1494.43	$3728.53	$4185.32	$5913.85
Ttl Return %	26.13%	29.45%	73.48%	82.49%	116.55%
"Divi-X" Rtrn	32.23%	36.33%	90.63%	101.73%	143.75%
Without "Divi-X"	27.55%	32.19%	77.45%	87.59%	122.72%
All returns are accumulated, not averaged.					

A few things to note about this chart:

1. We levered at 18.92%, or 18.92 shares.

2. Your money would have doubled approximately six months sooner than 'Without "Divi-X", but who's complaining? Everyone was a big winner with this stock. Bigger winner with "Divi-X." You know I had to say it.

3. Prime example of a little leverage going a long way. Our 18.92% in leverage reaped us an additional 21.03% over five years. That's enough for you to buy a copy of this book for everyone on your Christmas list.

UTX	United Technologies Corp	Purchase @ $ 74.95 share	Yield: 2.27%

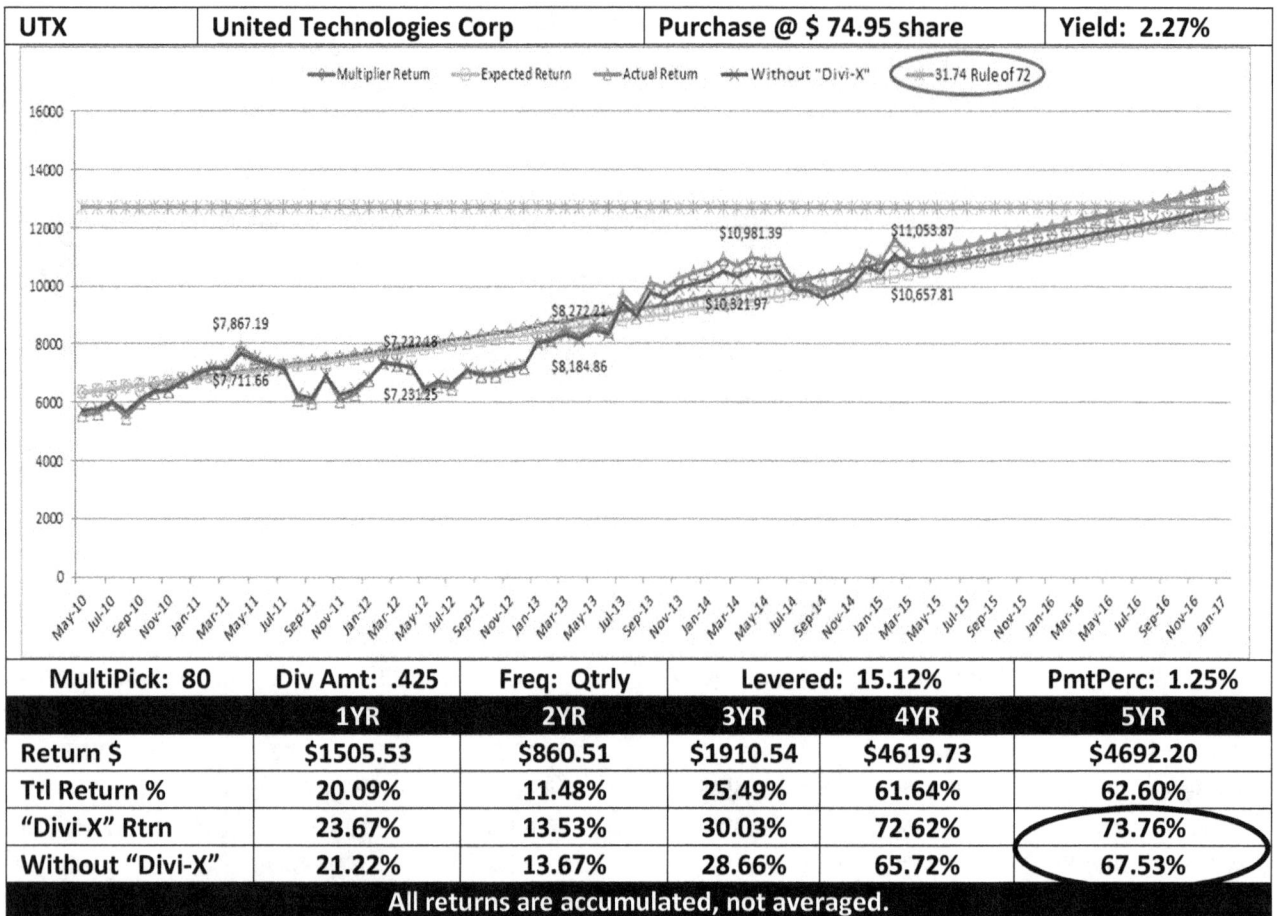

MultiPick: 80	Div Amt: .425	Freq: Qtrly	Levered: 15.12%		PmtPerc: 1.25%
	1YR	**2YR**	**3YR**	**4YR**	**5YR**
Return $	$1505.53	$860.51	$1910.54	$4619.73	$4692.20
Ttl Return %	20.09%	11.48%	25.49%	61.64%	62.60%
"Divi-X" Rtrn	23.67%	13.53%	30.03%	72.62%	73.76%
Without "Divi-X"	21.22%	13.67%	28.66%	65.72%	67.53%
All returns are accumulated, not averaged.					

A few things to note about this chart:

1. We levered at 15.12%, or 15.12 shares.

2. Again, it managed to meet or exceed your 'Expected Return,' so you would have to be pleased.

3. I couldn't think of much to say about this security, so to fill the white space I thought I would remind you again that the 'Ttl Return %' numbers are returns on the total shareholder value (not the cash value that the "Divi-X" returns are based on) with the added expense of margin interest. This figure will always trail the 'Without "Divi-X" figure because of the additional expense of margin interest. This is a good comparison when you want to know what kind of impact interest expense alone is having on total shareholder value, but is ultimately irrelevant as long as the "Divi-X" returns exceed the 'Without "Divi-X" returns.

4. Fill in the blank:
   a. Thanks to "_____", we beat 'Without "Divi-X," yet again. This time by 6.23%.

UNH	UnitedHealth Group Inc	Purchase @ $ 30.31 share	Yield: 1.65%

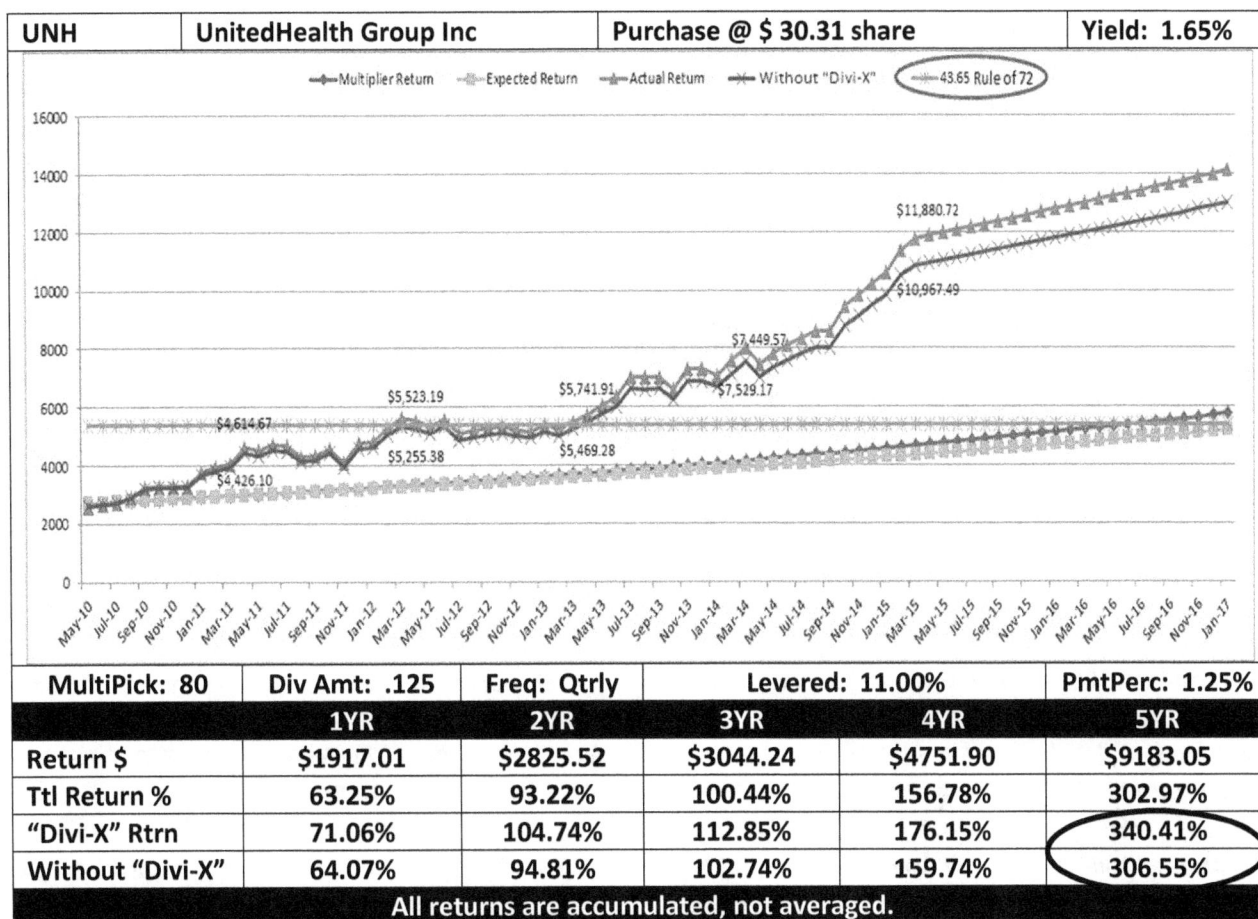

MultiPick: 80	Div Amt: .125	Freq: Qtrly	Levered: 11.00%		PmtPerc: 1.25%
	1YR	**2YR**	**3YR**	**4YR**	**5YR**
Return $	$1917.01	$2825.52	$3044.24	$4751.90	$9183.05
Ttl Return %	63.25%	93.22%	100.44%	156.78%	302.97%
"Divi-X" Rtrn	71.06%	104.74%	112.85%	176.15%	340.41%
Without "Divi-X"	64.07%	94.81%	102.74%	159.74%	306.55%
All returns are accumulated, not averaged.					

A few things to note about this chart:

1. The amazing performance of this one lifted our meager 11.0% leverage (or 11 shares) to an awesome 33.86% reward on top of the stellar 306.55% earned on its own.

2. Ok, I'm just nit-picking here, but after year two, even though 'Without "Divi-X" looks like it doubled your money, it fell short by $140. "Divi-X" did double your money by roughly $130. It wasn't until the following year that 'Without "Divi-X" managed to cross that milestone. Better late than never, but better sooner with "Divi-X" I now always say.

3. Another prime example why you shouldn't dismiss a small dividend yield:

	MSFT (pg.32)	UNH
Share Price	$30.96	$30.31
Div Yield	1.68%	1.65%
Leverage %	11.20%	11.00%
5 YR "Divi-X" Rtrn	77.91%	340.41%
Return on Leverage %	5.07%	33.86%

VZ	Verizon Communications Inc	Purchase @ $ 28.90 share	Yield: 6.57%

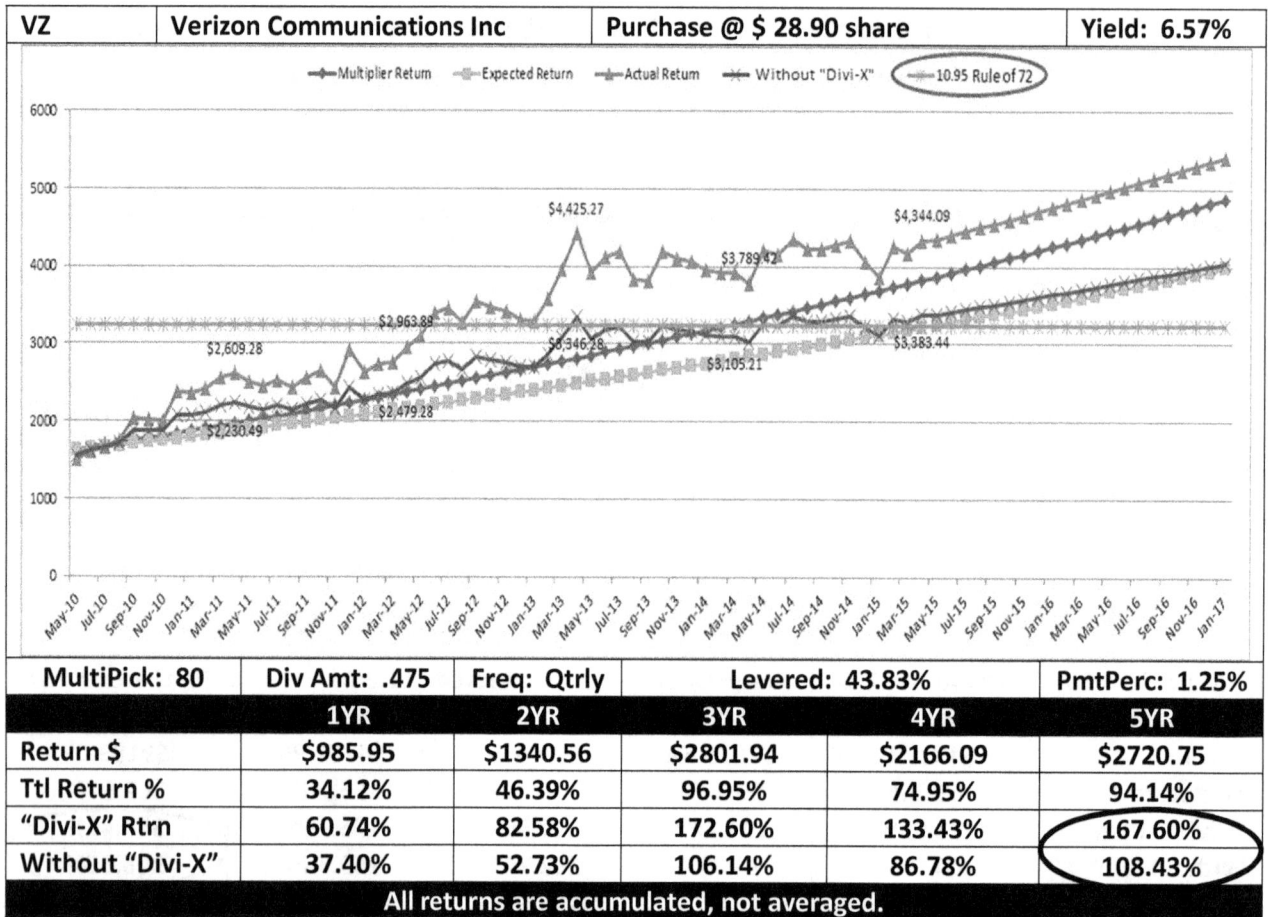

MultiPick: 80	Div Amt: .475	Freq: Qtrly	Levered: 43.83%		PmtPerc: 1.25%
	1YR	2YR	3YR	4YR	5YR
Return $	$985.95	$1340.56	$2801.94	$2166.09	$2720.75
Ttl Return %	34.12%	46.39%	96.95%	74.95%	94.14%
"Divi-X" Rtrn	60.74%	82.58%	172.60%	133.43%	167.60%
Without "Divi-X"	37.40%	52.73%	106.14%	86.78%	108.43%
All returns are accumulated, not averaged.					

A few things to note about this chart:

1. We levered at 43.83%, or 43.83 shares.
2. I love this one. The high yield on this well-known name paid for almost half of our shares at 43.83% leverage.
3. It doubled our money an entire year earlier than 'Without "Divi-X".
4. With a dividend yield of 6.57% allowing us to leverage such a large amount of our shares, our 'Actual Return' on our cash investment (not total shareholder value) is practically begging to double within 5 years with any modest increase in the share price whether or not there is an increase of dividend payouts in the future. This is hinted at by looking at the 5 year trend line of our 'Expected Return' rate which eventually crosses the 'Rule of 72' just after the five year time frame. Almost six years sooner than the 'Rule of 72' said we would double our money.
5. In the end, a 59.17% lead over 'Without "Divi-X" or, $960.65.

V	Visa Inc	Purchase @ $22.558 share	Yield: 0.56%

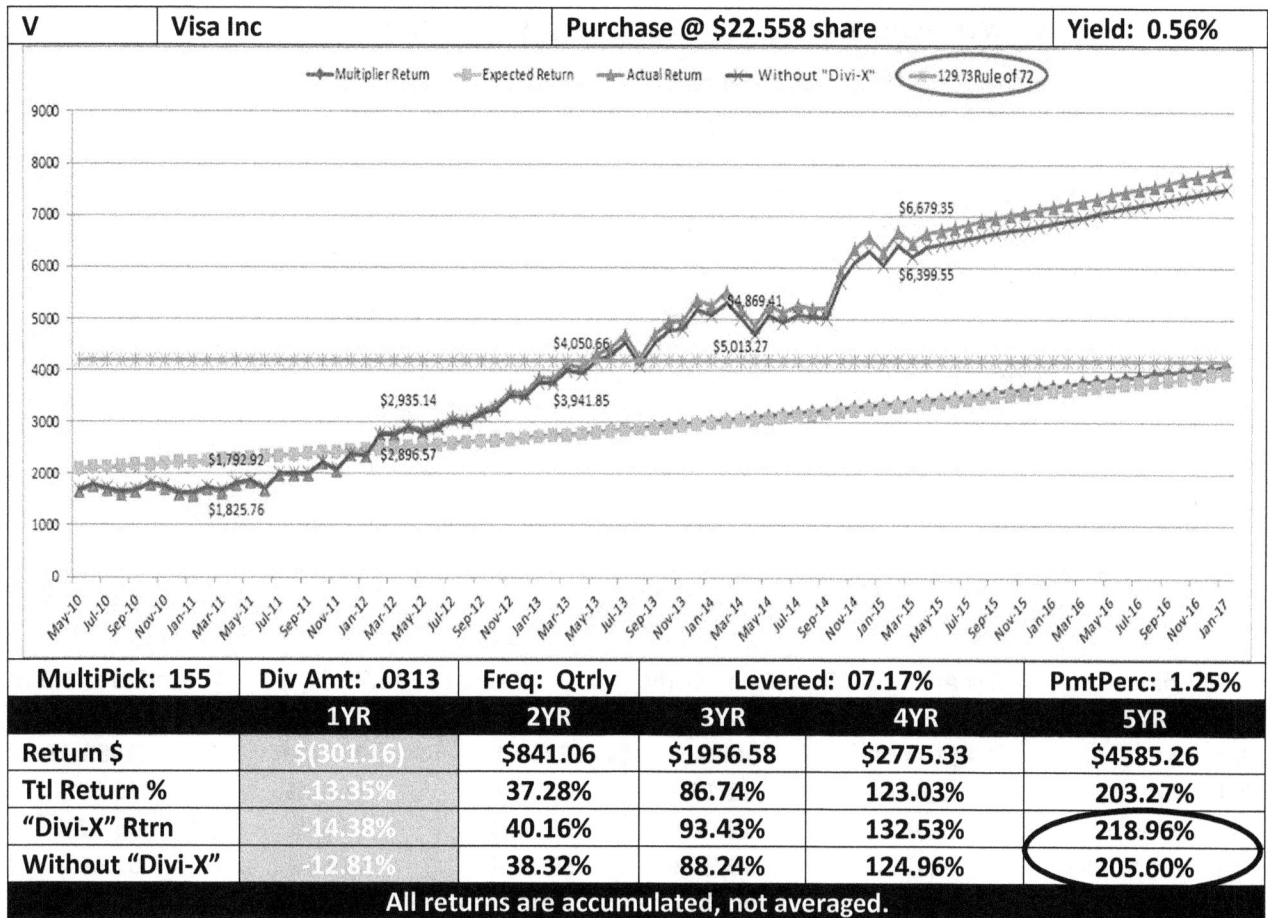

MultiPick: 155	Div Amt: .0313	Freq: Qtrly	Levered: 07.17%		PmtPerc: 1.25%
	1YR	**2YR**	**3YR**	**4YR**	**5YR**
Return $	$(301.16)	$841.06	$1956.58	$2775.33	$4585.26
Ttl Return %	-13.35%	37.28%	86.74%	123.03%	203.27%
"Divi-X" Rtrn	-14.38%	40.16%	93.43%	132.53%	218.96%
Without "Divi-X"	-12.81%	38.32%	88.24%	124.96%	205.60%
All returns are accumulated, not averaged.					

A few things to note about this chart:
1. We levered at 7.17%, or 7.17 shares.
2. Not much to brag about here but you have to admit, a 13.36% edge using only 7.17% leverage (and that's with a 155 "Multiplier Pick") is impressive even though it pales in comparison to the overall return.
3. The actual leverage dollar amount borrowed for this security was $161.72. The actual return on borrowed money is $279.80. That's 73% more than you borrowed and 173% actually earned on the borrowed $161.72. In other words, we would not have to pay back the $161.72 from the $279.90 because the returns shown are already net. How's that for perspective?
4. Anyway, once again "Divi-X" takes the lead.

WMT	Wal-Mart Stores Inc	Purchase @ $ 54.53 share	Yield: 2.22%

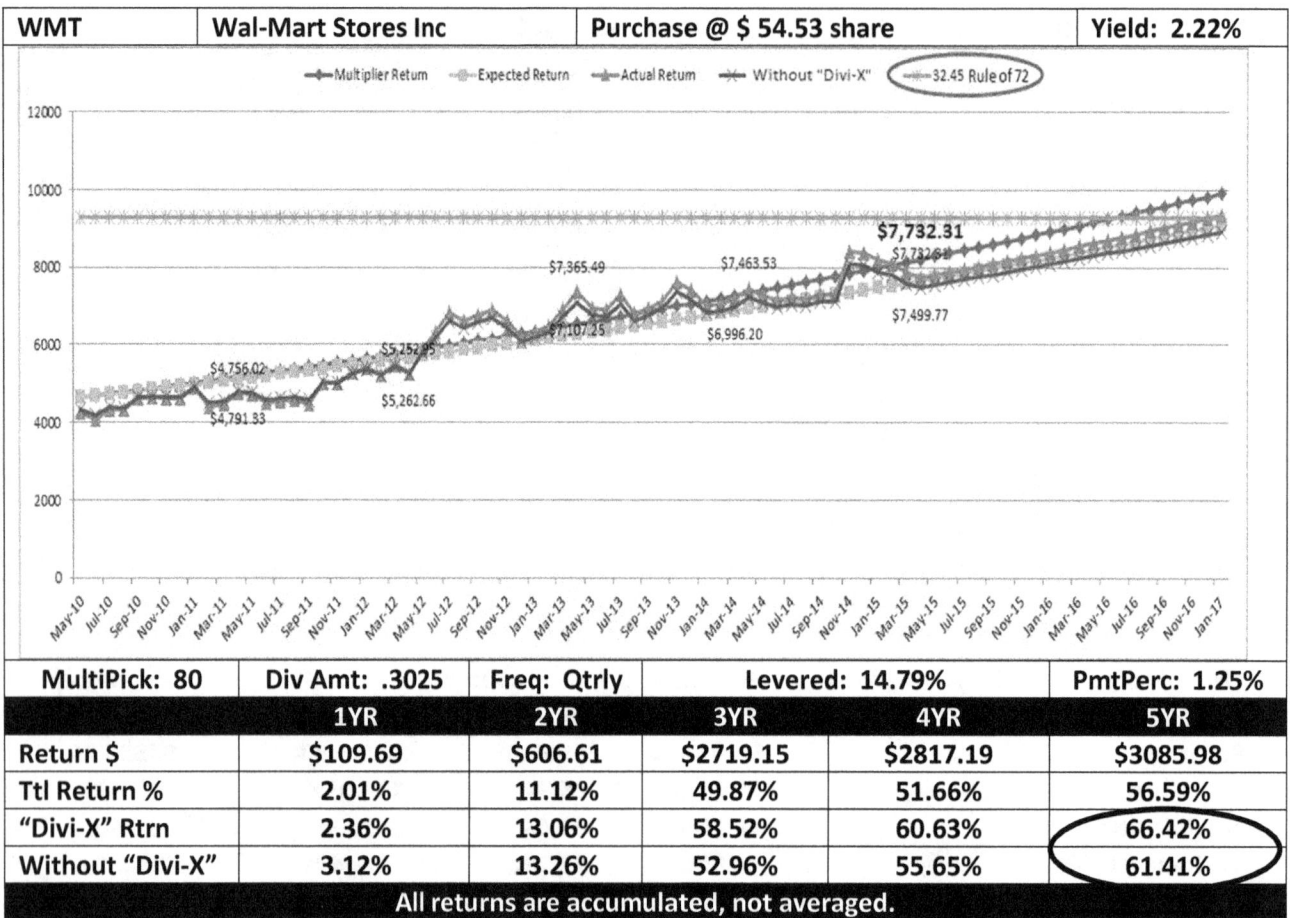

MultiPick: 80	Div Amt: .3025	Freq: Qtrly	Levered: 14.79%		PmtPerc: 1.25%
	1YR	**2YR**	**3YR**	**4YR**	**5YR**
Return $	$109.69	$606.61	$2719.15	$2817.19	$3085.98
Ttl Return %	2.01%	11.12%	49.87%	51.66%	56.59%
"Divi-X" Rtrn	2.36%	13.06%	58.52%	60.63%	66.42%
Without "Divi-X"	3.12%	13.26%	52.96%	55.65%	61.41%
All returns are accumulated, not averaged.					

A few things to note about this chart:

1. We levered at 14.79%, or 14.79 shares.
2. We didn't lever much on this stock and for the first couple of years it actually looked to work in our favor because the stagnant share price along with the added margin expense had us trailing, ever so slightly 'Without "Divi-X." In year one, 'Without "Divi-X" outperformed us by 0.76% and by a smaller 0.20% in the second year. In the following year, although not an earth shattering turn around, things started looking up. "Divi-X" had leap-frogged 'Without "Divi-X" for a modest 5.56% advantage.
3. Fortunately, with a little patience, we were both fairly rewarded in the long run with a slight 5.01% advantage to "Divi-X."

DIS	Walt Disney Co	Purchase @ $ 36.84 share	Yield: 1.09%

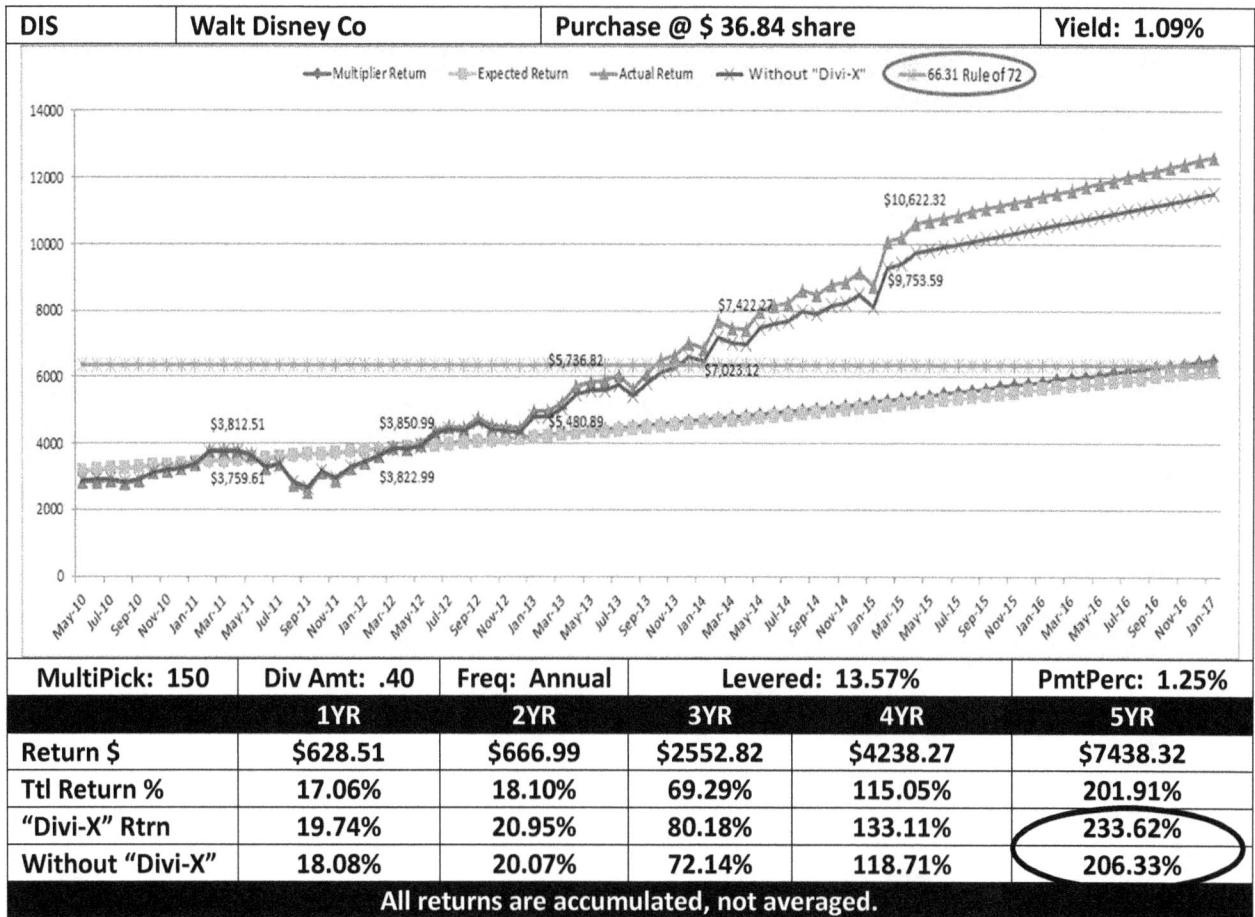

MultiPick: 150	Div Amt: .40	Freq: Annual	Levered: 13.57%		PmtPerc: 1.25%
	1YR	2YR	3YR	4YR	5YR
Return $	$628.51	$666.99	$2552.82	$4238.27	$7438.32
Ttl Return %	17.06%	18.10%	69.29%	115.05%	201.91%
"Divi-X" Rtrn	19.74%	20.95%	80.18%	133.11%	233.62%
Without "Divi-X"	18.08%	20.07%	72.14%	118.71%	206.33%
All returns are accumulated, not averaged.					

A few notes about this chart:

1. We levered at 13.57%, or 13.57 shares with a "Multiplier Pick" of 150.
2. Another example why you shouldn't dismiss a small yield and low leverage on a security. I don't think anyone would complain about an $868.73 net return on $500 borrowed. A 173.7% return on borrowed money alone.
3. And of course we have to mention the final tally. "Divi-X" with a 27.29% lead over 'Without "Divi-X" and while only leveraging 13.57%. Remarkable.

The "Divi-X" System Workbook: Once you enter the basic security information, you're almost no longer needed for "Divi-X" to do its job.

Chapter 3
How It Works

How It Works

The key to the "Divi-X" system is simply this:

The total monthly dividend is multiplied by a "Multiplier Pick" of your choosing to determine how much leverage you will actually borrow to achieve the results you hope for.

1. Any "Multiplier Pick" chosen should be able to cover the associated margin loan payment with the anticipated monthly dividend income you expect from the security.

2. You can purchase the maximum number of shares that the dividend payment can afford and that you are comfortable with borrowing against.

3. A "Multiplier Pick" in excess of 100 may have to be tweaked by you to come up with the scenario you want.

   a. There is no set rule of thumb as to the "Multiplier Pick." I try to keep the "Multiplier Pick" within a certain range of leverage. The higher the risk I feel for a particular security, the lower the leverage amount; therefore a lower "Multiplier Pick."

   b. On low yielding stocks, I'll likely pick as high a "Multiplier Pick" as possible as long as the interest is covered. This could possibly mean picking a "Multiplier Pick" well in excess of 100.

   c. You may want to go even higher if you're convinced the stock will payoff big soon. This might involve a "Multiplier Pick" so high that it doesn't even cover the interest on the margin loan.

   d. Or you may want to use a "Multiplier Pick" in the range of say 1 (yes you can go that low) to 15 until you become more familiar with the "Divi-X" System and the idea of using margin.

Walkthrough from Start to Finish

It might help to reference Fig. 3.2 while we go over this.

Determine your goal. Are you investing for income, short-term capital gains, long-term growth, or growth and income. Even though this program is suited for all investment goals and allows flexibility along the way, the numbers you choose in the beginning will have long-term effects on the actual results.

1. Pick your security
2. Record share price
    a. For reason of simplification, if you wish to account for trade commissions, I would include that in the cost basis of your purchase. For example, if you purchase 100 shares of XYZ Corp. @ $10/share and your trade commission is $7.00, divide that $7.00 among the total shares purchased which would give you a cost per share basis of 10.07/share.
3. Record the total number of shares purchased.
4. Record your Purchase Date.
5. Record total purchase price with or without commission (applies if you are using manual form).
6. Record the dividend amount and payout frequency (i.e., monthly, quarterly, semi-annual, etc.).
    a. Regardless of payout frequency, "Divi-X" breaks the dividends down to a monthly basis. Even though you may not receive them that often, it's easier to keep track of things because when you amortize, you'll be taking into account monthly debt service payments (even monthly debt service is not required but again, for simplification). You will find out later on that this is strictly a record-keeping procedure ("Divi-X" takes care of this) to track your investments progress. If you choose to break it down according to the actual frequency payout, you can do that to. Over the life of the holding, the difference in return is negligible on a percentage basis.
    b. By default, brokerage firms usually sweep any dividends received to the outstanding margin balance. That's not a big deal, it just reduces your principal balance but you can still use it by drawing on margin as the dividend payments make new margin available. As a matter of fact, the automatic sweep feature reduces your average daily balance which could offset the difference pointed out above, but again both are negligible.
7. Record your margin rate
    a. This number divided by twelve is what you multiply your outstanding margin balance by every month to derive the monthly interest amount associated with your security purchase ("Divi-X" Lite and the Workbook does this for you).
        i. For the purposes of this program, it is imperative that you learn that there are two separate margin balances.
            1. Your total outstanding margin balance
                a. This is the sum of all of your margin draws. This is the amount your brokerage firm charges interest on.
            2. Total outstanding margin balance per security
                a. This is where you keep your focus. If you maintain your debt service payments established when you purchase a new security using the "Divi-X" System, the total outstanding margin balance will take care of itself.

8. Return Rate
    a. You may recall so far, that in most of the examples in this book, I used an eight or nine percent 'Return Rate.' This number is what I hope to beat, not make. This number is entirely up to you. There are several reasons why you might want to change it:
        i. You're not as greedy as I am.
        ii. You're greedier than I am and that's okay.
        iii. You just want to outpace inflation and preserve principal.
        iv. Fill in the blank: _____
    b. The number I choose is usually in relation to what I can realistically expect as a rate of return or my minimum threshold of what constitutes a decent investment. If my investments are more conservative, then obviously I would shoot for a lower number. If riskier, than higher.
9. Determining how much leverage/risk you are willing to take on and how much of a return you hope to gain. This part is easy in concept, but tedious by hand.
    a. Multiplier Pick
        i. This part is cool. All you do is multiply the total monthly dividend to come up with the amount of leverage you wish to take on.

> Let's say we own 100 shares of ABC, Inc. at $50 a share for a total of $5,000. Your monthly dividend is $.1667 a share (4.0% Yield) x 100 shares = $16.67 (ABC, Inc. actually pays quarterly which would make it $50 a quarter, but remember we break it down into monthly distributions).
> Licking our forefinger and holding it up to the wind, something tells us to give this stock a 25 x's Multiplier Pick.
>> $16.67 a month x Multiplier Pick of 25 = $416.75
>> $16.67 x 25 = $416.75
> So, of our $5000 stock purchase, we leverage $416.75 of it. $416.75 is a nice bit of help but it's not enough. To heck with the forefinger in the wind approach, let's try putting our ear to the ground. Do I hear a Multiplier Pick of 50? Let's see how that plays out.
>> $16.67 a month x Multiplier Pick of 50 = $833.33
>> $16.67 x 50 = $833.33
> So of our $5000 stock purchase, we now have leveraged $833.33 of it leaving us to put up the remaining $4166.67. Not bad, but the only problem is you don't get paid till Friday and you don't have the whole $4166.67 to put up right now and you don't think the stock is going to stay this low much longer. Clearly, putting your ear to the ground didn't help, so now what do you do? By now, your gut is telling you; that you should've listened to it in the first place and go in with a Multiplier Pick of 75.
>> $16.67 a month x Multiplier Pick of 75 = $1250

$$\$16.67 \times 75 = \$1250$$

$5000 less $1250 leveraged only requires you to put up $3750. That not only helps you buy the stock before pay day, but still leaves you enough to eat and by toilet paper.

  ii. You can multiply the total monthly dividend up to 100 x's and even more in some cases. Using the incredible ease of the "Divi-X" System Workbook, I toyed with dividend multiples in excess of 100. **I was startled to find that I could sometimes borrow one hundred percent of the stock purchase price and borrow additional money to put in my pocket and all I had to do was let the dividends pay for it all, provided the stock maintained its dividend**. In the interest of full disclosure, I am not using this as a selling point for the "Divi-X" System. The stocks in those scenarios are high-yield and very risky. It could work but for me personally, it is contrary to my belief of using leverage prudently. As of this writing, I do have some stocks leveraged as high as eighty percent using the "Divi-X" System. The results are mixed on capital appreciation but they are definitely meeting my income goals.

10. "PmtPerc"

  a. This is the monthly payment amount that you'll agree with yourself that you want to pay on the outstanding amortized loan balance associated with your security.

  b. The amortized loan amount will take on the form of a line of credit, but you will pay on it as if it were a credit card. Let me explain:

    i. Most lines of credit (just like your margin/brokerage account) will not require you to pay down principal, but instead, just have you make interest payments (individual terms may vary). You don't want to do this. By not paying down the principal, you will not be freeing up margin for future investments and the added interest will have a serious impact on your long-term results. Instead, you will want to:

    ii. Pay on it like a credit card. Traditionally, credit cards usually set payments as a percentage of the outstanding balance. The low percentage they use is designed to have you cover interest every month and reduce a very small amount of principal so you're basically paying on it forever. The payment percentage they use is in the area of one and a half percent (1.5%). Now, in reality, if you so choose to, you can apply the full amount of dividends toward the amortized loan and pay off the loan much quicker.

  c. To keep it simple, I usually limit the "PmtPerc" to one percent (1%) up to one and a half percent (1.5%), but I choose as my default, one and a quarter percent (1.25%). If you have access to the ease of the "Divi-X" Systems Workbook, you could play with numbers like .75%, 1.05%, 1.68%; anything you can think of within a matter of seconds. But if you choose to go it alone (filling in the form in the Appendix), I recommend limiting your choices to:

     i. All dividends paid

    ii. 1.00%

   iii. 1.25%

   iv. 1.50%

    v. "The "Divi-X" System Workbook" will allow you the flexibility to pay as much as you want as often as you want and have your results reflect the changes immediately.

d. Let's carry down our example from where we left off in the previous section, "Multiplier Pick." You had just purchased 100 shares of ABC, Inc. for $5000 using $1250 leverage and $3750 of your own money. That $1250 has to be paid back, and with interest. You just spent all of your money on food and toilet paper and your pay check on Friday has to pay the rent and you don't know if you'll have enough money for gas to get to and from work. What'll you do (if you haven't figured it out by now, this is my attempt at humor)?

Here's how it looks. You owe $1250. Your broker isn't harassing you for a payment because he has the security of ABC, Inc. shares sitting in his house (not his actual house) to secure your debt. Your $3750 upfront money far exceeds the $1250 you borrowed to get the $5000 in shares, so your broker is sleeping peacefully. Should that change, he has no problems selling your shares for you to satisfy your debt (that is a margin call and you do not ever want that to happen). Your confidence in ABC, Inc. doesn't really make that a concern for you.

You do, however, want to pay this balance down, because having margin tied up in ABC, Inc. won't allow you to deploy that margin elsewhere. Plus, the additional interest expense eats away at your returns. So what do you do? You treat your margin balance like a credit card. Regardless of the payment percentage you use, please at least try to cover the interest expense. Here's what the options I provided above would look like if you chose to elect one of them.

Dividends	PmtPerc	Payment	Principal*	Interest	Left Over*
$16.67	All DIV's	$16.67	$8.86	$7.81	$0.00
$16.67	1.00%	$12.50	$4.69	$7.81	$4.17
$16.67	1.25%	$15.63	$7.81	$7.81	$1.04
$16.67	1.50%	$18.75	$10.94	$7.81	$0.00

*'Principal' plus 'Left Over' = New margin available for investment elsewhere
Fig. 3.1

You may have noticed that the last option, the 1.50% payment option exceeds the dividend amount. That's ok. You would only pay up to the monthly dividend payout of $16.67, not a penny more. Over time, the reduction in principal will lower the payment to the selected 1.50% payment option chosen.

Honestly you don't have to do anything because your broker will automatically sweep all dividends to any outstanding balance you have on your margin/brokerage account. Should you need that money for gas, or whatever, most brokerages allow you to draw on that money for personal use (standard margin rates apply of course). This brings us to a very crucial learning point. **Why would you go through all the trouble of amortizing a margin loan when your broker automatically sweeps your dividends toward your margin balance and you still have the option to draw on it?**

When you open a margin/brokerage account at a brokerage firm, they keep track of your cost basis, realized/unrealized gains and losses, dividends received (some even project your dividend income by security) and margin interest expense. What they don't do is track the effects that dividends and margin expense have on the overall return of your individual securities. Once a dividend has been received by you, the only time you see it in any helpful way is when your broker itemizes it on your 1099 for tax purposes. Other than that, all they measure for you is how much you paid for a stock and the difference in the stock price at any given time. It does not account for the impact of dividends or margin interest expense on your individual securities. This alone could have negative consequences when it comes to making buy and hold decisions. Later in the book, I show you just how negative those consequences are. I think the results will surprise you.

That's all there is to it. Very rarely, will you find an investment opportunity and plug in the exact numbers in this system and be completely satisfied with the end result the first time you run the numbers. If you are going to use the manual form included in the back of this book, "tweaking" will almost be a necessity when it comes to customizing your investment structure using the "Divi-X" system. Every time you change one number, say the "PmtPerc" field, you will have to recalculate everything all over again.

e. If you are doing this program manually using the forms provided in the back, you might not have the patience to run every different scenario to your liking. However, I also provide you with a free offer in the back of the book for "Divi-X" Lite. A much more advanced version of the form version but not as sophisticated and in-depth as the full "Divi-X" System Workbook. I sincerely hope you'll take advantage of it.

f. Now it is very possible that you will be satisfied with your initial numbers, and later on I'll show you how to narrow your ranges to get positive results with little guess work; but imagine how much money you'll be leaving on the table because you settled for satisfactory results instead of ideal results. Why settle for, "I can live with that" instead of "That's just what I wanted"? "Divi-X" Lite streamlines this process to make it go much faster. The "Divi-X" System Workbook makes it ridiculously simple and helps you take advantage of the most efficient investment option available, allowing you to compare up to sixteen different outcomes at once.

During the holding period of your investment, things are likely to change. If you do not have the "Divi-X" System Workbook, any change in your investment will have to be manually taken into account by you. "Divi-X" Lite can help you considerably with this, but not with all of it.

What might change?

    i. Dividend Payments (you'll notice in the "Dow 30" examples that had happened frequently)

    ii. Margin Rate

    iii. Stock Split

    iv. Partial Divestiture

  g. In the "Divi-X" System Workbook, all these changes can be made with a simple entry. "Divi-X" Lite can do some of the same, but not all.

11. Actually, there is an additional twenty-three steps involved in filling out the user form. I'll refer you to the "**Leverage Security User Form**" in the Appendix at the back of the book for you to become more familiar with it. Don't let the form discourage you. You can always take advantage of "Divi-X" Lite for free.

Walkthrough from Start to Finish Using the "Divi-X" System Workbook

The steps involved using the "Divi-X" System Workbook are a little more streamlined than the walkthrough just lined out. Ok, a lot more streamlined.

	Ticker		Stock Price		No. Shares		Purch Date		End Date		DIV Pmt		Multiplier Start		Rtrn Rate?		% Levered
1	DIVX	2	100.0000	3	100	4	06/18/15		J-15	5	$ 0.9500	6	20	7	9.00%		25.33%
																	Rule 72
																	18.95
	12	Multiplier Pick		8	DIV Per/Year		Monthly DIV	9	Pmt Perc	10	Margin Rate	11	Multiplier Step		Mth DIV Ttl	Based on DIV	
		80			4		$ 0.3167		1.25%		7.75%		5		$ 31.67	On Est Rtrn	5.14
																On Act Rtrn	5.14

DIV Multiplier	Cash Out Of Pocket	Leverage Amt	Ttl Share Value	#Shares Purch by Leverage	DIV Yield	Min Pmt	Principal	Margin Interest	Net DIV Cash	Monthly Net Div Cash (1yr)	Monthly Net Div Cash (5yr)	Yield Less Margin Int	Yield Less Marg Int (1YR)	Yield Less Marg Int (5YR)	Leverage Ratio
0	20	$ 9,366.67	$ 633.33	$10,000.00	6.33	3.80%	$ 7.92	$ 3.83	$ 4.09	$ 23.75	$ 24.26	$ 26.13	3.04%	3.11%	3.35%	6.33%
1	25	$ 9,208.33	$ 791.67	$10,000.00	7.92	3.80%	$ 9.90	$ 4.78	$ 5.11	$ 21.77	$ 22.41	$ 24.75	2.84%	2.92%	3.22%	7.92%
2	30	$ 9,050.00	$ 950.00	$10,000.00	9.50	3.80%	$ 11.88	$ 5.74	$ 6.14	$ 19.79	$ 20.56	$ 23.36	2.62%	2.73%	3.10%	9.50%
3	35	$ 8,891.67	$ 1,108.33	$10,000.00	11.08	3.80%	$ 13.85	$ 6.70	$ 7.16	$ 17.81	$ 18.71	$ 21.98	2.40%	2.52%	2.97%	11.08%
4	40	$ 8,733.33	$ 1,266.67	$10,000.00	12.67	3.80%	$ 15.83	$ 7.65	$ 8.18	$ 15.83	$ 16.85	$ 20.59	2.18%	2.32%	2.83%	12.67%
5	45	$ 8,575.00	$ 1,425.00	$10,000.00	14.25	3.80%	$ 17.81	$ 8.61	$ 9.20	$ 13.85	$ 15.00	$ 19.21	1.94%	2.10%	2.69%	14.25%
6	50	$ 8,416.67	$ 1,583.33	$10,000.00	15.83	3.80%	$ 19.79	$ 9.57	$ 10.23	$ 11.88	$ 13.15	$ 17.82	1.69%	1.88%	2.54%	15.83%
7	55	$ 8,258.33	$ 1,741.67	$10,000.00	17.42	3.80%	$ 21.77	$ 10.52	$ 11.25	$ 9.90	$ 11.30	$ 16.44	1.44%	1.64%	2.39%	17.42%
8	60	$ 8,100.00	$ 1,900.00	$10,000.00	19.00	3.80%	$ 23.75	$ 11.48	$ 12.27	$ 7.92	$ 9.45	$ 15.06	1.17%	1.40%	2.23%	19.00%
9	65	$ 7,941.67	$ 2,058.33	$10,000.00	20.58	3.80%	$ 25.73	$ 12.44	$ 13.29	$ 5.94	$ 7.60	$ 13.67	0.90%	1.15%	2.07%	20.58%
10	70	$ 7,783.33	$ 2,216.67	$10,000.00	22.17	3.80%	$ 27.71	$ 13.39	$ 14.32	$ 3.96	$ 5.75	$ 12.29	0.61%	0.89%	1.89%	22.17%
11	75	$ 7,625.00	$ 2,375.00	$10,000.00	23.75	3.80%	$ 29.69	$ 14.35	$ 15.34	$ 1.98	$ 3.89	$ 10.90	0.31%	0.61%	1.72%	23.75%
12	80	$ 7,466.67	$ 2,533.33	$10,000.00	25.33	3.80%	$ 31.67	$ 15.31	$ 16.36	$ -	$ 2.04	$ 9.52	0.00%	0.33%	1.53%	25.33%
13	85	$ 7,308.33	$ 2,691.67	$10,000.00	26.92	3.80%	$ 33.65	$ 16.26	$ 17.38	$ (1.98)	$ 0.19	$ 8.13	-0.32%	0.03%	1.34%	26.92%
14	90	$ 7,150.00	$ 2,850.00	$10,000.00	28.50	3.80%	$ 35.63	$ 17.22	$ 18.41	$ (3.96)	$ (1.66)	$ 6.75	-0.66%	-0.28%	1.13%	28.50%
15	95	$ 6,991.67	$ 3,008.33	$10,000.00	30.08	3.80%	$ 37.60	$ 18.18	$ 19.43	$ (5.94)	$ (3.51)	$ 5.37	-1.02%	-0.60%	0.92%	30.08%
16	100	$ 6,833.33	$ 3,166.67	$10,000.00	31.67	3.80%	$ 39.58	$ 19.13	$ 20.45	$ (7.92)	$ (5.36)	$ 3.98	-1.39%	-0.94%	0.70%	31.67%

Fig. 3.2

1. Pick your security
2. Record share price
3. Record the total number of shares purchased

4. Record your Purchase Date
5. Record the dividend amount per share per actual pay period or "DIV Pmt"
6. "Multiplier Start" – This field is associated with the "Multiplier Step" field (#11) just below it. If you look at the "DIV Multiplier" column in **Fig. 3.2**, you'll notice the first number in the column is 20. That is the "Multiplier Start" and constitutes the first number in your "DIV Multiplier" column as the first projection out of the sixteen projections you can choose from. Also, you'll observe that every number below that in the "DIV Multiplier" column is in increments of 5 (25, 30, 35, 40, 45, 50, etc.); this is the "Multiplier Step." If the "Multiplier Step had been 10, the numbers under the "DIV Multiplier" column would be in sequences of 10 (30, 40, 50, 60, etc.). A "Multiplier Step" of 1 would give you 21, 22, 23, 24, etc. Both of these numbers are determined by you. You could have a "Multiplier Start" of 1 and a "Multiplier Step" of 1 or any other combination that makes sense for you.
7. "Rtrn Rte" or Return Rate - You may recall that in most of all the examples throughout this book, I used an eight or nine percent Return Rate. This number is what I hope to beat, not make. This number is entirely up to you.
8. "DIV Per/Year – Pretty self-explanatory. Just enter the number of times per year the security pays out a dividend.
9. "PmtPerc" - This is the monthly payment amount that you'll agree with yourself that you want to pay on the outstanding amortized loan balance associated with your security. For a more detailed explanation, see step 10 in the previous walkthrough.
10. "Margin Rate" – This is the annual rate your broker charges you on your outstanding loan balance. Check your statement every month because bells and whistles don't go off when this rate changes. It's up to you to stay on top of this.
11. "Multiplier Step" – See step 6 for explanation.
12. "Multiplier Pick" –This is the last step in the process. Taken all together, with the entry of a few fields, the "Divi-X" System Workbook offers you 16 different scenarios to choose from and the "Multiplier Pick" is your choice out of the 16 options. Don't like the options? Changing any field will give you 16 more options to choose from. It's ridiculously simple.

All of the other fields in **Fig. 3.2** are self-explanatory except for 'Net DIV Cash,' 'Monthly Net Div Cash (1Yr),' 'Monthly Net Div Cash (5YR),' 'Yield Less Margin Int,' 'Yield Less Margin Int (1Yr),' and 'Yield Less Margin Int (5Yr). These fields are extremely important when considering which 'Multiplier Pick' to choose. They basically tell you how much excess dividend cash you'll have every month after making a full debt service payment of interest and principal. For example, in **Fig. 3.2**, the user chose a "Multiplier Pick" of 80, and here's why:

If you follow the "Multiplier Pick" row of 80 all the way across to the 'Net DIV Cash' column, you see that the field is empty. That is because, on the first month, his monthly dividend payment was the exact amount of a full prinicple and interest payment on the margin loan. Had the user chose a "Multiplier Pick" of 75 (in the row above it), he/she would've had an excess dividend payment of $1.98 cents. A "Multiplier Pick" of 85 (the row below it) and it leaves a shortfall of ($1.98) cents.

Continue on to the next column, 'Monthly Net Div Cash (1YR)' and you see that there is a number indicating an excess of dividend cash, after a full interest and principal payment, of $2.04 cents. Had the user chose a "Multiplier Pick" of 85, he/she would now have an excess of $.19 cents instead of a negative amount of $(1.98). The numbers increase even further when you look under the 'Monthly Net Div Cash (5Yr)' column. The reason being, is because over time, as the outstanding margin loan balance gets paid down, the monthly payments decrease as the "PmtPerc" represents a percentage of a smaller loan balance. The remaining fields are just the projected yields on those excess dividend cash payments at 1Yr and 5Yr.

These fields are crucial when you are deciding on what "Multiplier Pick" to choose because it tells you how much leverage you can afford to have your dividends pay for. Later on, these numbers can be tinkered with and we'll go over that later, but you will notice me stress at times throughout this book: Treat any margin transaction within your own account as if you were borrowing outside funds that must be paid back. Do this, and you'll have a tremendous safety cushion should things take a negative turn down the road (ie., a dividend cut or elimination). This is a crucial element to using leverage wisely.

"Divi-X" System Workbook: The screenshot in **Fig. 3.2** is called the "Leverage Projection Worksheet." The manual walkthrough is a much more involved process than using the "Divi-X" System Workbook. Even the free "Divi-X" Lite version only offers you one scenario at a time. It is also important to note that the "Leverage Projection Worksheet" is just that; a projection and is only the first part of the process. The "Divi-X" System Workbook also gives you the ability to track and maintain your investments with the greatest of ease with just a simple entry every month to update the share price and maybe the occasional dividend or margin rate change.

Will The "Divi-X" System Work in a High Interest Rate Environment?

That's a good question. Let's explore that. In reality, if share price appreciation is high enough, than undoubtedly it'll work. But will it work better than without using the "Divi-X" System? Let's go back to the "Dow 30." In **Fig. 3.3**, I list a table of the "Dow 30" five year returns used in the beginning of the book. They all used a "Multiplier Pick" of 80 (except for (DIS)ney and (V)isa), a "PmtPerc" of 1.25% and a "Margin Rate" of 7.75%. We will compare them only changing the "Margin Rate" from 7.75% to 12.5%.

Ticker	"Multiplier Pick"	5YR Return w/o "Divi-X"	5YR Return @ 7.75%	5YR Return @ 12.50%
AXP	80	287.11%	348.69%	342.34%
BA	80	198.11%	247.89%	240.00%
CAT	80	232.63%	332.43%	319.35%
CVX	80	104.67%	130.85%	121.33%
CSCO	N/A	N/A	N/A	N/A
DD	80	211.43%	350.73%	330.30%
XOM	80	55.86%	60.22%	55.31%
GE	80	146.86%	179.16%	171.75%
GS	80	19.30%	17.23%	16.62%
HD	80	264.44%	343.44%	334.50%

Ticker	"Multiplier Pick"	5YR Return w/o "Divi-X"	5YR Return @ 7.75%	5YR Return @ 12.50%
MMM	80	159.81%	197.62%	189.82%
T	80	83.67%	126.28%	104.40%
INTC	80	12.24%	9.18%	5.23%
IBM	80	43.34%	45.00%	40.96%
JNJ	80	76.36%	88.99%	81.43%
JPM	80	51.62%	52.20%	51.40%
MCD	80	60.18%	67.42%	60.54%
MRK	80	85.89%	107.22%	96.73%
MSFT	80	72.84%	77.91%	74.60%
NKE	80	169.07%	182.97%	180.30%
PFE	80	139.09%	181.98%	171.42%
PG	80	48.51%	52.66%	45.83%
KO	80	72.42%	83.62%	76.25%
TRV	80	122.72%	143.75%	137.63%
UTX	80	67.53%	73.76%	69.09%
UNH	80	306.55%	340.41%	337.17%
VZ	80	108.43%	167.60%	147.14%
V	155	205.60%	218.96%	216.94%
WMT	80	61.41%	66.42%	61.86%
DIS	150	206.33%	233.62%	229.50%

Fig. 3.3

After reviewing the chart above, where returns were already close (as in (GS) and (INTC)) at a Margin Rate of 7.75%, the added interest expense made all the difference, but minimally. Again, had we put our hindsight genius caps on, I'm sure tweaking the variables, such as a higher "Multiplier Pick" or a lower "PmtPerc" would've provided us with entirely different results; but alas, we are fortune chasers, not fortune tellers.

Now, obviously, this is an oversimplification. Had interest rates risen to the rate of 12.5% during this five year period, the Dow might not have done nearly as well and we would be working with different five year results. But as to the performance of the "Divi-X" System with and without, I think you would have to conclude that it does work in a high-rate environment.

How About Conservative Investments in a High Interest Rate Environment?

Is there even such a thing as a conservative investment in a high interest rate environment? Anyway, instead of addressing the unlikely scenario of a conservative investment in a high interest rate environment using The "Divi-X" System, I instead, chose to find the most conservative investment you could invest in 'while' in a high interest rate environment and still come out ahead using The "Divi-X" System as opposed to not using it. Keep in mind, I'm not talking about breaking even, I'm talking about when "Divi-X" starts to exceed 'Without "Divi-X." We'll start with the table in **Fig. 3.4**.

If you have a dividend yield of	You would need a share price appreciation of*	Without "Divi-X" 5YR Ttl/5YR Avg	"Divi-X" 5YR Ttl/5YR Avg
2%	8.50%	61.66%/12.33%	62.09%/12.42%
3%	7.75%	61.20/12.24	61.80/12.36
4%	6.50%	57.54/11.51	57.07/11.41
5%	6.00%	59.21/11.84	59.42/11.88
6%	5.00%	57.80/11.56	57.13/11.43
7%	4.50%	59.71/11.94	60.50/12.10

*To match or beat the returns of 'Without "Divi-X"' @ a margin rate of 12.5% after five years.
Fig. 3.4

After you have reviewed the returns in **Fig. 3.4**, I want you to ask me the obvious question. Go ahead. Ask me why you should even bother with "Divi-X" if it's going to basically return the same results as if I hadn't used "Divi-X" at all? That's a good question. I'm glad you asked. And the simple answer is you wouldn't. The results above are intended to show you a minimum hurdle that would have to be overcome before you start receiving the benefit of "Divi-X" in a high interest rate environment. For example, in the case of the dividend yield at 5% in **Fig. 3.4**, once your share price appreciates greater than 6%, the wider the return gap between "Divi-X" and Without "Divi-X" in your favor. Read on to get a better idea of what I mean.

It is important to note that the only time since 1960, interest rates got this close and sometimes exceeded, was the period between 1980 and 1984. The average yield for the S&P during that time frame was 4.85% and the average earnings rate for the same period was 10.28% (source: http://pages.stern.nyu.edu/~adamodar/New_Home_Page/datafile/spearn.htm which obtained it from Bloomberg and S&P). We're going to round up that 4.85% dividend yield to an even 5%. If you look at the table in **Fig. 3.4** where the dividend is 5%, you see that you would only need a share price appreciation of 6% to match using **"Divi-X"** compared to **'Without "Divi-X."'** The average earnings yield during that time period was 10.28%.

If you had a dividend yield of	If you had a share price appreciation of	Without "Divi-X" 5YR Ttl/5YR Avg	"Divi-X" 5YR Ttl/5YR Avg
5%	10.28%	90.41%/18.08%	111.12%/22.22%

Fig. 3.5

Looking at **Fig 3.5**, it appears that for every 1% increase in share price appreciation above the 6%, **"Divi-X"** improves its return gap between **Without "Divi-X"** by roughly .83% a year on average. Also worth mentioning is that after 1984, interest rates have been in an aggressive steady decline ever since which would have further enhanced the "Divi-X" results in **Fig. 3.5,** but 'Without "Divi-X" would stay the same because it was an all cash investment not subject to interest expense.

Will "Divi-X" Work if My Share Price is Lower Then When I Purchased It?

This one is very cool. I was reading one of my regular investment sites and an author recommended **American Capital Mortgage Investment Crp (MTGE),** a real estate investment trust yielding a generous 11.6%. A large dividend doesn't scare me away from a security but again, remember high yield can be very high risk. Quickly, I look at the five year chart and the first thing I notice is that it hasn't even been trading for five years; just under four to be more precise. Again, this would not be a disqualifier for me.

The next thing I notice is that the current share price is lower than when it started trading publicly. I'm still not turned off just yet. I went to the company's web site to start digging through their 'Investor Relations' area and find that they highlight the total dividends paid out since their IPO in August 2011; a combined total of $10.75, not bad at all. Immediately, I start to wonder if they're pointing out the high dividend payout because their share price is trading lower than the IPO price. Long story short, for reasons not mentioned above, I decided not to invest in MTGE, but I thought it would make an excellent case study for the "Divi-X" system. Can you earn a respectable return using the "Divi-X" system if the share price is lower than your purchase price?

The reason that I find this to be an excellent example is because after its IPO in August 2011, it wasn't a high yielder at all. Had you purchased their shares at $18.63 when they went public, your yield would have been just over four and a quarter percent. As I'm writing this, your yield would be 11.6% on a share price of $17.24.

MTGE	American Capital Mortgage Investment Crp	Purchase @ $18.63 share	Yield: 4.29%

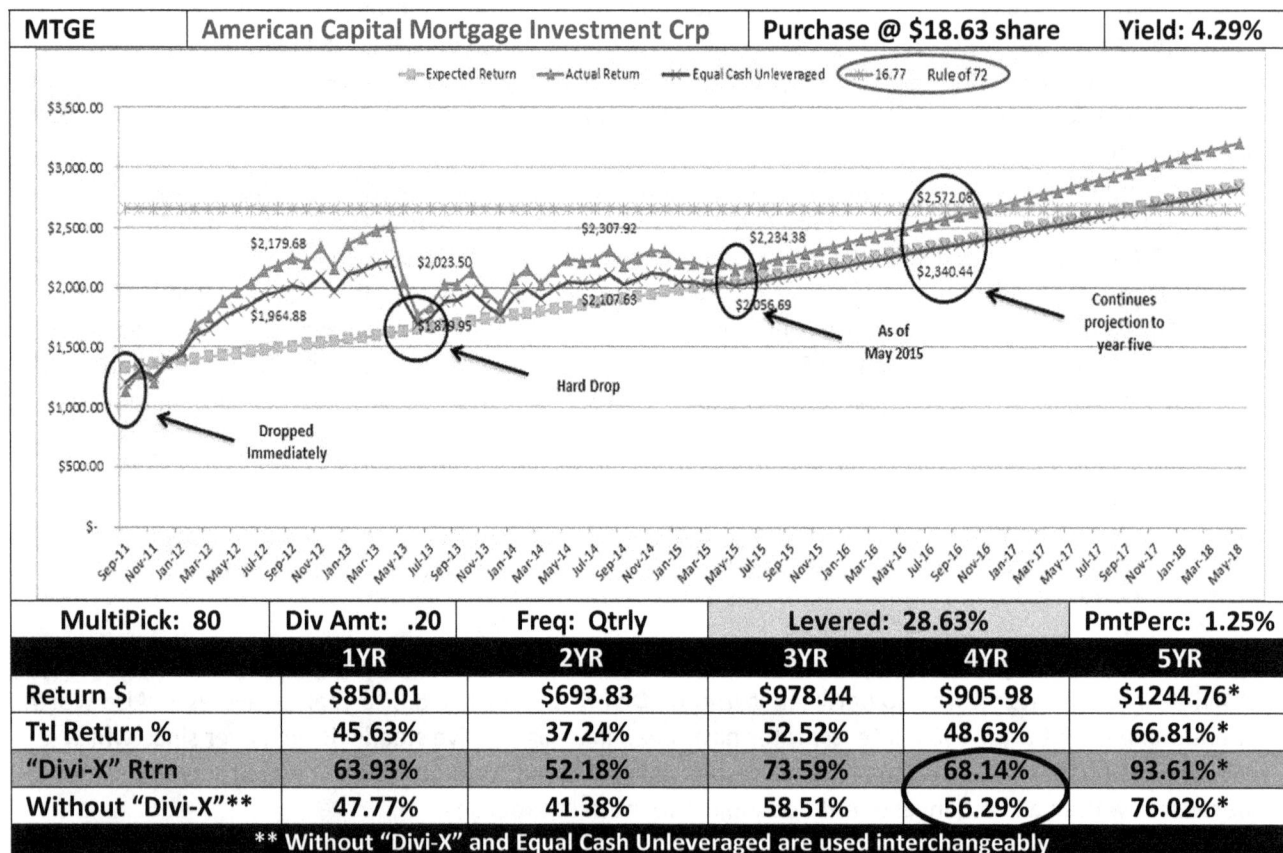

MultiPick: 80	Div Amt: .20	Freq: Qtrly	Levered: 28.63%	PmtPerc: 1.25%
	1YR	2YR	3YR	4YR	5YR
Return $	$850.01	$693.83	$978.44	$905.98	$1244.76*
Ttl Return %	45.63%	37.24%	52.52%	48.63%	66.81%*
"Divi-X" Rtrn	63.93%	52.18%	73.59%	68.14%	93.61%*
Without "Divi-X"**	47.77%	41.38%	58.51%	56.29%	76.02%*
** Without "Divi-X" and Equal Cash Unleveraged are used interchangeably					

*5YR numbers are projected

Fig. 3.6

As you can see, the returns are very respectable. After the four years since the IPO, your cash with the "Divi-X" system outpaced "Without "Divi-X"" by an average of about three percent a year. And because of the "Divi-X" system, and only because of the "Divi-X" system, our return rate managed to stay just above our "Expected Return" rate. We didn't double our money but you can't complain about a security that outpaces your expectations and we still have a year to go.

Chapter 4
Tips, Tricks, and Ideas

Suggestions for Low, Medium, and High-Yield Stocks

In all cases, it is recommended that the dividends cover, at the minimum, the monthly interest associated with the margin borrowed against the security purchased, but again, it all depends on your risk tolerance.

__A "Multiplier Pick" of 100 and a "PmtPerc" of 1.0% will cover the principal and interest payment of any security as long as the interest rate does not exceed 12.0%.__

For low-yielding stocks, below 2%, do not shy away from a "Multiplier Pick" in excess of 100 as long as it covers the associated monthly interest. Low yields, even with a high "Multiplier Pick" will always have you levered at a small percentage.

__A "Multiplier Pick" of 80 and a "PmtPerc" of 1.25% will cover the principal and interest payment of any security as long as the interest rate does not exceed 12.0%.__

With medium-yield stocks, yields between 2% and 6%, this is probably the sweet spot. You'll likely benefit from having a reasonable amount of leverage deployed without exposure to elevated risk from higher yields that allow you to borrow more against securities.

__A "Multiplier Pick" of 65 and a "PmtPerc" of 1.5% will cover the principal and interest payment of any security as long as the interest rate does not exceed 12.0%.__

We're going to classify high-yield (but not necessarily high-risk) as anything over 6.0%. This is the point where a "Multiplier Pick" of 100 will put you at or above 50% of leverage against a security. The higher the yield goes, the higher the leverage percentage goes. Use extreme caution when choosing a "Multiplier Pick" in excess of 100. Actually, use caution when any scenario has you levered over 60%.

What to Do If a Security Reduces or Eliminates its Dividend

This is one of the primary reasons why I advocate choosing a "Multiplier Pick" and "PmtPerc" that covers the monthly principal and interest associated with the security purchase. If a dividend is cut (not eliminated), there is a good possibility that even though the principal amount on your monthly margin payment will be reduced, there is a chance that an adjusted payment amount (reduced dividend) will cover the interest and possibly some of the principal allowing you to hold on to the stock if it is one you feel relatively positive about over the long-term.

You could even adjust the terms of the "Leverage Projection" (but not the 'Leverage Projection Worksheet') you initially setup when you purchased the security. Reducing the "PmtPerc" amount might help you maintain the loan as long as interest is still covered, or you could make an additional principal payment to reduce the required monthly payment amount on the loan.

The "Divi-X" System Workbook: CAUTION! Once you set up a "Leverage Projection Worksheet," it is never to be changed. The "Divi-X" System Workbook has a way for you to modify your initial terms without modifying the "Leverage Projection Worksheet."

If the dividend is cut altogether, then it gets big time serious. The entire premise of the "Divi-X" program is to have your dividends pay for the leveraged portion of your investment. If the dividend is cut entirely, it no longer makes sense to hold it in the context of this program and would need to be sold. However, if it is a security you still feel strongly about, you could take factors into consideration, such as, how long you have already held the security. If the security is almost paid off, you might be willing to put up the extra principal to maintain your position. If you feel the situation is only temporary, you might be willing to carry it a little longer on the assumption that dividends will resume in the near future.

Remember: All this finesse is necessary to keep track of the return of your individual investments. There are so many situations that would make the points made above seem completely unnecessary. For example, you may have so many dividends being paid out to you every month from so many different securities, that a dividend cut from one security would essentially be a non-event, but this goes back to my point: having all of your securities pooled into one margin account does not allow you to keep accurate measure of how well any specific security is doing. You could literally have a high yielding, poor performer covering the margin payment on a security that has cut its dividend but is increasing in value. Total chaos and many are ok with that. They see their account balance up, balance good, not a clue that balance should be higher than what it is.

Stock Splits

If you are doing this system by hand using the form in the back of this book, I implore you to invest in a spreadsheet program and upgrade to, at the least, the free "Divi-X" Lite version of the workbook. If there are any changes made to a security's status, whatever the change, a whole new form would have to be filled out or there will be a heck of a lot of erasing. You did use a pencil, right?

If you are fortunate enough to be using either of the workbooks, things get a bit easier to a lot easier. In the "Divi-X" Lite worksheet a stock split would be handled like this.

Let's say your stock split is 2:1 meaning for every one share you own, you now have two. If you purchased 100 shares, you now have 200 shares. Don't get excited, because now the share price will be halved and so will the dividend. All you would simply do is modify the original purchase details to reflect the split. Eventually the outcome is the same whether it was one hundred shares at $10 or 200 shares at $5. The full version of the "Divi-X" system offers you more flexibility. In 'The "Divi-X" System Workbook,' it also gives you the option to leave the original purchase info unchanged and instead, go to the actual time period of the split and make the adjustments there. Again, the return results are the same, but it gives you a little more detail about your securities performance and milestones, such as a stock split.

Lot Repurchases

Should you sell a security and repurchase it during the 'wash' period, at a lower or higher price, your broker will adjust your cost basis by the difference of when you first executed the trade and when you executed your next trade on the same security. Let's say you purchased a stock for $10 a share. You sold the shares at $9.50 for a loss of fifty cents a share. Before the wash period expires, you then purchase the shares back at $9.00 a share. You cannot claim a capital loss on the fifty cents a share when you sold your share, just like you wouldn't have to claim a fifty cent capital gain when you purchased the share again for less than when you sold it at $9.50 a share. Basically, what your broker will do is take that fifty cents and average down your purchase price. So instead of having a share that you purchased at $10 now worth a share of $9.00, you would have a share with a reduced cost basis of $9.50 worth $9.00. A 'wash sale' is a term, for IRS purposes, used when you buy or sell a security within a certain time period that excludes you from taking capital gains or losses on the difference in price between the two trades. See IRS guidelines for more info.

That is not how it's handled in the "Divi-X" system. All that hoop jumping is solely for the purpose of the IRS being able to sleep better knowing you're not getting an unwelcome break on your taxes. That is one beautiful thing about your broker. They keep track of all that nonsense so you don't have to. Just attach your 1099 to your taxes every year and be done with it.

In the "Divi-X" system, it's different. You can't adjust the cost basis because under no circumstance are you to ever modify the variables on the "Leverage Projection Worksheet" once you settled on terms (make a purchase) and account for your first margin loan payment. You can tweak it as much as you want before then but once you have recorded your first loan payment, don't fool with it anymore.

I want you to think of having two sets of books. There's the official set of books, the ones the IRS cares about, and there's the unofficial set of books, the ones only you care about. Don't worry, this is completely legal. You are not trying to hide anything from the IRS, because a) you don't want to and b) your broker won't let you.

I'm probably going into way more detail than needs to be on this subject but I want to be thorough. I want to paint you a picture. You purchase 1000 shares of Yummy Burger, Inc. for $10 a share. The next day you hear on the news that someone found a mouse tail inside their burger, and your shares drop to $8 a share. Personally, you make it a policy not to hold shares once they lose 15% of their value but the selling happened so fast, you weren't able to get out until you were down 20%. The company's fundamentals were solid. Who could've anticipated someone would find a mouse tail in their hamburger. You accept your loss knowing that you did your due diligence properly and if it weren't for that dang mouse tail.

Over the next few days, several more reports start to come in that others are finding mice tails in their hamburgers and now even their milk shakes. Yummy Burger's share price continues it's free fall until it hit's $5.50 a share. Something starts to sound fishy and you start to have your doubts about the claims of mice tails in people's food. You know the company's fundamentals are solid, if these claims turn out to be untrue, Yummy Burger would be at a screaming discount right now. So what do you do? You buy 2000 shares of Yummy Burger, Inc. at $5.50 a share, but we only care about the first 1000 shares for the purpose of this discussion.

A week later, the claims turned out to be unfounded. The whole thing was started as a vicious rumor that started on a social media site that went viral. Yummy Burger's price shoots back up to $11.50 a share and you live happily ever after, or as long as 2000 shares at $11.50 a share will let you.

As far as the IRS and your broker are concerned, you did not just get a screaming deal on the buyback of your shares. All they care about is that your transactions are recorded and reported to the IRS accurately. With the "Divi-X" system, all you do is treat it as a new investment and fill out a new "Leverage Projection Worksheet" under new terms.

If you repurchase shares outside of the 'wash' period, you would also treat it as an entirely new investment and would set up a new 'Leverage Projection Worksheet."

Special Dividends

Special dividends are probably the least involved. Simply add the special dividend amount to the existing dividend amount in the period in which it is paid.

Your Company Is Acquired

If your company is acquired and you continue to hold, you would change the ticker symbol in the 'Leverage Projection Worksheet' (the only time changing the original would be acceptable). Next, just simply change the share price to the company's new share price and follow the rules mentioned earlier under "Stock Splits" if the company acquired your company using shares that did not equal a 1:1 stock swap. If they paid a premium in the form of a special dividend, just add that to the current dividend in the time period in which it was paid. If they have a different dividend payout, change the dividend payout in the period the dividend was changed.

What's In a File Name?

If you choose to go the manual route and opt for the paper forms, this doesn't apply to you. Should you elect to use the free "Divi-X" Lite spreadsheet or if you use the full "Divi-X" System Workbook, you will find yourself running projections on literally hundreds of different securities. It's just so fun and easy.

When I first started using the system, unless I actually purchased the security, I wouldn't save my projections. As time went by, I would find myself re-examining many of the same securities, but because I didn't save the projections, I really didn't know if they were better buys or not since the last time I researched them. So I started saving all of my projections as well.

Here is a simple system to name your files that will be a huge help later down the road, whether you reference them a week later or even a year later.

Ticker	Date Reviewed	Share Price	DIV Yield	P/E Ratio
NYMT	093014	7.23	Yld 14.94	PE 5.98

Fig. 4.1

Or:

NYMT 093014 7.23 Yld 14.94 PE 5.98

Curiosity will always draw you back to these files and many times, you won't even have to open them because the majority of info you want to know is already in the file name.

Playing With the Numbers

Over the duration of holding a particular security, you may experience changes in variables that are unavoidable, such as the margin rate and the dividend paid out by the company you're invested in. But, two of the most important variables that give you some flexibility upfront are the dividend multiplier and the payment percentage amount. These two variables alone will tell you right away if your expectations of a security will have a greater chance of success or not. For example, below is a screenshot from one of my actual investments:

Ticker	Stock Price	No. Shares	Purch Date	End Date	DIV Pmt	Multiplier Start	Rtrn Rate?	% Levered
APTS	$ 8.1100	200	04/08/14	A-14	$ 0.1600	20	9.00%	42.75%

								Rule 72

Multiplier Pick	DIV Per/Year	Monthly DIV	Pmt Perc	Margin Rate	Multiplier Step	Mth DIV Ttl	Based on DIV	9.12
65	4	$ 0.0533	1.25%	7.75%	5	$ 10.67	On Est Rtrn	3.03
							On Act Rtrn	1.00

Screenshot © The Dividend Times, LLC

Fig. 4.2

The two most important variables we are concerned with here are the "Multiplier Pick" field and the "PmtPerc" field (The screenshot is for illustration purposes only. You do not need our program to take advantage of this investment technique but it would be much easier).

The amounts you select for these two fields will be critical in determining whether or not your security of choice is worth the effort or not, but more importantly, will allow you the flexibility to tweak the numbers until you come up with a desired profitability scenario if there is one.

Using the example above, let's check the different expected outcomes when we modify the "Multiplier Pick" and the "PmtPerc" fields.

Share Price	8.11	8.11	8.11	8.11
Dividend	.16	.16	.16	.16
Multiplier Pick	65	50	65	50
PmtPerc	1.25%	1.25%	1.00%	1.00%
Margin Rate	7.75%	7.75%	7.75%	7.75%
% Leveraged	42.75%	32.88%	42.75%	32.88%
Cash Appreciation 1YR	23.30%	20.95%	23.23%	20.90%
Total Return 1 YR	13.34%	14.06%	13.30%	14.03%
Cash Appreciation 5YR	142.23%	125.95%	140.53%	124.83%
Total Return 5 YR	81.44%	84.53%	80.46%	83.78%

Fig. 4.3

The biggest stand-out to me on this table is the differences between the Cash Appreciation returns and the Total Returns. They are huge! And that's just what you would want to see. The Cash Appreciation returns show your profit from using margin. The Total Returns is the cash on cash return on the full purchase price of the shares without using the "Divi-X" system. Anyway, back to the example about changing the "Multiplier Pick" and "PmtPerc" variables.

"PmtPerc" (Payment Percentage)

This is interesting. Looking back at Fig. **4.3,** it appears that a slight change in the "PmtPerc" field has very little effect on the eventual return results in the short-term and long-term. Or does it? All results do not include the reinvestment of dividends. That's because the dividends are used to service margin debt which is amortized when you set up your "Divi-X" system scenario for the security of your choice (I'll explain setting up amortization later). This debt service payment, and dividends in excess of the debt service payment, reduces your outstanding margin balance which makes it available for use again. This in turn can be reinvested.

Did I also mention that any cash deposits into your margin/brokerage account, whether it is direct deposits or dividends, might be matched, dollar for dollar, with more available margin? Anyway, I'm getting ahead of myself. This will all be explained in time when you get to the topic of Brokerage Accounts.

I don't know how long you have been involved in securities investing, but you don't have to be around long before you are made aware of the significance of reinvested dividends, and I concur. Without a better investment alternative, reinvesting your dividends is a very sound investment decision. But, let's imagine for a moment. What if we take that $100 in dividends, which could be matched by $100 dollars in margin availability for a total of $200 of fresh margin, but conservatively, we use only $50 in margin for a total of $150? And we repeat that process over and over and over again? Do you think that would make a big difference to your overall returns at some point in the future?

And while we are on the topic of "PmtPerc," the above example did not take into account larger "PmtPerc" differences. We only changed it one quarter of a percent. What if the difference was bigger? Say, between one percent and one and a half percent? What kind of effect would that have? Let's take a look.

Long-Term Effects of a Different "PmtPerc"
(on returns and yields)

	"PmtPerc"	"Multiplier Pick"	5YR Return in Dollars	5YR Total Returns	5YR "Divi-X" Rtrns in Percentages	5YR Dividend Yields	20YR Projected DIV Ylds
AXP	1.0%	100	$8728.54	278.59%	368.27%	2.82%	6.39%
	1.5%	65	$9029.70	282.29%	335.38%	3.47%	6.52%
BA	1.0%	100	$12,550.82	188.00%	264.43%	3.98%	11.26%
	1.5%	65	$13253.52	192.39%	236.90%	4.63%	10.82%
CAT	1.0%	100	$9303.49	218.08%	373.46%	7.51%	16.09%
	1.5%	65	$10,006.18	224.40%	307.58%	7.85%	14.42%
CVX	1.0%	100	$10,870.79	93.03%	139.48%	5.66%	12.27%
	1.5%	65	$12008.49	98.09%	125.19%	6.19%	11.60%
CISCO	1.0%	No Dividends Were Paid During Our Test Period in the Beginning and Did Not					
	1.5%	Qualify For the "DIVI-X" System.					
DD	1.0%	100	$5931.81	192.29%	424.78%	8.17%	20.13%
	1.5%	65	$6617.77	200.61%	311.38%	8.48%	16.45%

	"PmtPerc"	"Multiplier Pick"	5YR Return in Dollars	5YR Total Returns	5YR "Divi-X" Rtrns in Percentages	5YR Dividend Yields	20YR Projected DIV Ylds
XOM	1.0%	100	$9184.49	48.97%	60.99%	2.88%	6.33%
	1.5%	65	$9887.18	51.97%	59.60%	3.38%	6.44%
GE	1.0%	100	$2537.12	137.23%	189.40%	6.92%	13.75%
	1.5%	65	$2704.42	141.41%	172.26%	7.19%	13.04%
GS	1.0%	100	$15,932.07	16.52%	17.95%	1.01%	2.31%
	1.5%	65	$16,517.65	17.73%	18.70%	1.25%	2.47%
HD	1.0%	100	$7592.19	253.33%	371.27%	7.20%	15.78%
	1.5%	65	$7968.63	258.16%	325.33%	7.48%	14.65%
MMM	1.0%	100	$13,130.59	149.80%	209.90%	4.12%	10.68%
	1.5%	65	$13,983.87	154.15%	189.40%	4.74%	10.31%
T	1.0%	100	$2965.73	68.85%	126.28%	9.18%	19.41%
	1.5%	65	$3256.77	72.43%	114.87%	9.11%	17.53%
INTC	1.0%	100	$2892.17	6.52%	7.80%	2.16%	4.66%
	1.5%	65	$3155.68	9.01%	10.08%	2.61%	4.86%
IBM	1.0%	100	$15,708.78	37.51%	45.02%	2.78%	5.49%
	1.5%	65	$16796.29	40.05%	44.91%	3.20%	5.64%
JNJ	1.0%	100	$8910.62	66.57%	92.45%	3.56%	7.86%
	1.5%	65	$9814.09	70.83%	86.58%	4.23%	7.85%
JPM	1.0%	100	$6588.72	50.32%	52.26%	3.42%	5.46%
	1.5%	65	$6672.38	50.88%	52.14%	3.50%	5.49%
MCD	1.0%	100	$8832.64	51.10%	69.02%	4.10%	8.56%
	1.5%	65	$9752.84	55.04%	66.22%	4.66%	8.47%
MRK	1.0%	100	$4882.11	73.40%	114.19%	4.23%	9.92%
	1.5%	65	$5517.88	78.83%	102.66%	5.04%	9.56%
MSFT	1.0%	100	$4766.15	67.94%	79.00%	3.39%	6.42%
	1.5%	65	$4983.65	70.07%	77.08%	3.70%	6.49%
NKE	1.0%	100	$9872.82	165.03%	186.58%	2.14%	4.42%
	1.5%	65	$10,098.69	166.78%	180.32%	2.45%	4.56%
PFE	1.0%	100	$3187.88	126.55%	197.38%	8.73%	13.65%
	1.5%	65	$3489.03	132.00%	172.16%	8.81%	12.68%
PG	1.0%	100	$7064.06	39.48%	53.23%	3.37%	7.34%
	1.5%	65	$7870.15	43.40%	52.17%	4.00%	7.38%
KO	1.0%	100	$3617.26	62.82%	86.58%	3.95%	8.83%
	1.5%	65	$3985.33	66.99%	81.54%	4.57%	8.70%
TRV	1.0%	100	$9681.08	114.45%	149.90%	3.65%	7.55%
	1.5%	65	$10,283.40	118.04%	139.48%	4.19%	7.57%
UTX	1.0%	100	$10,644.49	60.92%	75.12%	2.47%	5.48%
	1.5%	65	$11,355.55	63.79%	72.73%	2.98%	5.65%
UNH	1.0%	100	$11,760.31	301.75%	349.84%	4.59%	8.15%

	"PmtPerc"	"Multiplier Pick"	5YR Return in Dollars	5YR Total Returns	5YR "Divi-X" Rtrns in Percentages	5YR Dividend Yields	20YR Projected DIV Ylds
	1.5%	65	$11,969.45	303.84%	333.65%	4.84%	8.13%
V	1.0%	100	$6857.28	205.60%	215.57%	1.73%	2.07%
	1.5%	65	$6805.31	204.69%	211.03%	1.86%	3.25%
VZ	1.0%	100	$3886.55	89.27%	197.44%	8.81%	19.51%
	1.5%	65	$4681.27	97.59%	151.57%	8.93%	16.00%
WMT	1.0%	100	$7440.93	54.95%	67.41%	2.87%	5.82%
	1.5%	65	$7947.04	57.76%	65.65%	3.33%	5.96%
DIS	1.0%	100	$11,168.70	206.33%	226.86%	2.29%	3.10%
	1.5%	65	$11,002.67	204.54%	217.32%	2.52%	4.89%

Fig. 4.4

As you reviewed the above table in **Fig. 4.4**, one of the most obvious things that might have stood out to you is the "Multiplier Pick." Why is there a "Multiplier Pick" of 100 when you use a "PmtPerc" of 1.0% and a "Multiplier Pick" of 65 when you use a "PmtPerc" of 1.5%. This is where the different "PmtPerc" becomes a huge deal. The reason for the difference is because you can afford a much higher "Multiplier Pick" with a "PmtPerc" of 1.0% than you can with a "PmtPerc" of 1.5%. For example, in the case of AXP, using a "PmtPerc" of 1.0% allowed us to purchase 24.35 additional shares on leverage compared to only 15.83 additional shares using a "PmtPerc" of 1.5%.

Let's dig a little deeper into our AXP example. If you'll notice, even though we were able to buy more shares using leverage (a higher "Multiplier Pick") with the 1.0% "PmtPerc," the **"5YR Total Returns"** was larger using the 1.5% "PmtPerc." So if the total return is higher using less leverage (a lower "Multiplier Pick") why would you use leverage at all? Good question. Let's dig deeper still.

Proceed to the next column with the heading **"5YR "Divi-X" Rtrns in Percentages."** This is the number that matters the most, the actual return on your cash. As you can see the returns are inverted. Now, the lower "PmtPerc" (higher "Multiplier Pick) is yielding you the higher returns and the differences are significant. This number represents the actual return you would have made on the actual cash you would have invested out of your pocket.

The "**5YR Total Returns**" column shows you the total returns divided by the full share purchase price of AXP. It's a good number to know but it's not how much you would have actually made and incidentally, this is the number your brokerage statement says you made. More so, your brokerage statement doesn't reflect interest expense associated with your specific securities so your brokerage statement returns would actually, but incorrectly, reflect even higher returns than the ones shown here.

Knowing what you know now, go back and review the list again and you'll get a better understanding of how useful the "Divi-X" system can be.

"Multiplier Pick"

When you're setting up your Leverage Projections, the idea is to pick a "Multiplier Pick" that covers the "PmtPerc" (total payment amount calculated by using "PmtPerc") you select when you set up your initial numbers. It is highly recommended that the "PmtPerc" that you select should cover at a minimum, the monthly interest on the outstanding margin balance associated with the particular security purchase and preferable that it covers some of the principal. When you borrow on margin, your broker does not harass you for payment every month. They do, however, automatically apply margin interest expense to your outstanding balance so you do not want to necessarily find yourself in a situation where your current month of interest is converted into next month's principal. In other words, don't let the interest pile up, it will eat away your returns.

Teaser: The final two columns, as indicated, show the Yields on your cash in 5YRs and the Projected Yields on your cash in twenty years. This is a fascinating subject that gets a chapter all to itself. Well worth the read. I can't wait till you get there.

Multiplier Picks in Excess of 100

Leveraging securities in excess of one hundred times the dividend is not possible when you are using the dividends to maintain the full principal and interest payments on your margin loans, but it is possible to use a multiplier pick in excess of one hundred as long as the monthly dividend payments cover, at the least, the monthly interest payments (technically, you can go higher but except in the instances of low yield, is high-risk and should require extra caution).

In some cases, in addition to using over one hundred times the multiplier pick, you may actually borrow money to put into your pocket and have the dividends pay for your stocks and a little extra spending money for yourself. This is a very high-risk option. The reason I'm pointing it out now, is that as you become more and more familiar with this system, that is a discovery you'll likely uncover on your own, and I'm letting you know up front, USE AT YOUR OWN PERIL! I'm not saying you shouldn't do it, but I'm begging you not to do it with money you can't afford to lose.

Below is a screenshot, in Fig. 4.5, from the "Divi-X" System Workbook. This is not a fictitious company. I have actually purchased this stock, but "not" using the scenario below. I want you to take notice of all the areas circled in gray.

Starting from top-left, you'll notice a "Multiplier Pick" of 150. This is a high-yielding stock. Using a 150 "Multiplier Pick" in this situation is only for those with ice in their veins. If you move to the far top-right, you'll see that the high "Multiplier Pick" of 150 allowed us to leverage an unbelievable 154.62% of the purchase price of 200 shares indicated by the circled "% Levered" field. That is more than what the total cost of the shares are.

Just below the "% Levered" field and slightly to the left, you can see our monthly dividend total, or "Mth DIV Ttl." This purchase of 200 shares nets us a monthly dividend total of $22.08. Now if you pan down to the center of the screen shot under the column heading "Margin Interest," you see that our monthly interest payment is $21.39, just slightly less than our monthly dividend total. After your first month, you not only made your interest payment but had $.69 left over to pay down some of the principal.

Ticker	Stock Price	No. Shares	Purch Date	End Date	DIV Pmt	Multiplier Start	Rtrn Rate?	% Levered
????	$ 10.7100	200	04/11/14	A-14	$ 0.1104	100	9.00%	154.62%

Rule 72

Multiplier Pick	DIV Per/Year	Monthly DIV	Pmt Perc	Margin Rate	Multiplier Step	Mth DIV Ttl		
150	12	$ 0.1104	1.25%	7.75%	5	$ 22.08	Based on DIV	5.82
							On Est Rtrn	-4.30
							On Act Rtrn	1.83

	DIV Multiplier	Cash Out Of Pocket	Leverage Amt	Ttl Share Value	#Shares Purch by Leverage	DIV Yield	Min Pmt	Principal	Margin Interest	Net DIV Cash	Monthly Net Div Cash (1yr)	Monthly Net Div Cash (5yr)	Yield Less Marg Int	Yield Less Marg Int (1YR)	Yield Less Marg Int (5YR)	Leverage Ratio
0	100	$ (66.00)	$ 2,208.00	$ 2,142.00	206.16	12.37%	$ 27.60	$ 13.34	$ 14.26	$ (5.52)	$ (9.11)	$ (2.41)	100.36%	165.66%	43.89%	103.08%
1	105	$ (176.40)	$ 2,318.40	$ 2,142.00	216.47	12.37%	$ 28.98	$ 14.01	$ 14.97	$ (6.90)	$ (10.45)	$ (3.61)	46.94%	71.10%	24.55%	108.24%
2	110	$ (286.80)	$ 2,428.80	$ 2,142.00	226.78	12.37%	$ 30.36	$ 14.67	$ 15.69	$ (8.28)	$ (11.74)	$ (4.57)	34.64%	49.13%	19.14%	113.39%
3	115	$ (397.20)	$ 2,539.20	$ 2,142.00	237.09	12.37%	$ 31.74	$ 15.34	$ 16.40	$ (9.66)	$ (13.03)	$ (5.54)	29.18%	39.38%	16.73%	118.54%
4	120	$ (507.60)	$ 2,649.60	$ 2,142.00	247.39	12.37%	$ 33.12	$ 16.01	$ 17.11	$ (11.04)	$ (14.32)	$ (6.50)	26.10%	33.86%	15.38%	123.70%
5	125	$ (618.00)	$ 2,760.00	$ 2,142.00	257.70	12.37%	$ 34.50	$ 16.68	$ 17.83	$ (12.42)	$ (15.62)	$ (7.47)	24.12%	30.32%	14.50%	128.85%
6	130	$ (728.40)	$ 2,870.40	$ 2,142.00	268.01	12.37%	$ 35.88	$ 17.34	$ 18.54	$ (13.80)	$ (16.91)	$ (8.43)	22.73%	27.85%	13.90%	134.01%
7	135	$ (838.80)	$ 2,980.80	$ 2,142.00	278.32	12.37%	$ 37.26	$ 18.01	$ 19.25	$ (15.18)	$ (18.20)	$ (9.40)	21.72%	26.03%	13.45%	139.16%
8	140	$ (949.20)	$ 3,091.20	$ 2,142.00	288.63	12.37%	$ 38.64	$ 18.68	$ 19.96	$ (16.56)	$ (19.49)	$ (10.36)	20.94%	24.64%	13.10%	144.31%
9	145	$ (1,059.60)	$ 3,201.60	$ 2,142.00	298.94	12.37%	$ 40.02	$ 19.34	$ 20.68	$ (17.94)	$ (20.78)	$ (11.33)	20.32%	23.53%	12.83%	149.47%
10	150	$ (1,170.00)	$ 3,312.00	$ 2,142.00	309.24	12.37%	$ 41.40	$ 20.01	$ 21.39	$ (19.32)	$ (22.07)	$ (12.29)	19.82%	22.64%	12.61%	154.62%
11	155	$ (1,280.40)	$ 3,422.40	$ 2,142.00	319.55	12.37%	$ 42.78	$ 20.68	$ 22.10	$ (20.70)	$ (23.36)	$ (13.26)	19.40%	21.89%	12.43%	159.78%
12	160	$ (1,390.80)	$ 3,532.80	$ 2,142.00	329.86	12.37%	$ 44.16	$ 21.34	$ 22.82	$ (22.08)	$ (24.65)	$ (14.23)	19.05%	21.27%	12.27%	164.93%
13	165	$ (1,501.20)	$ 3,643.20	$ 2,142.00	340.17	12.37%	$ 45.54	$ 22.01	$ 23.53	$ (23.46)	$ (25.94)	$ (15.19)	18.75%	20.74%	12.14%	170.08%
14	170	$ (1,611.60)	$ 3,753.60	$ 2,142.00	350.48	12.37%	$ 46.92	$ 22.68	$ 24.24	$ (24.84)	$ (27.23)	$ (16.16)	18.50%	20.28%	12.03%	175.24%
15	175	$ (1,722.00)	$ 3,864.00	$ 2,142.00	360.78	12.37%	$ 48.30	$ 23.35	$ 24.96	$ (26.22)	$ (28.53)	$ (17.12)	18.27%	19.88%	11.93%	180.39%
16	180	$ (1,832.40)	$ 3,974.40	$ 2,142.00	371.09	12.37%	$ 49.68	$ 24.01	$ 25.67	$ (27.60)	$ (29.82)	$ (18.09)	18.07%	19.53%	11.84%	185.55%

Fig. 4.5

Lastly, look over to your far left once again. Under the column heading, "Cash Out Of Pocket." It is a negative $(1,170.00). This is the amount borrowed in excess of the "Ttl Share Value" of $2,142.00 shown just to the right under the "Ttl Share Value" column. Now if you have the margin available, you could actually borrow this amount in addition to the shares already purchased and rely on the dividends to make that payment for you.

If you had unlimited margin availability, which you don't, thank goodness, you could take that amount and buy more shares creating the same scenario all over again. I won't post another screenshot, but you'll notice under the "#Shares Purch by Leverage" column, you could purchase another 109.24 shares with that borrowed money (309.24 purchased by leverage less the actual 200 share purchase you made) which would give you a "Cash Out Of Pocket" of an additional $(639.05) which would buy you even more shares.

Fortunately, brokers have margin limits in place which will minimize the damage if someone were to ever take on such a risky endeavor.

As a side note, this particular stock purchase that I made, the company cut its dividend eleven months later. For me personally, the cut still allows me to make the monthly interest payment with principal every month, but in the case we just outlined, it could've spelled serious trouble for that investor.

Holding Period

Stocks historically have done extremely well over the long-term. This system, likewise, will perform in kind. If your time horizon is short-term (less than 1 year), this system will still work for you (refer to the 1YR table columns in any of the Dow 30 "Multiplier Pick" chapters to get an idea of how much), but the longer you use it, the more you will likely make if your investment choices are sound.

Cut Your Losses

Have no illusions while using this or any other system. You will probably make purchases that perform badly for whatever reason. In addition, since this method employs leverage, if you don't cut your losses sooner rather than later, your losses could be significant. This doesn't mean to cut and run at the first sign of weakness. It would be unwise to think you will not experience some downturn in your holdings from time to time.

Five Year Past Histories

Five year histories, I think, provide a very useful tool to get a sense of how a particular security has behaved over time even though it is no indication of future performance. Personally, I needed the five year history of the securities for this book to see if the "Divi-X" system was even a viable system. When I first started this project, I manually entered all the historical data for each of the securities in this book. I dreaded the thought of inputting all that data just to come to the conclusion that I was wasting my time. Lucky for you too, because if it were any easier, there would've been a lot more charts included.

Actually, it is easier. I found a simpler way. Yahoo.com offers historical pricing that can be downloaded into an excel file with a .csv extension. All you have to do is click on the 'Historical Prices' tab of a particular security that you searched for. This information, historical share prices and dividend history, can be copied and pasted directly into The "Divi-X" System Workbook allowing you to create your own five year histories in a snap.

Security Screeners

If you have been investing on your own for a while, you may already be quite familiar with security screeners. If you are, the only thing I would suggest is to add dividend yield to your search and proceed to the next section. For those of you not familiar, there are a host of financial web sites that offer their own security screeners.

What these screeners allow you to do, is help you find securities that fall into a range of criteria set by you to help thin out the countless security options available. For example, if you wanted a list of securities that paid a dividend, the screener would likely not only return dividend paying securities, but also let you enter the yield range of the securities to return.

Some other popular criteria that many screeners have available are:

- P/E Ratio – Price to Earnings Ratio
- BV/Share – Book Value to Share Price
- EPS – Earnings Per Share
- D/E Ratio – Debt to Equity Ratio
- Volume
- Profit Margin %
- On and on and on…

The one I most often use is on Google, more so than my own broker's (your broker will likely have one also) simply because I don't have to log in every time I want to use it. After you check out the screener on Google, you can go to their search bar and simply type in "Stock Screener" to find other sites that offer them at no charge.

Closed-End Funds, Bonds, Mutual Funds, ETF's and REIT's

These types of securities are well known for their dividend payouts and many can also be found using screeners. Except for REIT's, one might choose these types of securities for the hands off approach required by the individual investor.

If you choose to use the "Divi-X" system on these types of investment vehicles, check with your broker on specifics. Some have margin limits on the type of security, as well as OTC (over the counter) securities and securities with a price below $5.

Some helpful sites with screeners are:

    Closed-End Funds:

        Closed-End Fund Screener @ www.cefconnect.com

    Bonds:

        Yahoo @ http://screener.finance.yahoo.com/bonds.html and Morningstar @ http://www.morningstar.com/bonds.html

    Mutual Funds and ETF's:

        Morningstar @ http://www.morningstar.com/tools.html

    REIT's:

        Any main portal's screener will do. REIT's are listed on the major exchanges with other stocks. If you are willing to do a little digging, a very cool place to go is https://www.reit.com/investing/investor-resources. This website is hosted by NAREIT. This website has all things REIT related. At the above link, you'll find lists of all REIT's, including Public Non-Listed REIT's and Private REIT's.

MoPays

A useful site packed with dividend related content is www.dividendchannel.com but the feature I find most helpful is their section on monthly paying dividend securities. That feature can be found @ http://www.dividendchannel.com/monthly-dividend/. As of this writing, dividendchannel currently lists one thousand three hundred fifty-seven monthly paying securities on the United States and Canadian markets. You will have to register but it's free, otherwise you can only view six pages of content per day. This is not enough to get full use out of the MoPay list. The list is broken down into sixty-eight pages starting with the highest yielding, highest risk securities.

More Useful Sites

MarketInOut has a useful stock screener @ http://www.marketinout.com/stock-screener/industry.php?picker=dps. Here you can search dividend paying stocks by amount, yield percentage, and payout ratio. No registration necessary.

Nasdaq's website is a wealth of information particularly @ http://www.nasdaq.com/dividend-stocks/. Here you'll find a list of the highest yielding stocks which can be downloaded in .csv format and viewed in a spreadsheet and a link to a "Dividend Calendar."

Chapter 5
Amortization and Dividend Reinvestment

Amortization

The definition of **'amortize'** according to Merriam-Webster is as follows:

> **1:** to pay off (as a mortgage) gradually usually by periodic payments of principal and interest or by payments to a sinking fund
>
> **2:** to gradually reduce or write off the cost or value of (as an asset) <*amortize* goodwill> <*amortize* machinery>

The first part of that definition is what we will focus on. You have some options when it comes to amortizing your margin loans.

1. Use all dividends to pay down the associated loan.
2. Use a "Fixed payment" established using the "PmtPerc" when you set up a Leverage Projection Worksheet.
3. Use a "PmtPerc" of the outstanding monthly balance to pay down the associated loan.
4. Pay "Interest Only" and not pay down the associated loan.

The "Divi-X" System Workbook: Offers you the flexibility to make sudden changes when the need arises on almost any possible situation. For example, if you opt to have all of your dividends pay down your outstanding margin loan balance, but find you need some of your dividends for personal expenses, you can account for that in the "Divi-X" System Workbook and all changes are reflected and projected immediately.

In reality, from a brokerage account standpoint, it doesn't matter which option you choose. Every month, the dividends get paid and your broker takes his interest.

However, from a record-keeping standpoint and for you personally, the option you choose is extremely important. Among the four options listed above, here are the differences:

1. Using all dividends pays the loan off much quicker than using the "PmtPerc" option. If there are dividend increases along the way and you choose to apply them to the outstanding loan balance it will be paid off quicker than the "Fixed Payment" option as well, but if the dividend is decreased it will take longer. If the dividend is decreased to the point it doesn't even cover the monthly interest or if it's eliminated altogether, repayment is in serious doubt unless the

dividend goes back up or is reinstated at an acceptable level to start reducing the principal. You may also have to consider changing the terms of your arrangement or selling.

2. "Fixed Payment" is middle of the road between options 1 and option 3. "Fixed Payment" doesn't take into account changes in the dividend. Once set, it would ideally remain fixed for the entirety of the loan whether there is an increase/decrease in the dividend or a change in the interest rate. However, the "Divi-X" system allows you to make changes whenever necessary to adapt to changing situations.

3. "PmtPerc" pays a percentage of the outstanding associated margin loan every month. As the balance decreases, so does the monthly payment. Depending on the size of your portfolio and your need for income, this might be your preference for your net income will increase every single month. This is the method of preferred use by "Divi-X." Even though the other methods may provide better returns in the long run, and by all means feel free to use the other methods, I find that this method strikes a very nice balance between increasing monthly income, equity appreciation and reduced risk by paying down the balance every month.

Here's how the three options play out using a stock that I've held for a very long time, Duke Energy Corp (DUK). The five year time frame is from May 2010 to April 2015. Again, we are using the usual "Multiplier Pick" of 80 and a 100 share purchase.

Throughout this book you will read phrases along the lines of "maintaining" or "keeping up with" your loan or amortization payments. This is just a little play on words. There are no actual checks to write or statements to reconcile. Once you set up a "Leverage Projection Worksheet," whether it's manually or through the free "Divi-X" Lite worksheet or 'The "Divi-X" System Workbook,' you are basically done. The only time you have to get involved is when there is a change in the margin rate or you decide to change your own terms, and even then, it requires nothing more than a couple of keystrokes.

Option 1 – All DIVs

	Actual Total Returns				
	1YR	**2YR**	3YR	**4YR**	5YR
$ Rtrn	$ 751.97	**$ 1,926.73**	$ 2,145.58	**$ 2,768.80**	$ 3602.95
"Divi-X" Rtrn	24.04%	**61.61%**	68.60%	**88.53%**	115.20%
Without "Divi-X"	17.94%	**44.14%**	50.86%	**65.48%**	84.01%
Ttl Rtrn	15.15%	**38.81%**	43.21%	**55.77%**	72.57%

Fig. 5.1

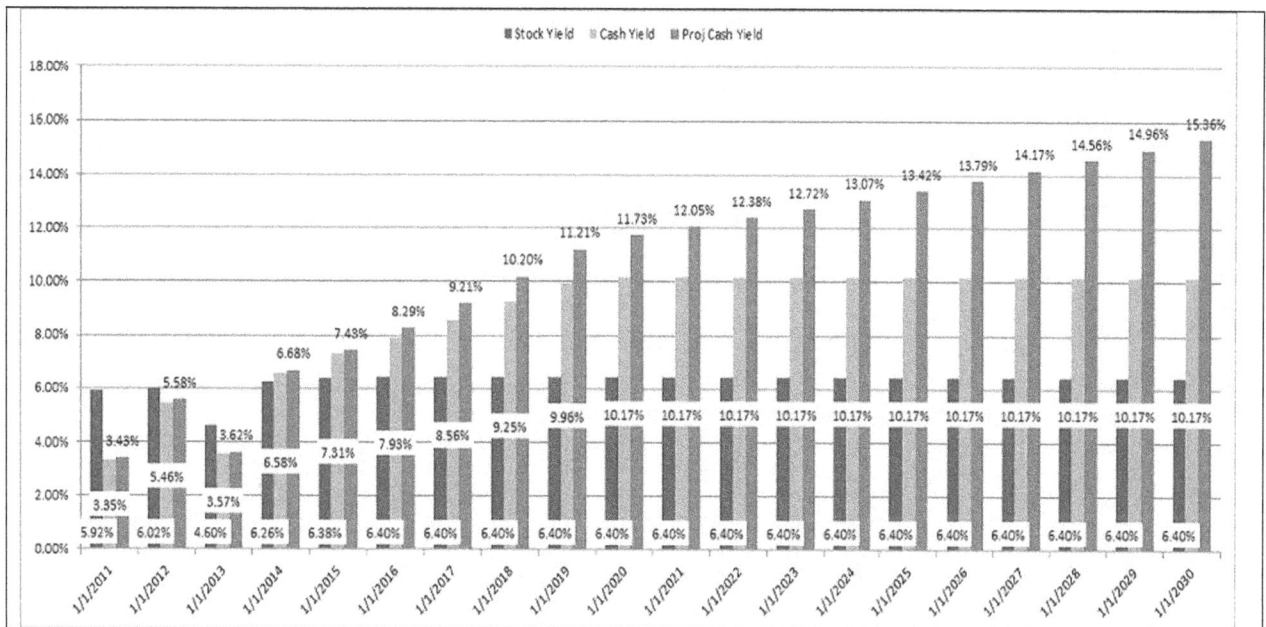

Fig. 5.2

A few things about this chart:
1. The first five years are derived from actual trade history data.
    a. Bottom yield number (5.92% - 6.40%) is the actual "Stock Yield."
    b. Middle yield number (3.35% - 10.17%) is the "Cash Yield."
    c. Top yield number (3.43% - 15.36%) is the "Proj Cash Yield," or the projected cash yield.
2. If you applied all dividends towards the margin loan, it would be paid off in about ten years. This is indicated in the chart when the maximum "Cash Yield" is reached at 10.17% in the year 2020. The reason the "Cash Yield" stops climbing after ten years is because:
    a. The "Cash Yield" is based on actual historical data and future data associated with the associated margin loan. After year 2020, there will be no more interest expense.

      b.   Dividends associated with "Cash Yield" reflect the actual cash on cash dividend rate less margin interest and do not include dividend increase projections.

3.   The 15.36% yield projected in twenty years is based on a reasonable assumption that the company will continue to increase dividends and that is approximately what the yield will earn on your initial cash investment.

      a.   The "Proj Cash Yield" is calculated the same as the "Cash Yield" except that it includes projected dividend increases.

      b.   The "Proj Cash Yield" will climb or fall as actual data replaces projected data (dividend increases/decreases).

Option 2 – Fixed Payments

Actual Total Returns					
	1YR	**2YR**	3YR	**4YR**	5YR
$ Rtrn	$ 753.60	**$ 1930.31**	$ 2,153.15	**$ 2,783.22**	$ 3,623.20
"Divi-X" Rtrn	24.10%	**61.72%**	68.85%	**88.99%**	115.85%
Without "Divi-X"	17.94%	**44.14%**	50.86%	**65.48%**	84.01%
Ttl Rtrn	15.18%	**38.88%**	43.37%	**56.06%**	72.97%

Fig. 5.3

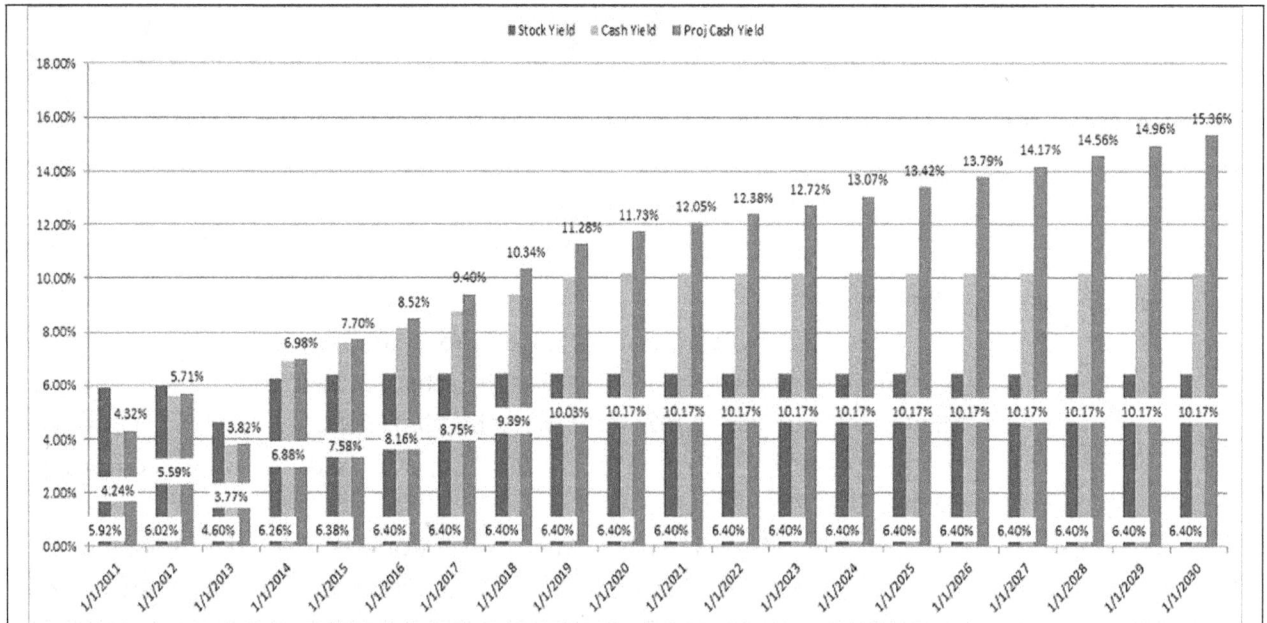

Fig. 5.4

A few things about this chart:

1.   The first five years are derived from actual trade history data.

2. If you chose the "Fixed Payment" option, even though the chart indicates it would be paid off in the same ten year period as the "All DIVs" option, it would actually be paid off two months later than the "All DIVs" option.
   a. The difference in the amount of time to pay off a loan between the "All DIVs" option and "Fixed Payment" option could vary dramatically depending on the dividend policy of a particular company's stock.
3. The slight increase in return between "All DIVs" and "Fixed Payment" is the amount of interest paid on the associated margin loan. Notice in **Fig. 5.4**, during the year of 2013, there was a dip in the dividend yield. As a result, the "All DIV's" option paid higher interest on the margin loan which had a slight negative effect on its returns.
4. The 15.36% yield projected in twenty years is based on a reasonable assumption that the company will continue to increase dividends and that is approximately what the yield will earn on your initial cash investment.

Option 3 – "PmtPerc"

Actual Total Returns					
	1YR	2YR	3YR	4YR	5YR
$ Rtrn	$ 752.73	**$ 1,925.63**	$ 2,140.01	**$ 2,755.24**	$ 3,572.24
"Divi-X" Rtrn	24.07%	**61.57%**	68.43%	**88.10%**	114.22%
Without "Divi-X"	17.94%	**44.14%**	50.86%	**65.48%**	84.01%
Ttl Rtrn	15.16%	**38.78%**	43.10%	**55.49%**	71.95%

Fig. 5.5

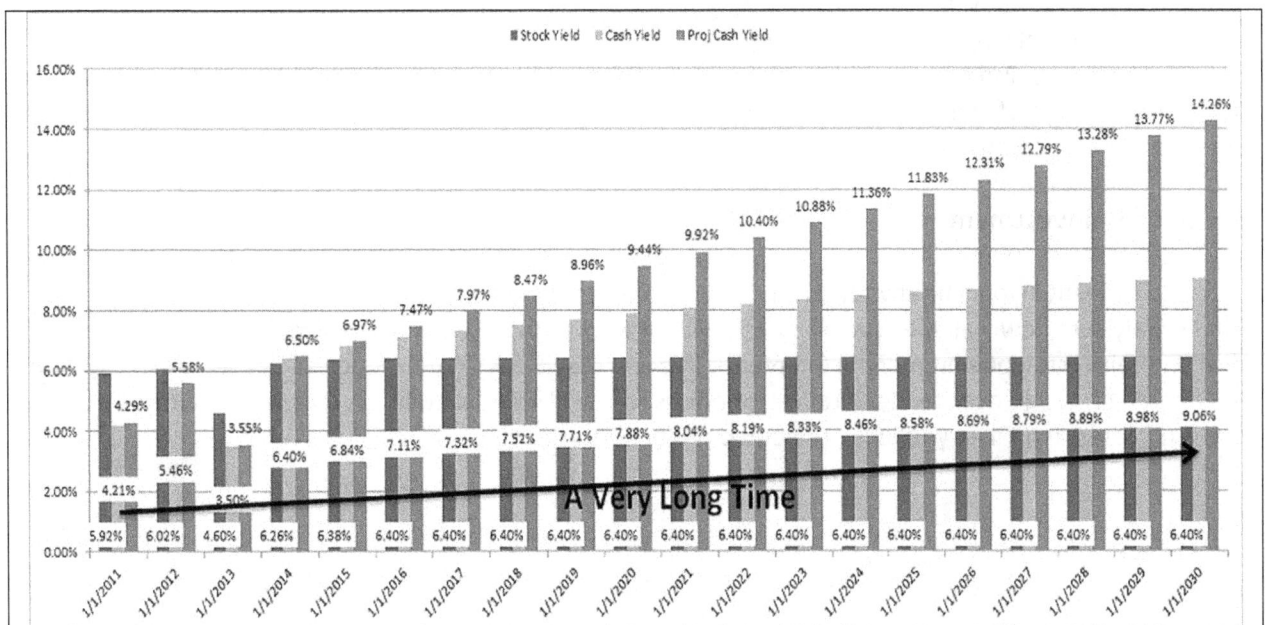

Fig. 5.6

A few things about this chart:
1. The first five years are derived from actual trade history data.
2. If you choose to use the "PmtPerc" option, then as you continue to pay down the margin associated with your stock's lot purchase, the monthly payment continues to decline which increases the amount of dividends you keep every month.
3. This is the ideal option if your primary goal is monthly income. Because you choose not to aggressively pay down the associated margin loan, you carry the balance almost indefinitely. As a result you increase your dividend income every month but at the expense of a small reduction in your "Divi-X" returns and a slight decrease in the long-term yield on your cash investment.
   a. Why would you want to carry a loan balance as long as possible instead of paying the loan down more aggressively? Opportunity cost. The longer you carry a balance on a security, the longer you can invest your free cash elsewhere. If there comes a time when you feel good opportunities have dried up, then you can change your focus to a more aggressive payback.

Notice that in all three scenarios, your actual 'Cash Yield' exceeded the 'Stock Yield' after year four. Also notice that in all three scenarios the 'Cash Yield' over the 'Stock Yield' widens year, after year, after year. That yield will continue to widen as long as there is an outstanding loan, but as the loan is paid down and the interest expense decreases, the rate at which the yield widens will become slower.

Even though there is nothing to stop you from fudging the numbers down the road, it is very important that you maintain discipline when it comes to using margin. Not just in this system but in any system. Once you start using margin and your investments are pooled together in your brokerage account, there is very little to help you keep track of how your investments are actually doing. It simply isn't enough to look at your brokerage statement, see that some shares are up, some shares are down, and be content that your overall balance is up.

There may also come a time when you have to tap your margin for personal use. This adds an additional element of confusion. Also consider that there could be tax ramifications when you start to use your margin for personal use. Always consult a professional in these matters.

Dividend Reinvestment

I thought I would briefly touch on dividend reinvestment using the "Divi-X" System. In truth, I'm not entirely sure how well the "Divi-X" system would work with dividend reinvestment. I touch on dividend reinvestment a bit more in Chapter 8: **'Margin'** but it does not include use of the "Divi-X" system. In Chapter 11, we go over dividend reinvestment using the "Divi-X" system in great detail, but its actual use is untested and I'll let you judge the outcome for yourself.

My personal thoughts on dividend reinvestment, is that if you're going to purchase a couple of stocks and keep reinvesting the dividends, you don't really have much use for a system like this. However, if your reinvested dividends help you acquire a reasonably large amount of shares or a few high priced shares every distribution, it might be worth it. I don't know how much good that would do you though other than personal curiosity since you will obviously be committed to just a couple of stock names. In Chapter 11, I do give it my best attempt to come up with a workable dividend reinvestment plan using the "Divi-X" system. It seems very doable. It does involve a little extra work. Anyway, we'll worry about that when we get to it.

Below is a simple flow chart of how the "Divi-X" System works. Aside from a little detour for Margin Interest Expense, all the money comes flowing back to your Margin Account for future reinvestment.

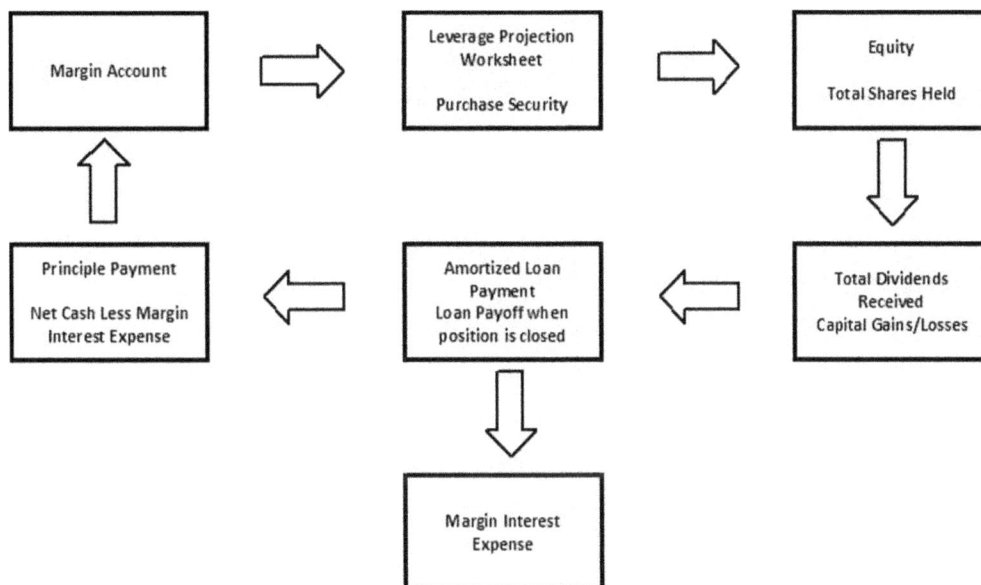

```
┌──────────────────┐        ┌──────────────────┐        ┌──────────────────┐
│                  │   ⇒    │ Leverage         │   ⇒    │   Equity         │
│  Margin Account  │        │ Projection       │        │                  │
│                  │        │ Worksheet        │        │ Total Shares Held│
│                  │        │ Purchase Security│        │                  │
└──────────────────┘        └──────────────────┘        └──────────────────┘
         ⇑                                                         ⇓
┌──────────────────┐        ┌──────────────────┐        ┌──────────────────┐
│ Principle Payment│   ⇐    │ Amortized Loan   │   ⇐    │ Total Dividends  │
│                  │        │ Payment          │        │ Received         │
│ Net Cash Less    │        │ Loan Payoff when │        │ Capital Gains/   │
│ Margin Interest  │        │ position is      │        │ Losses           │
│ Expense          │        │ closed           │        │                  │
└──────────────────┘        └──────────────────┘        └──────────────────┘
                                     ⇓
                            ┌──────────────────┐
                            │ Margin Interest  │
                            │ Expense          │
                            └──────────────────┘
```

Fig. 5.7

In the event of dividend reinvestment, the dividends received would flow back to "Equity." If your dividend reinvestment program provides you the option, and many of them do, of allocating what percentage of dividends you would like to reinvest, you could divide the dividend up to cover the margin interest expense and have the rest reinvested.

A transaction like that would look something like this:

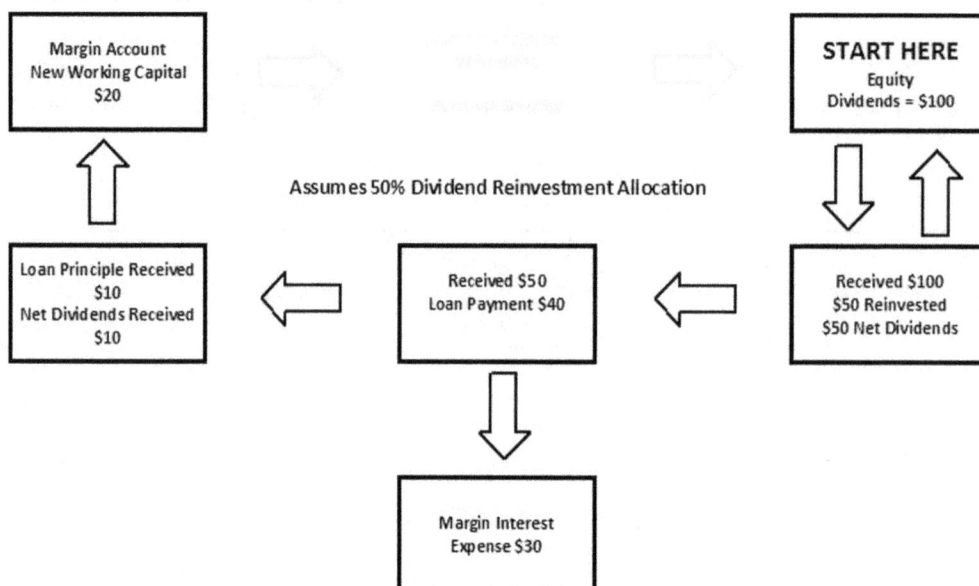

```
┌──────────────────────┐                                    ┌──────────────────────┐
│   Margin Account      │                                    │     START HERE        │
│ New Working Capital   │                                    │       Equity          │
│        $20            │                                    │  Dividends = $100     │
└──────────────────────┘                                    └──────────────────────┘
          ⬆                                                       ⬇      ⬆
                        Assumes 50% Dividend Reinvestment Allocation
┌──────────────────────┐      ┌──────────────────────┐      ┌──────────────────────┐
│ Loan Principle Received│     │   Received $50        │      │   Received $100       │
│        $10            │ ⬅   │  Loan Payment $40     │ ⬅   │   $50 Reinvested      │
│ Net Dividends Received │     └──────────────────────┘      │   $50 Net Dividends   │
│        $10            │              ⬇                     └──────────────────────┘
└──────────────────────┘      ┌──────────────────────┐
                              │   Margin Interest     │
                              │    Expense $30        │
                              └──────────────────────┘
```

Fig. 5.8

If you choose to have all of your dividends reinvested, you would then have the option of letting the interest accumulate, which I personally would not have any interest in doing; or you could introduce outside funds to cover the interest expense. I would anticipate that most people would be making regular contributions to their margin accounts already so this seems to be a sensible choice. Here's what that would look like:

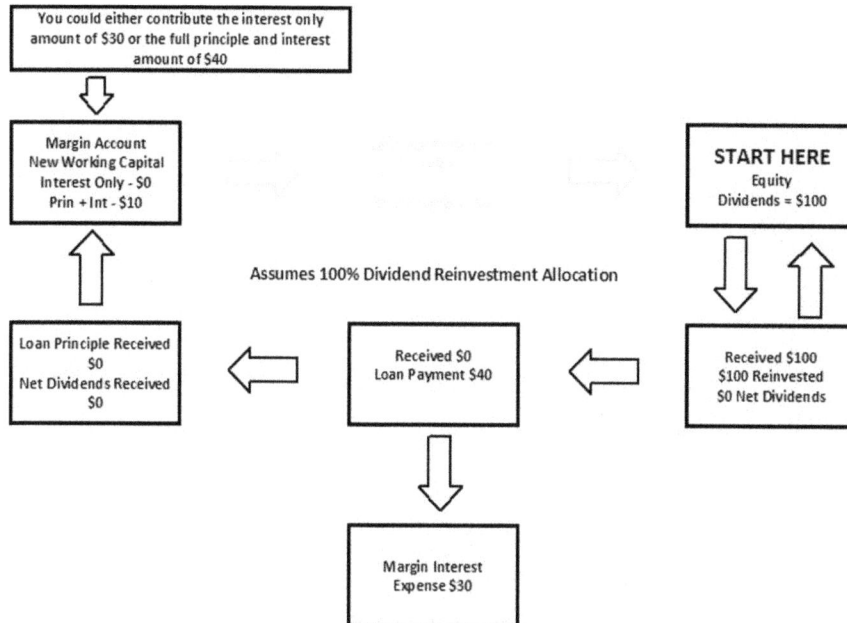

Fig. 5.9

In the Margin Account/New Working Capital box that shows Interest Only - $0/Prin + Int - $10, those figures assume that you did make the $40 contribution. The Interest Only line states $0 because the actual $30 interest expense was reflected in the "Margin Interest Expense" box. The $10 in the line Prin + Int is the remainder of the $40 contribution and what is left after you deduct the $30 interest expense. If you had only contributed the interest expense of $30, that line would be $0 as well.

The "Divi-X" System Workbook: Even breaks down the returns on borrowed funds.

Chapter 6
Yields

Yields over Time Using the "Divi-X" System

Following is the Dow 30 using the same Dow 30 data as before, and as will be the case in all of our Dow 30 examples. The purpose of the following charts is to show you how the effects of using the "Divi-X" System, effects the yield on your cash investment over time. Twenty years to be more precise.

The first five years of every chart uses actual stock history data and the remaining fifteen years is projected. You were introduced to these charts in Chapter 5.

The actual historical data speaks for itself. The future data makes the following assumptions, and in the absence of any changes to the following variables, the predictions regarding "Cash Yield" can be viewed as attainable but not guaranteed regardless of the share price.

1. You use the "PmtPerc" option (you'll do equally as well or better using either option; 'All DIV's' or 'Fixed Pmt').
2. No change in interest rates. This is unlikely and will change the eventual outcome.
3. No decrease in the company's dividend.
4. Company has a history of increased dividends and it is believed that the company will continue to do so.
5. You stick to the plan (there is so much flexibility built into the "Divi-X" System Workbook, that any change you make to the plan will automatically be reflected in any future outlook).
6. The companies continue to trade as public entities for the entirety of the projection period.

You will notice in the vast majority of the times, your "Cash Yield" will eventually outpace the stated annual "Stock Yield" of the actual companies. The primary reason for this is because over time as you decrease your margin balance associated with each stock, the monthly margin payment decreases as well. This effect actually causes your yield to rise every single month for the duration of your holding period or until the loan is paid off.

AXP	American Express	Purchase @ 24.64 share	Yield 2.92%

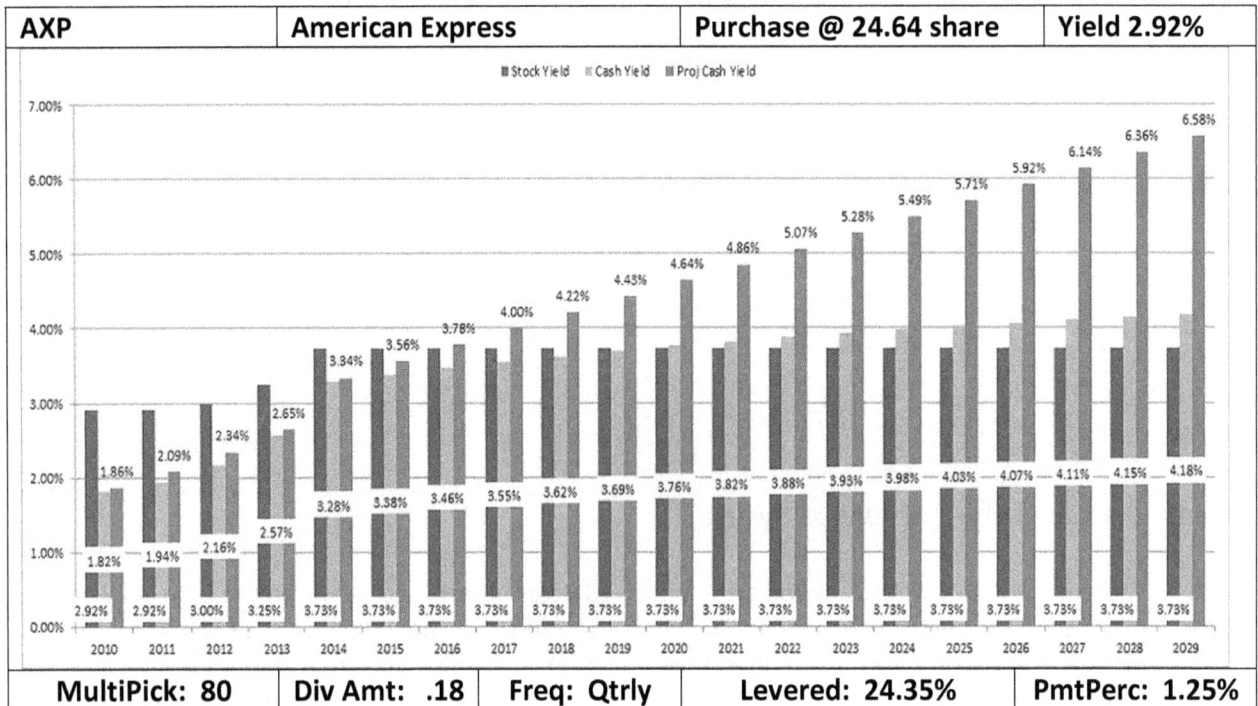

MultiPick: 80	Div Amt: .18	Freq: Qtrly	Levered: 24.35%	PmtPerc: 1.25%

'Stock Yield' bottom % number   'Cash Yield' middle % number   'Proj Cash Yield' top % number

BA	Boeing Co.	Purchase @ 48.88 share	Yield 3.47%

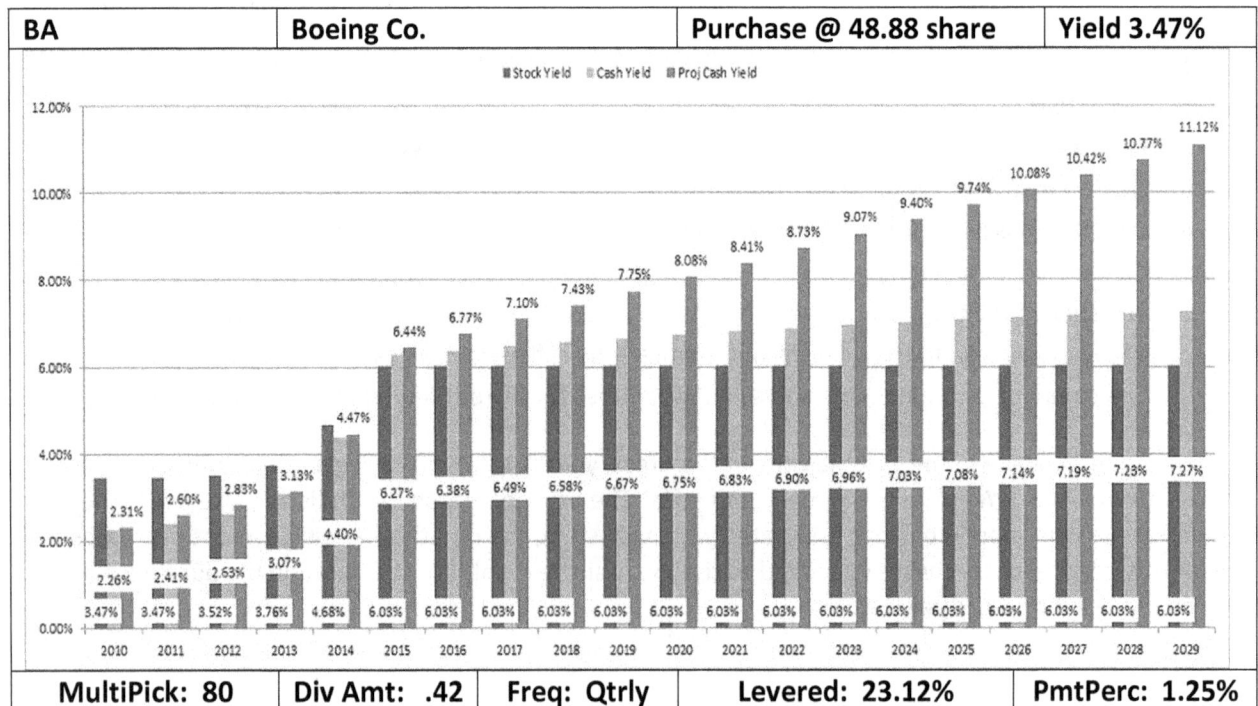

MultiPick: 80	Div Amt: .42	Freq: Qtrly	Levered: 23.12%	PmtPerc: 1.25%

CAT	Caterpillar	Purchase @ 33.65 share	Yield 4.99%

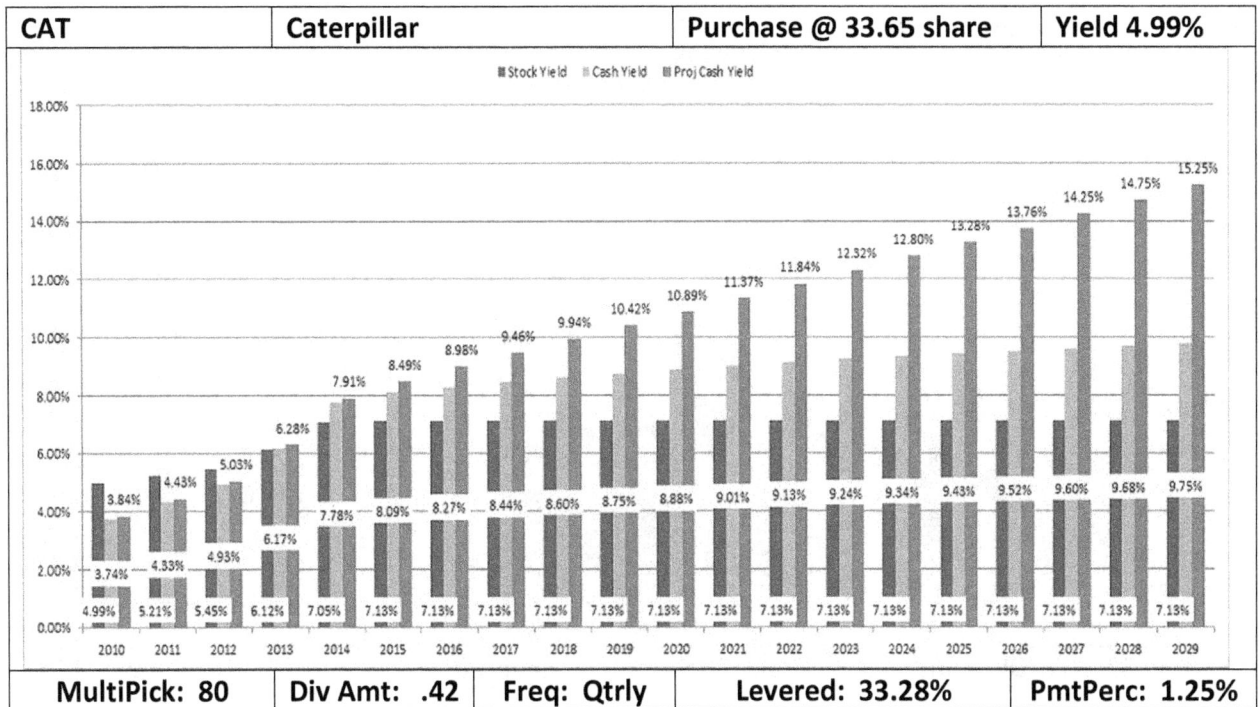

Stock Yield ■ Cash Yield ■ Proj Cash Yield

	2010	2011	2012	2013	2014	2015	2016	2017	2018	2019	2020	2021	2022	2023	2024	2025	2026	2027	2028	2029
Proj Cash Yield		3.84%	4.43%	5.03%	6.28%	7.91%	8.49%	8.98%	9.46%	9.94%	10.42%	10.89%	11.37%	11.84%	12.32%	12.80%	13.28%	13.76%	14.25%	14.75%	15.25%
Cash Yield		3.74%	4.33%	4.93%	6.17%	7.78%	8.09%	8.27%	8.44%	8.60%	8.75%	8.88%	9.01%	9.13%	9.24%	9.34%	9.43%	9.52%	9.60%	9.68%	9.75%
Stock Yield	4.99%	5.21%	5.45%	6.12%	7.05%	7.13%	7.13%	7.13%	7.13%	7.13%	7.13%	7.13%	7.13%	7.13%	7.13%	7.13%	7.13%	7.13%	7.13%	7.13%

MultiPick: 80	Div Amt: .42	Freq: Qtrly	Levered: 33.28%	PmtPerc: 1.25%

CSCO   Cisco Systems, Inc.   Paid no dividends during our time window and would not work.

CVX	Chevron Corporation	Purchase @ $68.06 Share	Yield: 4.0%

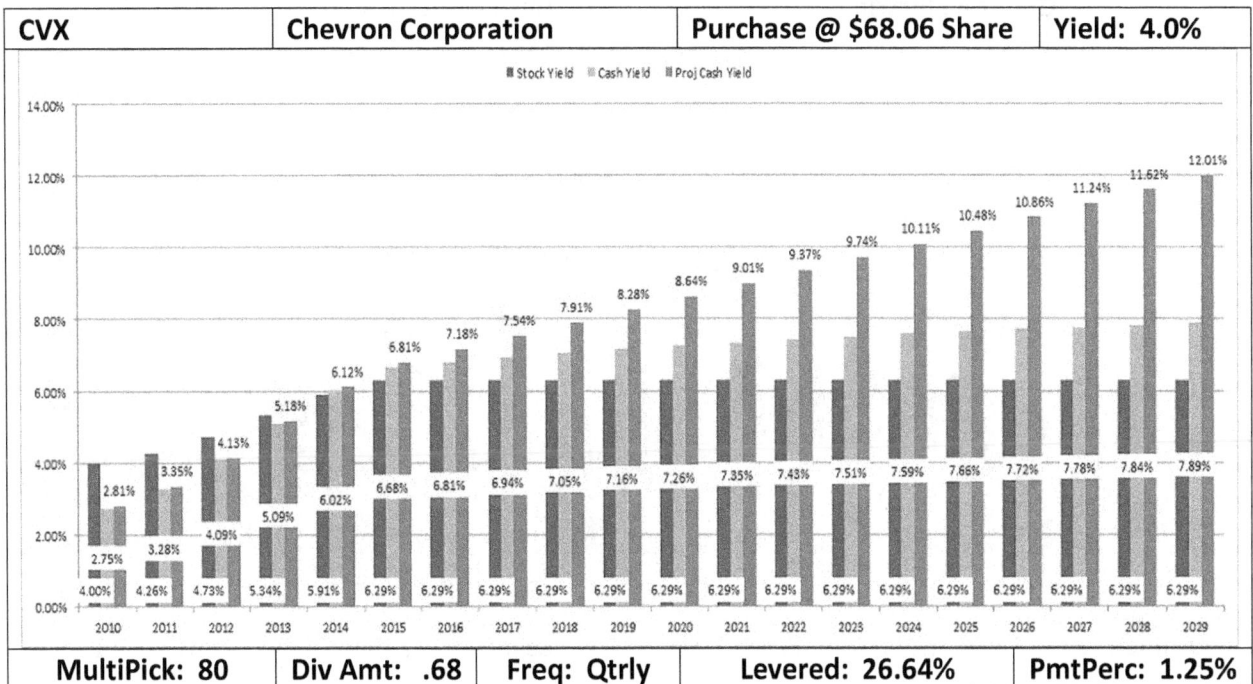

Stock Yield ■ Cash Yield ■ Proj Cash Yield

	2010	2011	2012	2013	2014	2015	2016	2017	2018	2019	2020	2021	2022	2023	2024	2025	2026	2027	2028	2029
Proj Cash Yield		2.81%	3.35%	4.13%	5.18%	6.12%	6.81%	7.18%	7.54%	7.91%	8.28%	8.64%	9.01%	9.37%	9.74%	10.11%	10.48%	10.86%	11.24%	11.52%	12.01%
Cash Yield		2.75%	3.28%	4.09%	5.09%	6.02%	6.68%	6.81%	6.94%	7.05%	7.16%	7.26%	7.35%	7.43%	7.51%	7.59%	7.66%	7.72%	7.78%	7.84%	7.89%
Stock Yield	4.00%	4.26%	4.73%	5.34%	5.91%	6.29%	6.29%	6.29%	6.29%	6.29%	6.29%	6.29%	6.29%	6.29%	6.29%	6.29%	6.29%	6.29%	6.29%	6.29%

MultiPick: 80	Div Amt: .68	Freq: Qtrly	Levered: 26.64%	PmtPerc: 1.25%

| DD | E I Dupont De Nemours and Co | Purchase @ $24.97 share | Yield: 6.57% |

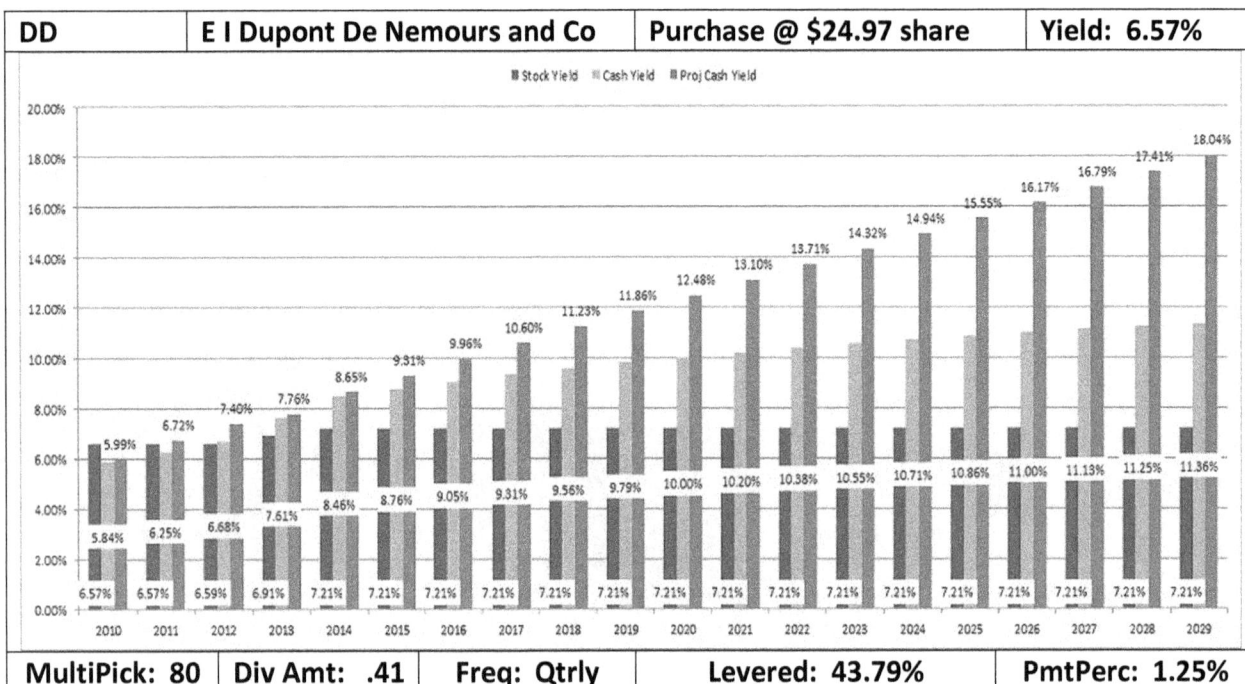

Stock Yield   Cash Yield   Proj Cash Yield

| MultiPick: 80 | Div Amt: .41 | Freq: Qtrly | Levered: 43.79% | PmtPerc: 1.25% |

| GE | General Electric | Purchase @ 12.10 share | Yield: 3.31% |

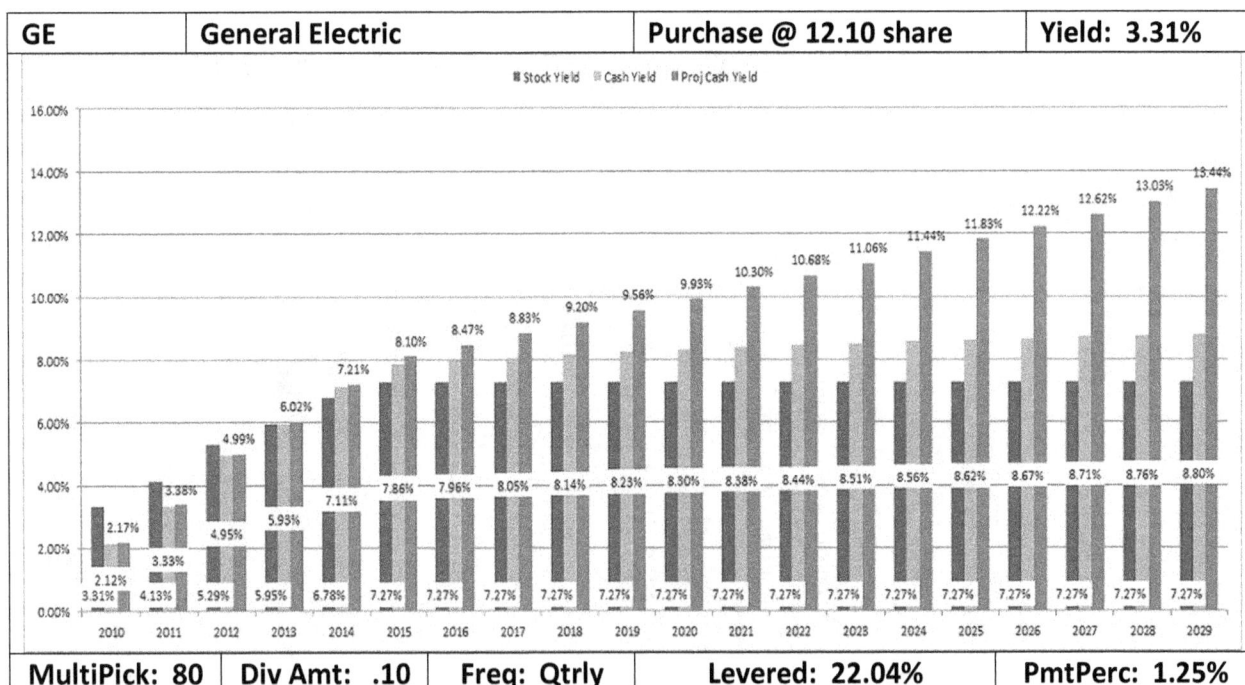

Stock Yield   Cash Yield   Proj Cash Yield

| MultiPick: 80 | Div Amt: .10 | Freq: Qtrly | Levered: 22.04% | PmtPerc: 1.25% |

GS	Goldman Sachs Group, Inc.	Purchase @ $146.74	Yield: 0.95%

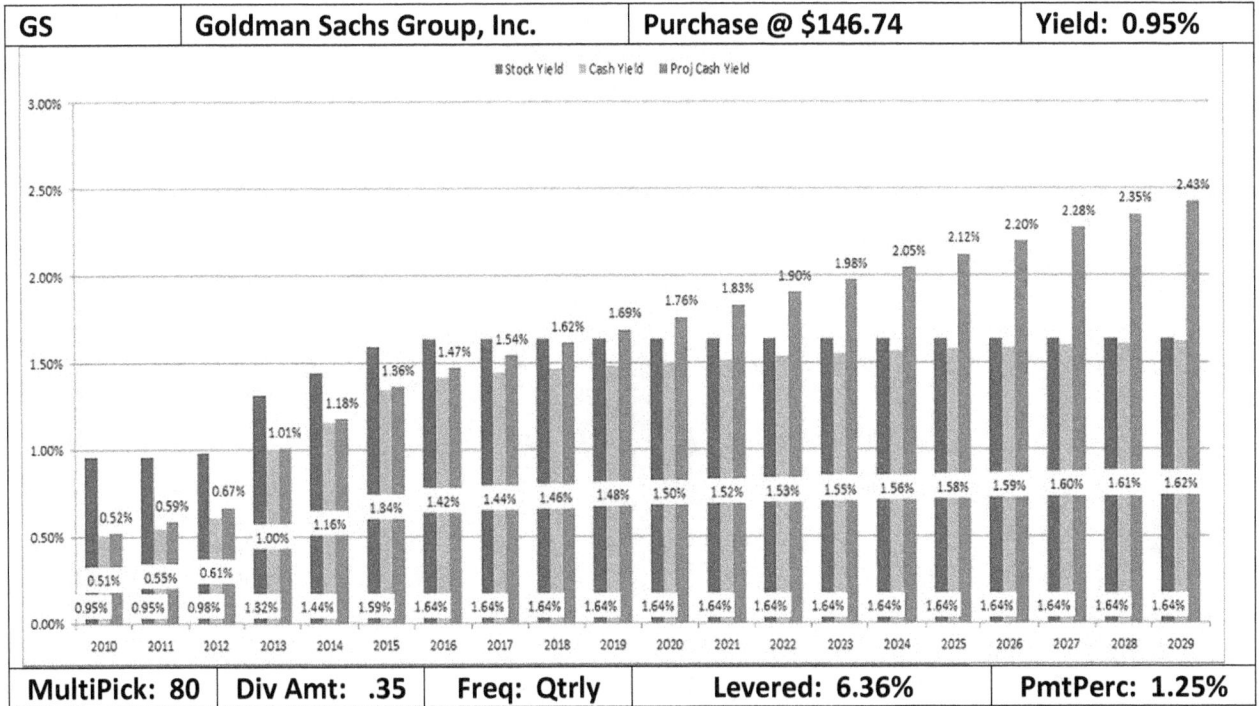

MultiPick: 80	Div Amt: .35	Freq: Qtrly	Levered: 6.36%	PmtPerc: 1.25%

HD	Home Depot	Purchase @ $23.61	Yield: 3.81%

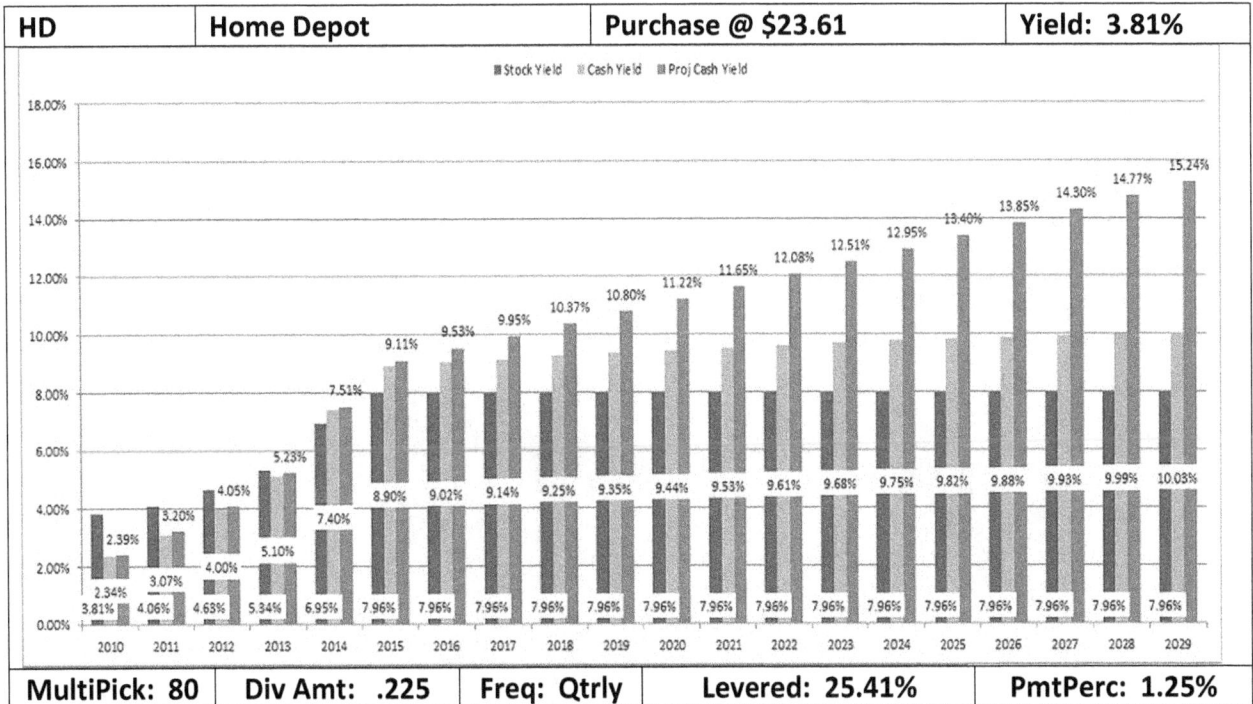

MultiPick: 80	Div Amt: .225	Freq: Qtrly	Levered: 25.41%	PmtPerc: 1.25%

MMM	3M Co	Purchase @ $59.37	Yield: 3.44%

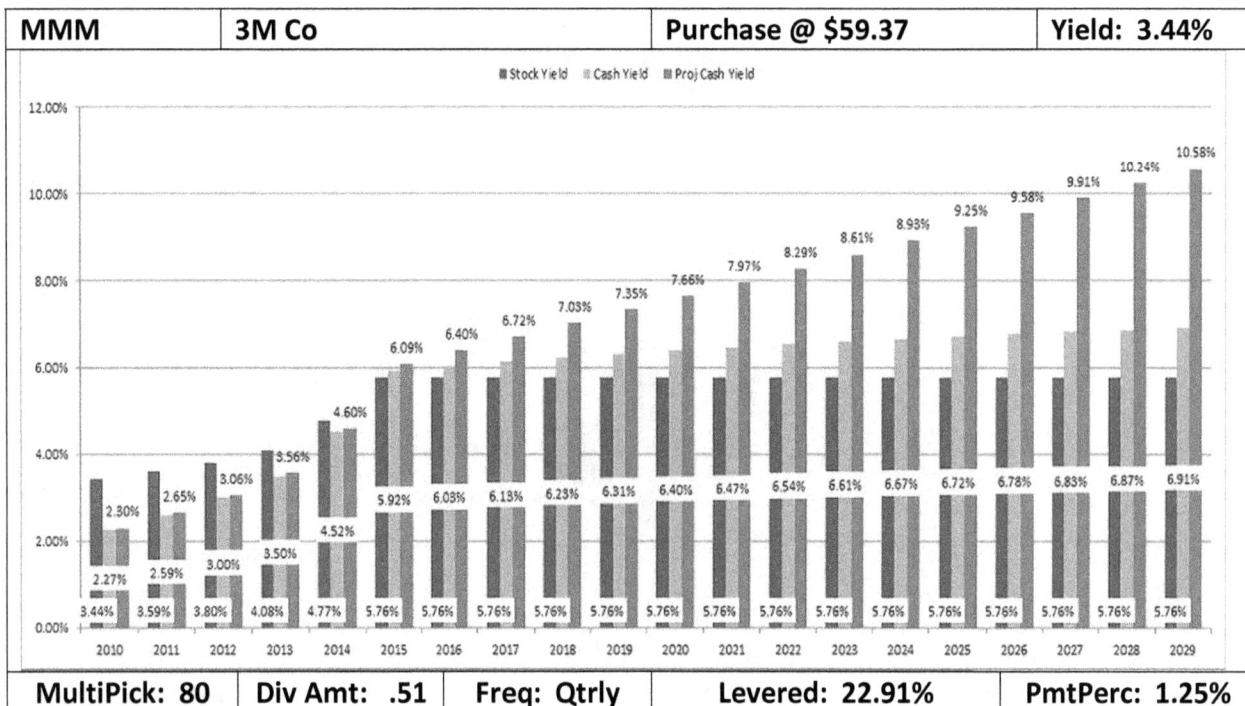

MultiPick: 80	Div Amt: .51	Freq: Qtrly	Levered: 22.91%	PmtPerc: 1.25%

T	AT&T	Purchase @ $24.04	Yield: 6.82%

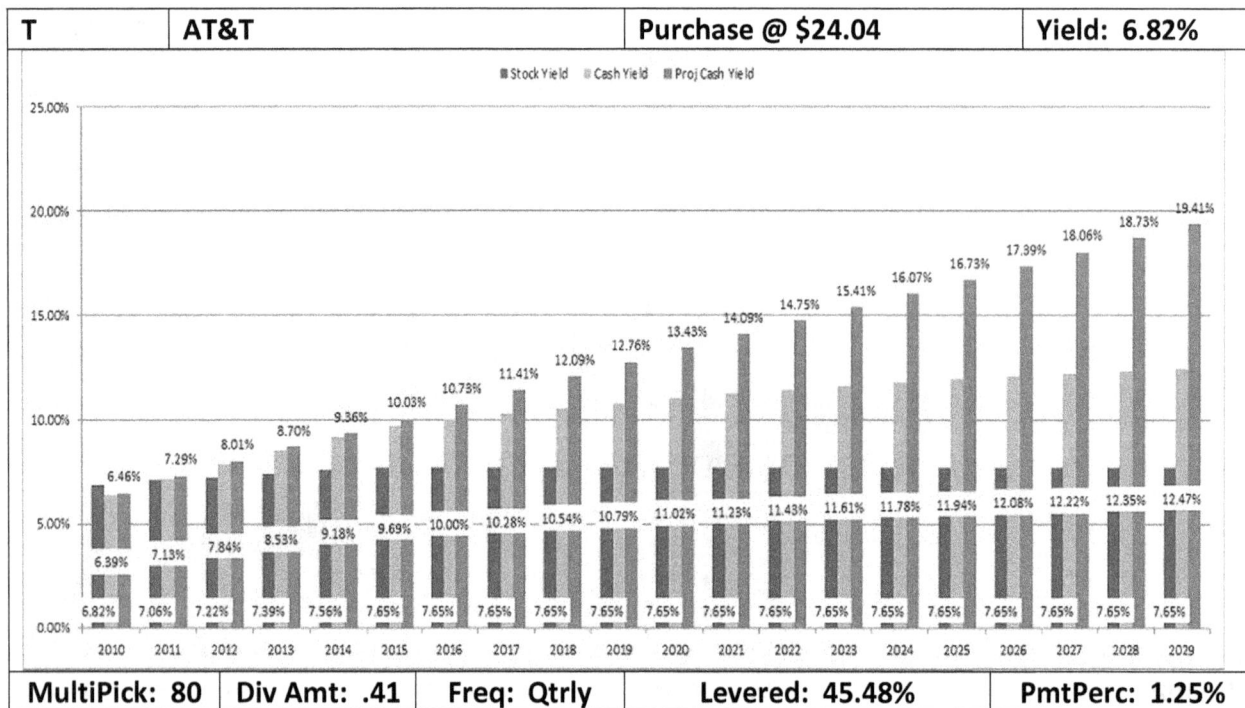

MultiPick: 80	Div Amt: .41	Freq: Qtrly	Levered: 45.48%	PmtPerc: 1.25%

INTC	Intel Corporation	Purchase @ $32.08	Yield: 1.96%

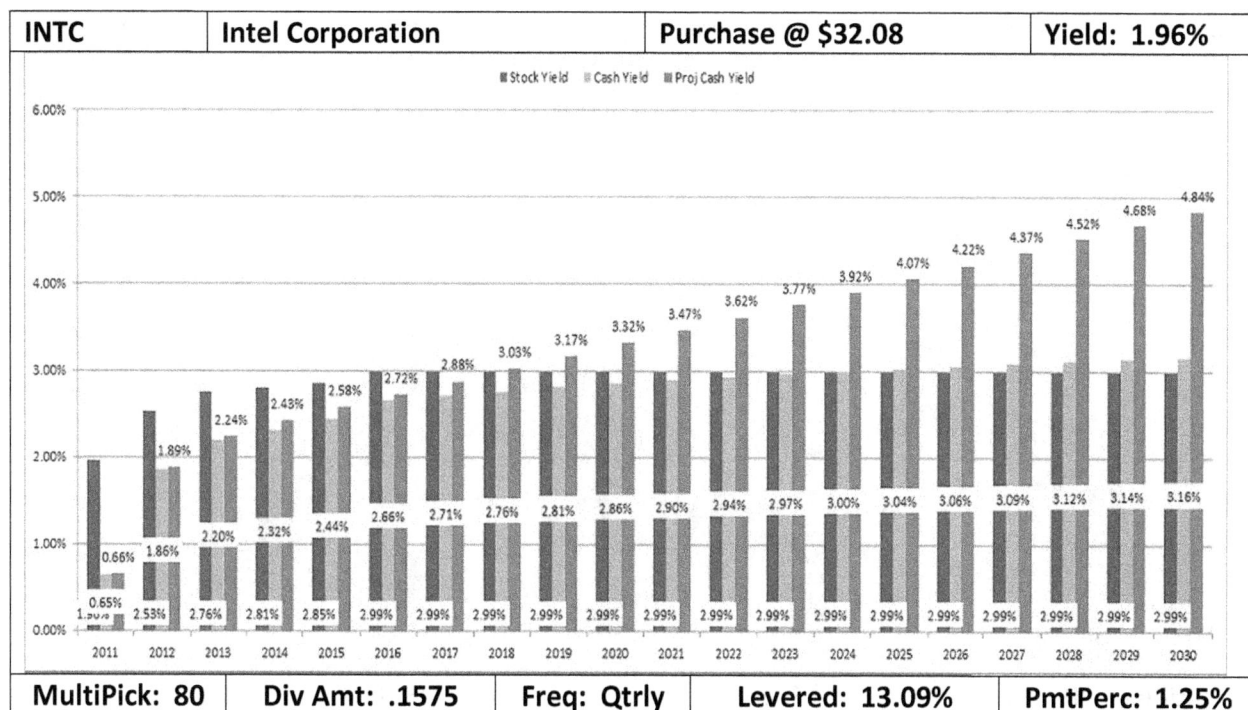

MultiPick: 80	Div Amt: .1575	Freq: Qtrly	Levered: 13.09%	PmtPerc: 1.25%

XOM	Exxon Mobile Corporation	Purchase @ $71.05 share	Yield: 2.36%

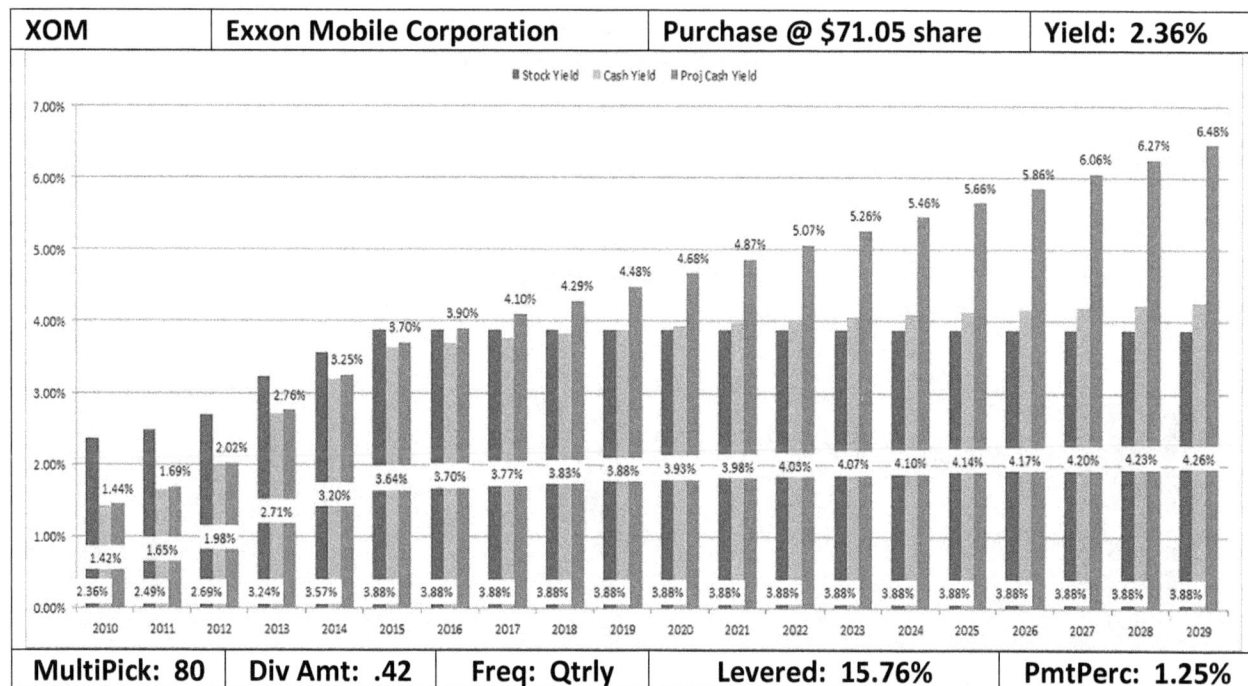

MultiPick: 80	Div Amt: .42	Freq: Qtrly	Levered: 15.76%	PmtPerc: 1.25%

IBM	International Business Machines Corp.	Purchase @ $129.99 share	Yield: 2.00%

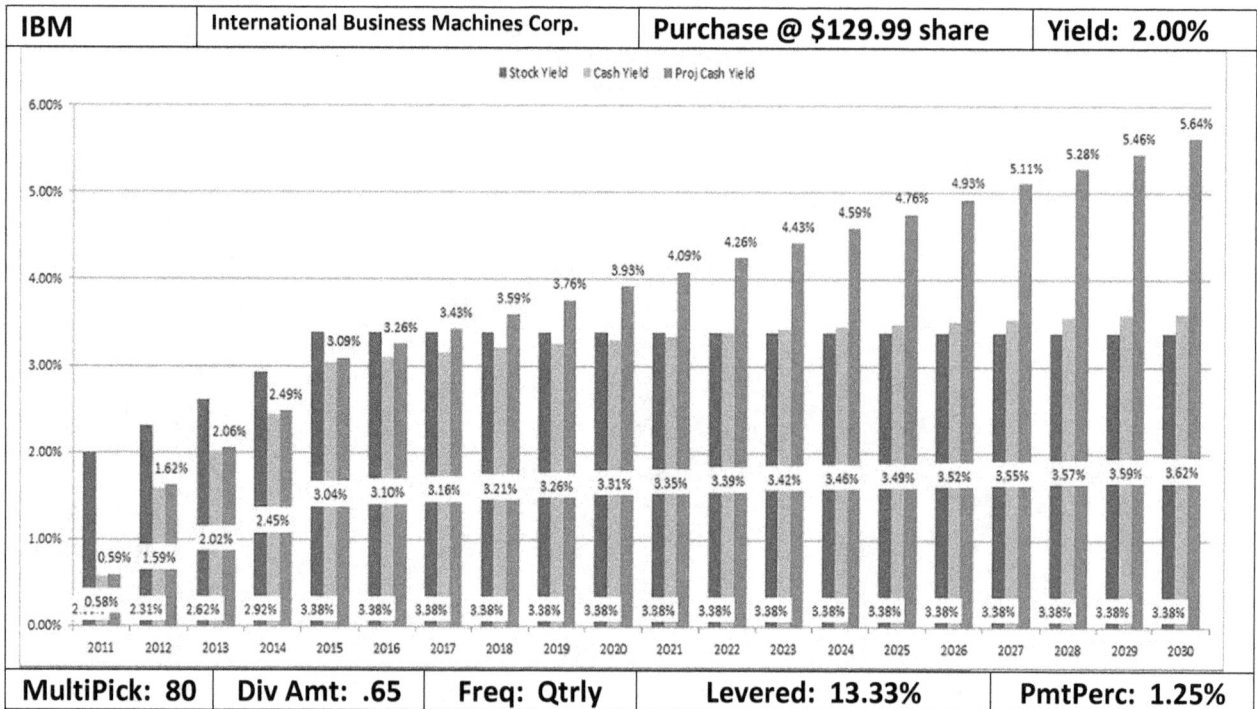

MultiPick: 80	Div Amt: .65	Freq: Qtrly	Levered: 13.33%	PmtPerc: 1.25%

JNJ	Johnson & Johnson	Purchase @ $ 64.30 share	Yield: 3.36%

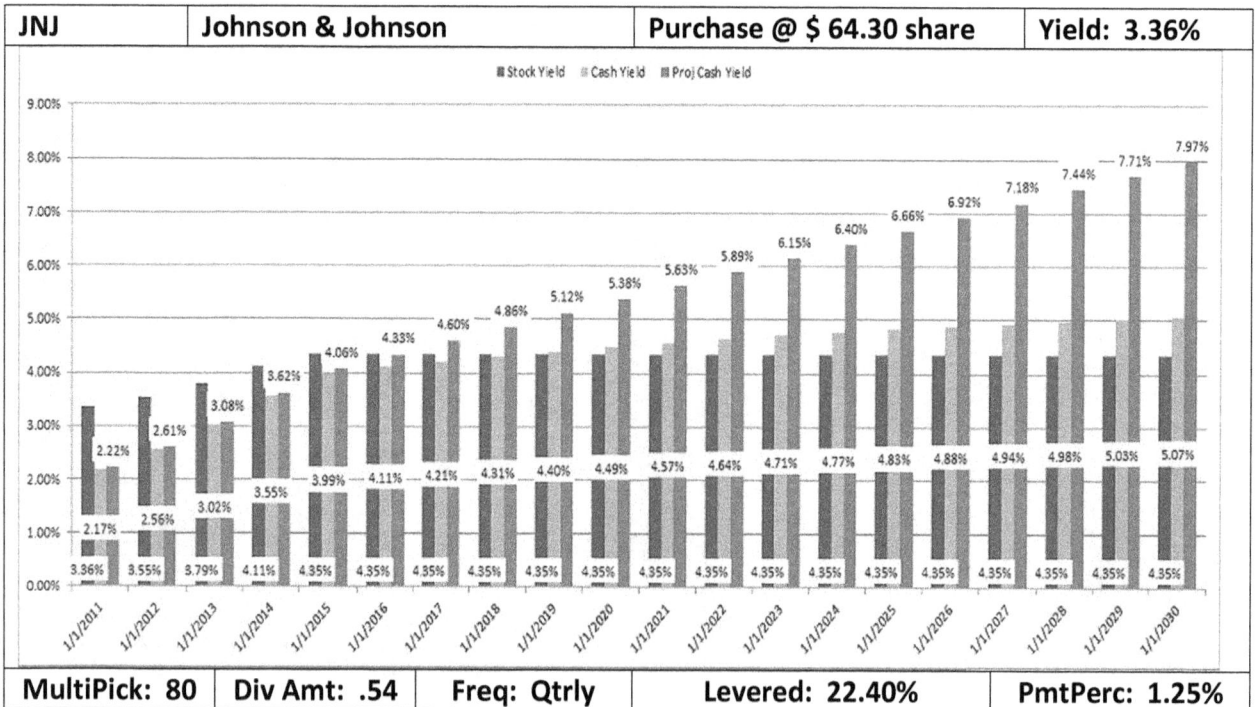

MultiPick: 80	Div Amt: .54	Freq: Qtrly	Levered: 22.40%	PmtPerc: 1.25%

JPM	JPMorgan Chase & Co.	Purchase @ $ 44.94 share	Yield: 0.45%

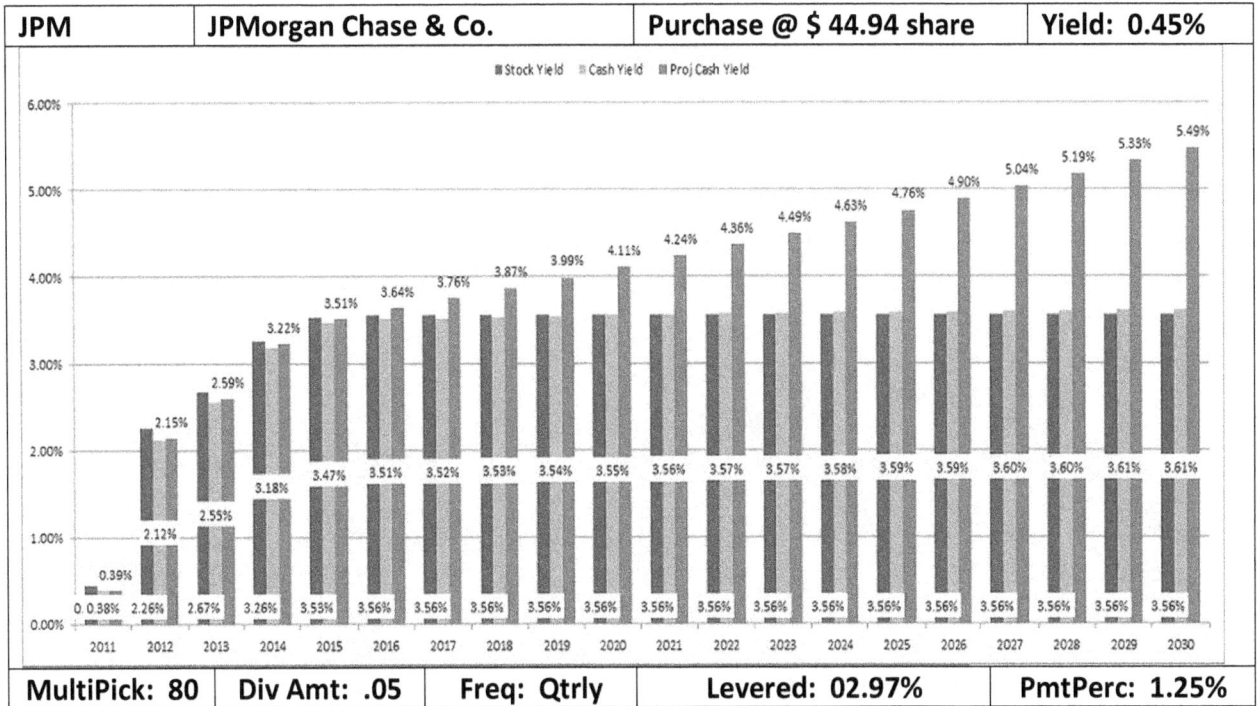

MultiPick: 80	Div Amt: .05	Freq: Qtrly	Levered: 02.97%	PmtPerc: 1.25%

MCD	McDonald's Corporation	Purchase @ 70.59 share	Yield: 3.12%

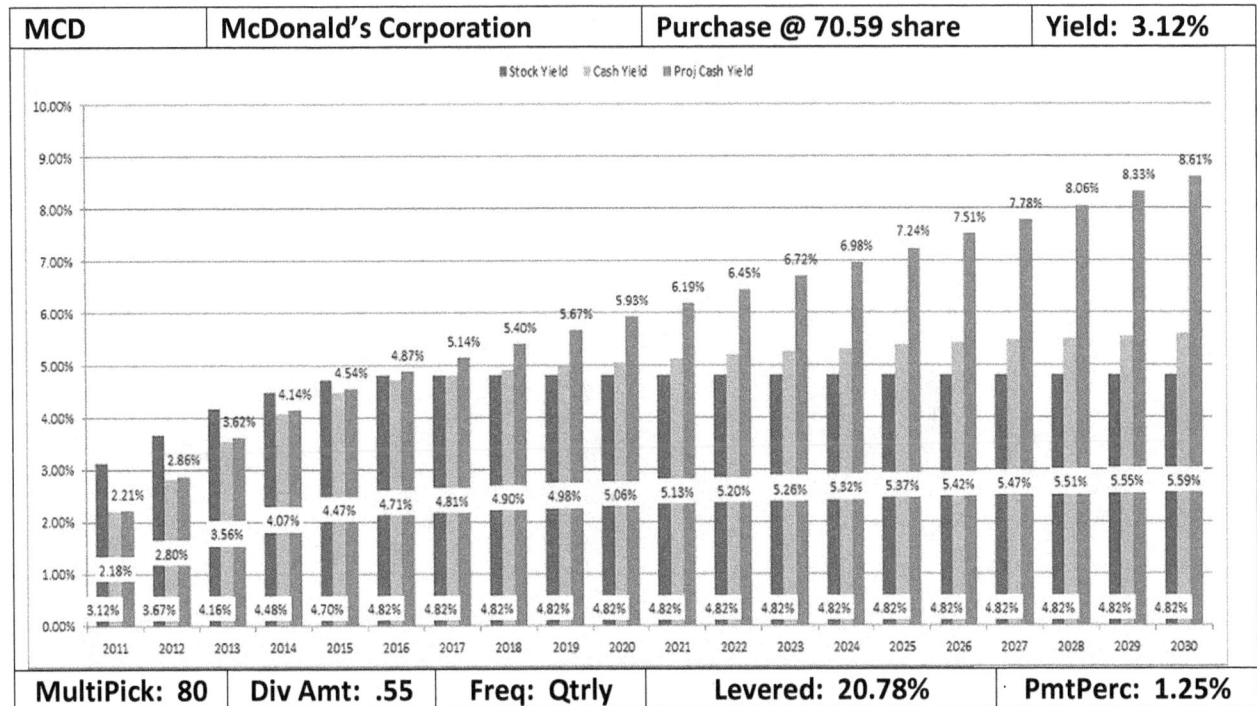

MultiPick: 80	Div Amt: .55	Freq: Qtrly	Levered: 20.78%	PmtPerc: 1.25%

MRK	Merck & Co Inc	Purchase @ $ 35.46 share	Yield: 4.29%

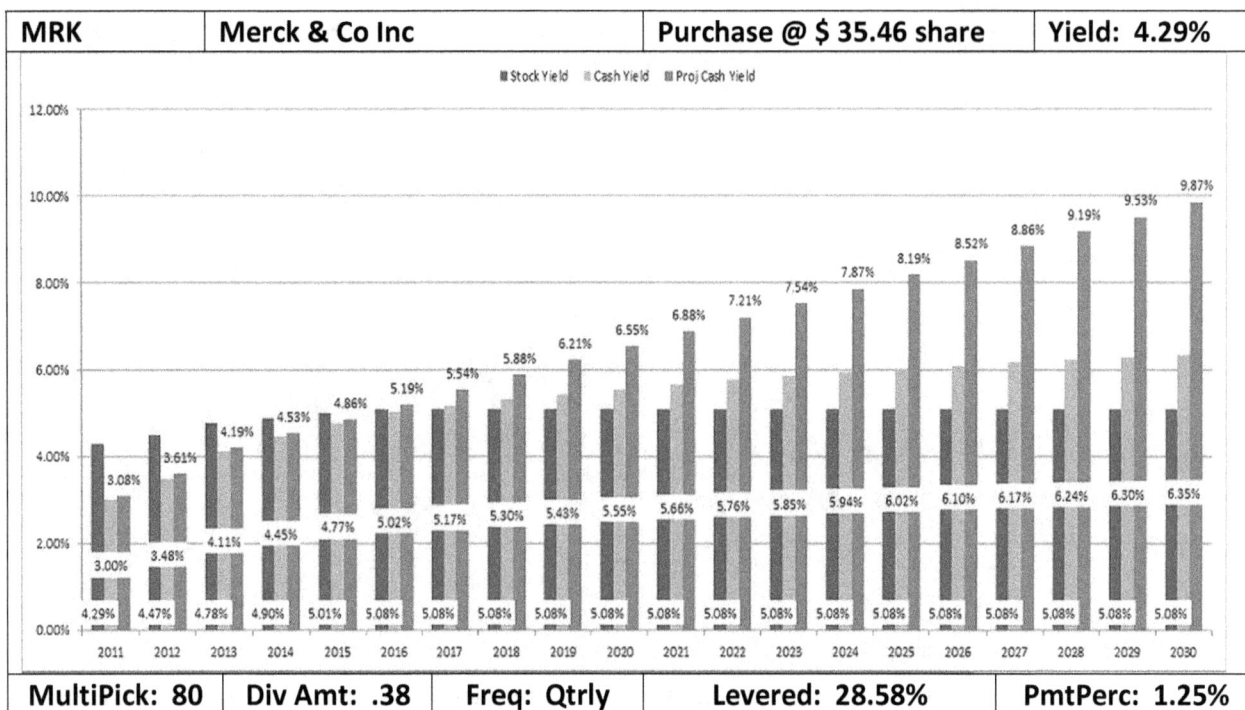

MultiPick: 80	Div Amt: .38	Freq: Qtrly	Levered: 28.58%	PmtPerc: 1.25%

MSFT	Microsoft Corporation	Purchase @ $ 30.96 share	Yield: 1.68%

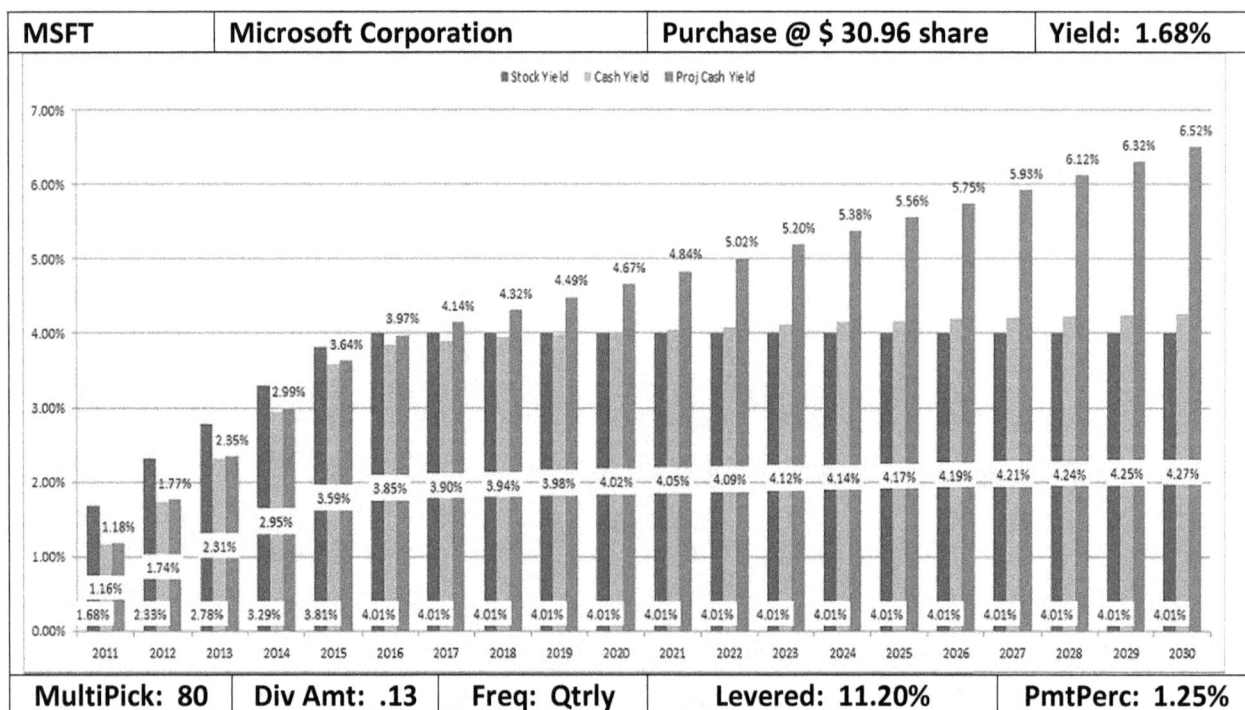

MultiPick: 80	Div Amt: .13	Freq: Qtrly	Levered: 11.20%	PmtPerc: 1.25%

NKE	Nike Inc	Purchase @ $ 38.95 share	Yield: 1.39%

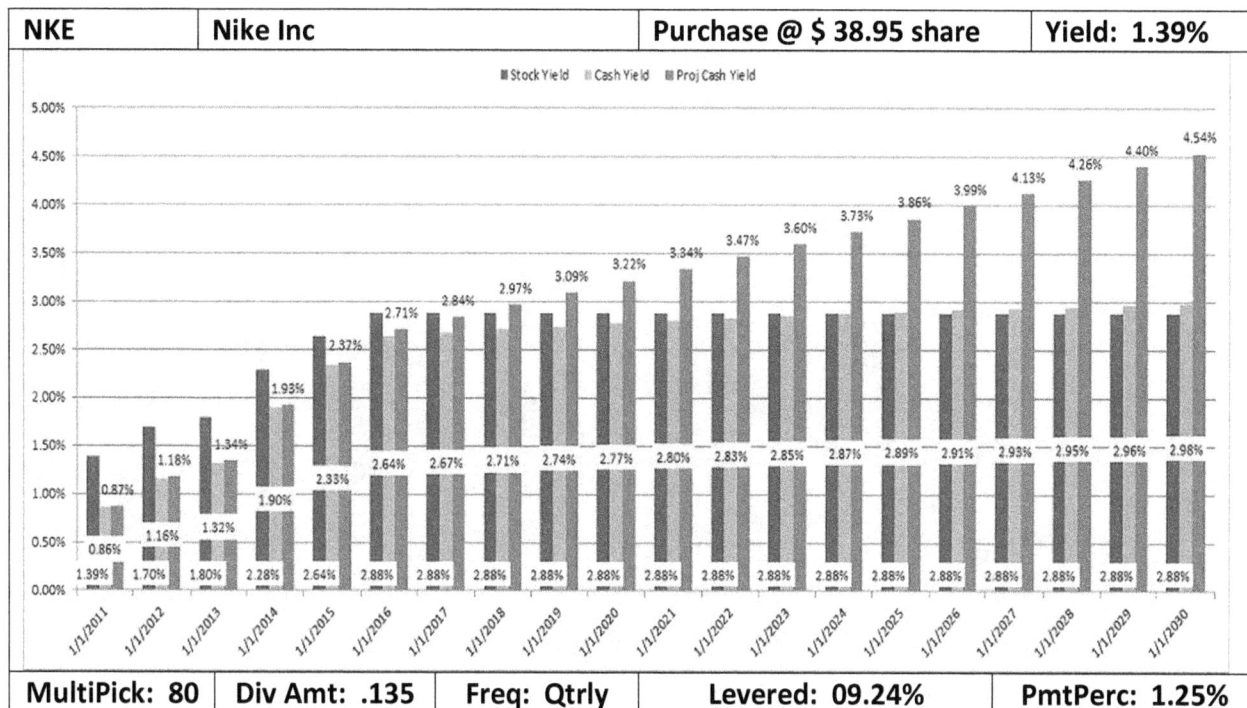

MultiPick: 80	Div Amt: .135	Freq: Qtrly	Levered: 09.24%	PmtPerc: 1.25%

PFE	Pfizer Inc	Purchase @ $ 16.72 share	Yield: 4.31%

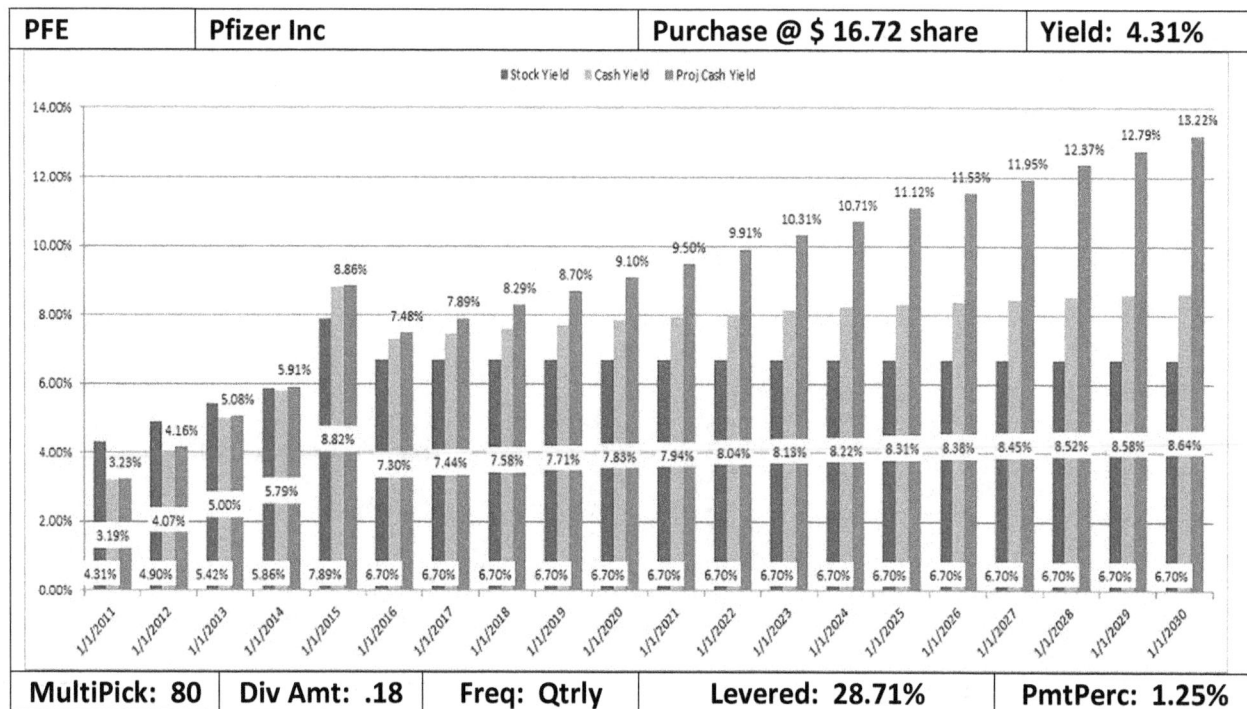

MultiPick: 80	Div Amt: .18	Freq: Qtrly	Levered: 28.71%	PmtPerc: 1.25%

PG	Procter & Gamble & Co	Purchase @ $ 62.16 share	Yield: 3.10%

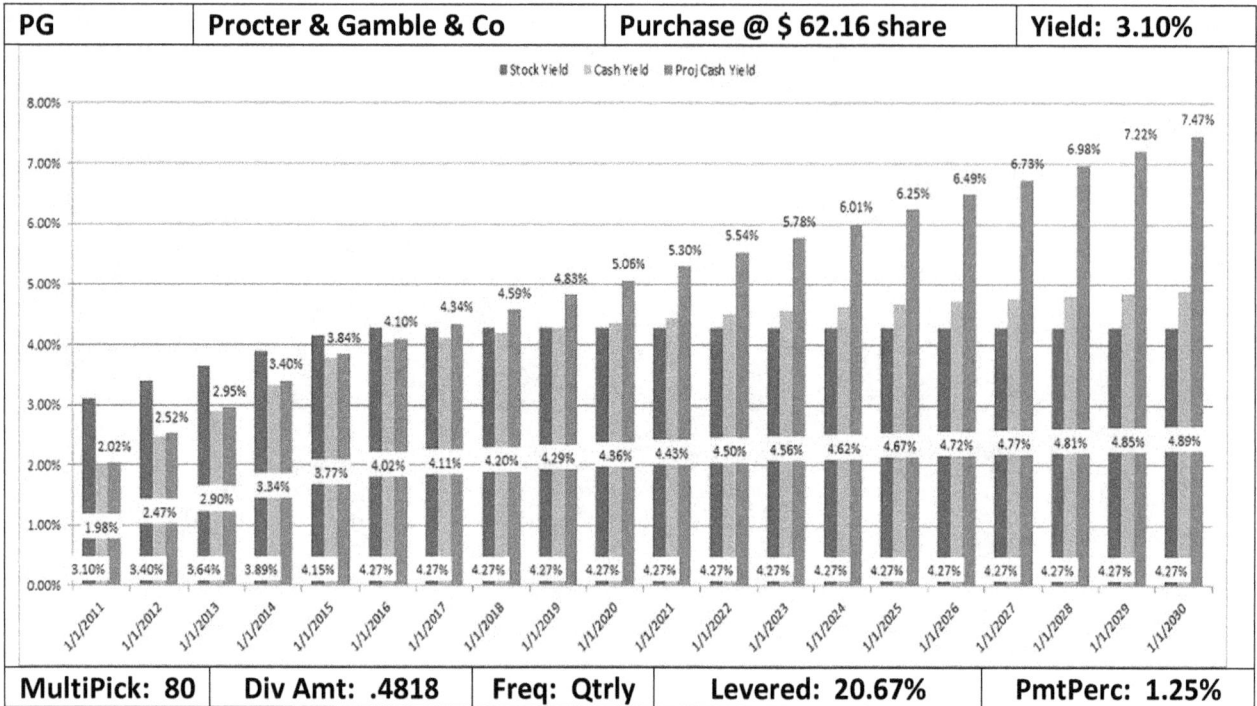

Stock Yield ■ Cash Yield ■ Proj Cash Yield

MultiPick: 80	Div Amt: .4818	Freq: Qtrly	Levered: 20.67%	PmtPerc: 1.25%

KO	The Coca-Cola Co	Purchase @ $ 26.72 share	Yield: 3.29%

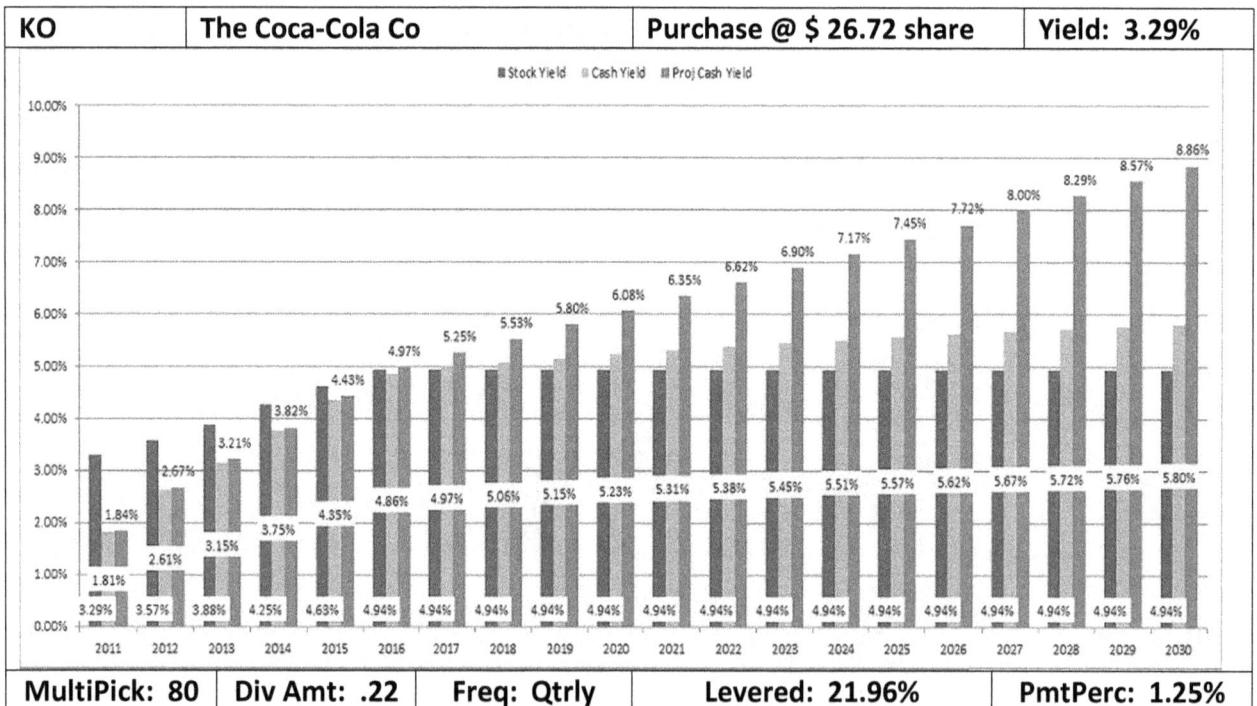

Stock Yield ■ Cash Yield ■ Proj Cash Yield

MultiPick: 80	Div Amt: .22	Freq: Qtrly	Levered: 21.96%	PmtPerc: 1.25%

TRV	Travelers Companies Inc	Purchase @ $ 50.74 share	Yield: 2.84%

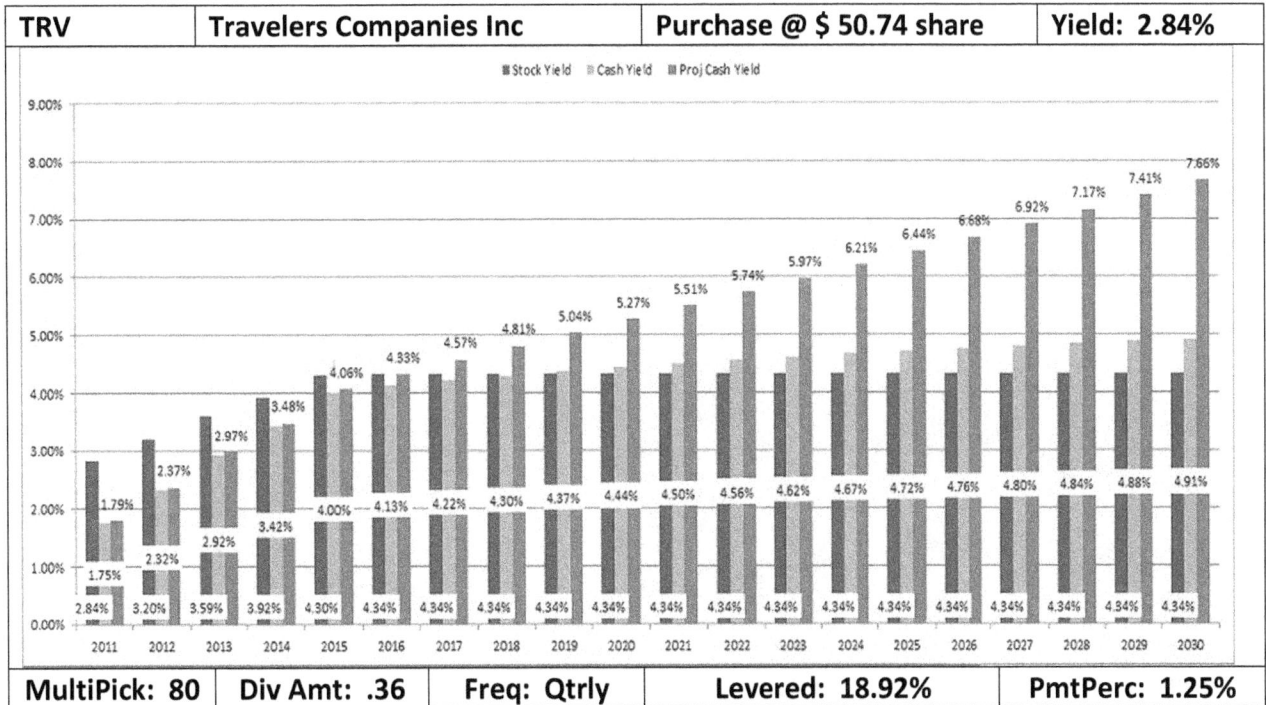

MultiPick: 80	Div Amt: .36	Freq: Qtrly	Levered: 18.92%	PmtPerc: 1.25%

UTX	United Technologies Corp	Purchase @ $ 74.95 share	Yield: 2.27%

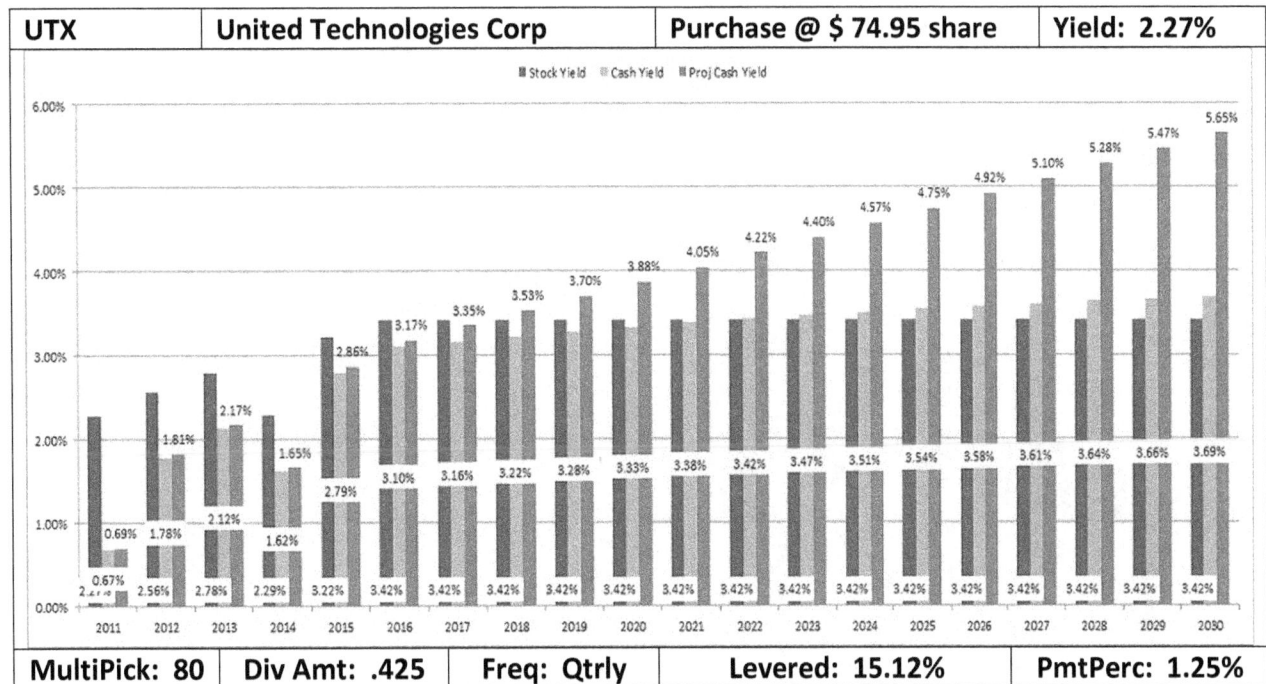

MultiPick: 80	Div Amt: .425	Freq: Qtrly	Levered: 15.12%	PmtPerc: 1.25%

UNH	UnitedHealth Group Inc	Purchase @ $ 30.31 share	Yield: 1.65%

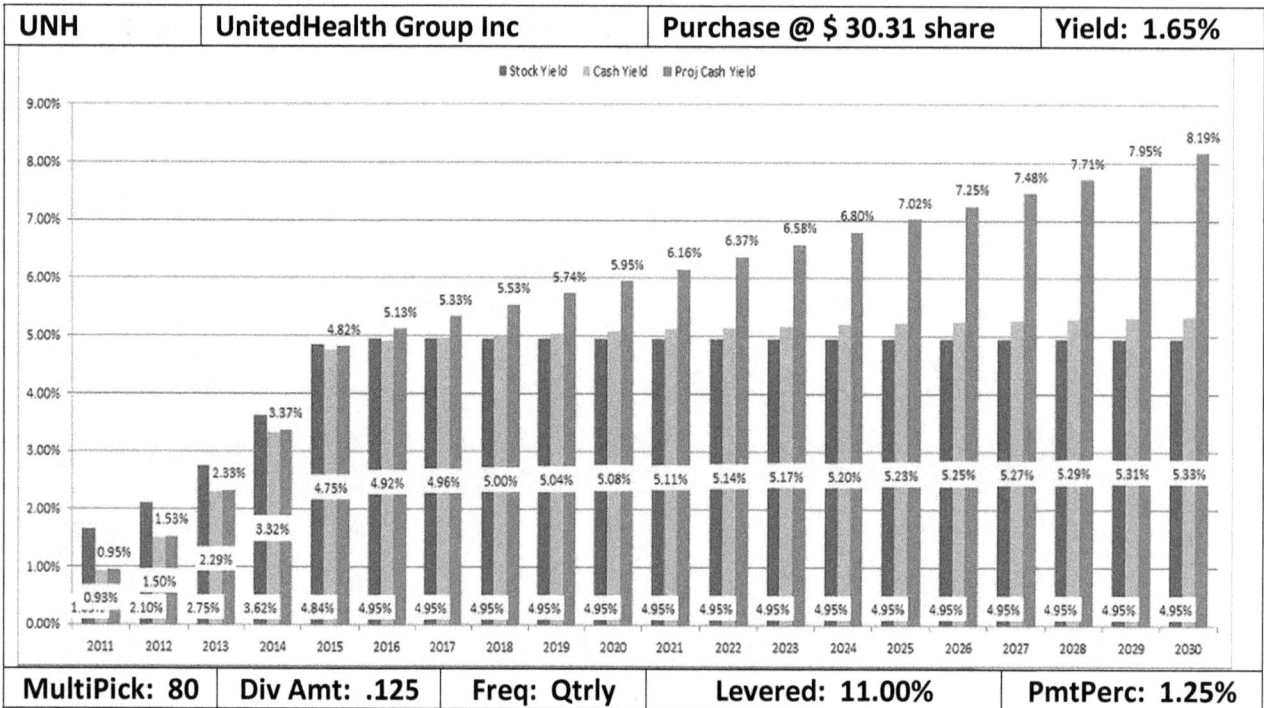

MultiPick: 80	Div Amt: .125	Freq: Qtrly	Levered: 11.00%	PmtPerc: 1.25%

VZ	Verizon Communications Inc	Purchase @ $ 28.90 share	Yield: 6.57%

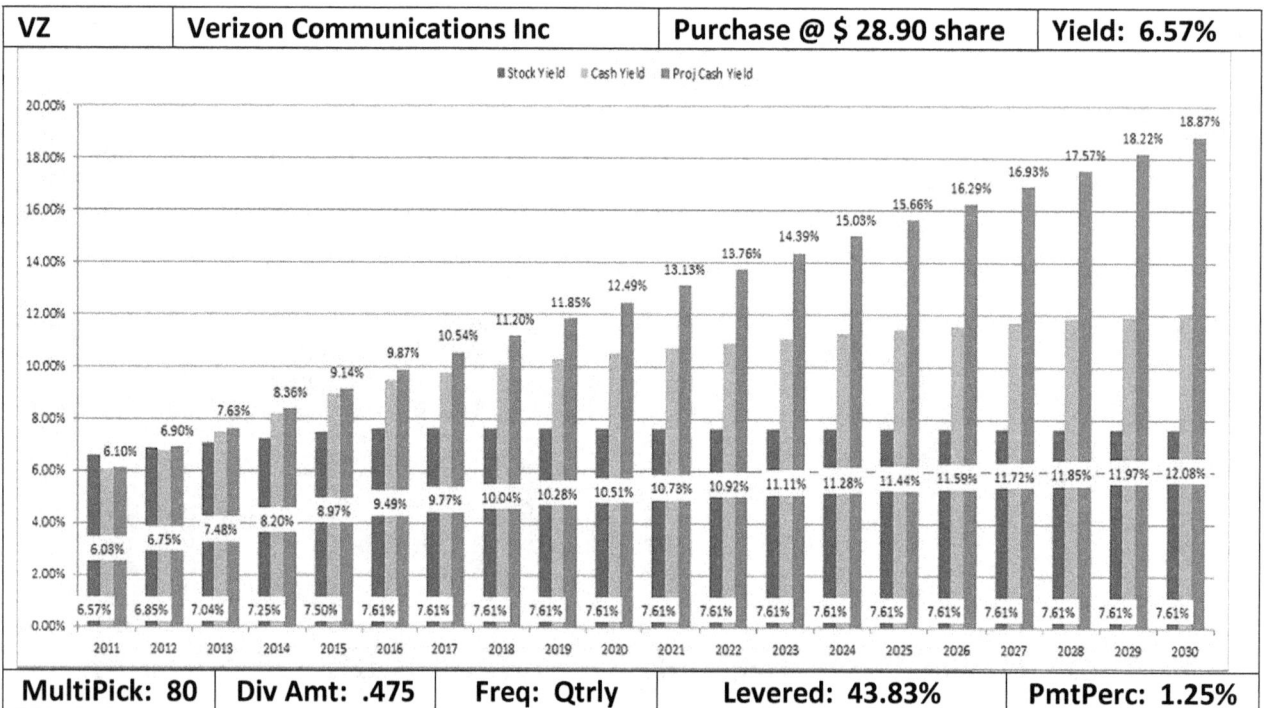

MultiPick: 80	Div Amt: .475	Freq: Qtrly	Levered: 43.83%	PmtPerc: 1.25%

V	Visa Inc	Purchase @ $22.558 share	Yield: 0.56%

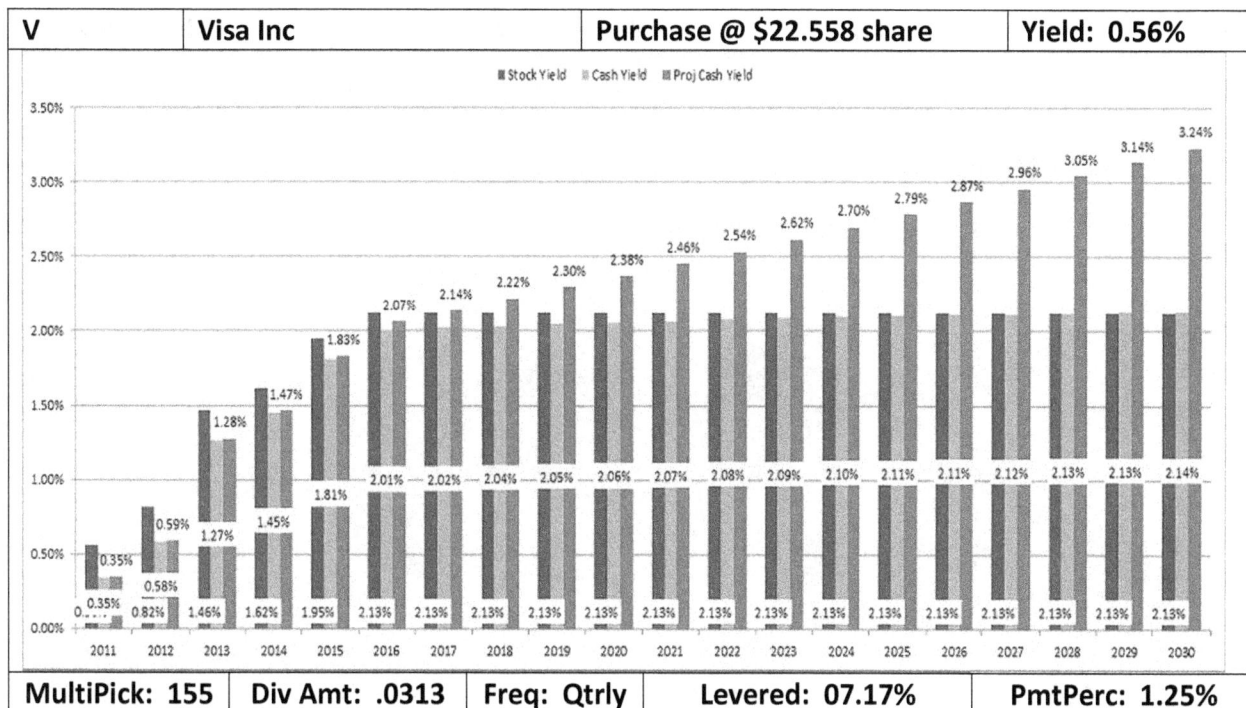

Stock Yield   Cash Yield   Proj Cash Yield

MultiPick: 155	Div Amt: .0313	Freq: Qtrly	Levered: 07.17%	PmtPerc: 1.25%

WMT	Wal-Mart Stores Inc	Purchase @ $ 54.53 share	Yield: 2.22%

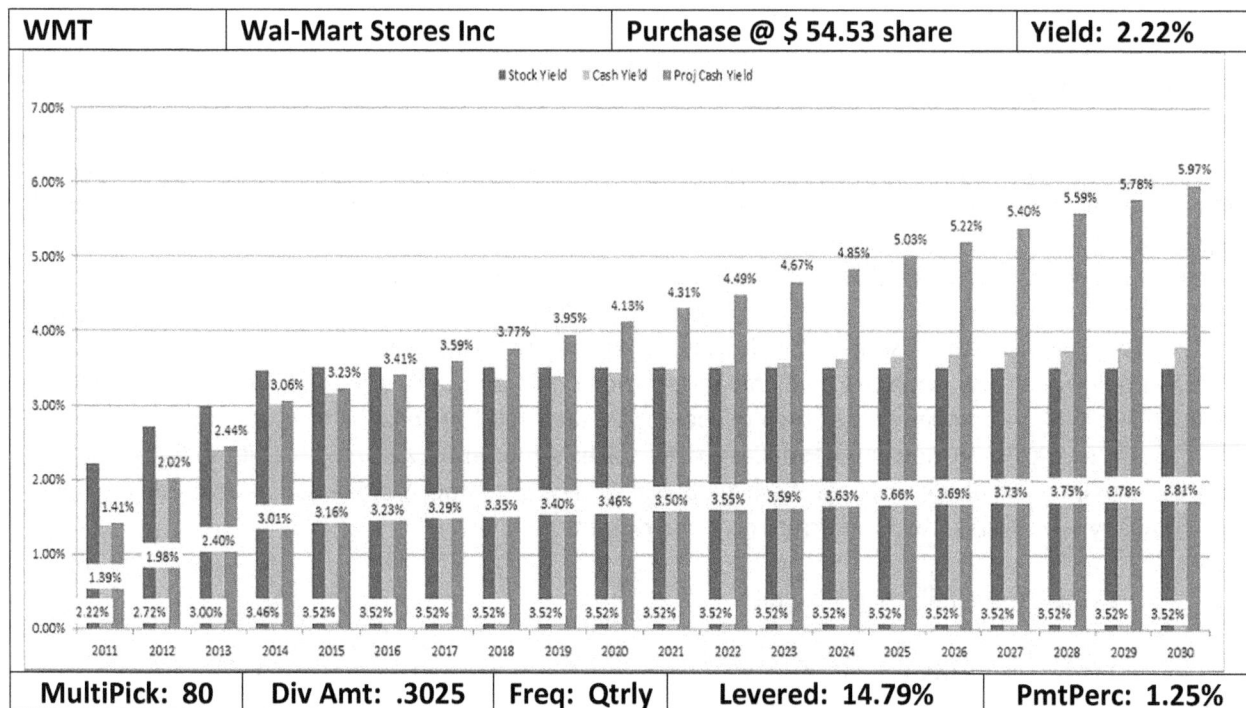

Stock Yield   Cash Yield   Proj Cash Yield

MultiPick: 80	Div Amt: .3025	Freq: Qtrly	Levered: 14.79%	PmtPerc: 1.25%

DIS	Walt Disney Co	Purchase @ $ 36.84 share	Yield: 1.09%

■ Stock Yield ▨ Cash Yield ▨ Proj Cash Yield

Stock Yield / Cash Yield / Proj Cash Yield by year:

Year	Proj Cash Yield	Cash Yield	Stock Yield
2011	0.60%	0.59%	—
2012	0.90%	0.87%	1.31%
2013	1.46%	1.43%	1.80%
2014	1.89%	1.86%	2.16%
2015	2.47%	2.43%	2.66%
2016	3.04%	2.96%	3.12%
2017	3.16%	2.99%	3.12%
2018	3.29%	3.01%	3.12%
2019	3.41%	3.04%	3.12%
2020	3.53%	3.06%	3.12%
2021	3.66%	3.08%	3.12%
2022	3.79%	3.10%	3.12%
2023	3.92%	3.12%	3.12%
2024	4.05%	3.14%	3.12%
2025	4.18%	3.15%	3.12%
2026	4.32%	3.17%	3.12%
2027	4.45%	3.18%	3.12%
2028	4.59%	3.20%	3.12%
2029	4.74%	3.21%	3.12%
2030	4.88%	3.22%	3.12%

MultiPick: 150	Div Amt: .40	Freq: Annual	Levered: 13.57%	PmtPerc: 1.25%

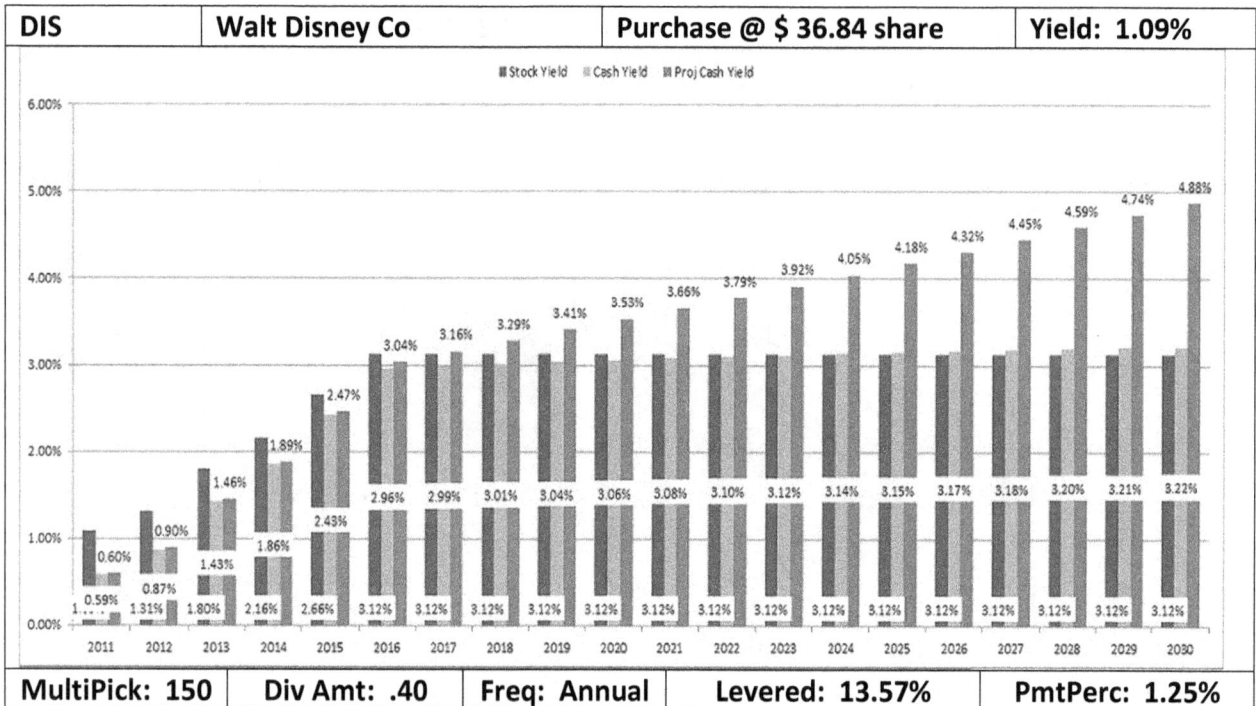

It's worth pointing out that in all the examples just shown, the 'Cash Yield' ultimately passed the 'Stock Yield' in all cases except one, Goldman Sachs (GS). The gap narrowed every year for twenty years but not fast enough to pass it within that time frame.

Going All the Way

Let's first address the huge gap between the "Stock Yield" and the "Cash Yield." Early on, because you are using dividends to actually pay for additional shares, you are sacrificing current yield for future capital appreciation. Eventually, the goal is to benefit from the best of both worlds; higher capital appreciation and higher yield returns as indicated in most of the charts referenced by the 'Proj Cash Yield's.'

You'll notice in the vast majority of these charts that from the years six through twenty, the "Divi-X" 'Cash Yield' inevitably surpasses the companies 'Stock Yield.' Also, you will notice in the years one through five, when a company raises their dividend, you see a modest spike in the 'Stock Yield,' but the increase in "Divi-X" 'Cash Yield' and 'Proj Cash Yield' spikes significantly, meaning that if the company continues to increase dividends, your 'Cash Yield' will surpass the 'Stock Yield' much more quickly than if the company were to maintain its current dividend rate throughout.

Let's look at the following example:

In the five years used in our window of time, Johnson & Johnson raised their dividend approximately six percent a year for the first five years. If we were to assume the same consistency over the remaining fifteen years, **Fig. 6.1** is what it would look like. This is assuming no change in interest rates.

JNJ	Johnson & Johnson	Purchase @ $ 64.30 share	Yield: 3.36%

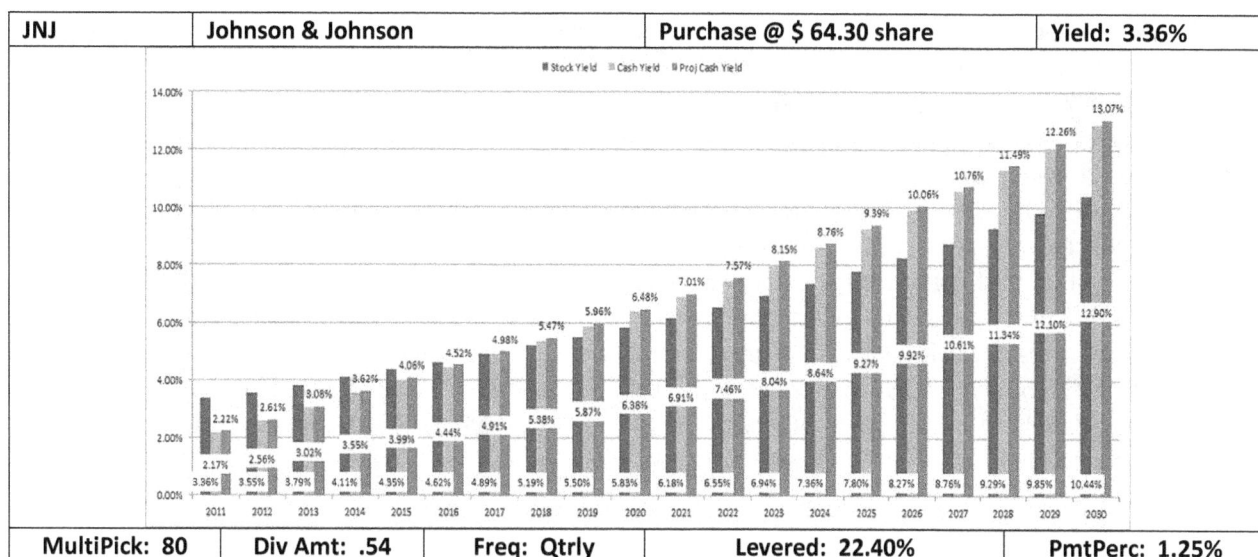

MultiPick: 80	Div Amt: .54	Freq: Qtrly	Levered: 22.40%	PmtPerc: 1.25%

Fig. 6.1

You can see in the first five years that, even though the actual 'Cash Yield' was gaining on the company's 'Stock Yield,' it didn't quite surpass it; nor did it in year six. However, in year seven it managed to just eke by and from that point on, even if Johnson & Johnson kept the dividend the same, our 'Cash Yield' would continue to widen its yield margin over the company's 'Stock Yield.' If they continued with their average annual dividend increase, which was 5.9% year over year in 2015, at the end of twenty years, your annual 'Cash Yield' would earn you approximately 2.46% more than someone who used all cash to purchase their shares. If you held past twenty years, that gap would widen further still.

It's important to point out that these yields are irrespective of the company's share price. Whether the share price goes up, goes down, or just lingers in a tight pattern, as long as the dividend policy stays in place your yield would continue to outpace the company's 'Stock Yield' and eventually surpass it. Even in the event of rising interest rates, your yield would continue to outpace the company's 'Stock Yield,' just at a slower pace.

Let's look at one more:

VZ	Verizon Communications Inc	Purchase @ $ 28.90 share	Yield: 6.57%

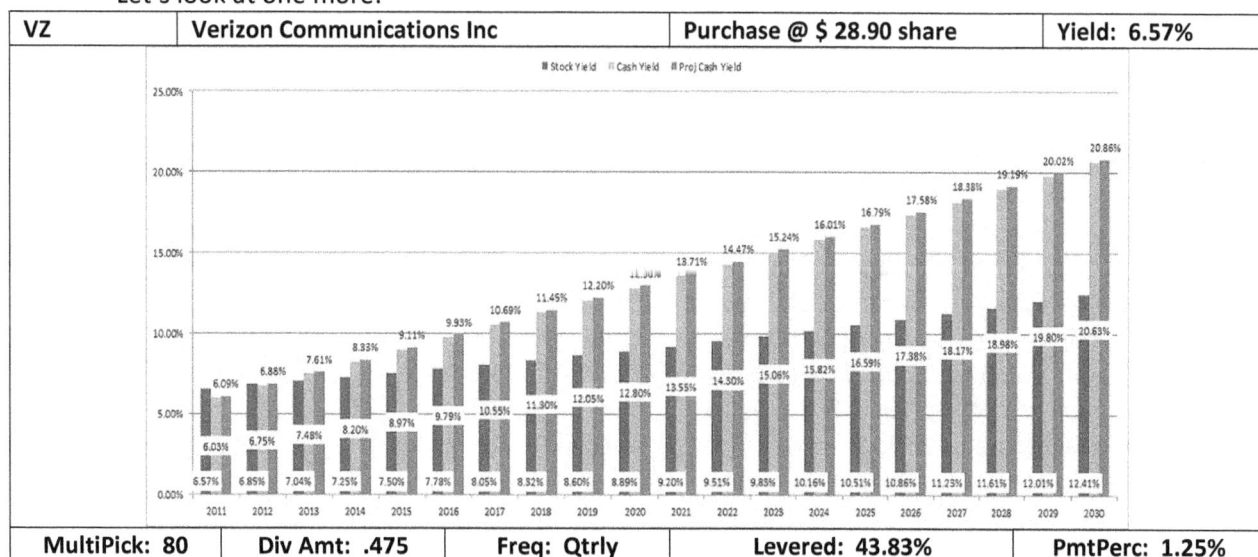

MultiPick: 80	Div Amt: .475	Freq: Qtrly	Levered: 43.83%	PmtPerc: 1.25%

Fig. 6.2

Now, in **Fig. 6.2**, our projected dividend increases were based on the fifth year company's actual dividend increase percentage of 3.89% and projected going forward for the remaining twenty years.

Look how huge the spread is after twenty years between the 'Stock Yield' and the 'Cash Yield.' The primary reasons for this stems from the initial high 'Stock Yield' Verizon(VZ) was already paying. This would have allowed you to leverage much more shares resulting in a total higher yield on a much smaller cash outlay from you. That, coupled with the constant paying down of the margin loan, which reduces interest expense every month, both contributed to (VZ)'s impressive 'Cash Yield.' In the case of (VZ), after twenty years, your 'Cash Yield' could be earning over 8% more a year (in addition to a nice 12+% 'Stock Yield') in yield than someone who invested all cash; a very satisfying 20+%, and again, its irrespective of the company's share price as long as the company's dividend policy stays intact.

What if a company's dividend policy doesn't stay intact? That's a good question and a very real possibility. Let's look at a case where (VZ) cut's their dividend in half about ten years later and there were no further dividend increases for the remainder of 20 years. How would that look?

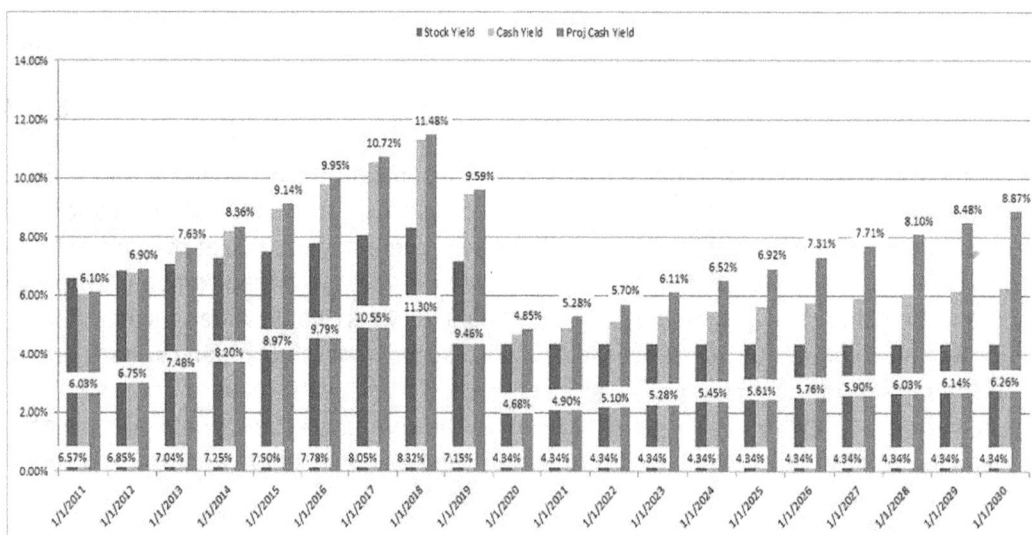

Fig. 6.3

It looks pretty much the same, only cut in half. The gap between 'Cash Yield' and 'Proj Cash Yield' widens because even though the dividend has been cut, 'Proj Cash Yield' assumes regular dividend increases. The 'Cash Yield' does continue to climb at a slower pace, in the absence of regular dividend increases, because the margin loan is still being paid down and reducing interest expense.

Granted, that on a percentage basis, the dividend cut has a drastic effect on the long-term yield but that is not the point. The point is that even though the overall yields have declined significantly, the "Divi-X" systems 'Cash Yield' *spread* is still significantly higher than the company's 'Stock Yield.' Albeit, the spread was not unscathed as a result of the dividend cut and the dividend increase suspension but it still fared much better than the 'Stock Yield' alone. In **Fig. 6.2,** after twenty years, the 'Yield Spread' was 40% above the company's 'Stock Yield.' In **Fig. 6.3,** after the drastic change in dividend policy and after twenty years, the "Divi-X" systems 'Yield Spread' was still at a hefty 31% above the company's 'Stock Yield.'

Chapter 7
Margin and Margin Accounts

How Margin Works

It's really pretty simple. Let's say you deposit $10,000 into a brokerage account, your funds are often matched with a so-called line of credit equal to your deposit of $10,000, making available to you, a total purchasing power of $20,000. Depending on your feelings about credit and your confidence in investing, that concept might excite you or scare the hell out of you.

I'm going to show you a breakdown of a couple of trades to show you how margin works in your account.

Trade #1: You purchase 100 shares of ABC, Inc. for $200 a share for a total of $20,000. Of that $20,000, half of it (your deposit of $10,000) comes from you and the remainder comes from the margin availability of your broker. Oh yeah, don't forget to deposit a little extra for your broker's commission.

Trade #2: You purchase 100 shares of XYZ, LLC for $150 a share for a total of $15,000. Of that $15,000, half of it ($7,500) comes from you, right? Wrong. Your whole $10,000 deposit goes towards the purchase and your broker covers the remaining $5,000 on margin. As a result, all of your cash is fully invested and you have now borrowed against half of your margin capacity, which would leave you $5,000 remaining to borrow against. In this example, you don't have to worry about depositing a little extra for commission because that can come out of the $5,000 margin you have remaining. So if, let's say, your commission is $8 a trade, you now have the borrowing capacity of $4,992.

Moving on, let us assume that in Trade #2 there is no commission and you have the full borrowing power of $5,000 still remaining, that means you could purchase another $5,000 in securities (but seriously, don't forget about the commission) on margin. How is that possible if you needed cash for the previous two trades but you don't need your own cash for this trade? It's because you still have the matching availability on your margin, and in lieu of a cash balance in your account, you now have the equity in your securities as collateral.

Now this part is interesting. You would think that because all of your cash is now fully invested in securities and you've used all of the matching margin funds to purchase even more securities that would be it. Not necessarily, but before I continue, just a reminder that you're already at a debt to equity ratio of 0.5, or fifty percent of your total equity. In other words, you already owe half of what your assets are worth. I don't know what your comfort level is but always be mindful of what this number is. This figure is easily found by dividing your outstanding margin loan balance by the total amount of assets (including cash) in your account.

Anyway, as I was saying, you would think that since all of your cash and margin has been used up, the only thing left to do now is wait for the dividends and hope your investments go in the right direction, but as you glance at your brokerage statement, you notice that you still have margin buying power left. I don't know what your broker does, but mine actually breaks this balance into two categories, and it goes something like this; of the $5000 remaining on margin, I can use the full $5000 to purchase more securities in my account or I can borrow only half of it for non-marginable transactions (i.e., mad money, debt reduction, down payment on a car, basically anything). Just be mindful that this is a margin loan and interest rates do apply.

Several factors will modify this figure. It will increase when dividends are received (plus matching cash) and decrease when interest is added at the end of the month. Margin maintenance requirements can significantly alter this figure. The initial (FED) requirement is to maintain 50% of marginable securities but your broker might be a little more lenient after the initial (FED) requirement has been met. I'll dig a little deeper on that later in this chapter.

Why Use Margin at All? Isn't it Risky?

I'm not here to talk you into investing using margin. I mentioned at the very beginning of this book that this material is offered up as a means to enhance investment returns using margin in a simple, systematic fashion. There will always be risk associated with anything where the future is unknown. It is the assumption of the author (that's me) that you are already well aware of the pros and cons of investing in the securities market and hoping to get a little more out of your investment dollars, or yen, or pesos, or whatever.

But to answer your question, I'll just have to refer you to the following table in **Fig. 7.1**.

Value of $10,000 after 5 Years ("PmtPerc" = 1.25%)
(Results do not include reinvested dividends)

The following table shows the results of a $10,000 investment using the Multiplier Picks exhibited throughout this book. If you'll recall, you are not limited to these Multiplier Picks. Using the "Divi-X" system, you have complete flexibility over "PmtPerc" and "Multiplier Pick." Either can range from zero to as high as you want to go, but it's ultimately up to you as to what makes good investment sense for you.

Ticker	Without "Divi-X"	Multiplier Pick 25	Multiplier Pick 65	Multiplier Pick 80	Multiplier Pick 100	Multiplier Pick Maxed	Maxed Leverage %
AXP	$38,711	$40,361	$43,497	$44,869	$46,904	$53,839	37.50
BA	$29,811	$31,100	$33,640	$34,789	$36,539	$42,896	44.51
CAT	$33,263	$35,585	$40,678	$43,243	$47,516	$68,512	64.07
CVX	$20,467	$21,122	$22,459	$23,085	$24,067	$27,807	51.29
DD	$31,143	$33,978	$41,019	$45,073	$52,766	$125,805	84.29
XOM	$15,586	$15,707	$15,928	$16,022	$16,157	$16,497	30.34
GE	$24,686	$25,531	$27,179	$27,916	$29,031	$32,931	42.42
GS	$11,930	$11,903	$11,858	$11,840	$11,816	$11,712	12.24
HD	$36,444	$38,444	$42,447	$44,344	$47,238	$58,421	48.92
MMM	$25,981	$26,962	$28,891	$19,761	$31,087	$35,829	44.10

Ticker	Without "Divi-X"	Multiplier Pick 25	Multiplier Pick 65	Multiplier Pick 80	Multiplier Pick 100	Multiplier Pick Maxed	Maxed Leverage %
T	$18,367	$19,213	$21,361	$22,628	$25,097	$52,609	87.55
INTC	$11,224	$11,137	$10,982	$10,918	$10,826	$10,459	25.20
IBM	$14,334	$14,381	$14,465	$14,499	$14,549	$14,623	25.67
JNJ	$17,636	$17,965	$18,610	$18,899	$19,339	$20,773	43.11
JPM	$15,162	$15,179	$15,208	$15,220	$15,235	$15,263	5.71
MCD	$16,018	$16,209	$16,579	$16,742	$16,986	$17,698	40.00
MRK	$18,589	$19,112	$20,201	$20,723	$21,552	$24,816	55.01
MSFT	$17,284	$17,429	$17,686	$17,790	$17,938	$18,324	21.55
NKE	$26,907	$27,313	$28,016	$28,298	$28,689	$29,809	17.79
PFE	$23,909	$24,959	$27,149	$28,200	$29,870	$36,773	55.26
PG	$14,851	$14,962	$15,173	$15,267	$15,406	$15,747	39.79
KO	$17,242	$17,535	$18,106	$18,362	$18,748	$19,984	42.27
TRV	$22,272	$22,838	$23,910	$24,374	$25,065	$27,299	36.42
UTX	$16,753	$16,927	$17,242	$17,376	$17,568	$18,090	29.11
UNH	$40,655	$41,632	$43,344	$44,042	$45,021	$47,949	21.17
VZ	$20,843	$22,045	$25,037	$26,760	$30,032	$60,500	84.37
V	$30,560	$30,763	$31,094	$31,223	$31,399	$31,869	7.12
WMT	$16,141	$16,281	$16,535	$16,642	$16,796	$17,194	28.48
DIS	$30,633	$31,112	$31,718	$31,991	$32,362	$33,408	13.93

Fig. 7.1

CSCO did not pay dividends at the start of our sample window of time and therefore did not qualify for the "Divi-X" system.

The final two columns show the maximum "Multiplier Pick" you can choose that will just cover the interest (generally around 154 or 155 at a "PmtPerc" of 1.25%) and what the leverage percentage would be if you had chosen the maximum "Multiplier Pick."

Using Margin

Maintain discipline at all times when you use margin. One of the worse things that can happen is you overextend yourself at the wrong time. If the market tanks it could increase your margin ratio (same as debt to equity or debt ratio) considerably, prompting your broker to issue a margin call. In order to satisfy a margin call, you can be forced, if your broker doesn't do it for you, to sell securities within your portfolio and that can have severe consequences at tax time. Not to mention, that once you're forced to sell, that money is gone. You can no longer wait for the market to come back to recuperate your losses. It's possible that you could deposit more cash or equity to satisfy a margin call but simply making a deposit may not be enough to do the trick because some brokers put such a long hold time on new deposits those funds may not be available fast enough.

I strongly suggest that when purchasing securities using margin, you make certain that the total dividends at least cover the monthly interest amount associated with the securities and ideally cover the minimum principal and interest payment without overleveraging your position. I would like to point out, at this time, that in all of the Dow 30 examples introduced to you earlier in Chapter 2, margin did not exceed 50.00% of the total share purchase price when using a "Multiplier Pick" of 80 and a "PmtPerc" of 1.25%. If your "Divi-X" portfolio is similar in nature, this adds an added layer of protection against a margin call since you will have at least a fifty percent interest in your portfolio that is not leveraged, allowing it further to fall in nightmare scenarios. It is not up to me to tell you if you should've sold by then or not.

Also, if you are maintaining the amortization payments associated with your "Divi-X" portfolio, the loan balance is continuously being paid down, further increasing your margin of safety against a margin call.

Margin Requirements

Check with your broker regarding margin requirements. They can vary slightly from broker to broker but they all have the 'Initial (FED) Requirement.' Most brokers ease up on requirements after the 'Initial (FED) Requirement' has been met in some cases but not all. Let's compare an example of the 'FED' requirements and my current broker (I doubt this structure will change much from broker to broker).

Common and Preferred Stock $5 a share and up – The 'Initial (FED) Requirement' is 50% of market value but my broker eases that restriction to a maintenance requirement of 30% of market value. In other words, initially I am required to have $50 in equity for every $100 in marginable securities for securities priced $5 and up. My broker eases that requirement to $30 for every $100.

My personal rule of thumb regarding margin limits is 50%/50%/100%. That is a maximum of 50% equity, 50% margin to 100% of total security value. I could go as high as 35% equity/65% margin/100% total security value. These numbers can fluctuate a bit, plus 5 or 10% on the margin side, reducing by 5% – 10% on the equity side, but only temporarily. That is on the total account balance, not individual securities. That is my comfort zone. You'll have to find your own.

Cheaper Margin

I won't spend too much time on this. It's almost too obvious but I'll mention it anyway.

Friends & Family – It's quite possible this can be obtained interest free but I wouldn't recommend being so stingy with people you care about.

Home Equity Line of Credit – You can do the math. If your broker is charging 7.5% and you can get a line of equity on your home currently at 4.82% (source: internet search June 2015) with good credit, something to seriously consider.

Again, refer to the disclaimer, but for me personally, I would treat borrowed money from any outside source towards my margin limit. I would not treat outside borrowed money as new principal to be borrowed against for matching margin in my brokerage account. That just makes poor investment sense to me.

This is the reason why I tell you to treat all of your margin borrowings as outside loans. Because, they just might be one day.

Margin Rates

I have only researched a handful of different brokerage firms for the purpose of this book. The few that I researched based their margin rates on various market factors, economic conditions and the ability to be competitive. That surprised me a bit. I had expected it to be tied to a certain benchmark such as the Fed Funds Rate or LIBOR (London Interbank Offered Rate).

Another thing that they have in common is that your rate is tied to your balance; the bigger the balance, the lower the rate. With most of the companies I looked at, there wasn't much of a difference in rates on accounts with balances less than $500,000, maybe a quarter to a half of a percentage point. Once your account reaches $500,000, that's when you start to see significant variances in the rates offered; possibly as high as two percentage points, or as they like to say in the world of finance, two hundred basis points.

Advantages of Using Margin/Leverage

1. No Red Tape – Once you set up your margin brokerage account, you do not need to reapply for a new loan every time you wish to use margin.
2. No Fees – No new loan applications and no new fees other than the monthly interest.
3. Easily Accessible – Online, it's just a matter of point and click. Other means of access may be available. Check with your broker on terms and conditions.
4. Flexible – Paying down the balance replenishes its availability for use again. Cash contributions to your margin account are matched with additional margin availability (limited to buying securities within your own account).
5. Doesn't Show Up On Your Credit if Maintained in Good Standing – This is helpful when applying for credit outside of your brokerage account. A lot of creditors look at certain ratios when determining how much credit you're eligible for and how expensive that credit is going to be. This does not affect those ratios.
6. Can Be Used For Personal Needs – In this sense I'm referring to easy access to funds for investments you wish to make outside of your brokerage account where other funding is not so easily available, such as starting a new business or a down payment on a piece of real estate.
7. More Purchase Power – Self-explanatory.
8. Covered by Equity So a Reduced Risk of Default – Your broker will likely see to this with the use of margin calls, then automatic liquidation if necessary.
9. No Late Payments – There are no due dates so there is no chance of missing a payment and being late.
10. Able To Take Advantage Of Time Sensitive Opportunities – Just having the funds available immediately can allow you to take advantages of opportunities that might not be available if it relies on loan approval and time to receive funds (unless your broker provides you with a checking account feature, you may have to request funds through wire transfer or other means which will take a couple of business days to complete).

11. Can Use to Invest Outside of Your Brokerage Account – There is a limit to how much you can actually borrow on margin outside of your brokerage account because once funds leave your account it calls into question your brokers ability to cover any shortfall that happens in your account.

Disadvantages of Using Margin/Leverage

I believe that I can best illustrate this topic with a simple example. So far, we've seen the rosy side of things, but when your positions aren't doing so well, you feel anything but rosy. Such is the case for a particular Oil & Gas company whose name I'm withholding as to protect their identity. What I'm about to show you may shock you. If you have any small children in the room, you may want to ask them to leave the room. The story I'm about to show you is based on actual events that took place between July 2010 and July 2015. Warning! These images are graphic! Reader discretion is advised.

In the interest of full disclosure, I took a position in this particular security. I got out before the worse happened but not without some cuts and bruises. What you are about to witness, are events that may have happened with an individual, we'll call him Mr. Jones, that happened to be a little greedier than I was. This individual threw caution to the wind and leveraged the maximum amount of shares he could purchase with the yield that was provided. This is his story.

Oil & Gas Stock	Oil & Gas Stock	Purchase @ 30.69 share	Yield 8.21%

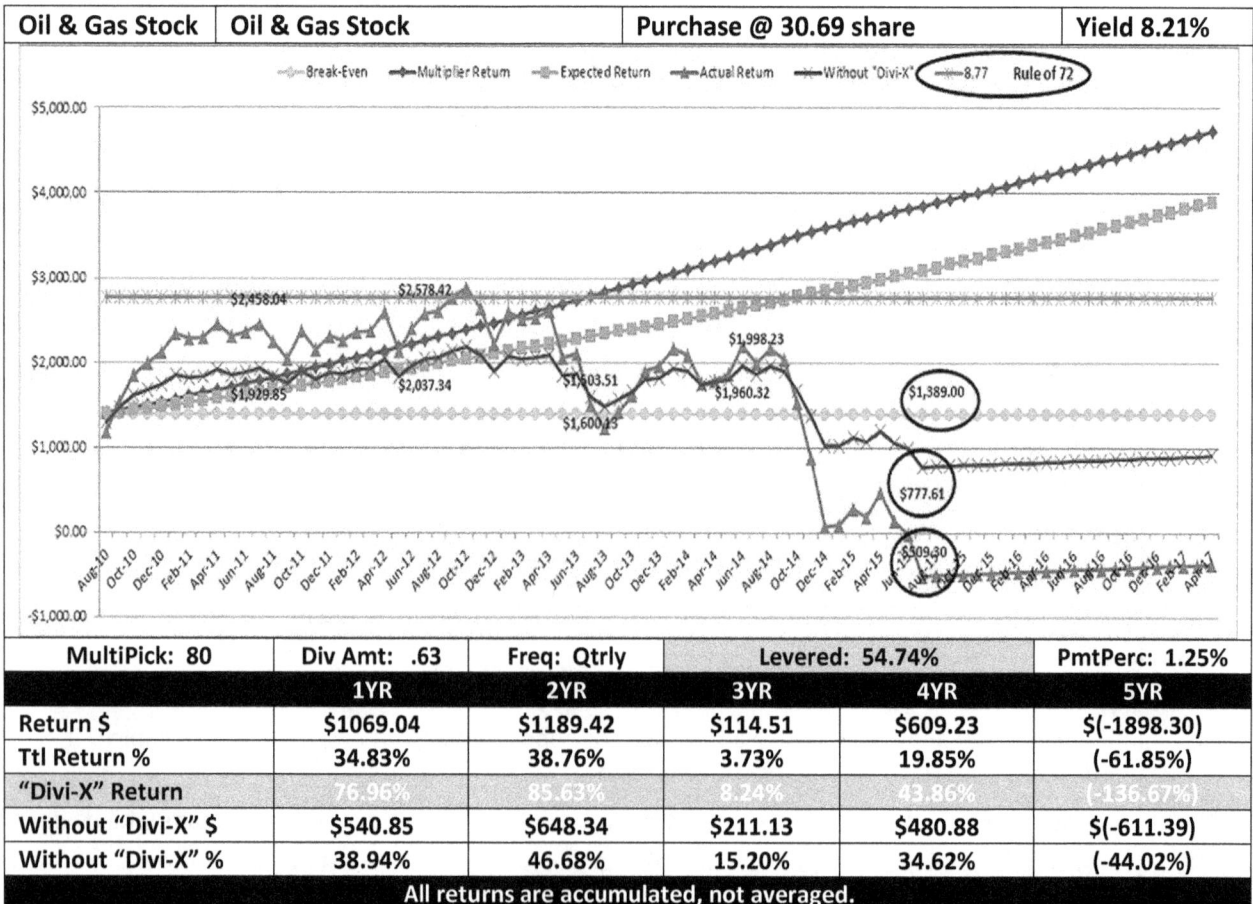

MultiPick: 80	Div Amt: .63	Freq: Qtrly	Levered: 54.74%		PmtPerc: 1.25%
	1YR	**2YR**	**3YR**	**4YR**	**5YR**
Return $	$1069.04	$1189.42	$114.51	$609.23	$(-1898.30)
Ttl Return %	34.83%	38.76%	3.73%	19.85%	(-61.85%)
"Divi-X" Return	76.96%	85.63%	8.24%	43.86%	(-136.67%)
Without "Divi-X" $	$540.85	$648.34	$211.13	$480.88	$(-611.39)
Without "Divi-X" %	38.94%	46.68%	15.20%	34.62%	(-44.02%)
All returns are accumulated, not averaged.					

Fig. 7.2

As you can see from the "Break-Even" line, circled in the chart above **(Fig. 7.2)**, Mr. Jones initially invested $1389.00 of his own cash. The dividend afforded him the ability to leverage this security at 54.74%, or $1680.00, for a total shareholder value of $3069.00 for one hundred shares. In the beginning, it looked like a fairly good investment. After a couple of years, you can see that he actually doubled his money (if he had sold) when the cash value (not the shareholder value) crossed the "Rule of 72" around October of 2012. Almost six full years before the "Rule of 72" predicted. Not being a complete amateur, Mr. Jones knew that after such a decent run up, a pull-back (decline) may soon be in the cards and almost as soon as he thought it, it happened.

Immediately after the new high in October of 2012, the stock pulled back for the following two months and finally stopped to rest just above his "Expected Return" in December of 2012. The following month, the stock bounced back with a nice spike adding to Mr. Jones's confidence that he made a wise investment. For the next few months, it didn't really move too much in either direction and that was okay, because while he waited for the stock to make its next move in either direction, Mr. Jones was content to wait with the peace of mind knowing that he was collecting nearly a 13% yield on his cash investment, as shown in year 2013 in the chart below **(Fig. 7.3)**. Notice the 'Cash Yield' was higher than the 'Stock Yield' already after the first year and considerably higher than the 9.45% 'Stock Yield' in year 2013.

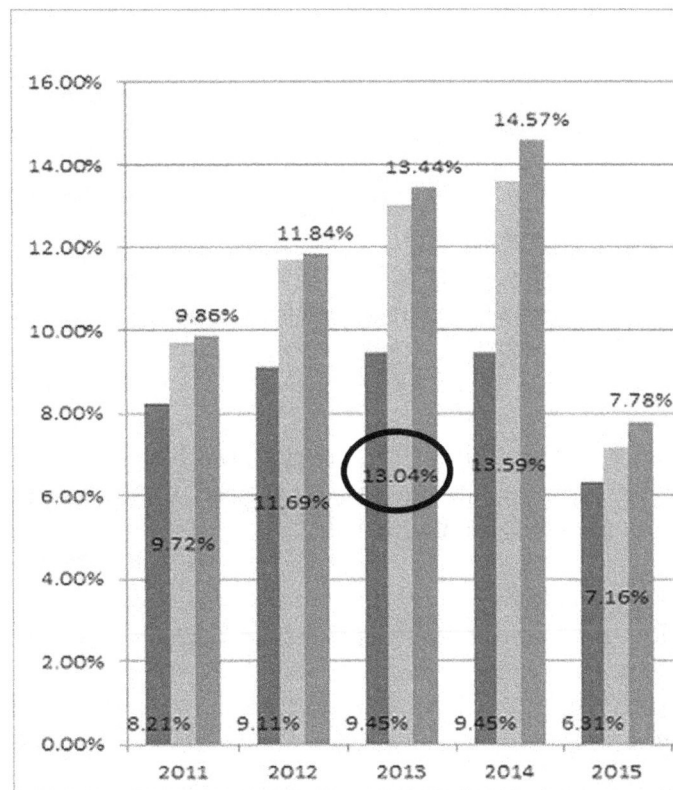

Fig. 7.3

In May 2013, that peace of mind quickly turned to self-doubt as he watched nearly half of all his returns disappear. In June 2013, Mr. Jones tried to recompose himself and reevaluate his position logically. He gained little comfort from the slight increase during the month for he was now below his "Expected Return." Weighing it all, Mr. Jones eventually concluded that he'll maintain his position. Maybe it would climb as fast as it had in the past. After all, he was collecting that 13%+ yield. Besides, absent the economy crashing, surely this had to be a fluke.

The following month, Mr. Jones quickly realized just how wrong he is. Things had gone from bad, to really bad. On the close of his third year of holding this stock, all he had to show for all that time, was a measly $114.51 and that included his 13%+ yield. Now, at this point, you would think that most people would be inclined to sell and take their lumps, not so.

People will always find a rationale to keep holding after such a destructive loss. Maybe they figure at least they're still in the black, no matter how small. Surely, it has reached a bottom by now. There is still that very enticing yield which is now at approximately 13 ½%, or the ever popular, oil always comes back. Whatever the reason, Mr. Jones continued to hold still.

The following month, he went in the red. Fortunately, for Mr. Jones, that also may have signaled a bottom because for the next several months, his holding improved and by the end of year 4, Mr. Jones was sitting on nearly a 44% return on his invested cash. Far below his previous highs and still below his "Expected Return," but an annual return rate of 11% a year (minus the ulcer medication) was something he could live with and further justified why he should continue to hold.

That justification was short lived, for not before long, things took a dramatic turn for the worse. In October 2014, the oil market went into free fall because of oversupply, increased competition from shale drilling and OPEC's unwillingness to curb its own production. By December 2014, Mr. Jones's holding was only worth pennies. His entire cash investment was wiped out on paper (no pun intended). Oil & Gas cut its distribution in half, reducing Mr. Jones's yield to around 7%. A respectable yield but of no comfort to a disgusted Mr. Jones whose holding was worthless (on paper). The shares still had value, but if Mr. Jones sold them, all the proceeds would go to pay off the outstanding margin loan.

In January 2015, the stock managed to squeeze out a very short-lived and meager rally but if Mr. Jones continued to hold, which he did, and the price took another dive, which it did after the elimination of the distribution, Mr. Jones would then have to pay for the shortfall. Oil continues to fall as of this writing and Mr. Jones would now be in debt for $509 if he sold now. Does Mr. Jones face a margin call and have to sell? No.

Because Mr. Jones has other securities in his brokerage account that are not doing nearly as bad as this one, the worth of those securities and the match by his broker on those securities more than cover the $509 negative balance on this one security. Should Mr. Jones sell now? I don't know. It's not my place to tell you that.

I have personally felt some of the carnage of this particular security when it entered its freefall. Fortunately, I got out without too much bloodshed, but I continued to track this security looking for a possible re-entry point. I also frequent the company's message boards to get a feel for investor sentiment. It has been heartbreaking to witness investors constantly rationalize holding this security as it continues to go down. I hope in the end, they eventually find themselves on the right side of the argument, but only time will tell.

How to D.R.I.P. on Margin

This nifty little idea allows you to use your personal brokerage account to take advantage of commission free investments with companies outside of your brokerage account (depends on individual company's plan requirements) using margin. Some brokerage accounts may already allow you to reinvest dividends for free, but not allow you to make regular monthly contributions. This also eliminates the option to be able to leverage your monthly contributions.

If you give, or would like to start giving, regular contributions to a company's dividend reinvestment program (D.R.I.P.), see if your broker will allow direct debits to your brokerage account. If they do, make your monthly deposit or your unleveraged contribution portion of the D.R.I.P directly into your brokerage account. If they do not allow it, they may have a feature that allows a linked checking account. If that's the case, you can make your unleveraged contribution portion of the D.R.I.P to your linked checking account and before the company debits your account for the full amount, you can transfer the leveraged portion of funds to your checking account from your margin/brokerage account. Note: Whenever a withdrawal is taken from your margin/brokerage account, the interest clock starts ticking.

> **"Divi-X" System Workbook:** Doing a separate "Leverage Projection Worksheet" every month for each separate purchase made to your D.R.I.P account would be a huge pain, even with the super simplicity of using the "Divi-X" System Workbook. I would recommend doing one initial leverage projection (I'll explain why in detail later in this segment) and review its progress on a regular basis (maybe annually or when something fundamental about the security changes, such as a dividend increase/decrease). Should the stocks fundamentals change and you wish to reallocate your leverage percentage, then you could do another "Leverage Projection Worksheet."

Getting Started on Your D.R.I.P.

You want to contribute $100 a month to General Electric's D.R.I.P. (I chose GE at random and have no idea what their plan specifics are. Do you research before you choose any company sponsored D.R.I.P.) You do a leverage projection and settle on a "Multiplier Pick" of 80 which breaks your monthly unleveraged contribution down to $77.96 out of pocket and a margin contribution of $22.04. There, you just purchased $100 worth of shares for $77.96 cash out of pocket.

The interest clock starts when that $22.04 goes outstanding after your D.R.I.P withdraws your contribution or you manually transfer the funds to your linked checking account from your margin account.

The "Divi-X" System uses dividends to make margin payments but with any type of dividend reinvestment program, dividends are primarily used to buy more stock. So how do we pay back the margin balance?

As of this writing, my margin/brokerage account charges me interest at a rate of 7.50% annually. On a $22.04 balance that amounts to a whopping $.14 (fourteen cents) a month in interest. With a "PmtPerc" of 1.25% of the outstanding balance, that's a principal and interest payment of $.28 (twenty-eight cents) a month.

Keep in mind that this would be a recurring monthly event so if you choose to cover interest only, you must cover an additional fourteen cents each and every month. Principal and interest is an additional twenty-eight cents each and every month.

Here's how it looks for the first year:

	Cash Contribution	Margin Contribution	Interest Only	Contribution + Int Pmt	Int + Principal	Contribution + Int & Principal
1st Month	$77.96	$22.04	.14	$78.10	.28	$78.24
2nd	$77.96	$22.04	.28	$78.24	.56	$78.52
3rd	$77.96	$22.04	.42	$78.38	.84	$78.80
4th	$77.96	$22.04	.56	$78.52	1.12	$79.08
5th	$77.96	$22.04	.70	$78.66	1.40	$79.36
6th	$77.96	$22.04	.84	$78.80	1.68	$79.64
7th	$77.96	$22.04	.98	$78.94	1.96	$79.92
8th	$77.96	$22.04	1.12	$79.08	2.24	$80.20
9th	$77.96	$22.04	1.26	$79.22	2.52	$80.48
10th	$77.96	$22.04	1.40	$79.36	2.80	$80.76
11th	$77.96	$22.04	1.54	$79.50	3.08	$81.04
12th	$77.96	$22.04	1.68	$79.64	3.36	$81.32

Fig. 7.4

Notice under the "**Contribution + Int Pmt**" column and the "**Contribution + Int & Principal**" column that the monthly payment amount increases every month by a few cents, but in either column, the payment amount is well under $100 a month. If you chose to pay the "**Contribution + Int & Principal**" every month it would take you 78.71 months ($22.04 ÷ .28 cents) of regular increased contributions before your monthly contribution amount, out of pocket, reached the $100 a month being withdrawn from you monthly by the D.R.I.P. That's over five and a half years of contributions, or $1,734.77 of extra shares purchased (78.71 months x 22.04 a month), assuming all things stated remained unchanged (actually it takes a bit longer since the principal and interest payments modestly slow the rate at when you would reach $100 a month out of pocket but the impact is so minute and the math too extensive to break down for a simple example).

If you paid the "**Contribution + Interest Pmt**" only, it would take 157.43 months ($22.04 ÷ .14 cents) before you reached $100 a month out of pocket. That's just over thirteen years and $3469.76 (157.43 months x $22.04 a month) in extra shares purchased (actually it takes a bit less since the principal does not get paid down so with each additional D.R.I.P contribution the principal increases raising the monthly interest amount, but the impact is so minute and the math too extensive to break down for a simple example).

You have a few options to choose from before you set up a D.R.I.P. and just so you know, I picked (GE) just because. I have no idea what their D.R.I.P. requirements are. For any D.R.I.P., you should get the specific details directly from the company sponsoring the D.R.I.P.

1. Some D.R.I.P programs allow you to allocate a percentage of dividends for reinvestment and receive the remainder back to you to spend however you wish. Simply opt for a percentage that will cover the margin payment for the first year or two and reassess at a later date. If we use the data in Fig. 7.4 above, here's how that would play out:

   a. "**Contribution + Int Pmt**" – The first month of interest is only $.14. If we go back to our Dow 30 examples in Chapter 2, we see that (GE) was paying an annual dividend per share of $.40 a year which breaks down to $.035 (three and a half cents) a share per month. Our share price in Chapter 2 was $12.10 each. If we did not make an initial share purchase, which some D.R.I.P.'s require, our first $100 monthly contribution would have purchased us a total of 8.26 shares. The monthly dividend on those 8.26 shares would be $.289 cents (8.26 shares x $.035) a month. We would then figure out the percentage of interest to our monthly dividend: $.14 interest ÷ $.289 monthly dividend = 48.4%, or rounded down, just 48%. So, initially, we would set up our D.R.I.P. with a dividend reinvestment of 52% and have the other 48% returned to us so we could maintain the interest payments.

    b. **"Contribution + Int & Principal"** – The combined interest + principal is almost equal to the monthly dividend. We would have to request 100% of our dividends to maintain our full interest and principal payments. I'm not sure a D.R.I.P would allow 100%, so in this case, you might have to request as much as you can which may help with the principal or... see number 2.

2. Just suck it up and just fork over the few extra cents every month out of your own pocket.
    a. You could pay the full $.28/month out of pocket, or
    b. Have the 48% of dividends returned to you to cover interest and pay the remaining $.149 cents of principal out of your own pocket.

3. Reduce your "Multiplier Pick." It will reduce the monthly interest and principal payments but increase the amount out of pocket to make your minimum monthly contribution.

4. Don't do anything. If you currently have dividend income coming into your margin/brokerage account from other securities, it'll likely cover the difference. Make certain funds are there before you make this assumption. This is a deviation from "Divi-X" protocol, but so is the use of a D.R.I.P. account. At this point, you're winging it.

If you opt to use margin to finance stock purchases outside of your margin/brokerage account
1. You need assets in your margin/brokerage account to secure your outstanding balance (check with your broker on rules and restrictions)
2. Funding assets outside of your margin/brokerage account reduces your margin availability for other investments
3. You could have your D.R.I.P. held at your brokerage firm and that will count as equity towards margin availability, but there could be a fee involved for servicing your D.R.I.P., making this option less attractive.

It is too impractical for 'The "Divi-X" System' to track your investment progress in a D.R.I.P. unless your monthly contributions are large enough to justify the trouble. It can help you with projections like the case above. I hope to add the feature in the future if there is enough demand for it.

Two Sets of Books

I'm not suggesting you need to keep two set of books, nor even one set for that matter. Once you set up your leverage projection worksheets and make your purchases, aside from updating share prices (monthly), dividends (when they change) and margin rate changes (when they change), there is little else that's needed from you.

I, on the other hand, have taken the "Divi-X" system to the extreme and have actually set up a mock company using a popular business accounting program to track my results. I don't know what kind of traction this program might take on, but I hope to use those results for future use to bolster the program even more.

I made a case in Chapter 4 why two sets of books is actually a good thing but to touch on it a little more, if you'll recall, I mentioned that there is an automatic sweep of dividends to any outstanding margin balance. If your entire cash balance is tied up in securities, any dividends you receive will automatically go towards your outstanding margin balance. You will still have access to those funds should you want them (they will be withdrawn in the form of margin and add to your outstanding balance), but the margin/brokerage account is where it sits till you use it. It's kind of like extra principal payments. As a result, this has the effect of actually lowering the interest expense that you actually pay on all of your investments. The difference, depending on the balance you carry might not make much of a difference, but if you ever tried to reconcile your investment results per each individual investment with your margin/brokerage account, it would never be equal simply because the full sweep of dividends towards the total outstanding margin balance will reflect a lower, overall interest expense than what the total sum of your "Divi-X" investments will show. Don't panic by this insignificant discrepancy. It's not like you have to worry about being audited (seriously, you don't).

Finally, on Margin

Margin can be an unbelievable ally in your endeavor to create above average wealth but it is not a toy to be played with. Constantly educate yourself on the topic. This program will aid you in that endeavor. Just using the examples in this book will give you valuable insight into what margin will do to your portfolio in several different scenarios. Keep in mind that margin can also serve many purposes outside of your margin account as well, whether it be an external D.R.I.P. or two, a down payment on an investment property or just for pleasure and in worst cases, for emergencies.

Be ever vigilant when using margin. As wonderful as margin is in helping you create wealth, it can be unforgiving when it mercilessly rips your existing wealth away as seen in our Oil & Gas example earlier in this chapter.

Chapter 8
Multiplier Pick 100

Multiplier Pick 100: Dow 30 Comparisons

Until you develop a history with your stock picks using the "Divi-X" System or had time to play around with different results, which is actually kind of fun using 'The "Divi-X" System Workbook', I thought I would show you some "what-if's" using different variables on the same Dow 30 results we showed you earlier, just to give you some idea of the flexibility this system allows you.

Following is the same Dow 30 history results as before but now we are using a "Multiplier Pick" of 100 instead of 80 as in the earlier examples. The overall dollars returned are smaller than they are when you use the 80 "Multiplier Pick" because we are using less of our own dollars (more leverage), but the percentage returns are bigger, which is what you want. In other words, you are getting a higher percentage return with fewer dollars. That's always a good thing. Plus, there is nothing stopping you from using more dollars to earn the new higher percentage rate (i.e., buy more shares than the one hundred shares used in all the examples). **Caution: We are looking at these scenarios in hindsight. They are no indication of future performance.**

Remember: "Equal Cash Unleveraged" and 'Without "Divi-X" are used interchangeably.

AXP	American Express	Purchase @ 24.64 share	Yield 2.92%

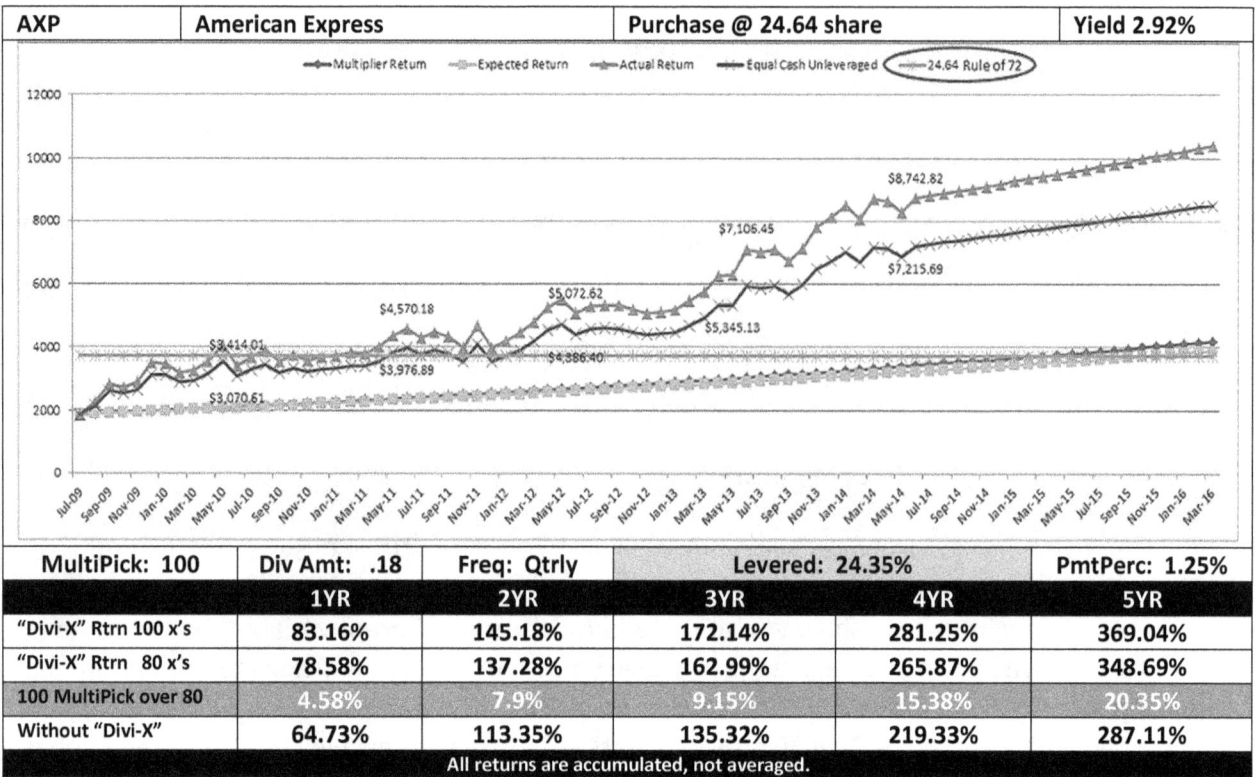

MultiPick: 100	Div Amt: .18	Freq: Qtrly	Levered: 24.35%		PmtPerc: 1.25%
	1YR	2YR	3YR	4YR	5YR
"Divi-X" Rtrn 100 x's	83.16%	145.18%	172.14%	281.25%	369.04%
"Divi-X" Rtrn 80 x's	78.58%	137.28%	162.99%	265.87%	348.69%
100 MultiPick over 80	4.58%	7.9%	9.15%	15.38%	20.35%
Without "Divi-X"	64.73%	113.35%	135.32%	219.33%	287.11%
All returns are accumulated, not averaged.					

BA	Boeing Co.	Purchase @ 48.44 share	Yield 3.47%

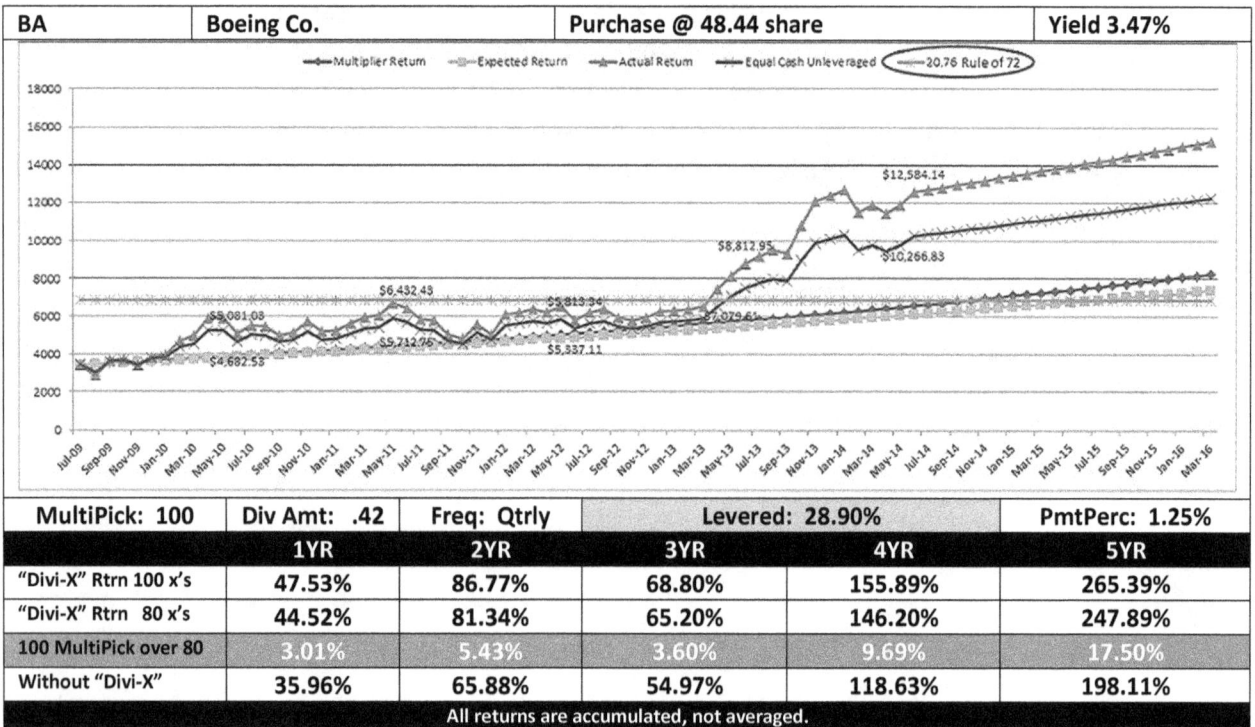

MultiPick: 100	Div Amt: .42	Freq: Qtrly	Levered: 28.90%		PmtPerc: 1.25%
	1YR	2YR	3YR	4YR	5YR
"Divi-X" Rtrn 100 x's	47.53%	86.77%	68.80%	155.89%	265.39%
"Divi-X" Rtrn 80 x's	44.52%	81.34%	65.20%	146.20%	247.89%
100 MultiPick over 80	3.01%	5.43%	3.60%	9.69%	17.50%
Without "Divi-X"	35.96%	65.88%	54.97%	118.63%	198.11%
All returns are accumulated, not averaged.					

CAT	Caterpillar	Purchase @ 33.65 share	Yield 4.99%

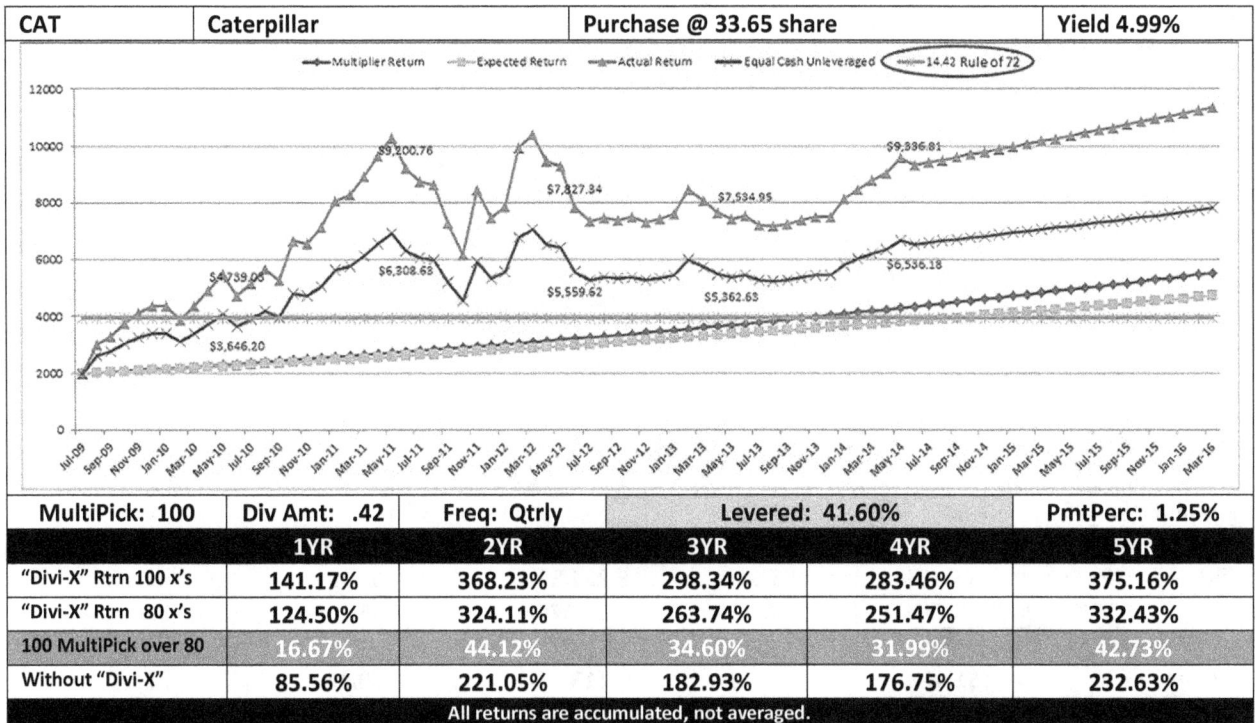

MultiPick: 100	Div Amt: .42	Freq: Qtrly	Levered: 41.60%		PmtPerc: 1.25%
	1YR	2YR	3YR	4YR	5YR
"Divi-X" Rtrn 100 x's	141.17%	368.23%	298.34%	283.46%	375.16%
"Divi-X" Rtrn 80 x's	124.50%	324.11%	263.74%	251.47%	332.43%
100 MultiPick over 80	16.67%	44.12%	34.60%	31.99%	42.73%
Without "Divi-X"	85.56%	221.05%	182.93%	176.75%	232.63%
All returns are accumulated, not averaged.					

CVX	Chevron Corporation	Purchase @ 68.06 share	Yield: 4.0%

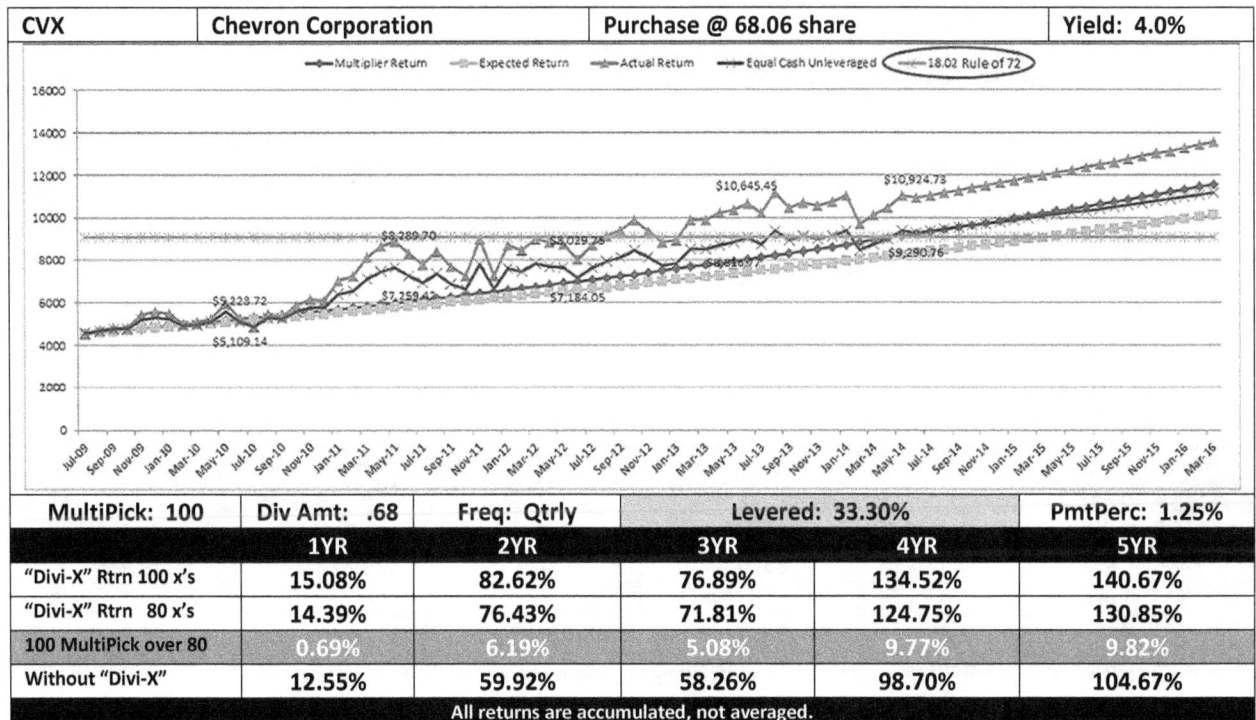

MultiPick: 100	Div Amt: .68	Freq: Qtrly	Levered: 33.30%		PmtPerc: 1.25%
	1YR	2YR	3YR	4YR	5YR
"Divi-X" Rtrn 100 x's	15.08%	82.62%	76.89%	134.52%	140.67%
"Divi-X" Rtrn 80 x's	14.39%	76.43%	71.81%	124.75%	130.85%
100 MultiPick over 80	0.69%	6.19%	5.08%	9.77%	9.82%
Without "Divi-X"	12.55%	59.92%	58.26%	98.70%	104.67%
All returns are accumulated, not averaged.					

DD	E I Dupont De Nemours and Co	Purchase @ $24.97 share	Yield: 6.57%

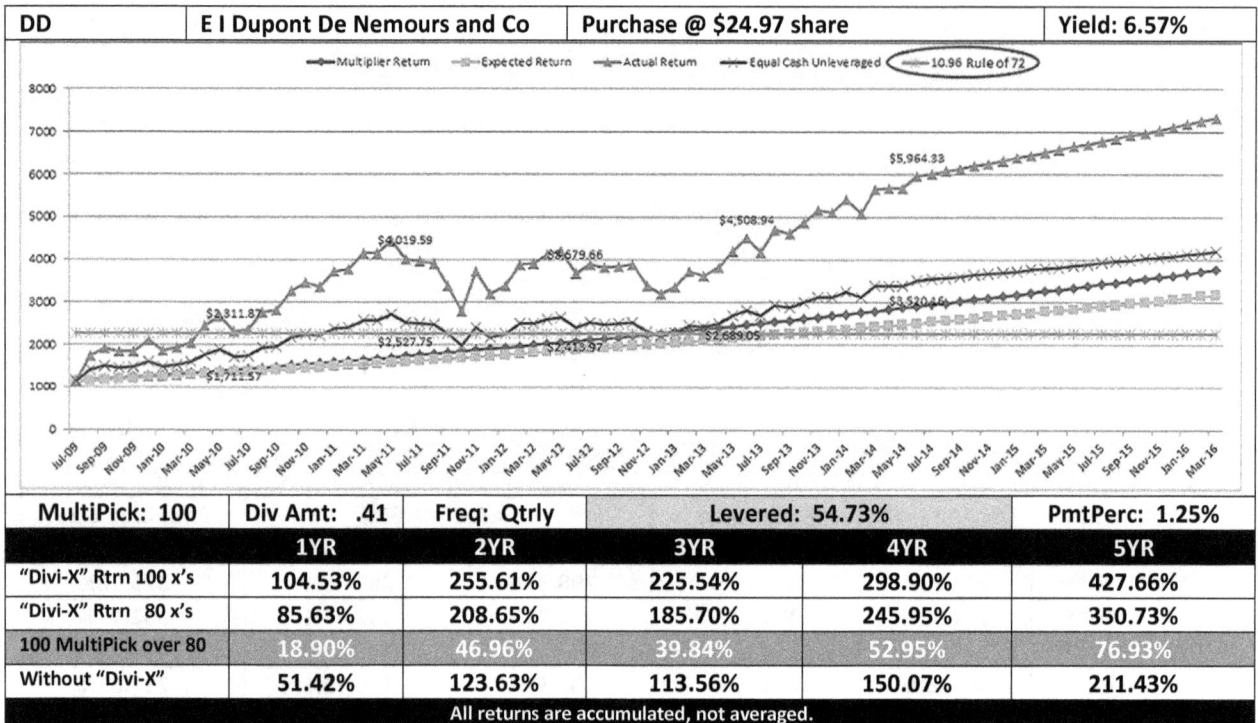

MultiPick: 100	Div Amt: .41	Freq: Qtrly	Levered: 54.73%			PmtPerc: 1.25%
	1YR	**2YR**	**3YR**	**4YR**		**5YR**
"Divi-X" Rtrn 100 x's	104.53%	255.61%	225.54%	298.90%		427.66%
"Divi-X" Rtrn 80 x's	85.63%	208.65%	185.70%	245.95%		350.73%
100 MultiPick over 80	18.90%	46.96%	39.84%	52.95%		76.93%
Without "Divi-X"	51.42%	123.63%	113.56%	150.07%		211.43%
All returns are accumulated, not averaged.						

GE	General Electric	Purchase @ $12.10 share	Yield: 3.31%

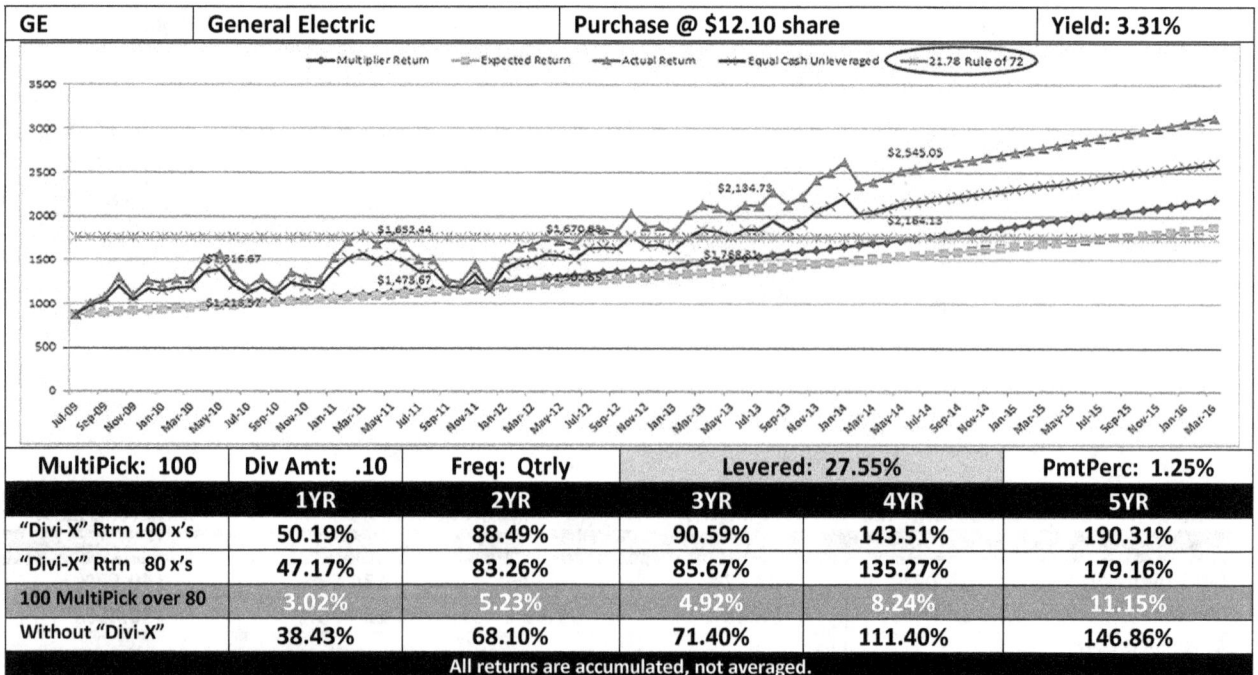

MultiPick: 100	Div Amt: .10	Freq: Qtrly	Levered: 27.55%			PmtPerc: 1.25%
	1YR	**2YR**	**3YR**	**4YR**		**5YR**
"Divi-X" Rtrn 100 x's	50.19%	88.49%	90.59%	143.51%		190.31%
"Divi-X" Rtrn 80 x's	47.17%	83.26%	85.67%	135.27%		179.16%
100 MultiPick over 80	3.02%	5.23%	4.92%	8.24%		11.15%
Without "Divi-X"	38.43%	68.10%	71.40%	111.40%		146.86%
All returns are accumulated, not averaged.						

GS	Goldman Sachs Group, Inc.	Purchase @ $146.74 share	Yield: 0.95%

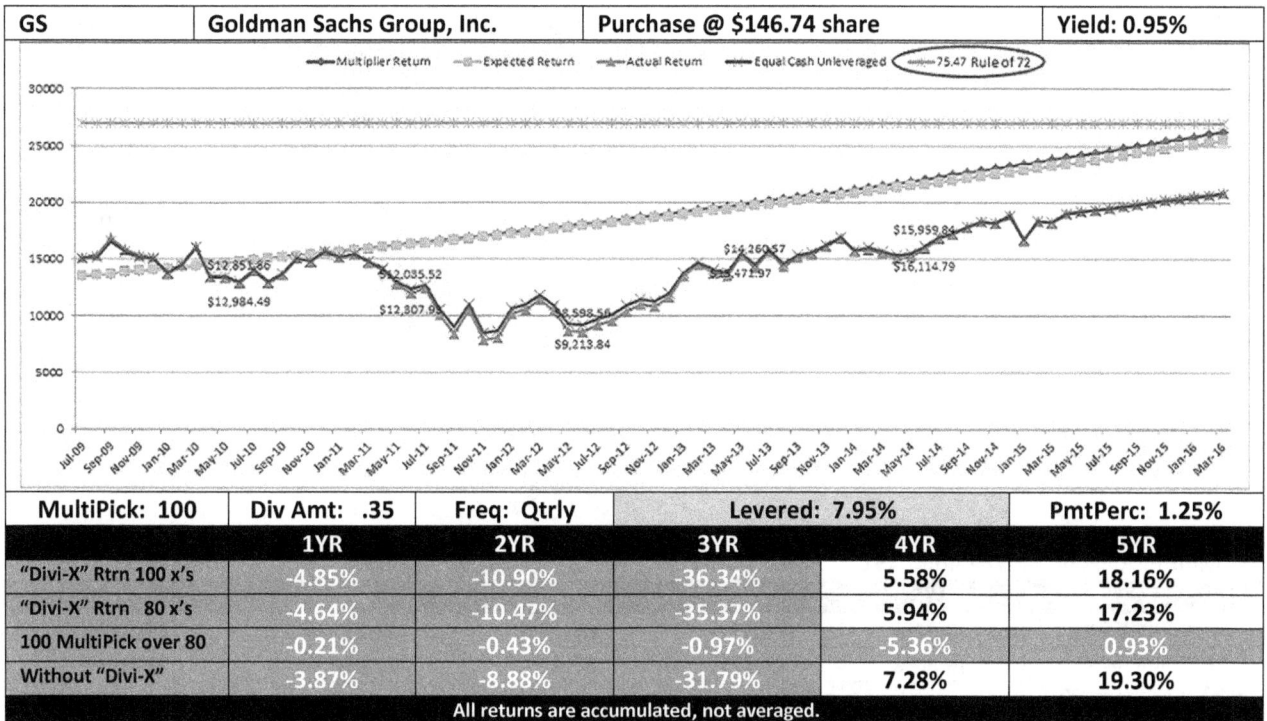

MultiPick: 100	Div Amt: .35	Freq: Qtrly	Levered: 7.95%		PmtPerc: 1.25%
	1YR	2YR	3YR	4YR	5YR
"Divi-X" Rtrn 100 x's	-4.85%	-10.90%	-36.34%	5.58%	18.16%
"Divi-X" Rtrn 80 x's	-4.64%	-10.47%	-35.37%	5.94%	17.23%
100 MultiPick over 80	-0.21%	-0.43%	-0.97%	-5.36%	0.93%
Without "Divi-X"	-3.87%	-8.88%	-31.79%	7.28%	19.30%
All returns are accumulated, not averaged.					

HD	Home Depot	Purchase @ $23.61 share	Yield: 3.81%

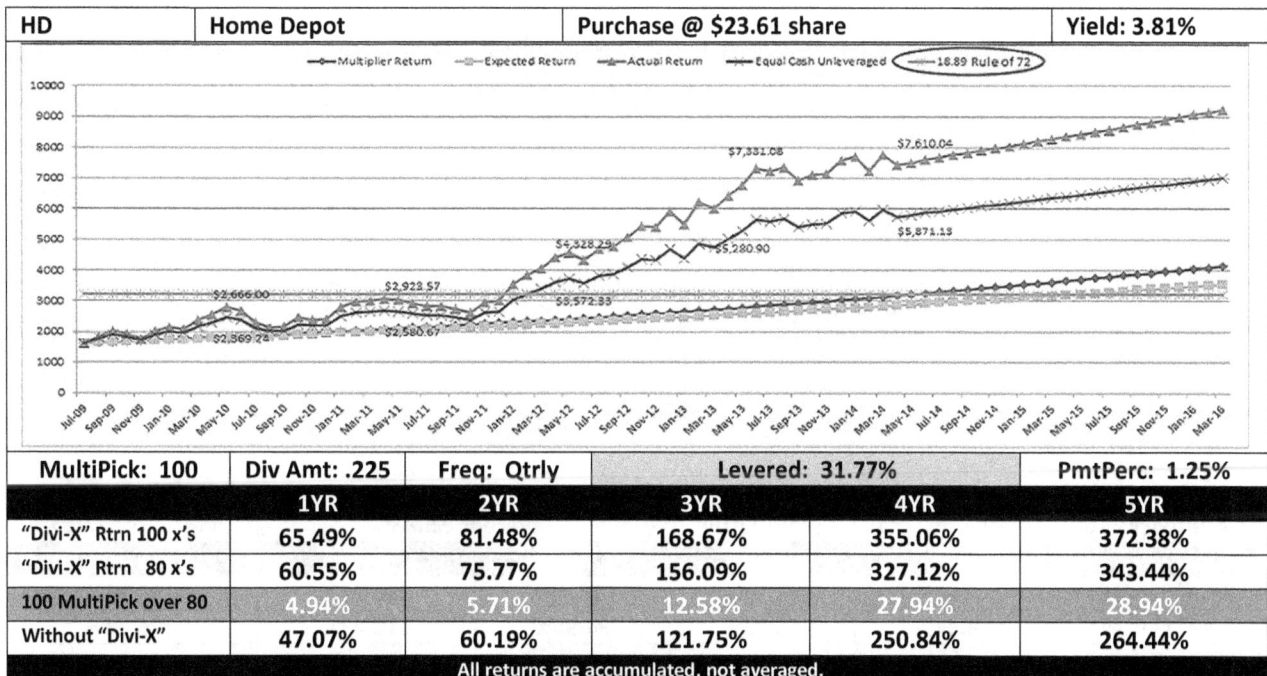

MultiPick: 100	Div Amt: .225	Freq: Qtrly	Levered: 31.77%		PmtPerc: 1.25%
	1YR	2YR	3YR	4YR	5YR
"Divi-X" Rtrn 100 x's	65.49%	81.48%	168.67%	355.06%	372.38%
"Divi-X" Rtrn 80 x's	60.55%	75.77%	156.09%	327.12%	343.44%
100 MultiPick over 80	4.94%	5.71%	12.58%	27.94%	28.94%
Without "Divi-X"	47.07%	60.19%	121.75%	250.84%	264.44%
All returns are accumulated, not averaged.					

MMM	3M Co	Purchase @ $59.37share	Yield: 3.44%

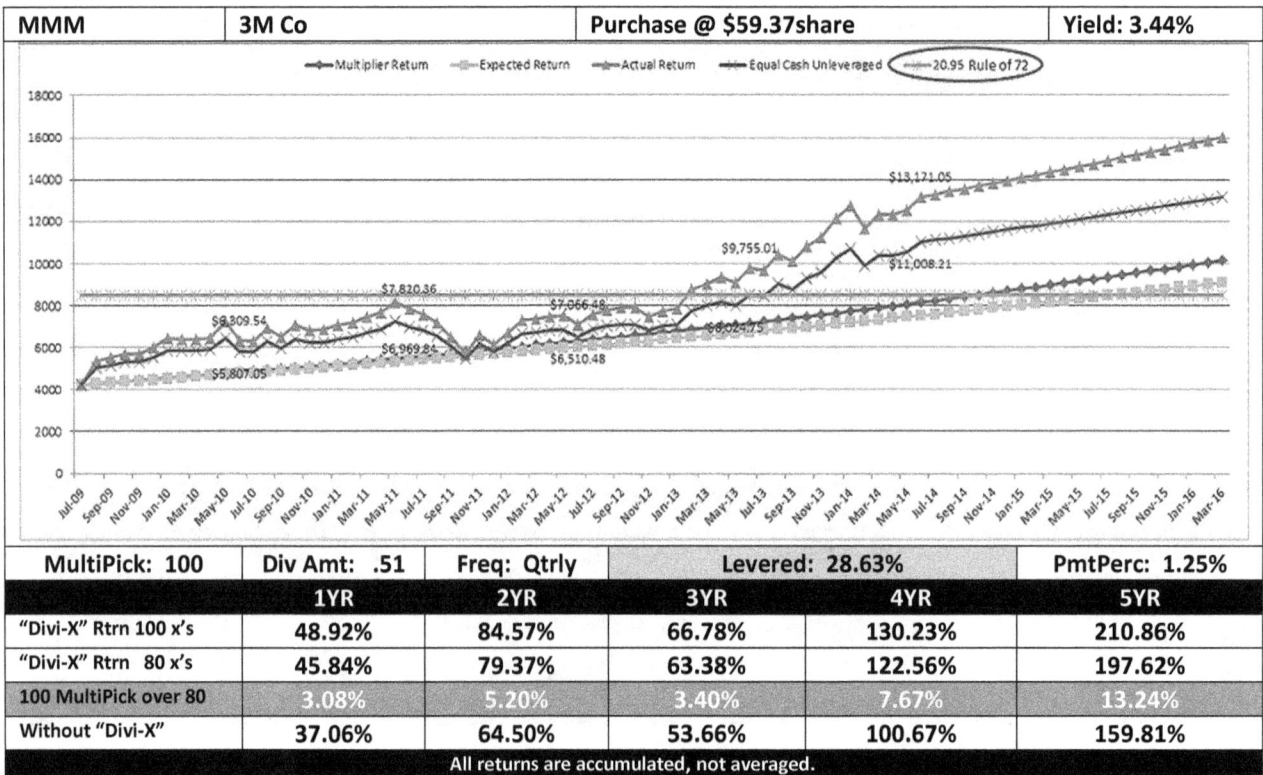

MultiPick: 100	Div Amt: .51	Freq: Qtrly	Levered: 28.63%		PmtPerc: 1.25%
	1YR	**2YR**	**3YR**	**4YR**	**5YR**
"Divi-X" Rtrn 100 x's	48.92%	84.57%	66.78%	130.23%	210.86%
"Divi-X" Rtrn 80 x's	45.84%	79.37%	63.38%	122.56%	197.62%
100 MultiPick over 80	3.08%	5.20%	3.40%	7.67%	13.24%
Without "Divi-X"	37.06%	64.50%	53.66%	100.67%	159.81%
All returns are accumulated, not averaged.					

T	AT&T	Purchase @ $24.04 share	Yield: 6.82%

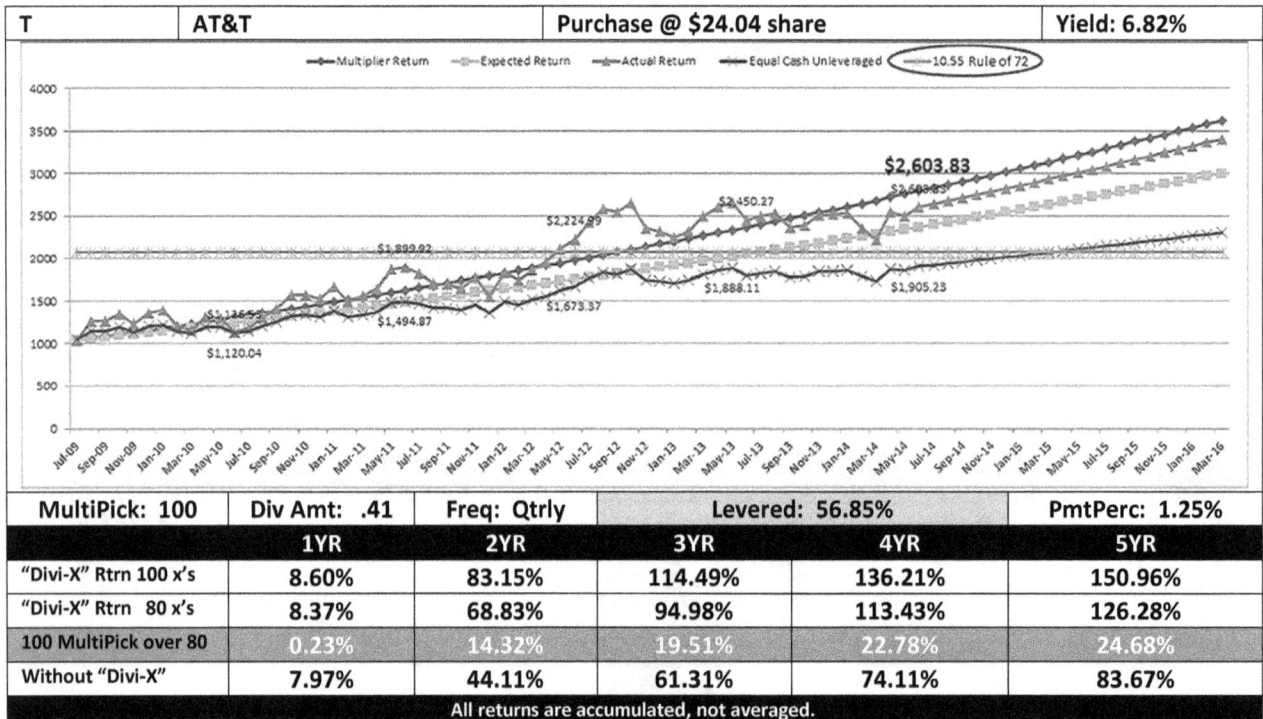

MultiPick: 100	Div Amt: .41	Freq: Qtrly	Levered: 56.85%		PmtPerc: 1.25%
	1YR	**2YR**	**3YR**	**4YR**	**5YR**
"Divi-X" Rtrn 100 x's	8.60%	83.15%	114.49%	136.21%	150.96%
"Divi-X" Rtrn 80 x's	8.37%	68.83%	94.98%	113.43%	126.28%
100 MultiPick over 80	0.23%	14.32%	19.51%	22.78%	24.68%
Without "Divi-X"	7.97%	44.11%	61.31%	74.11%	83.67%
All returns are accumulated, not averaged.					

INTC	Intel Corporation	Purchase @ $32.08 share	Yield: 1.96%

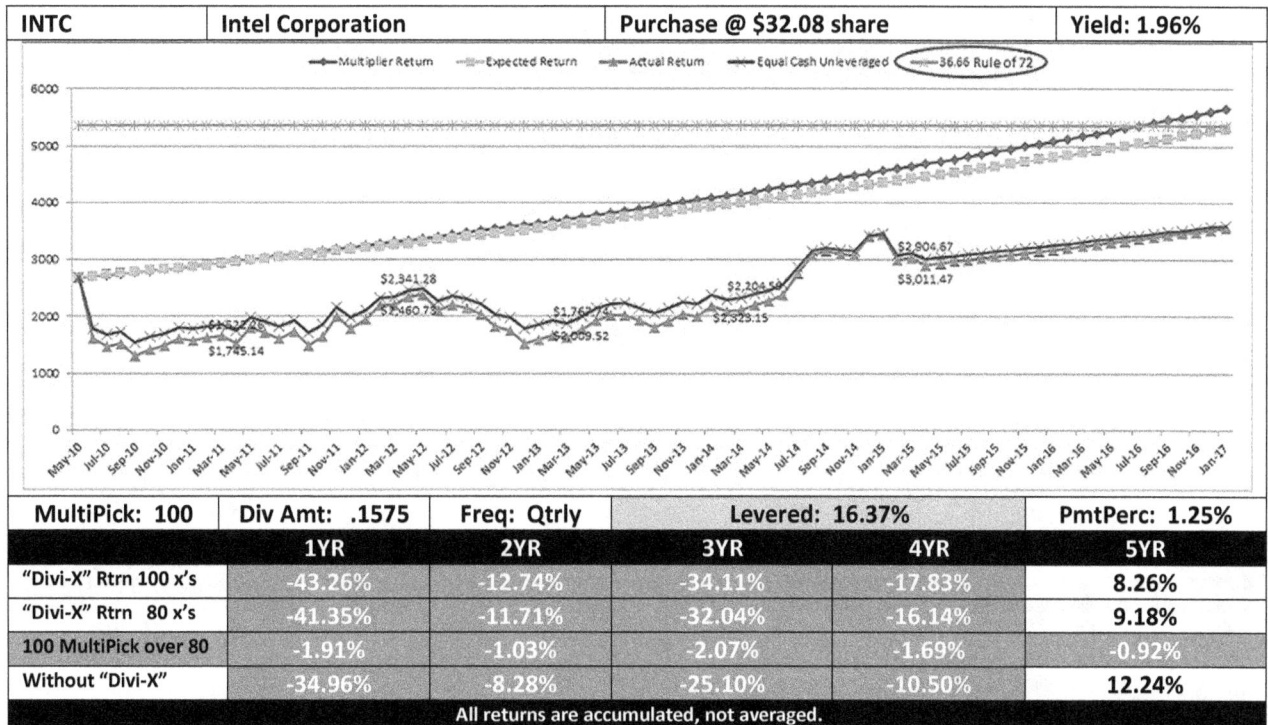

MultiPick: 100	Div Amt: .1575	Freq: Qtrly	Levered: 16.37%		PmtPerc: 1.25%
	1YR	2YR	3YR	4YR	5YR
"Divi-X" Rtrn 100 x's	-43.26%	-12.74%	-34.11%	-17.83%	8.26%
"Divi-X" Rtrn 80 x's	-41.35%	-11.71%	-32.04%	-16.14%	9.18%
100 MultiPick over 80	-1.91%	-1.03%	-2.07%	-1.69%	-0.92%
Without "Divi-X"	-34.96%	-8.28%	-25.10%	-10.50%	12.24%
All returns are accumulated, not averaged.					

XOM	Exxon Mobile Corporation	Purchase @ $71.05 share	Yield: 2.36%

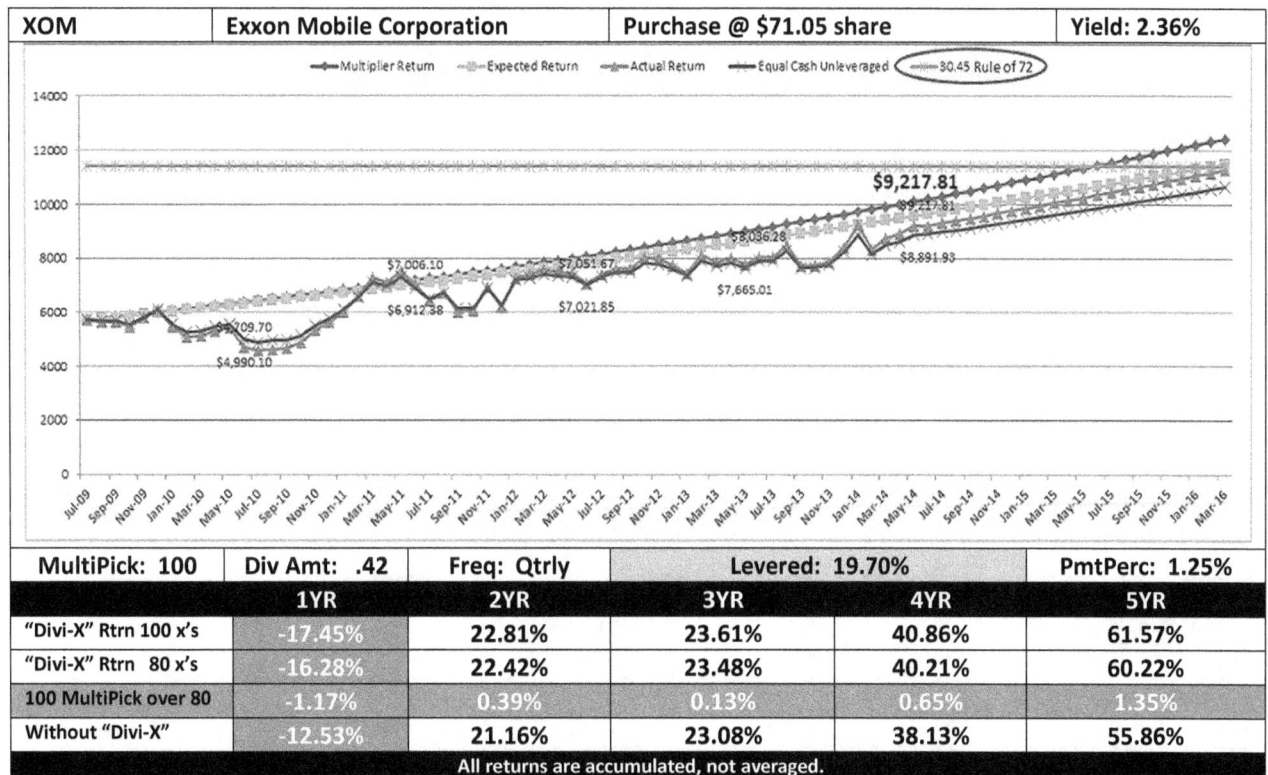

MultiPick: 100	Div Amt: .42	Freq: Qtrly	Levered: 19.70%		PmtPerc: 1.25%
	1YR	2YR	3YR	4YR	5YR
"Divi-X" Rtrn 100 x's	-17.45%	22.81%	23.61%	40.86%	61.57%
"Divi-X" Rtrn 80 x's	-16.28%	22.42%	23.48%	40.21%	60.22%
100 MultiPick over 80	-1.17%	0.39%	0.13%	0.65%	1.35%
Without "Divi-X"	-12.53%	21.16%	23.08%	38.13%	55.86%
All returns are accumulated, not averaged.					

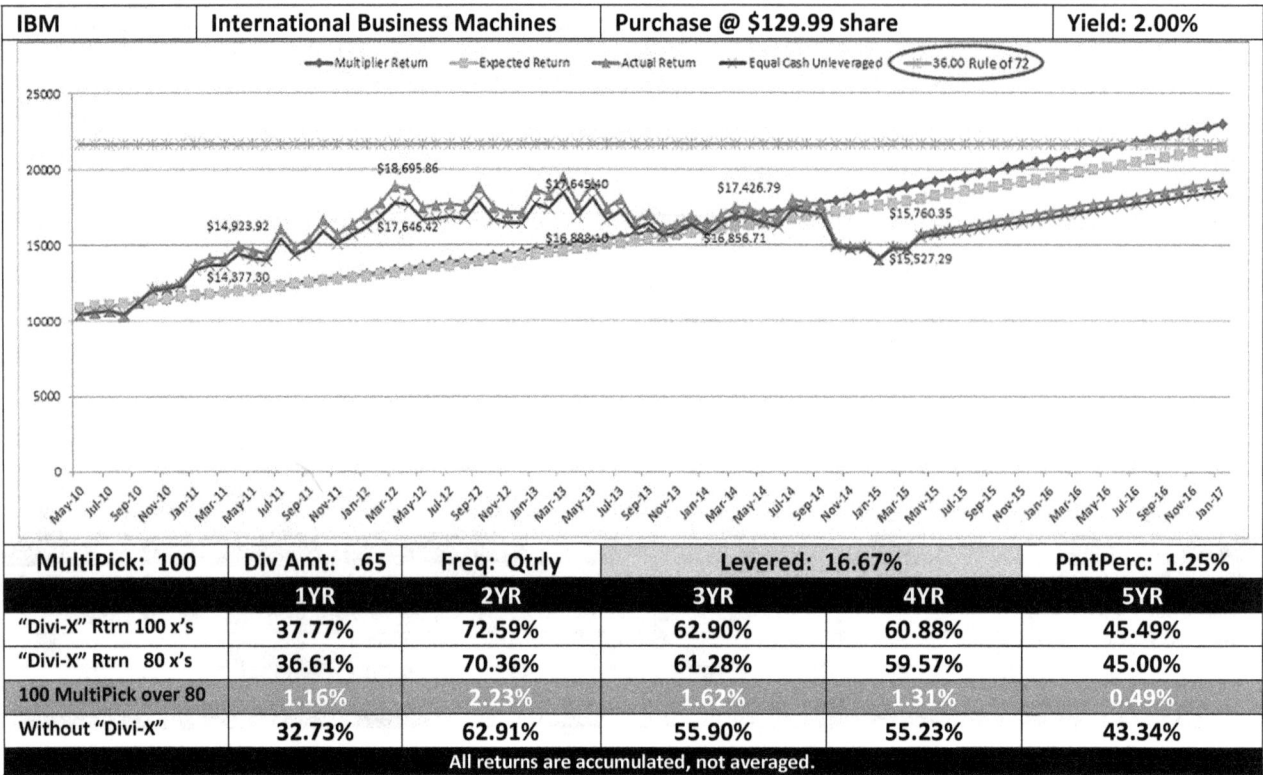

IBM	International Business Machines	Purchase @ $129.99 share		Yield: 2.00%

MultiPick: 100	Div Amt: .65	Freq: Qtrly	Levered: 16.67%		PmtPerc: 1.25%
	1YR	2YR	3YR	4YR	5YR
"Divi-X" Rtrn 100 x's	37.77%	72.59%	62.90%	60.88%	45.49%
"Divi-X" Rtrn 80 x's	36.61%	70.36%	61.28%	59.57%	45.00%
100 MultiPick over 80	1.16%	2.23%	1.62%	1.31%	0.49%
Without "Divi-X"	32.73%	62.91%	55.90%	55.23%	43.34%
All returns are accumulated, not averaged.					

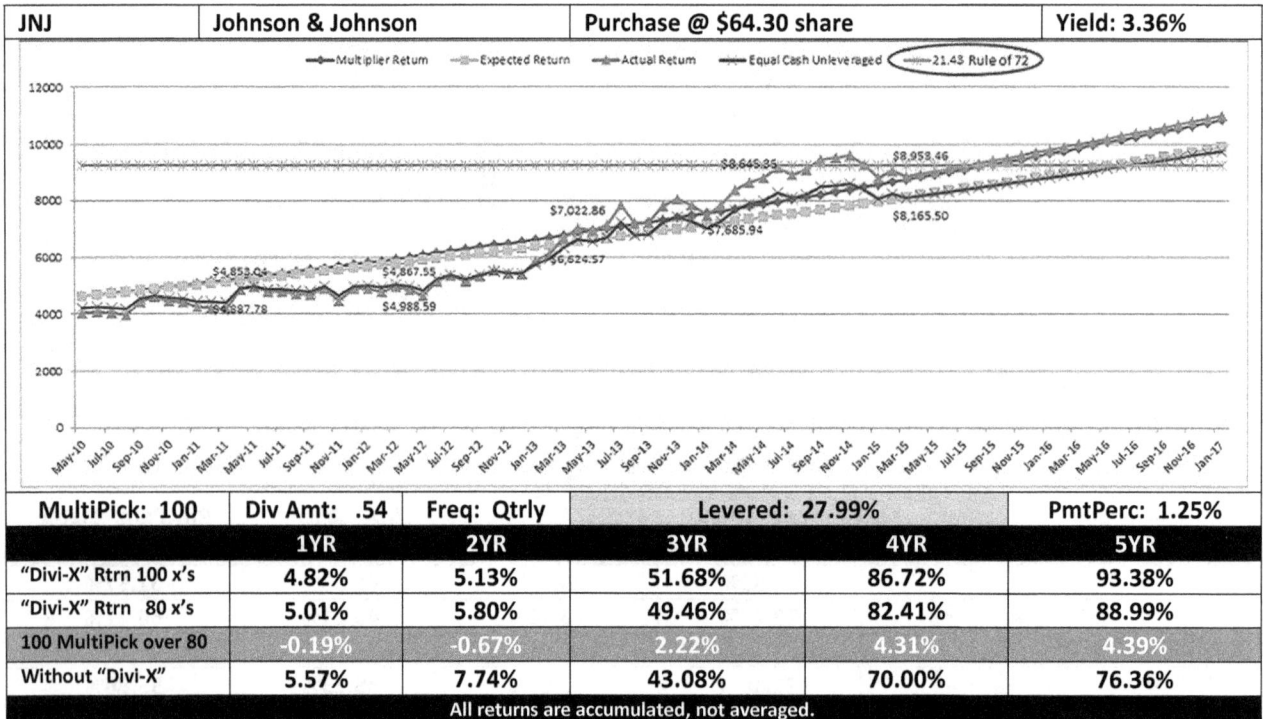

JNJ	Johnson & Johnson	Purchase @ $64.30 share		Yield: 3.36%

MultiPick: 100	Div Amt: .54	Freq: Qtrly	Levered: 27.99%		PmtPerc: 1.25%
	1YR	2YR	3YR	4YR	5YR
"Divi-X" Rtrn 100 x's	4.82%	5.13%	51.68%	86.72%	93.38%
"Divi-X" Rtrn 80 x's	5.01%	5.80%	49.46%	82.41%	88.99%
100 MultiPick over 80	-0.19%	-0.67%	2.22%	4.31%	4.39%
Without "Divi-X"	5.57%	7.74%	43.08%	70.00%	76.36%
All returns are accumulated, not averaged.					

JPM	JPMorgan Chase & Co.	Purchase @ $44.94 share	Yield: 0.45%

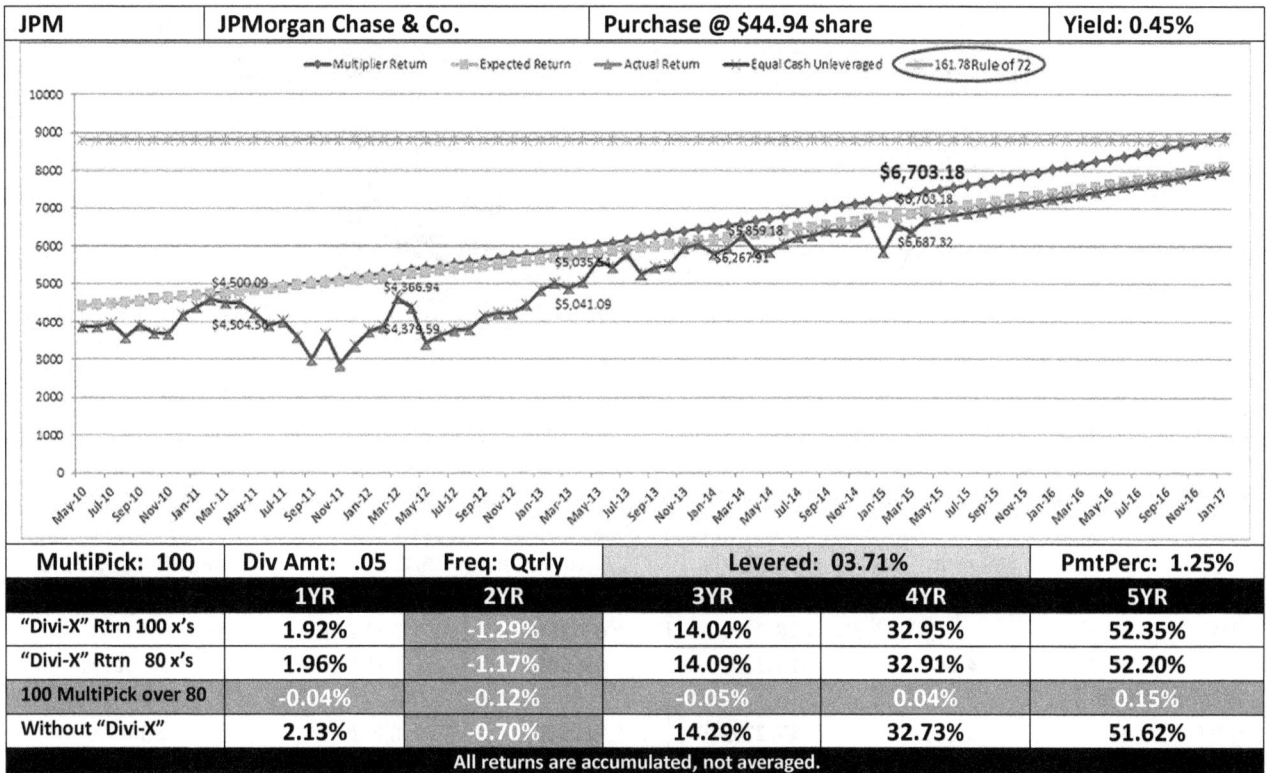

Legend: Multiplier Return — Expected Return — Actual Return — Equal Cash Unleveraged — 161.78 Rule of 72

Chart values: $4,500.09, $4,504.50, $4,366.94, $4,379.59, $5,041.09, $5,035.41, $6,267.91, $5,859.18, $6,703.18, $6,687.32

MultiPick: 100	Div Amt: .05	Freq: Qtrly	Levered: 03.71%		PmtPerc: 1.25%
	1YR	2YR	3YR	4YR	5YR
"Divi-X" Rtrn 100 x's	1.92%	-1.29%	14.04%	32.95%	52.35%
"Divi-X" Rtrn 80 x's	1.96%	-1.17%	14.09%	32.91%	52.20%
100 MultiPick over 80	-0.04%	-0.12%	-0.05%	0.04%	0.15%
Without "Divi-X"	2.13%	-0.70%	14.29%	32.73%	51.62%
All returns are accumulated, not averaged.					

MCD	McDonald's Corporation	Purchase @ $70.59 share	Yield: 3.12%

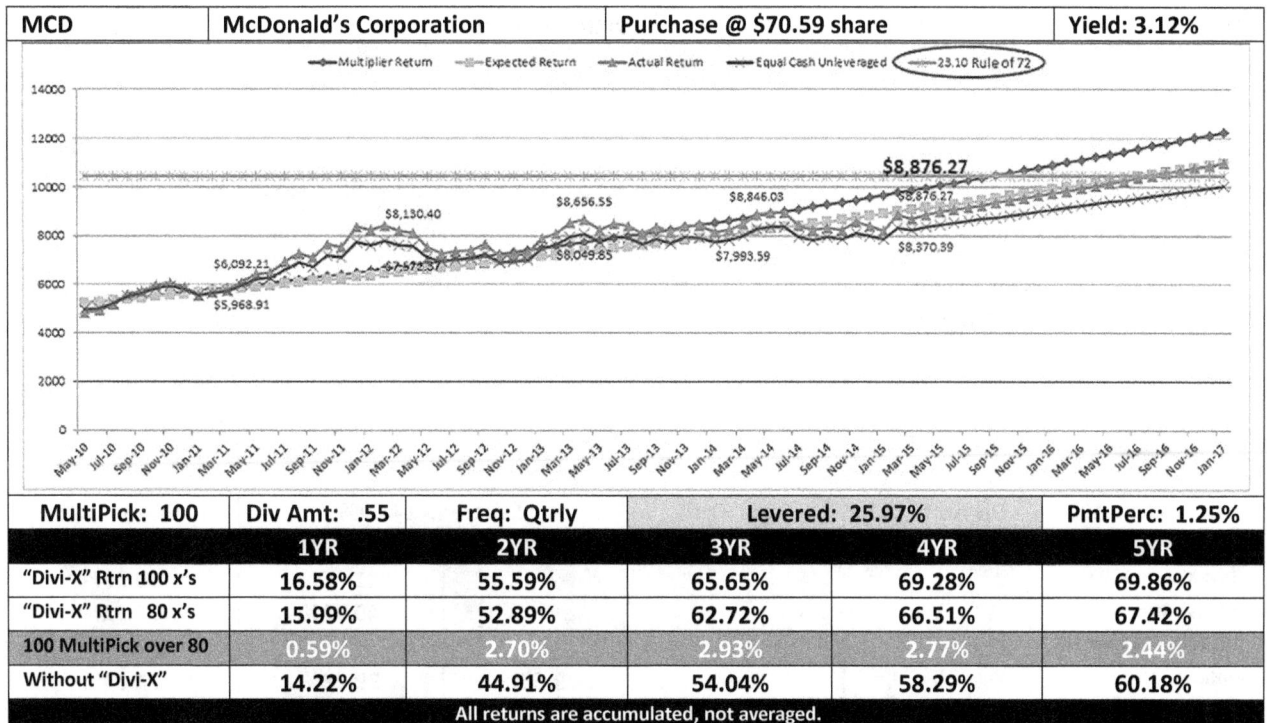

Legend: Multiplier Return — Expected Return — Actual Return — Equal Cash Unleveraged — 23.10 Rule of 72

Chart values: $6,092.21, $5,968.91, $8,130.40, $7,572.37, $8,656.55, $8,049.85, $8,846.03, $7,993.59, $8,876.27, $8,370.39

MultiPick: 100	Div Amt: .55	Freq: Qtrly	Levered: 25.97%		PmtPerc: 1.25%
	1YR	2YR	3YR	4YR	5YR
"Divi-X" Rtrn 100 x's	16.58%	55.59%	65.65%	69.28%	69.86%
"Divi-X" Rtrn 80 x's	15.99%	52.89%	62.72%	66.51%	67.42%
100 MultiPick over 80	0.59%	2.70%	2.93%	2.77%	2.44%
Without "Divi-X"	14.22%	44.91%	54.04%	58.29%	60.18%
All returns are accumulated, not averaged.					

| MRK | Merck & Co Inc | Purchase @ $35.46 share | Yield: 4.29% |

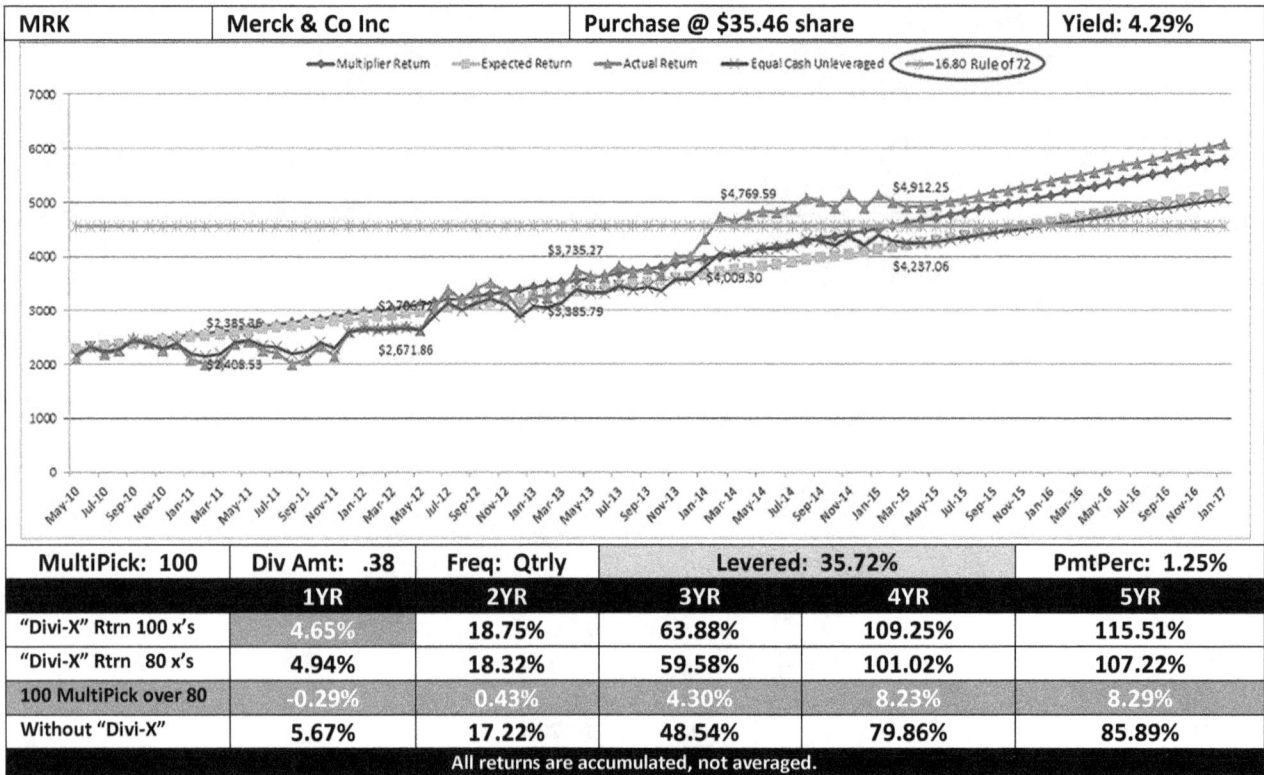

MultiPick: 100	Div Amt: .38	Freq: Qtrly	Levered: 35.72%		PmtPerc: 1.25%
	1YR	2YR	3YR	4YR	5YR
"Divi-X" Rtrn 100 x's	4.65%	18.75%	63.88%	109.25%	115.51%
"Divi-X" Rtrn 80 x's	4.94%	18.32%	59.58%	101.02%	107.22%
100 MultiPick over 80	-0.29%	0.43%	4.30%	8.23%	8.29%
Without "Divi-X"	5.67%	17.22%	48.54%	79.86%	85.89%
All returns are accumulated, not averaged.					

| MSFT | Microsoft Corporation | Purchase @ $30.96 share | Yield 1.68% |

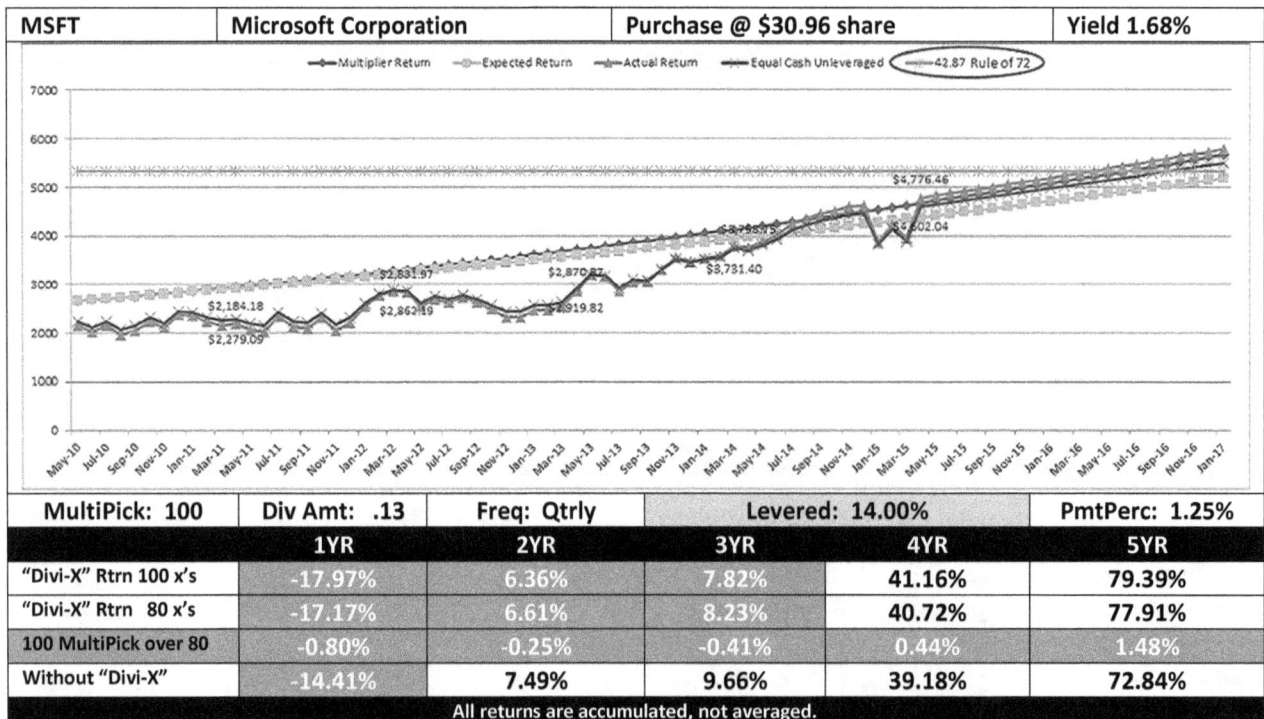

MultiPick: 100	Div Amt: .13	Freq: Qtrly	Levered: 14.00%		PmtPerc: 1.25%
	1YR	2YR	3YR	4YR	5YR
"Divi-X" Rtrn 100 x's	-17.97%	6.36%	7.82%	41.16%	79.39%
"Divi-X" Rtrn 80 x's	-17.17%	6.61%	8.23%	40.72%	77.91%
100 MultiPick over 80	-0.80%	-0.25%	-0.41%	0.44%	1.48%
Without "Divi-X"	-14.41%	7.49%	9.66%	39.18%	72.84%
All returns are accumulated, not averaged.					

NKE	Nike Inc	Purchase @ $38.95 share	Yield: 1.39%

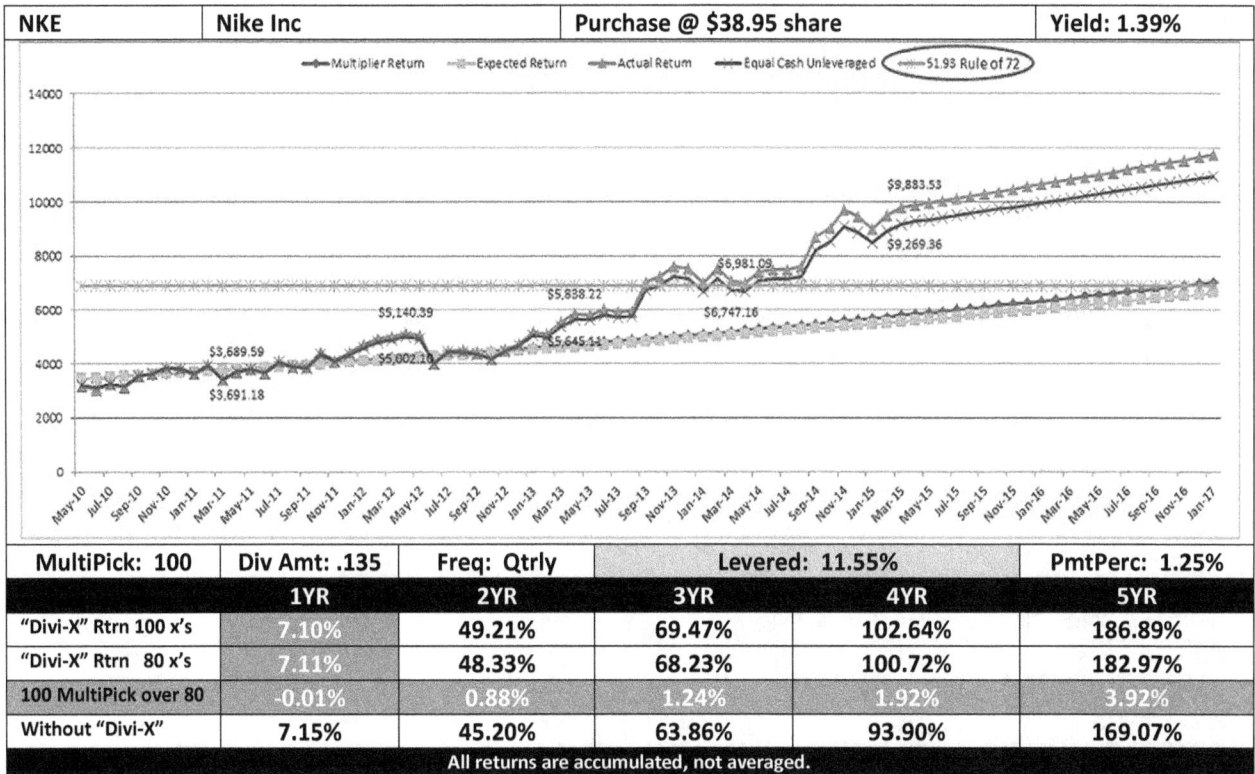

Multiplier Return — Expected Return — Actual Return — Equal Cash Unleveraged — 51.93 Rule of 72

$9,883.53
$9,269.36
$6,981.09
$5,838.22
$6,747.16
$5,140.39
$5,645.11
$5,002.16
$3,689.59
$3,691.18

MultiPick: 100	Div Amt: .135	Freq: Qtrly	Levered: 11.55%		PmtPerc: 1.25%
	1YR	2YR	3YR	4YR	5YR
"Divi-X" Rtrn 100 x's	7.10%	49.21%	69.47%	102.64%	186.89%
"Divi-X" Rtrn 80 x's	7.11%	48.33%	68.23%	100.72%	182.97%
100 MultiPick over 80	-0.01%	0.88%	1.24%	1.92%	3.92%
Without "Divi-X"	7.15%	45.20%	63.86%	93.90%	169.07%
All returns are accumulated, not averaged.					

PFE	Pfizer Inc	Purchase @ $16.72 share	Yield: 4.31%

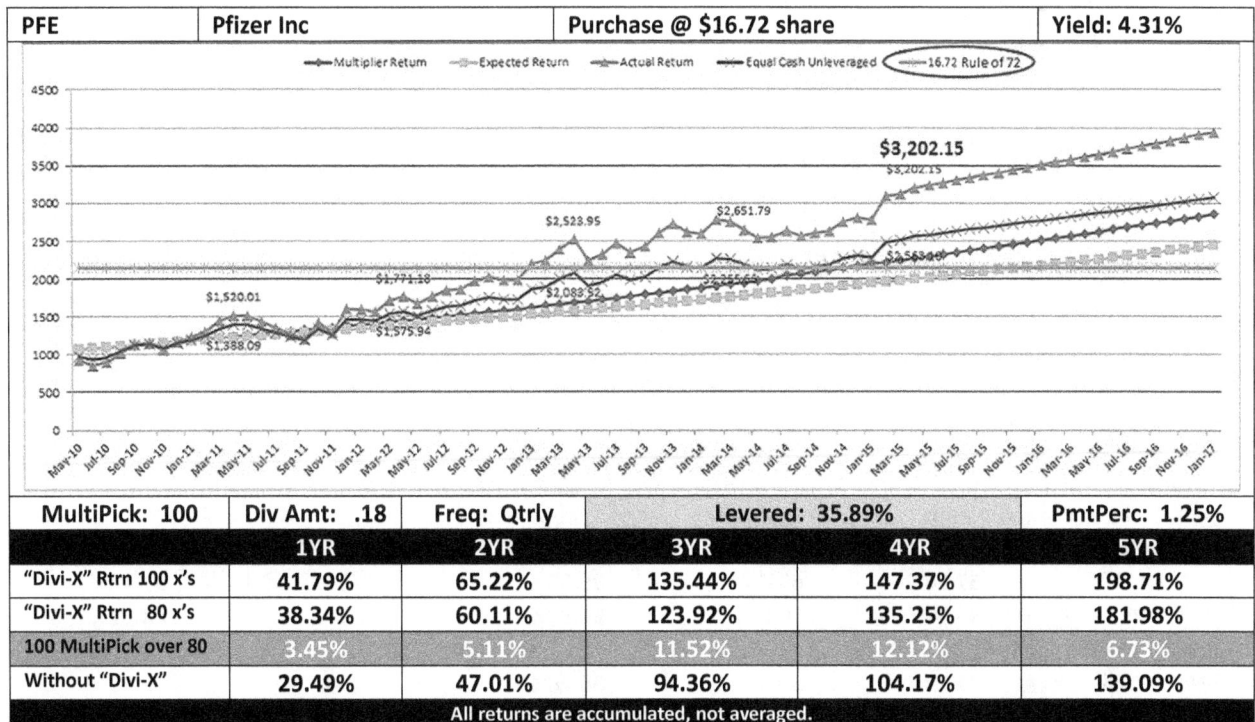

Multiplier Return — Expected Return — Actual Return — Equal Cash Unleveraged — 16.72 Rule of 72

$3,202.15
$3,202.15
$2,651.79
$2,523.95
$1,771.18
$2,088.52
$2,563.
$1,520.01
$1,575.94
$1,388.09

MultiPick: 100	Div Amt: .18	Freq: Qtrly	Levered: 35.89%		PmtPerc: 1.25%
	1YR	2YR	3YR	4YR	5YR
"Divi-X" Rtrn 100 x's	41.79%	65.22%	135.44%	147.37%	198.71%
"Divi-X" Rtrn 80 x's	38.34%	60.11%	123.92%	135.25%	181.98%
100 MultiPick over 80	3.45%	5.11%	11.52%	12.12%	6.73%
Without "Divi-X"	29.49%	47.01%	94.36%	104.17%	139.09%
All returns are accumulated, not averaged.					

PG	Proctor & Gamble & Co	Purchase @ $62.16 share	Yield: 3.10%

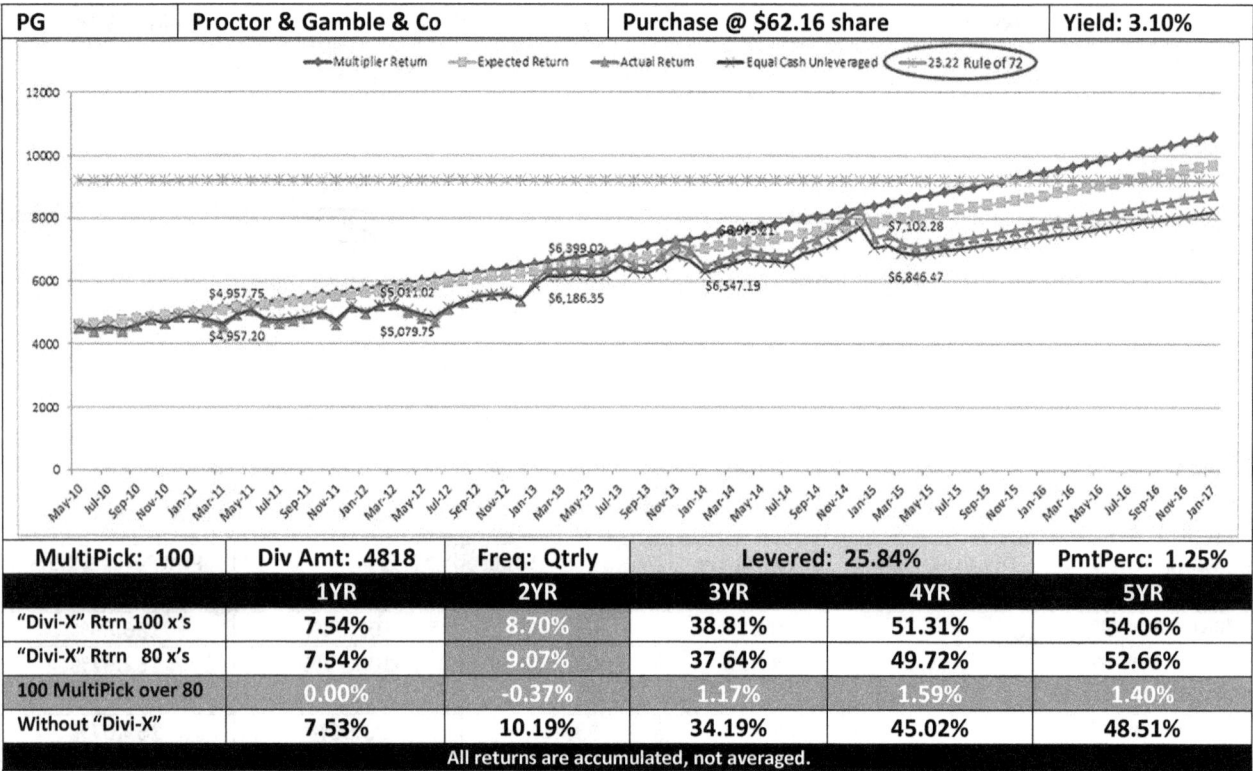

MultiPick: 100	Div Amt: .4818	Freq: Qtrly	Levered: 25.84%		PmtPerc: 1.25%
	1YR	2YR	3YR	4YR	5YR
"Divi-X" Rtrn 100 x's	7.54%	8.70%	38.81%	51.31%	54.06%
"Divi-X" Rtrn 80 x's	7.54%	9.07%	37.64%	49.72%	52.66%
100 MultiPick over 80	0.00%	-0.37%	1.17%	1.59%	1.40%
Without "Divi-X"	7.53%	10.19%	34.19%	45.02%	48.51%
All returns are accumulated, not averaged.					

KO	The Coca-Cola Co	Purchase @ $26.72 share	Yield: 3.29%

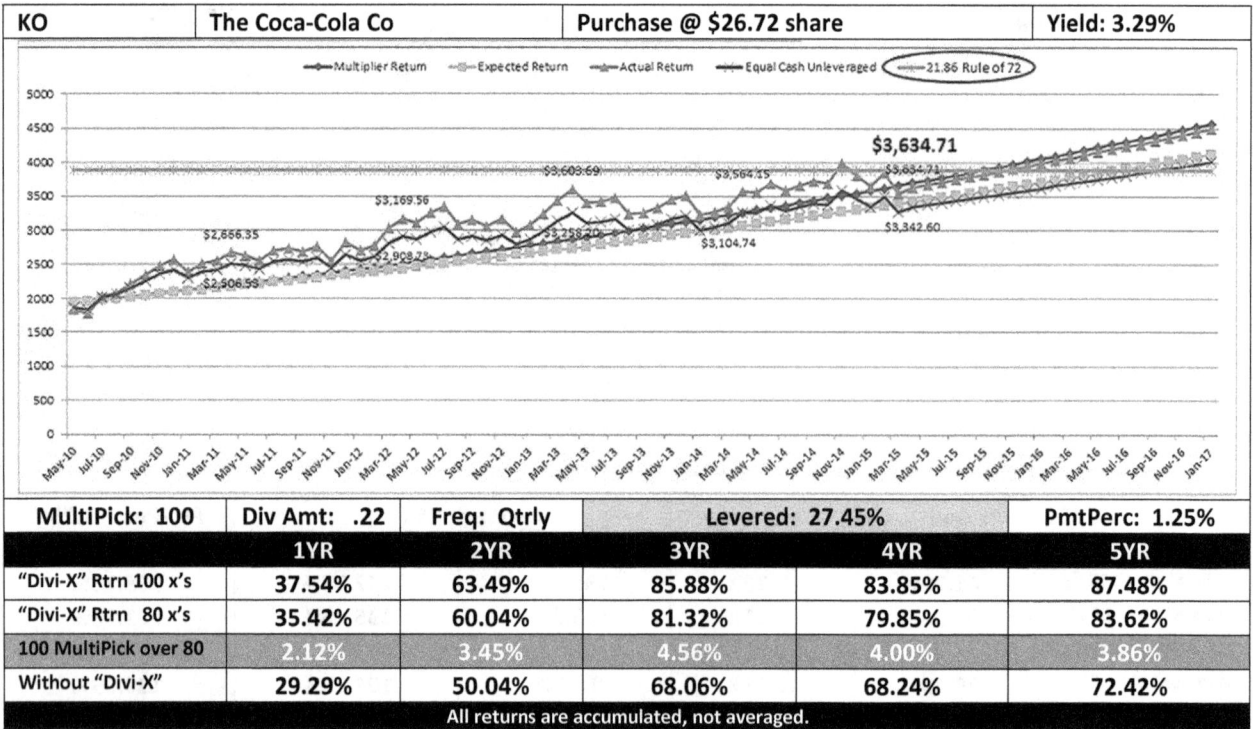

MultiPick: 100	Div Amt: .22	Freq: Qtrly	Levered: 27.45%		PmtPerc: 1.25%
	1YR	2YR	3YR	4YR	5YR
"Divi-X" Rtrn 100 x's	37.54%	63.49%	85.88%	83.85%	87.48%
"Divi-X" Rtrn 80 x's	35.42%	60.04%	81.32%	79.85%	83.62%
100 MultiPick over 80	2.12%	3.45%	4.56%	4.00%	3.86%
Without "Divi-X"	29.29%	50.04%	68.06%	68.24%	72.42%
All returns are accumulated, not averaged.					

TRV	Travelers Companies Inc	Purchase @ $50.74share	Yield: 2.84%

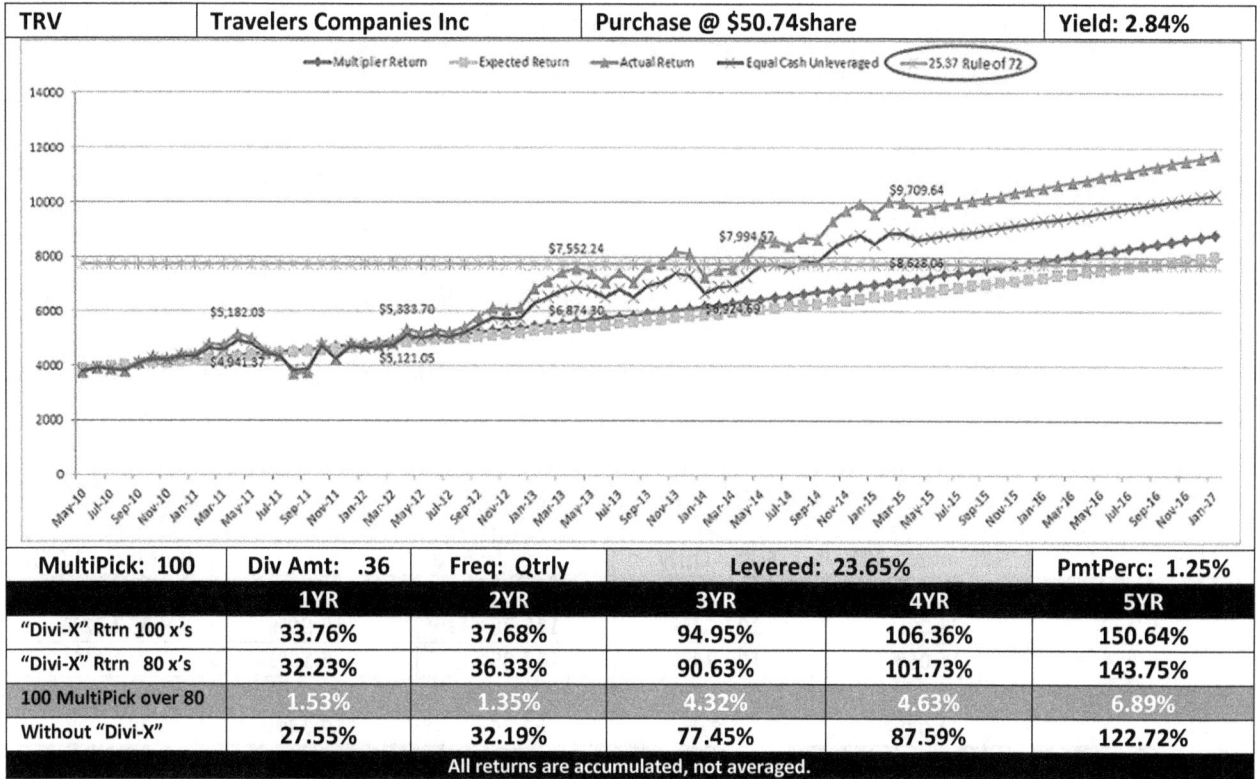

Legend: Multiplier Return — Expected Return — Actual Return — Equal Cash Unleveraged — 25.37 Rule of 72

Data labels visible: $5,182.03, $4,941.37, $5,121.05, $5,333.70, $6,874.30, $6,724.59, $7,552.24, $7,994.87, $8,628.06, $9,709.64

MultiPick: 100	Div Amt: .36	Freq: Qtrly	Levered: 23.65%		PmtPerc: 1.25%
	1YR	2YR	3YR	4YR	5YR
"Divi-X" Rtrn 100 x's	33.76%	37.68%	94.95%	106.36%	150.64%
"Divi-X" Rtrn 80 x's	32.23%	36.33%	90.63%	101.73%	143.75%
100 MultiPick over 80	1.53%	1.35%	4.32%	4.63%	6.89%
Without "Divi-X"	27.55%	32.19%	77.45%	87.59%	122.72%
All returns are accumulated, not averaged.					

UTX	United Technologies Corp	Purchase @ $74.95 share	Yield: 2.27%

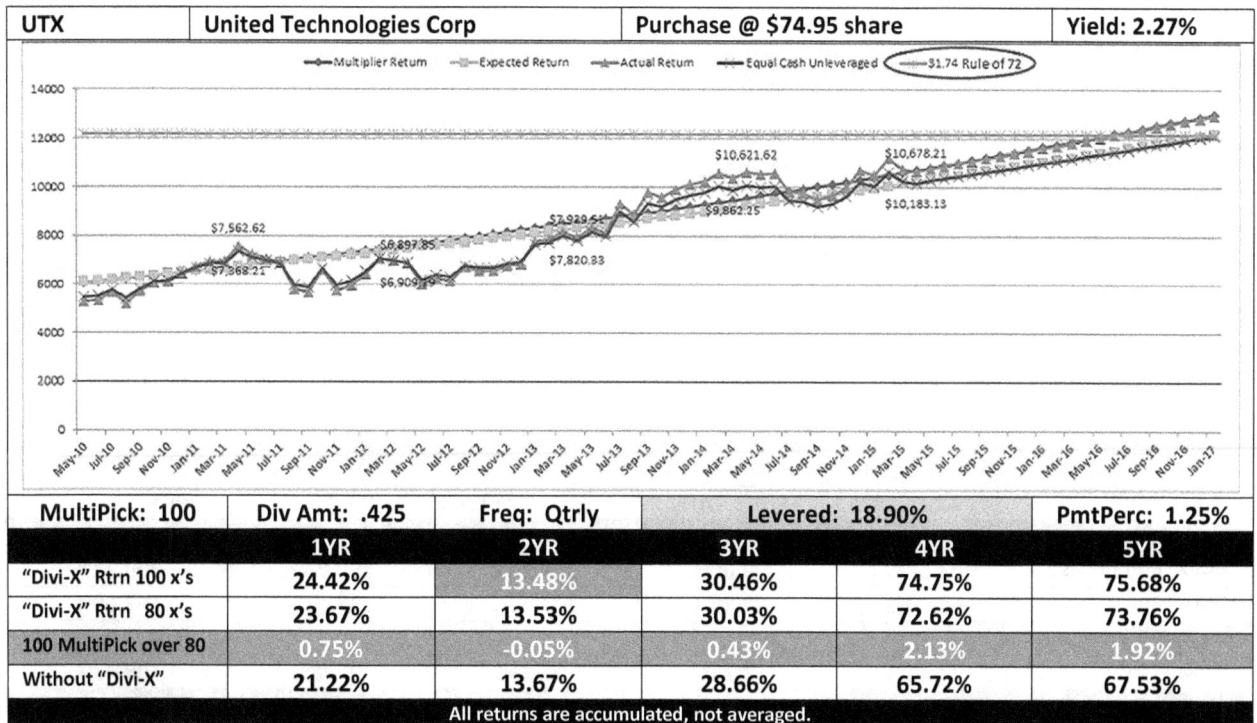

Legend: Multiplier Return — Expected Return — Actual Return — Equal Cash Unleveraged — 31.74 Rule of 72

Data labels visible: $7,562.62, $7,368.21, $6,897.85, $6,909.19, $7,929.41, $7,820.83, $9,862.15, $10,621.62, $10,183.13, $10,678.21

MultiPick: 100	Div Amt: .425	Freq: Qtrly	Levered: 18.90%		PmtPerc: 1.25%
	1YR	2YR	3YR	4YR	5YR
"Divi-X" Rtrn 100 x's	24.42%	13.48%	30.46%	74.75%	75.68%
"Divi-X" Rtrn 80 x's	23.67%	13.53%	30.03%	72.62%	73.76%
100 MultiPick over 80	0.75%	-0.05%	0.43%	2.13%	1.92%
Without "Divi-X"	21.22%	13.67%	28.66%	65.72%	67.53%
All returns are accumulated, not averaged.					

UNH	UnitedHealth Group Inc	Purchase @ $30.31 share	Yield: 1.65%

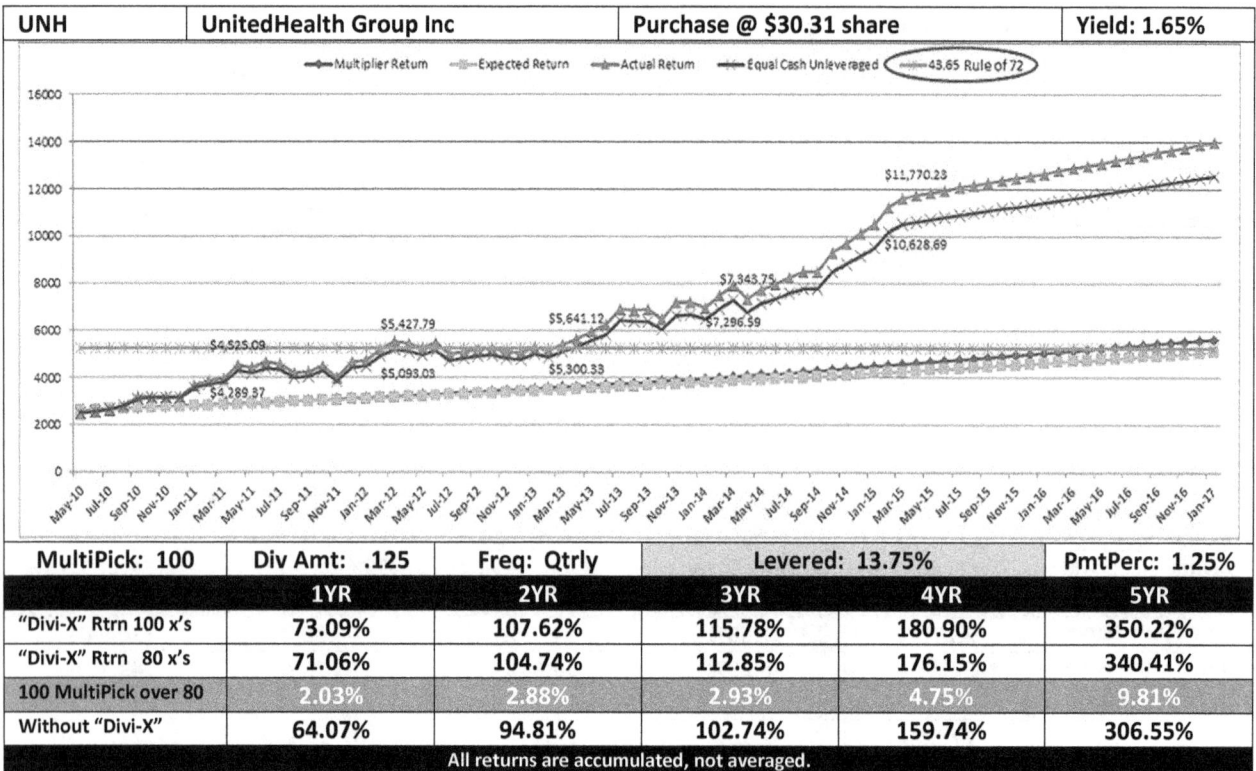

MultiPick: 100	Div Amt: .125	Freq: Qtrly	Levered: 13.75%		PmtPerc: 1.25%
	1YR	2YR	3YR	4YR	5YR
"Divi-X" Rtrn 100 x's	73.09%	107.62%	115.78%	180.90%	350.22%
"Divi-X" Rtrn 80 x's	71.06%	104.74%	112.85%	176.15%	340.41%
100 MultiPick over 80	2.03%	2.88%	2.93%	4.75%	9.81%
Without "Divi-X"	64.07%	94.81%	102.74%	159.74%	306.55%
All returns are accumulated, not averaged.					

VZ	Verizon Communications Inc	Purchase @ $28.90 share	Yield: 6.57%

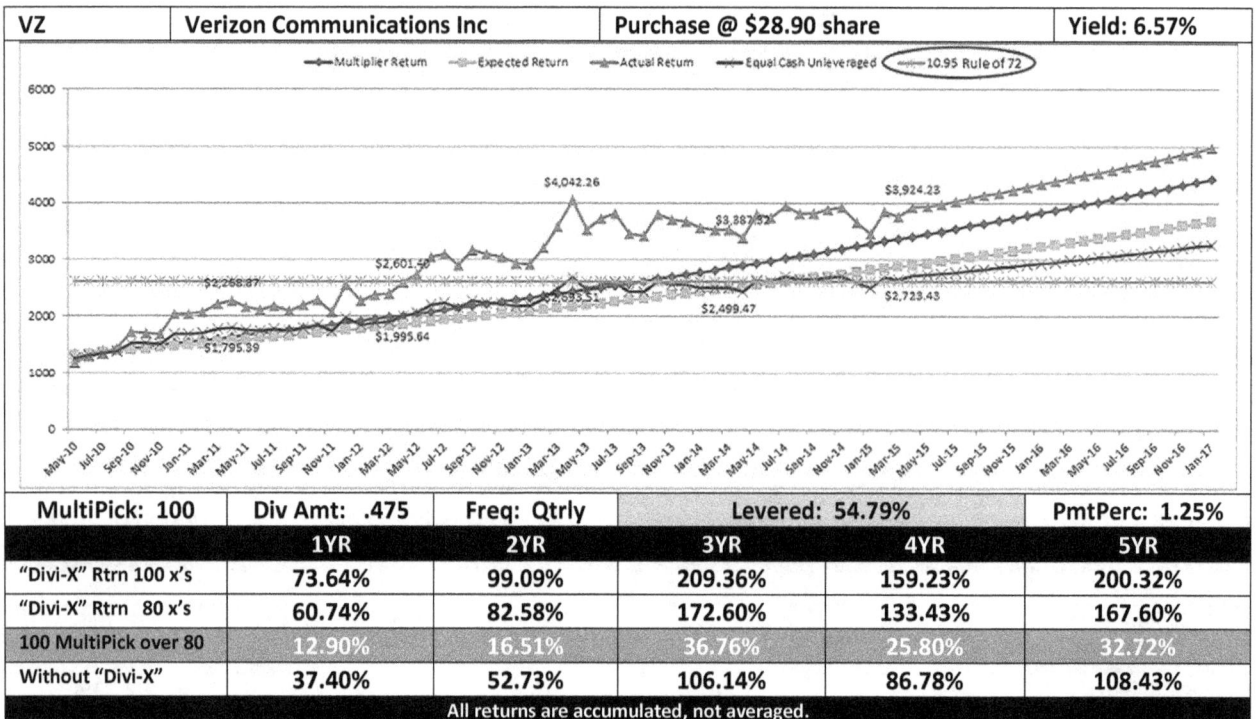

MultiPick: 100	Div Amt: .475	Freq: Qtrly	Levered: 54.79%		PmtPerc: 1.25%
	1YR	2YR	3YR	4YR	5YR
"Divi-X" Rtrn 100 x's	73.64%	99.09%	209.36%	159.23%	200.32%
"Divi-X" Rtrn 80 x's	60.74%	82.58%	172.60%	133.43%	167.60%
100 MultiPick over 80	12.90%	16.51%	36.76%	25.80%	32.72%
Without "Divi-X"	37.40%	52.73%	106.14%	86.78%	108.43%
All returns are accumulated, not averaged.					

V	Visa	Purchase @ $22.558 share	Yield: 0.56%

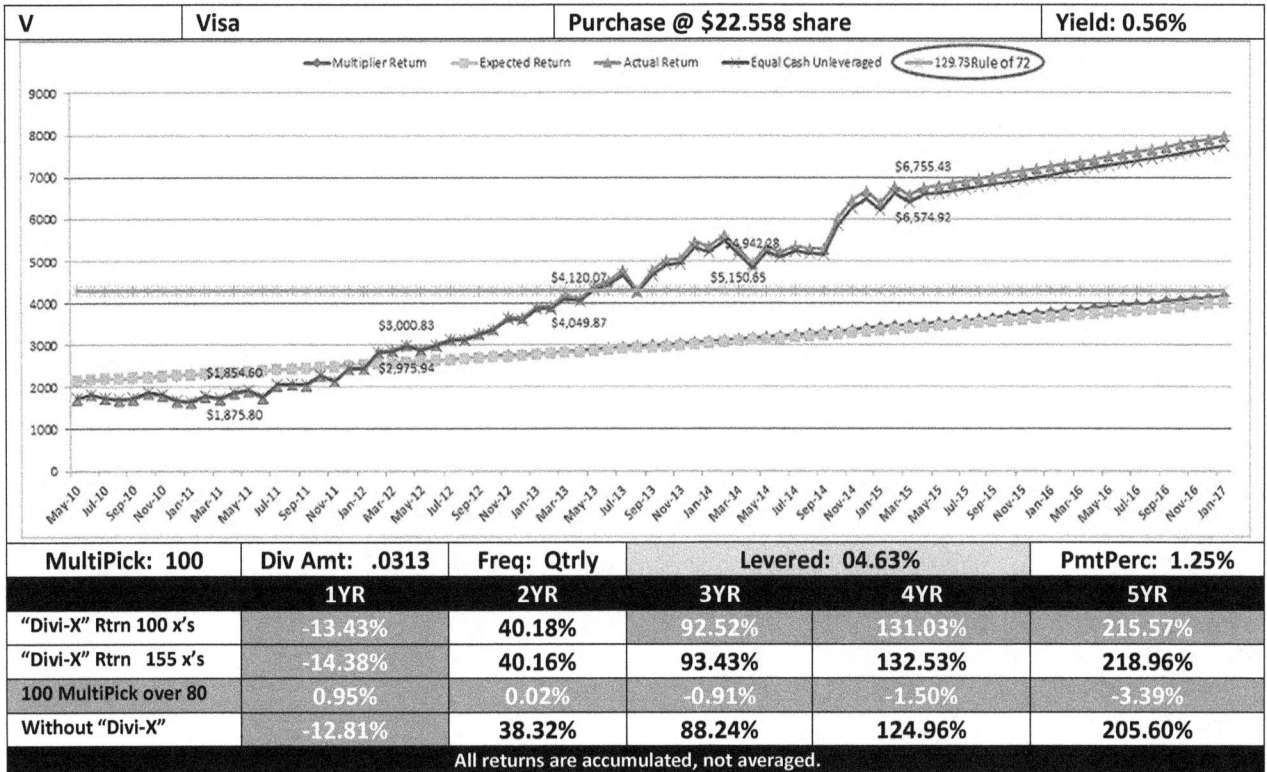

Legend: Multiplier Return — Expected Return — Actual Return — Equal Cash Unleveraged — 129.73 Rule of 72

Chart labels: $1,854.60, $1,875.80, $2,975.94, $3,000.83, $4,049.87, $4,120.07, $4,942.08, $5,150.65, $6,574.92, $6,755.43

MultiPick: 100	Div Amt: .0313	Freq: Qtrly	Levered: 04.63%		PmtPerc: 1.25%
	1YR	2YR	3YR	4YR	5YR
"Divi-X" Rtrn 100 x's	-13.43%	40.18%	92.52%	131.03%	215.57%
"Divi-X" Rtrn 155 x's	-14.38%	40.16%	93.43%	132.53%	218.96%
100 MultiPick over 80	0.95%	0.02%	-0.91%	-1.50%	-3.39%
Without "Divi-X"	-12.81%	38.32%	88.24%	124.96%	205.60%
All returns are accumulated, not averaged.					

WMT	Wal-Mart Stores Inc	Purchase @ $54.53 share	Yield: 2.22%

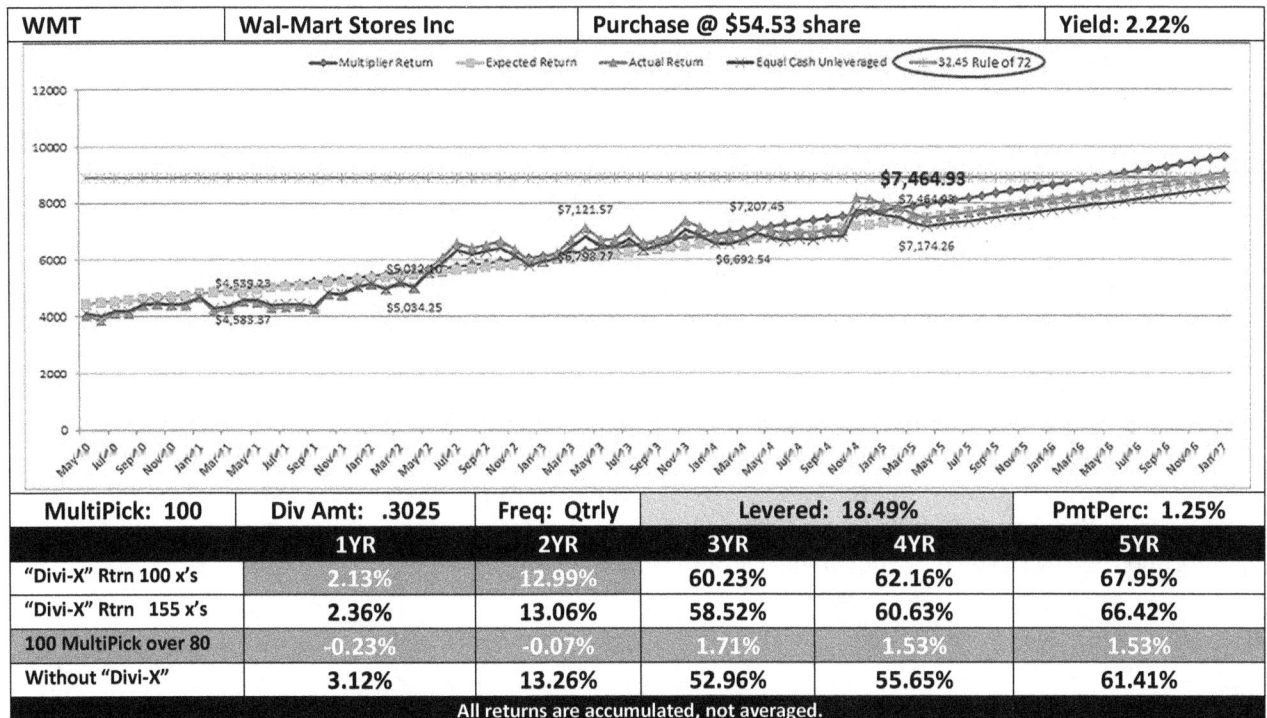

Legend: Multiplier Return — Expected Return — Actual Return — Equal Cash Unleveraged — 32.45 Rule of 72

Chart labels: $4,539.23, $4,583.37, $5,012.40, $5,034.25, $6,798.77, $7,121.57, $6,692.54, $7,207.45, $7,464.93, $7,464.93, $7,174.26

MultiPick: 100	Div Amt: .3025	Freq: Qtrly	Levered: 18.49%		PmtPerc: 1.25%
	1YR	2YR	3YR	4YR	5YR
"Divi-X" Rtrn 100 x's	2.13%	12.99%	60.23%	62.16%	67.95%
"Divi-X" Rtrn 155 x's	2.36%	13.06%	58.52%	60.63%	66.42%
100 MultiPick over 80	-0.23%	-0.07%	1.71%	1.53%	1.53%
Without "Divi-X"	3.12%	13.26%	52.96%	55.65%	61.41%
All returns are accumulated, not averaged.					

DIS	Walt Disney Co	Purchase @ $36.84 share	Yield: 1.09%

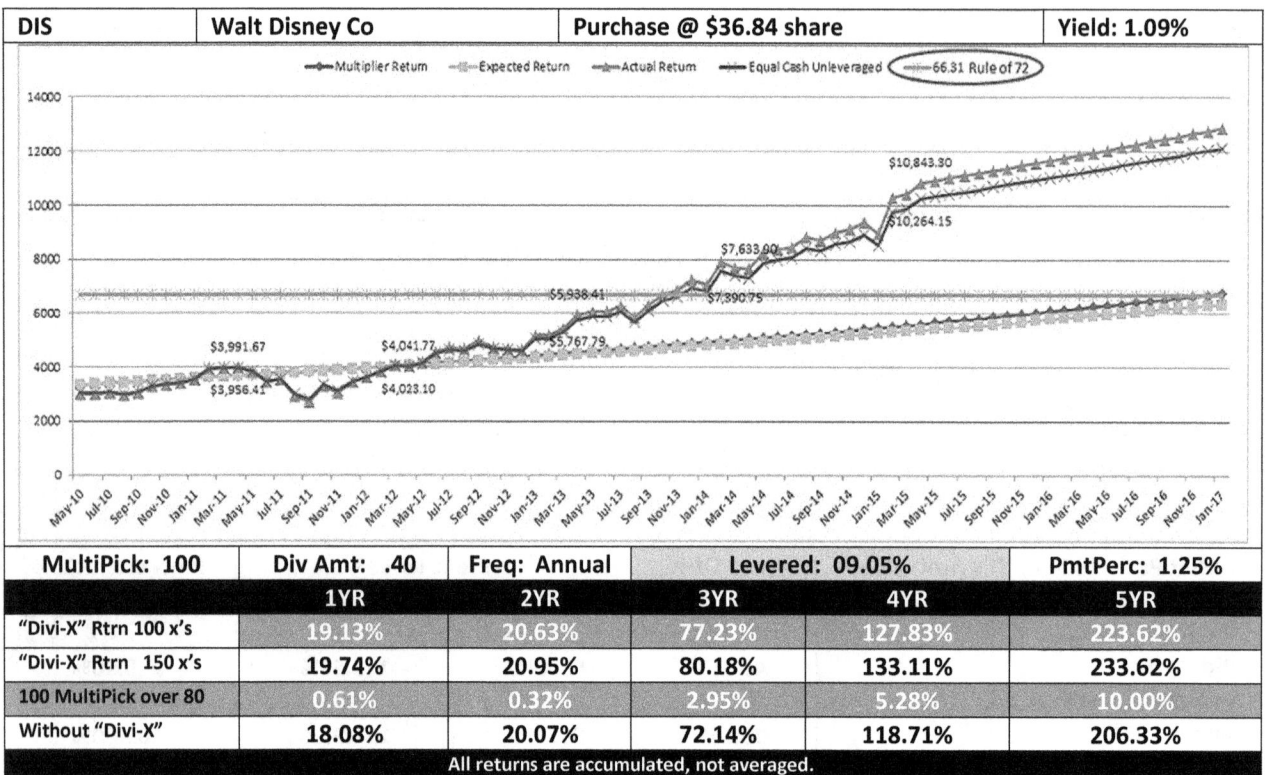

Legend: Multiplier Return · Expected Return · Actual Return · Equal Cash Unleveraged · 66.31 Rule of 72

(chart data labels: $3,991.67, $3,956.41, $4,041.77, $4,023.10, $5,938.41, $5,767.79, $7,390.75, $7,633.00, $10,264.15, $10,843.30)

MultiPick: 100	Div Amt: .40	Freq: Annual	Levered: 09.05%		PmtPerc: 1.25%
	1YR	2YR	3YR	4YR	5YR
"Divi-X" Rtrn 100 x's	19.13%	20.63%	77.23%	127.83%	223.62%
"Divi-X" Rtrn 150 x's	19.74%	20.95%	80.18%	133.11%	233.62%
100 MultiPick over 80	0.61%	0.32%	2.95%	5.28%	10.00%
Without "Divi-X"	18.08%	20.07%	72.14%	118.71%	206.33%
All returns are accumulated, not averaged.					

A few things to note about these charts:

There is no difference in the 'Without "Divi-X" returns from the "Multiplier Pick" of 80 examples because the only variables that change in all of these examples, is the amount of leverage used with "Divi-X." 'Without "Divi-X" does not use leverage so the percentage returns would be the same if you invested one dollar or one million dollars.

It's also worth mentioning that any increase in the "Multiplier Pick" also changes, and in most cases, greatly improves the outcome of yields over time highlighted earlier in Chapter 6. I thought I would point that out in lieu of posting more charts, although I could look at them all day, but maybe I'm biased. In these examples, increasing the "Multiplier Pick" from 80 to 100 increased the yields over time, primarily because you used less cash out of pocket for the same amount of shares and the higher margin balances were reduced faster because of the larger payments as a result of keeping the "PmtPerc" variable at the same 1.25% of the outstanding balance.

It's also worth noting that in the vast majority of these Dow 30 examples, increasing the "Multiplier Pick" to 100 still kept the leverage percentage below fifty percent. In the three (DuPont, AT&T, and Verizon) that exceeded fifty percent, it was by a very modest amount, maybe five or six percentage points and they all kicked butt (not an indicator for future performance).

Chapter 9
"Divi-X" – Is it Magic?

It Just Seems Too Good To Be True

This program has evolved considerably since I began writing this book over a year ago. I have added so many features and functionality in the program that I had not even considered when I started this project. Payment options, dividend reinvestment, twenty year yield projections, these were not part of the original program. And even though I have added these really cool features to offer you maximum flexibility to invest the way that is most comfortable to you, I really do not want the original premise of the "Divi-X" system to be overlooked.

The most significant and major underlying principal behind the "Divi-X" system is to earn income while your investments pay for themselves. To maximize yield on your investment dollars regardless of the direction of the market and hopefully, in the long-term, walk away with a nice profit when you cash out.

To accomplish the above, the "Divi-X" system was developed to utilize the "PmtPerc" function without 'dividend reinvestment.' I have built tremendous flexibility into the "Divi-X" system which will allow you to go off in a direction that was not the original goal of this program and that's okay if it works for you because ultimately, the whole purpose of this program is to create value for you. But to benefit from the majority of the material in this book, utilizing "PmtPerc" without 'dividend reinvestment' is the most prudent use of the program.

Upping the Ante

I've been using one hundred share lots throughout this book to keep it simple, but I'm going to up the ante a little bit on this one just to make it look a little bit more impressive. For this example, I thought I would us one thousand shares.

Let's say we purchased one thousand shares of **ABC, Incorporated (ABC)** at $10.00 a share with an annual yield of 6.4%, or $ .16 a share quarterly. A couple of months after you purchased it, **XYZ, LLC (XYZ)** files a lawsuit claiming **ABC, Incorporated** is using **XYZ, LLC's** "LMNOP" technology in its educational software and it immediately drops to $8.00 a share, a twenty percent drop. Educational software isn't ABC, Inc.'s only source of revenue, maybe less than seven percent of it, so it isn't like the lawsuit puts the company in any real danger of going out of business, nonetheless the market saw fit to punish ABC's share price.

Now here is another gem of beauty in the "Divi-X" system. Sure we would have liked to purchase ABC, Inc. after the drop (if you decided to still hold after a twenty percent drop), but I'm sure you already know, "@#&%" happens and here we are. If you had paid for the full one thousand shares with cash, out of pocket, and you sold on the drop, you would already be out of $2000. If you continued to hold, you would only be down $2000. If you used the "Divi-X" system and sold on the hit, you would still be out $2000. "Divi-X" is an investment enhancer, and while it may seem to work magic, it is not a miracle worker. However, if you decided to hold, here's how the two different scenarios would look like.

In this situation, without "Divi-X" and with "Divi-X" both decide to hold and wait for the share price to recover. Part of that decision was reached because ABC, Incorporated has a history of increasing its annual dividend since its inception twenty-five years ago. The increase we use here is $.01 cent a year.

	Without "Divi-X"	With "Divi-X"
Purchased 1000 @ $10/share	$10,000	$5733.33
Dividends Received YR1	$640	$640
Margin Interest Expense YR1	$0	$319.90
Net Dividend Income YR1	$640	320.10
Yield On Cash Invested YR1	**6.40%**	**5.58%**
Dividends Received YR2	$759.96	759.96
Margin Interest Expense YR2	$0	$297.46
Net Dividend Income YR2	$759.96	$462.50
Yield On Cash Invested YR2	**7.6%**	**8.07%**

Fig. 9.1

You can see that while both scenarios wait for the share price to recover, after the second year, "Divi-X" is already earning a greater percentage on its money than without "Divi-X." This spread will widen every year whether the company increases its dividends or not because as the interest payments get smaller, the yield continues to get bigger. Oh, and let's not forget about the potential returns on the other investments "Divi-X" purchased with the other $4266.67 ($10,000 - $5733.33).

Fig. 9.2, on the next page, is what a twenty year chart of yields on ABC, Incorporated (ABC) would look like. The most notable points are year two (2017) when the "Divi-X" 'Cash Yield' of 8.07% surpasses the 'Stock Yield' of 7.60%. Next is year five because five year time horizons are what we look at the most in this book and are the maximum time frame that the "Divi-X" System Workbook tracks (I actually expanded the program for twenty years but the files were too massive). Here, the "Divi-X" 'Cash Yield' has widened its margin over the 'Stock Yield' by 4.16% to an impressive 15.36%. And lastly, the twenty year yields. "Divi-X" does not track individual investments that far out, but I had to add this feature because the results are too compelling to ignore. After twenty years, if everything plays out as planned (but never does), the "Divi-X" 'Cash Yield' is now at a whopping 49.53% of actual cash invested compared to the still impressive 29.20% 'Stock Yield,' an unbelievable 20.33% lead.

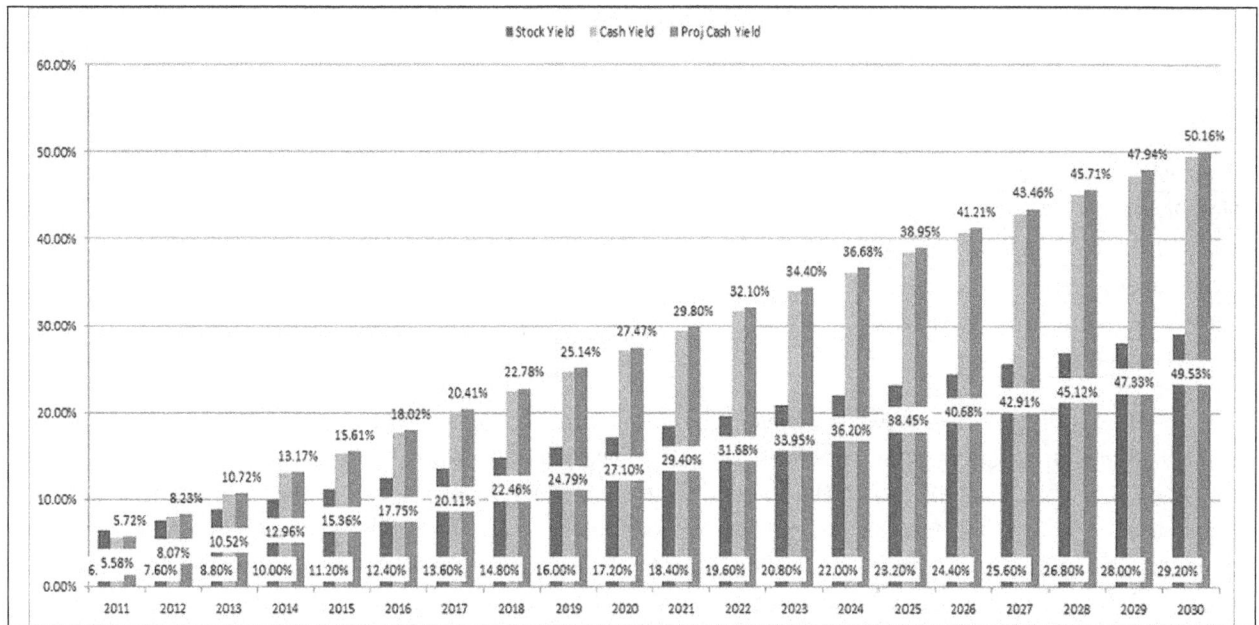

Figure 9.2

Believe it or not, if you were to continue to hold ABC, Incorporated (ABC) for longer than twenty years, that margin would widen still. It would widen at a slower pace because as the interest payments get smaller, its contribution to yield slows down.

By now you are probably wondering what has happened to the share price of ABC, Incorporated (ABC) and believe it or not, after five long years, it has finally managed to get back up to exactly $10 a share after the verdict came back in favor of ABC, Inc. and found they were not using XYZ's "LMNOP" technology after all. This news has come just in time to. You had every intention of holding ABC, Inc. until retirement, but XYZ, LLC just released "LMNOP 2.0." There's no way ABC, Inc. can compete with that so you decide it's in your long-term best interest to sell ABC, Inc. (goodbye 15.36% yield ☹) and reinvest it into XYZ,LLC. Here's where it gets very confusing so pay close attention.

Without "Divi-X" it's pretty cut and dry. He invested $10,000 cash, collected some nice dividends along the way and he gets his $10,000 cash back. His overall return after five years came to 44% even, or an average of 8.8% a year.

With "Divi-X" is not so simple. Don't get me wrong, it isn't hard either. If the day were to come when you decided to sell a security using the "Divi-X" system, this is how it would play out.

When you purchased ABC, Incorporated (ABC), you borrowed $4266.67 ($10,000 - $5733.33). That money has to be paid back. When you set your purchase up using the "Divi-X" system, you set up the terms of how you were going to pay it back. For example, if you chose the "Interest Only" option you decided that you would pay back the loan when you sell the securities. If you chose the "PmtPerc" option you decided you would pay down the balance with dividends while you held the security. This is how either option would look on paper after five years.

	"Divi-X" Interest Only	"Divi-X" PmtPerc
Purchase 1000 shares @ $10 share	$10,000	$10,000
Borrowed On Margin	$4266.67	$4266.67
Dividends for five years	$4399.84	$4399.84
Interest Paid for five years	$1653.33	$1390.31
Net Dividends after five years	$2746.51	$1300.61
Loan Balance after five years	$4266.67	$3002.22
Net Proceeds from sale after margin	$5733.33	$6997.78
"Divi-X" Returns after five years	47.90%	52.49%
Five year average returns	9.58%	10.5%

Fig. 9.3

Now, to look at these two examples, you could draw a couple of conclusions. If I choose "Interest Only" I'll net more income while I hold ABC, Inc. If I pay down the balance by choosing "PmtPerc" I'll get a bigger payoff when I sell (of course that is only if the share price recovers) but it doesn't matter. When all is said and done, the only figures that matter are your sell price and interest expense. When you receive a dividend while you are borrowing on margin, your broker doesn't itemize things such as loan payments or break out how much interest you are paying on a specific security. All of your margin activity is just lumped together. That dividend you just received went towards paying down your margin balance as a whole, not the self-imposed loan you put on ABC, Inc. but as soon as it lowers your margin balance, it's available for use again immediately. At the end of the month, your broker takes his due interest on your entire margin balance so ultimately, it is in your best interest to keep interest to a minimum. Therefore, using the "PmtPerc" option is always preferable to the "Interest Only" option unless you have more profitable prospects to invest your extra cash in.

Why It Should Matter?

The relationship between you and your broker is a little like you and your boss. He makes available your standard of living by exchanging your wages for your employment. It's not his place to see how you are spending your paycheck so if some of that check happens to buy food for the family, your boss doesn't care what kind of food or how much food you spend your money on. If your car breaks down and you have to take a cab to work all he cares about is that you made it to work. In other words, it's entirely up to you to make sure your money is being used wisely.

Here's a snapshot of a portfolio after five years. These are all fictitious companies. I apologize but screening over 30,000 securities to find examples to make my point here would be extremely tedious and as you all know, I'm trying to get this book out the door. Also, for simplicity sake, these thinly traded, fictitious stocks only had two trading days; the day they were purchased, and the exact day five years later.

Security Name	Purchase Date	Purchase Price	Qty	Share Value	Current Price	Current Value	% Gain/ Loss
ABC, Inc. (ABC)	7/26/10	10.00	1000	10,000.00	10.25	10,250.00	2.5%
Water Treader's Franchise (WTF)	7/26/10	74.95	500	37,475.00	82.00	41,000.00	8.6%
M. T. Bank (MTB)	7/26/10	122.43	250	30,607.50	129.58	32,395.00	5.3%
Down The Drain Plumbing(DDP)	7/26/10	26.99	100	$2699.00	29.66	2966.00	9.0%
U. R. Broker, Inc. (URB)	7/26/10	50.05	50	2502.50	100.10	5005.00	100.0%
				83,284.00		91,616.00	9.1%
						5YR AVG	1.82%

Fig. 9.4

Here's the story behind our fictitious portfolio. Mr. Smith just inherited $50,000 from a distant relative. Making, what he thinks is, a wise decision, Mr. Smith puts his money to work for him immediately by opening a margin account under the advice of his new broker at U.R. Broker, Inc. (URB). Upon opening his new account, he notices that the broker has made a huge mistake. They accidentally doubled his deposit, allowing Mr. Smith to invest as much as $100,000! Being the honest person that he is, he hurriedly called his broker to report their error. Imagine his shock when his broker informs him that it was no error and then proceeds to explain to Mr. Smith, the concept of margin.

Recognizing the potential of this new, very powerful tool made available to him he asks his broker to show him a handful of good stock picks. His broker then shows him a list of consistent dividend plays as well as making a recommendation that he take a position in U.R. Broker, Inc. (URB) (which pays no dividend) as well. Sensing a slight sales pitch, but appreciative for the effort his broker has spent with him, Mr. Smith agrees to take a small position and will consider increasing it if his portfolio does well.

After tallying up the total of all the picks recommended to him, he notices right away that he is going to have to take advantage of the margin extended to him. Here's how that would look:

Cash in Account:	$ 50,000	Cash Used in Purchase:	$50,000
Available Margin:	$ 50,000	Margin Used:	$33,284
Total Buying Power:	$100,000	Total Purchase:	$83,284

Notice that all of his cash was invested first and then the balance was covered by margin. Now, if you want to hold on to some of your cash, simply do not put it all in your margin account. You could take $5000 out of your margin account, leaving a cash balance of $45,000 and a match of $45,000, giving you $90,000 of purchasing power instead of $100,000. It's still enough to cover this example and would look like this:

Cash in Account:	$45,000	Cash Used in Purchase:	$45,000
Available Margin:	$45,000	Margin Used:	$38,284
Total Buying Power:	$90,000	Total Purchase:	$83,284

Other than paying additional interest in the second example, either way doesn't matter much. Had you used the first example and you later needed the cash, your margin account likely would allow you to draw on it for use outside of the account, most likely, not the whole $16,716, but probably half of that amount. Again, check with your broker for details.

If you plan on using "Divi-X" or not, and you plan on using a leverage ratio of less than 50% on all of your purchases, you could keep all of your cash in a separate account, with a transfer feature between it and your margin account, and simply add the cash to your margin account when you want to make a purchase. Since the amount you deposit covers at least, or more than, 50% of the purchase amount, you will never use any more margin than you intended to and will always have access to your cash.

Mr. Smith Five Years Later

Fast forward five years (**Fig. 9.4**), we get to see how well Mr. Smith's portfolio stood a test of time. Looking at his most recent statement, he really wishes he put more into (URB) when his broker recommended it, that literally doubled. Next, he sees that his portfolio did no better than an average annual return of 1.82% a year, shown in **Fig. 9.4**. Somewhat dismayed, he calls his broker to express his dissatisfaction. His broker calmly reminds him that the majority of his shares paid dividends and that's not accounted for in his total returns. Feeling a bit embarrassed for overlooking something so obvious, he asks his broker how much his actual returns are when factoring in the dividends but his broker can't tell him because they don't track that much information. After Mr. Smith hangs up with his broker, he tries to determine the real rate of return on his investments with the dividends included (Mr. Smith would already know this if he used 'The "Divi-X" System Workbook').

After spending a whole day going through the year-end statements for the last five years, Mr. Smith retrieved the exact amount that was paid on each security in dividends, and this time, had the foresight to make note of the margin interest he paid every year as well.

In Reality

In the real world we usually lump everything together and average it all out and hope we finish off better than when we started. But in reality, is that always the best thing to do? Personally, I'm not opposed to the concept. I think it's a good barometer to let you know when your good decisions have surpassed your bad ones and vice versa.

In the case of Mr. Smith, the real world has told him that his "stock selections" have averaged 3.7% a year for the last five years (**Fig. 9.5**). Now that he's accounting for dividends it just slightly doubles the 1.82% average he thought he had. But in reality, did his "portfolio" earn 3.7% a year for the last five years? I'm sure you noticed in **Fig. 9.5**, that I left the "Margin Exp" and the "Net Return" fields empty. You may be suspecting that I did that because I'm about to drop a "Dun, Dun, Dunnnnn!!!" moment on you, and you're right. Are you ready?

Security Name	Share Value	Unrealized Gain	Dividends	Total Return	% Gain/Loss
ABC, Inc. (ABC)	10,000.00	250.00	1280.00*	1530.00	15.3%
Water Treader's Franchise (WTF)	37,475.00	3525.00	4249.80	7774.00	20.7%
M. T. Bank (MTB)	30,607.50	1787.50	800.00*	2587.50	8.5%
Down The Drain Plumbing(DDP)	$2699.00	267.00	720.00	987.00	36.6%
U. R. Broker, Inc. (URB)	2502.50	2502.50	0.00	2502.50	100.0%
	83,284.00	8332.00	7049.80	15,381.80	18.5%

Total Return	15,381.80
Margin Exp.	
Net Return	
5YR AVG	3.7%

*dividend reduced or eliminated

Fig. 9.5

Once you factor in "Margin Exp," his actual return is dramatically less than, not the 3.7% he thought he had after he added dividends, but dramatically less than the 1.82% he thought he initially had in **Fig. 9.4**! "Dun, Dun...." Wait. That's not it. You see, Mr. Smith opted to "let it ride." He figured the dividend payments would pay at least the interest on the margin loan and his gains would eventually, more than pay off the outstanding balance and leave him with a very nice profit. The only problem was that (wait for it... wait for it) the dividend payments **didn't even cover the monthly interest on his margin loan. "Dun, Dun, Dunnnnn!!!** Because he failed to cover the monthly interest on his margin loan, the balance kept going higher, and so did his interest expense **(Fig. 9.6)**.

Security Name	Share Value	Unrealized Gain	Dividends	Total Return	% Gain/Loss
ABC, Inc. (ABC)	10,000.00	250.00	1280.00*	1530.00	15.3%
Water Treader's Franchise (WTF)	37,475.00	3525.00	4249.80	7774.00	20.7%
M. T. Bank (MTB)	30,607.50	1787.50	800.00*	2587.50	8.5%
Down The Drain Plumbing(DDP)	$2699.00	267.00	720.00	987.00	36.6%
U. R. Broker, Inc. (URB)	2502.50	2502.50	0.00	2502.50	100.0%
	83,284.00	8332.00	7049.80	15,381.80	18.5%
				Total Return	15,381.80
				Margin Exp	13,275.18
				Net Return	2.5%
				5YR AVG	**0.5%**

*dividend reduced or eliminated

Fig. 9.6

What Went Wrong?

In the real world, I'm certain it wouldn't have taken Mr. Smith five years to notice that his portfolio balance was going down from time to time, but would he have known this was the problem? Or would he have just assumed his picks were having a bad month, or year, or whatever?

I'm going to try to walk through this in chronological order. When Mr. Smith made his purchases, they were made in the exact order listed in **Fig. 9.7**. Now, we're not assuming for the sake of assuming. If you were to do what I'm about to show you, it would play out in a very similar fashion, but for this example, let's just assume the purchases were made as listed in **Fig. 9.7**.

Security Name	Share Value	Cash Used	Leverage Amount	Total Return (Incl. DIV's)	% Gain/Loss	Margin Expense	Real Returns
ABC, Inc. (ABC)	10,000.00	10,000	0.00	1530.00	15.3%	0.00	15.3%
Water Treader's Franchise (WTF)	37,475.00	37,475.00	0.00	7774.00	20.7%	0.00	20.7%
M. T. Bank (MTB)	30,607.50	2525.00	28,082.50	2587.50	8.5%	12,453.09*	(-32.2%)
Down The Drain Plumbing(DDP)	$2699.00	0.00	2699.00	987.00	36.6%	1073.12	(-3.2%)
U. R. Broker, Inc. (URB)	2502.50	0.00	2502.50	2502.50	100.0%	1134.37	54.7%
	83,284.00	50,000.00	33,284.00	15,381.80	18.5%		
				Total Return	15,381.80		
				Margin Exp	13,275.18	14660.58	
				Net Return	2.5%		
				5YR AVG	**0.5%**		

*Interest on 91.75% of total

Fig. 9.7

In the real world we usually lump everything together and average it all out and hope we finish off better than when we started. But in reality, is that always the best thing to do? Suppose Mr. Smith were to stagger his purchases instead of purchasing them all at once, do you think he would have invested in M.T. Bank, Down The Drain Plumbing, or even U.R. Broker, for that matter, knowing they would be 100% levered (91.75% in the case of M.T. Bank because he still had a couple thousand of his own cash to put toward that purchase) as shown in **Fig. 9.7.**?

If you are wondering why the "Margin Expense" is higher now ($14,660.58) than in **Fig. 9.6**, it's because we broke out the actual "Margin Expense" associated with each security. In **Fig. 9.6**, the figure was lower because the dividends from all securities went toward the outstanding balance. In **Fig. 9.7**, we only applied the dividends paid by the securities that used margin, essentially making them pull their own weight. U.R. Broker's return drops dramatically because it paid no dividend and now it actually reflects the interest that would have been paid for the last five years but wasn't accurately accounted for in the previous scenario. Still pretty, but not as nice as when Mr. Smith had the blinders on.

What Can "Divi-X" Do For You?

I would like to take the time to point out that as I am writing this for you, I have no idea what the final results of this section will be. I have so much confidence in this system, that everything you have read up till now and everything you will read after, I am learning the results the same way you are, as you read it and as I write it. I am not manufacturing probabilities to get the outcomes that I want. That is why I used the Dow 30 for most of the examples in this book. That information is easily verifiable if you wish to check it. I admitted to making up these fictitious companies for this section for simplicity, and even then, I think you can agree, it's quite involved. I knew I would be spending an abundance of time to make these points and I really didn't want to spend several more hours looking for real companies that fit the profile of these fictitious companies. What we will be diving into next, is how "Divi-X" would have guided you through the situation that Mr. Smith was, sadly, ill-informed to deal with.

Mr. Smith just inherited $50,000 from a distant relative. Making, what he thinks is, a wise decision, Mr. Smith puts his money to work for him immediately by opening a margin account under the advice of his new broker at U.R. Broker, Inc. (URB) by depositing the minimum $2000 initial deposit and then putting the remaining $48,000 in a checking account with an automatic transfer/sweep option. Upon opening his new margin account, he notices that the broker has made a huge mistake. They accidentally doubled his deposit, allowing Mr. Smith to invest as much as $4,000! Being the honest person that he is, he hurriedly called his broker to report their error. Imagine his shock when his broker informs him that it was no error and then proceeds to explain to Mr. Smith, the concept of margin.

Recognizing the potential of this new, very powerful tool made available to him he asks his broker to show him a handful of good stock picks. His broker then shows him a list of consistent dividend plays as well as making a recommendation that he take a position in U.R. Broker, Inc. (URB) (which pays no dividend) as well. Armed with a copy of 'The "Divi-X" System' that he purchased after his friend recommended it to him while fishing on his friends yacht and reading the thousands upon thousands of favorable reviews posted online, Mr. Smith would normally decline to take his broker up on the offer to invest in U.R. Broker, Inc. (URB) because it didn't pay a dividend and couldn't help Mr. Smith pay for it (I didn't say "Divi-X" was perfect). Mr. Smith did agree to give serious consideration to the other recommendations and would be in touch after he had some time to do some due diligence on them.

One at a time, Mr. Smith felt comfortable with the picks his broker made, and made the purchases after each review. He even opted for the shares of U.R. Broker, Inc. (URB) because of all the trouble his broker went through. In every purchase, he opted to use a "Multiplier Pick" of "80" and a "PmtPerc" of "1.25%," and (URB) had to be all cash because dividends wouldn't help him pay for the shares. He then deposited no more than the actual cash amount required to his brokerage account via online transfer. Here is how it all plays out and remember, for simplicity sake, these thinly traded, fictitious stocks only had two trading days; the day they were purchased, and the exact day five years later.

Security Name	Purchase Date	Purchase Price	Qty	Share Value	Cash Used	Leverage Used	Gain/Loss (net Marg. Exp.)	"Divi-X" Gain/Loss %*
ABC, Inc. (ABC)	7/26/10	10.00	1000	10,000.00	5733.33	4266.67	330.77	5.8%
Water Treader's Franchise (WTF)	8/02/10	74.95	500	37,475.00	31,808.33	5666.67	5998.39	18.9%
M. T. Bank (MTB)	8/09/10	122.43	250	30,607.50	27,940.83	2666.67	427.47	1.5%
Down The Drain Plumbing (DDP)	8/16/10	26.99	100	$2699.00	1739.00	960.00	686.02	39.4%
U. R. Broker, Inc. (URB)	8/24/10	50.05	50	2502.50	2502.50	0	2502.50	100.0%
				83,284.00	69,723.50	13,560.01	9945.15	14.3%
						5YR AVG		2.9%

*% is Return on Cash Used

Fig. 9.8

Using **Fig. 9.8**, you see that ABC, Inc. realized a 5.8% return because ABC, Inc. reduced its dividend after year one. This event caused the dividend to not be able to maintain margin payments and had to be sold. I realize that a dividend reduction would likely have a dramatic impact on a stock to the downside (not always), but I didn't punish the stock in the previous example, so I didn't punish it here.

Water Treader's Franchise was held for the entire five years with a gain of 18.9%.

M.T. Bank eliminated its dividend after year two, and as in the case of ABC, Inc., was sold because the dividends weren't there to maintain debt service payments. If you go back to **Fig. 9.7**, you'll see that M.T. Bank lost Mr. Smith (-32.2%) and "Divi-X" earned him 1.5%. Of course, you can't get rich off of a 1.5% return, but you could certainly get a whole lot poorer on a (-32.2%) loss. In addition, because M.T. Bank was sold, that principal was no longer exposed to risk (the same for ABC, Inc.) and we can therefore remove the cash paid from our total "Cash Used" column, changing that figure to $36,049.34. **As a result, our total return is not 14.3% of $69,723.50, but actually 27.6% of $36,049.34, or 5.5% for a five year average.** And as an added bonus, that $33,674.16 you cashed out could've been redeployed garnering you even higher returns to add to your 27.6%! I was going to create another fictitious company to demonstrate returns on that, but I think you get the picture.

Down The Drain Plumbing was held for the entire five years and earned Mr. Smith a very decent 39.4% on his cash investment. U.R. Broker, Inc. doubled and this time you got to keep it all because you didn't leverage any of it.

Now look, this is actually quite beautiful. Maybe its coincidence, maybe it isn't. If you look at the "Cash Used" column in **Fig. 9.8**, you notice right away that we didn't have enough cash to purchase all of these stocks using the "Divi-X" system. We had plenty of margin available, but not enough cash. Maybe that is telling us that Mr. Smith was way overleveraged in the previous scenario. After all, the dividends on his securities weren't able to even make the interest payments on the margin balance in **Fig. 9.7**. Let's tweak it a bit so our cash can cover our purchases (**Fig. 9.9**). Since we made our purchases in chronological order, we're already invested in ABC and Water Treader's. We don't have the cash "Divi-X" says we would need when we consider purchasing 250 shares of M.T. Bank, so we're going to have to reduce our purchase if we really want it.

Let's review our standing. We purchased (ABC) and (WTF) already. That leaves us with a cash balance of $12,458.34 ($50,000 – (ABC) $5733.33 and (WTF) $31,808.33). If we intend to purchase as much stock as we can using our remaining $12,458.34, using the "Divi-X" system, that allows us to purchase a total of only 111 (one hundred eleven) shares of M.T. Bank. Here is what the new scenario would look like using the "Divi-X" system the way it is meant to be used:

Security Name	Purchase Date	Purchase Price	Qty	Share Value	Cash Used	Leverage Used	Gain/Loss (net Marg. Exp.)	"Divi-X" Gain/Loss %*
ABC, Inc. (ABC)	7/26/10	10.00	1000	10,000.00	5733.33	4266.67	330.77	5.8%
Water Treader's Franchise (WTF)	8/02/10	74.95	500	37,475.00	31,808.33	5666.67	5998.39	18.9%
M. T. Bank (MTB)	8/09/10	122.43	111	13,589.73	12,405.73	1184.00	189.80	1.53%
Down The Drain Plumbing (DDP)					0.00	0.00		0.00%
U. R. Broker, Inc. (URB)	8/24/10	50.05	50	2502.50	0.00	2502.50	2502.50	54.7%
				66,266.23	49,947.39	13,619.84	9021.46	18.1%
						5YR AVG		3.62%

*% is Return on Cash Used
Fig. 9.9

We would have had to pass on Down The Drain Plumbing because the dividends would not have supported the interest payments associated with a margin loan at one hundred percent. We would have had to leverage it at 100% because we had already used all of our cash in our first three investments. We would also have had to pass on U.R. Broker, Inc. because it paid no dividend and we had no cash. However, if you really, really, wanted to buy it, you could and the dividends from your other investments would cover the debt service even after the (ABC) dividend cut and the (MTB) dividend elimination. Just remember though, five years ago you didn't know it was going to double in price.

Now the actions taken in the above paragraph pertaining to (URB) are an unofficial recommendation of how to use the "Divi-X" system, the way it was intended to be used in order to have your investments help pay for themselves. I am not saying, however, that you should exclude yourself from investment opportunities because they don't pay dividends. Once you start using the program yourself, it's entirely up to you on how to use it. If you decide to purchase securities that do not cover at least the minimum interest payments or if you choose to invest in securities that pay no dividends, you should still fill out a "Leverage Projection Worksheet." In doing so, you will still be able to track actual results of your securities by monitoring the impact interest is having on your returns.

One final point about **Fig. 9.9** and we'll rap this up. Just like in the example in **Fig. 9.8**, because Mr. Smith sold his position in M.T. Bank (MTB) when they eliminated the dividend and ABC Inc. when it reduced its dividend, the cash paid portion in our "Cash Used" column gets removed from the total leaving only $31,808.33 exposed to risk (the leverage amount would be removed as well making it available for use elsewhere, as well as, lowering our interest expense and adding to our total return but I'm not going to count that figure here). **As a result, our total return is not 18.1% of $49,947.39, but actually 28.4% on $31,808.33, or 5.7% for a five year average.** Also, note that you have more cash and now you can pay off the margin on U.R. Broker, Inc. saving on the interest expense associated with that and adding another half a percent to your annual average returns.

I think you would have to agree that "Divi-X" left Mr. Smith in a far better position at 5.7% a year than going it alone and only realizing a pittance of a return at 0.5% a year.

In Closing

I hope that in this chapter, I showed you some of the tremendous potential the "Divi-X" can provide you. I also realize that some of you may be thinking this is all smoke and mirrors or some type of accounting trickery, but nothing is further from the truth. By using the "Divi-X" system, you are treating the funds in your account as if you were borrowing external money and some of you will indeed be using external money if the rates justify it. If you maintain discipline while using the "Divi-X" system, the potential for returns showcased in this book are very real. It gives you much more awareness than just relying on the generic information provided to you on your brokerage statement. Don't get me wrong, I'm not knocking brokerage firms. I consider the margin they extend to me a wonderful gift, but just like it isn't your boss's job to tell you how to spend your pay check, it's not your brokers job to tell you how to invest.

The "Divi-X" System gives you the power to no longer have to settle for overall results based on the average returns of your portfolio. "Divi-X" gives you the power to project, lever, and track your securities' performances on a very precise level, granting you the ability to pinpoint weakness in your portfolio at any time and alerting you to investments that are falling short of your expectations.

Chapter 10
"Divi-X" to the Max

"Divi-X" to the Max

Please take note of the following assumptions:

1. The following charts assume a "PmtPerc" of 1% as opposed to the 1.25% in all of the previous examples. The reason for this is because a "PmtPerc" of 1% is just enough to cover the monthly interest associated with the margin loan with a few pennies to spare.

2. Margin Rate is assumed at 7.75% as in all examples in this guide. Be mindful, if you are a long-term holder, this rate will change periodically. Also, if you are fortunate enough to keep increasing your margin account balance, you rate will likely go down simply by passing balance thresholds. If not, shop for another broker.

3. The "Multiplier Pick" is maxed up to the point that at least all interest is covered by the dividends. That "Multiplier Pick" is 154.

4. Do not be discouraged from using such a high "Multiplier Pick" in your investments. If a company pays a low yield, a very high "Multiplier Pick" would still keep leverage levels well within reason.

5. Some of the returns in this chapter are absolutely mind-blowing, but showcasing them here is not an endorsement to always use a maximum "Multiplier Pick."

Remember: "Equal Cash Unleveraged" and 'Without "Divi-X" are used interchangeably

AXP	American Express		Purchase @ 24.64 share		Yield 2.92%

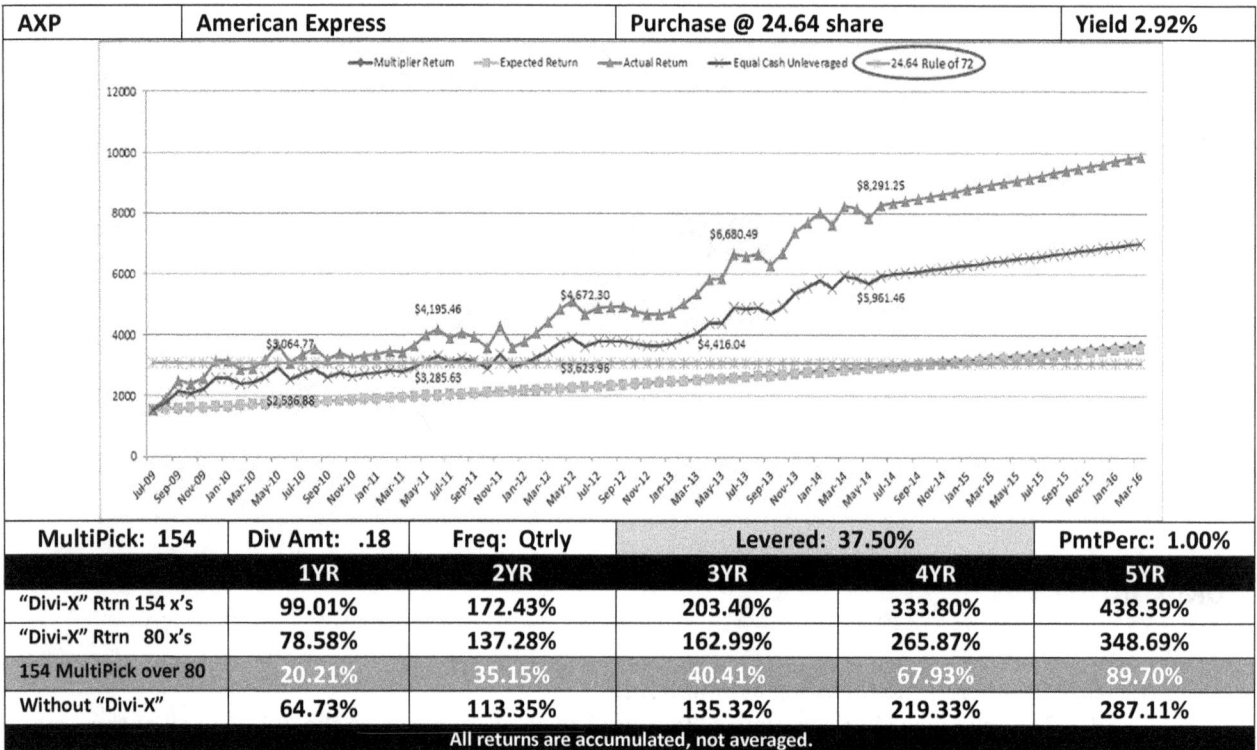

MultiPick: 154	Div Amt: .18	Freq: Qtrly	Levered: 37.50%		PmtPerc: 1.00%
	1YR	2YR	3YR	4YR	5YR
"Divi-X" Rtrn 154 x's	99.01%	172.43%	203.40%	333.80%	438.39%
"Divi-X" Rtrn 80 x's	78.58%	137.28%	162.99%	265.87%	348.69%
154 MultiPick over 80	20.21%	35.15%	40.41%	67.93%	89.70%
Without "Divi-X"	64.73%	113.35%	135.32%	219.33%	287.11%
All returns are accumulated, not averaged.					

BA	Boeing Co.		Purchase @ 48.44 share		Yield 3.47%

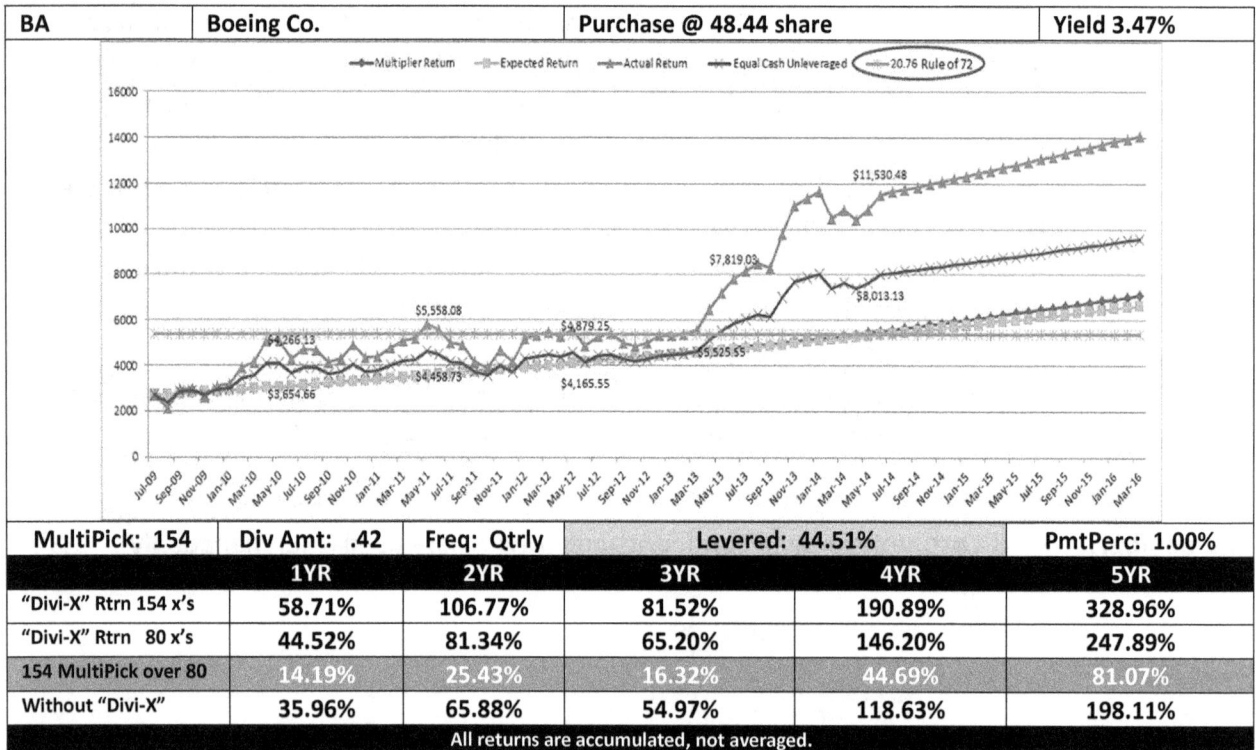

MultiPick: 154	Div Amt: .42	Freq: Qtrly	Levered: 44.51%		PmtPerc: 1.00%
	1YR	2YR	3YR	4YR	5YR
"Divi-X" Rtrn 154 x's	58.71%	106.77%	81.52%	190.89%	328.96%
"Divi-X" Rtrn 80 x's	44.52%	81.34%	65.20%	146.20%	247.89%
154 MultiPick over 80	14.19%	25.43%	16.32%	44.69%	81.07%
Without "Divi-X"	35.96%	65.88%	54.97%	118.63%	198.11%
All returns are accumulated, not averaged.					

CAT	Caterpillar	Purchase @ 33.65 share	Yield 4.99%

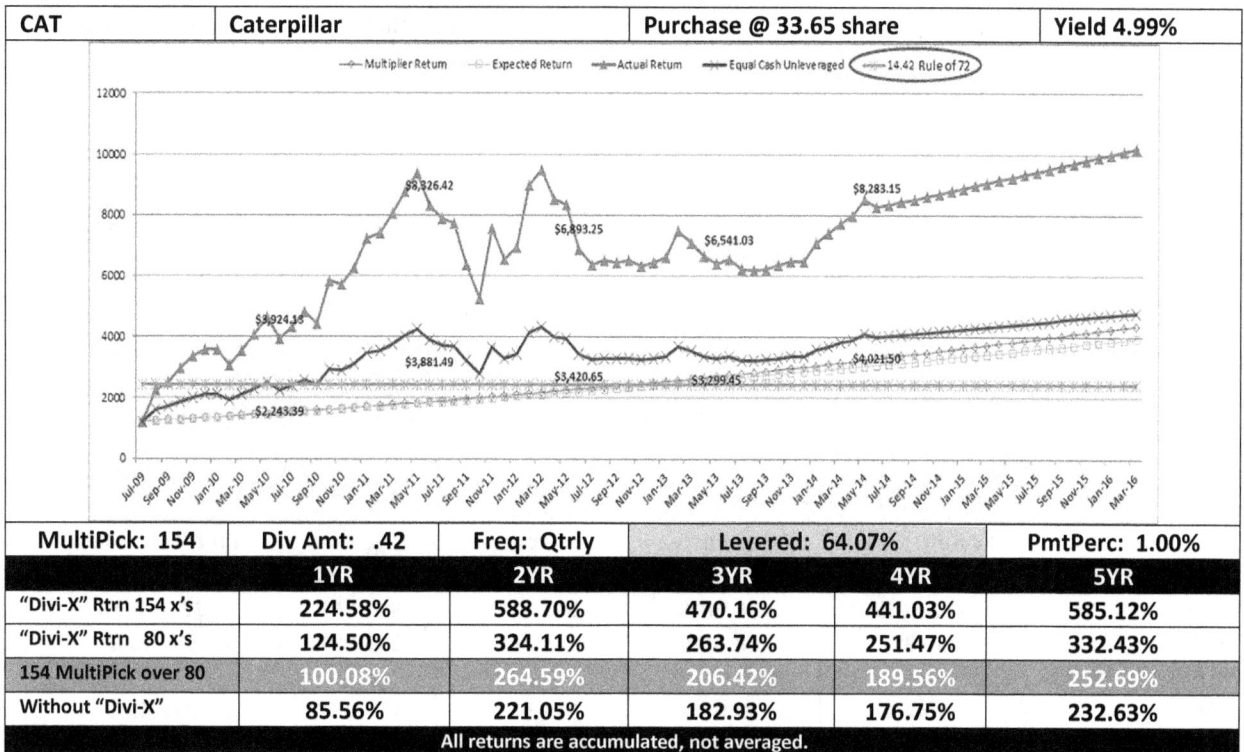

MultiPick: 154	Div Amt: .42	Freq: Qtrly	Levered: 64.07%		PmtPerc: 1.00%
	1YR	2YR	3YR	4YR	5YR
"Divi-X" Rtrn 154 x's	224.58%	588.70%	470.16%	441.03%	585.12%
"Divi-X" Rtrn 80 x's	124.50%	324.11%	263.74%	251.47%	332.43%
154 MultiPick over 80	100.08%	264.59%	206.42%	189.56%	252.69%
Without "Divi-X"	85.56%	221.05%	182.93%	176.75%	232.63%
All returns are accumulated, not averaged.					

CVX	Chevron Corporation	Purchase @ 68.06 share	Yield: 4.00%

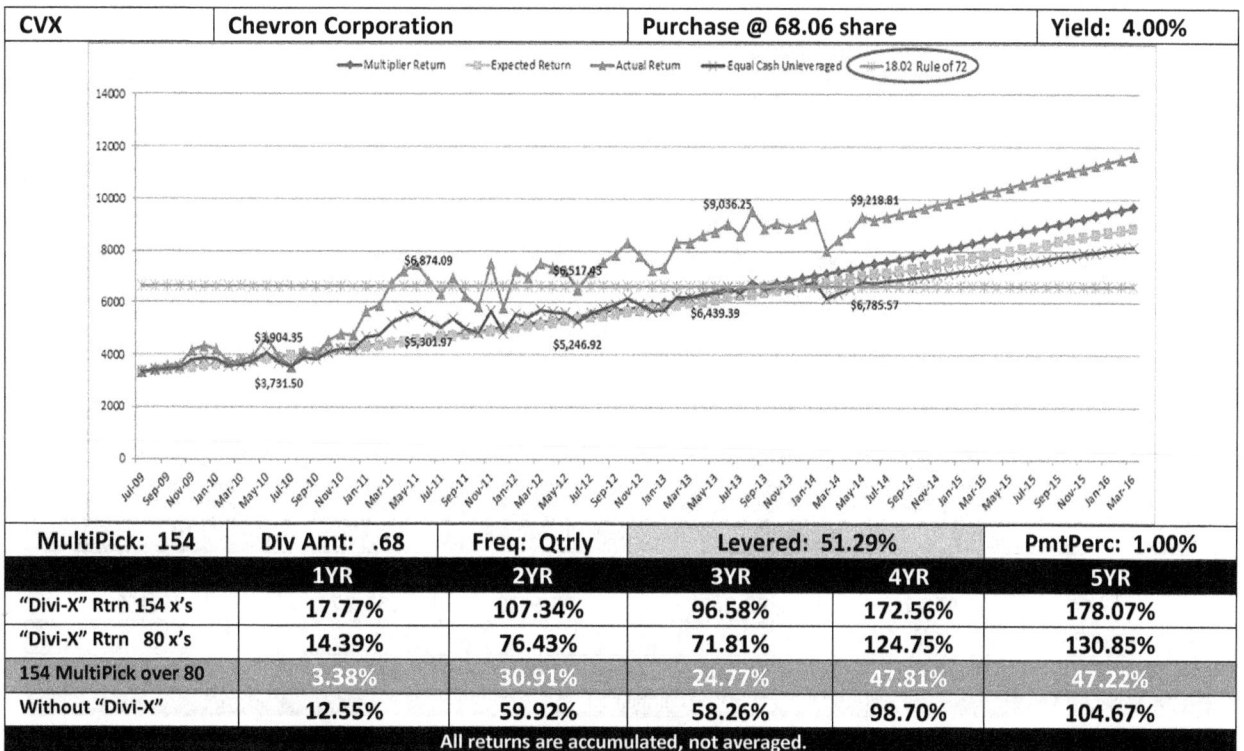

MultiPick: 154	Div Amt: .68	Freq: Qtrly	Levered: 51.29%		PmtPerc: 1.00%
	1YR	2YR	3YR	4YR	5YR
"Divi-X" Rtrn 154 x's	17.77%	107.34%	96.58%	172.56%	178.07%
"Divi-X" Rtrn 80 x's	14.39%	76.43%	71.81%	124.75%	130.85%
154 MultiPick over 80	3.38%	30.91%	24.77%	47.81%	47.22%
Without "Divi-X"	12.55%	59.92%	58.26%	98.70%	104.67%
All returns are accumulated, not averaged.					

DD	E I Dupont De Nemours and Co	Purchase @ $24.97 share	Yield: 6.57%

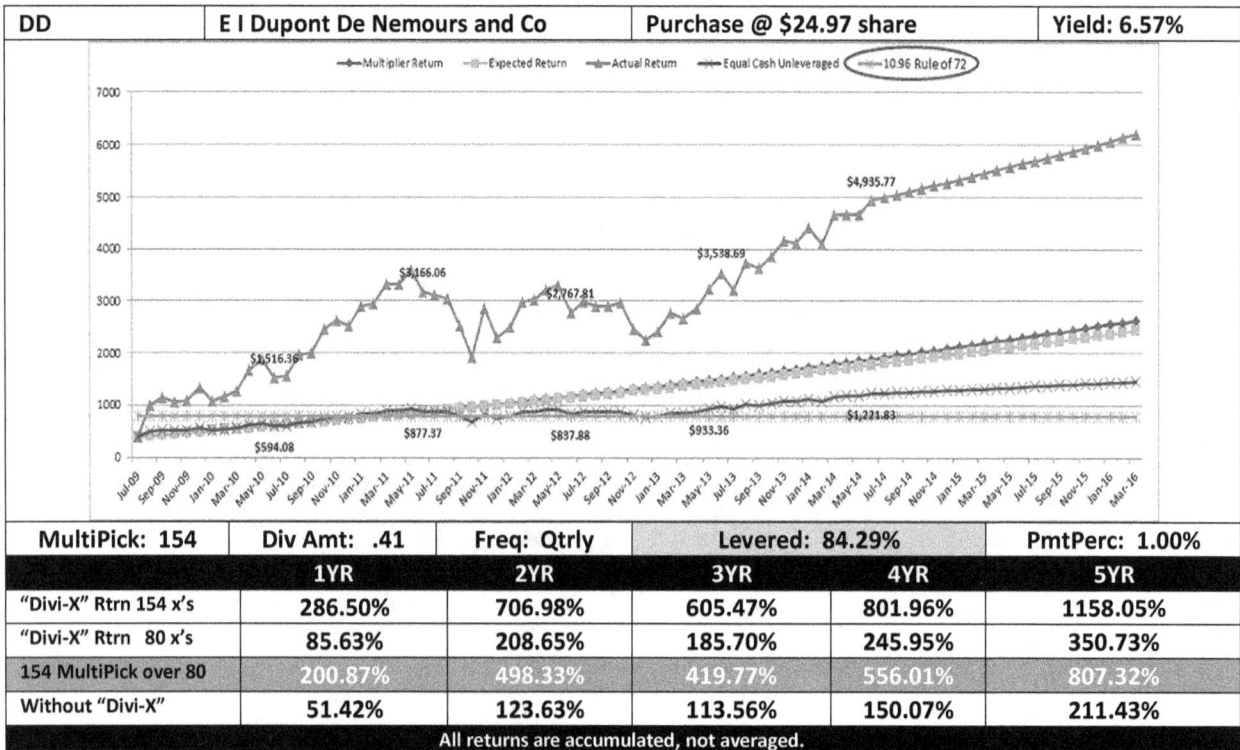

Multiplier Return — Expected Return — Actual Return — Equal Cash Unleveraged — 10.96 Rule of 72

$4,935.77
$3,538.69
$3,166.06
$2,767.81
$1,516.36
$877.37
$837.88
$933.36
$594.08
$1,221.83

MultiPick: 154	Div Amt: .41	Freq: Qtrly	Levered: 84.29%		PmtPerc: 1.00%
	1YR	2YR	3YR	4YR	5YR
"Divi-X" Rtrn 154 x's	286.50%	706.98%	605.47%	801.96%	1158.05%
"Divi-X" Rtrn 80 x's	85.63%	208.65%	185.70%	245.95%	350.73%
154 MultiPick over 80	200.87%	498.33%	419.77%	556.01%	807.32%
Without "Divi-X"	51.42%	123.63%	113.56%	150.07%	211.43%
All returns are accumulated, not averaged.					

GE	General Electric	Purchase @ $12.10 share	Yield: 3.31%

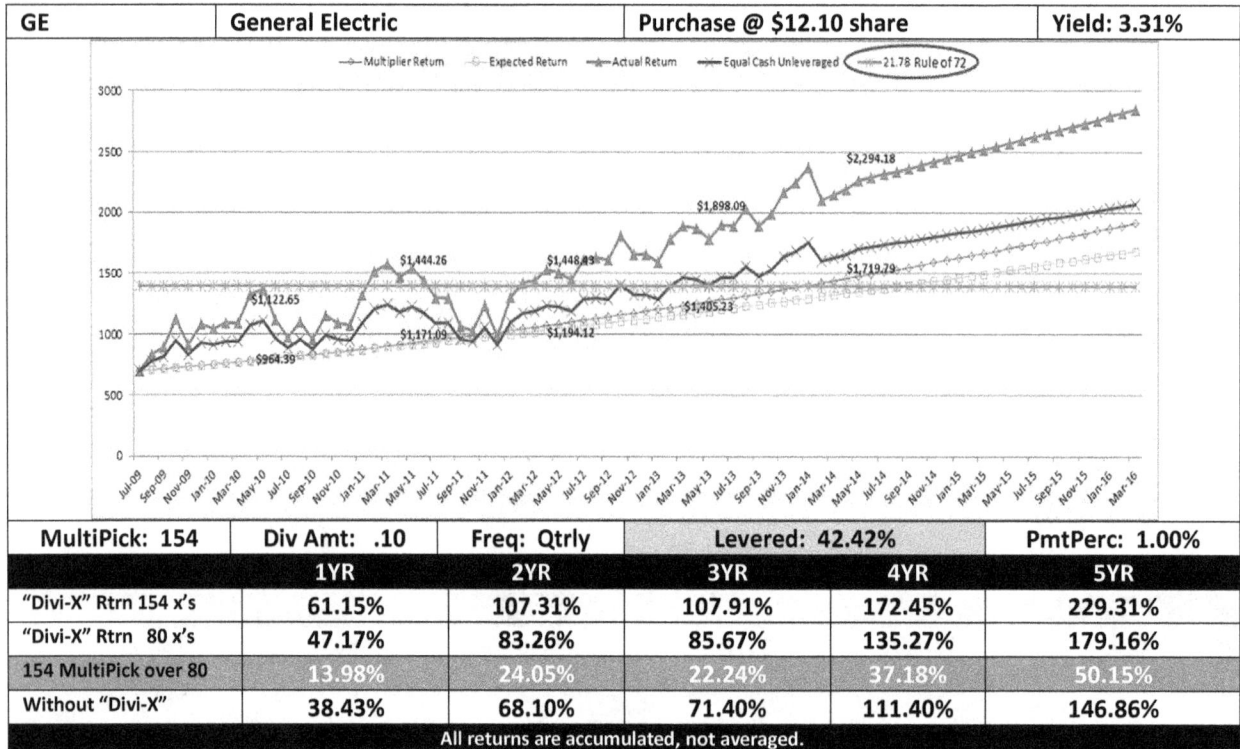

Multiplier Return — Expected Return — Actual Return — Equal Cash Unleveraged — 21.78 Rule of 72

$2,294.18
$1,898.09
$1,448.83
$1,444.26
$1,719.79
$1,122.65
$1,405.23
$1,171.09
$1,194.12
$964.39

MultiPick: 154	Div Amt: .10	Freq: Qtrly	Levered: 42.42%		PmtPerc: 1.00%
	1YR	2YR	3YR	4YR	5YR
"Divi-X" Rtrn 154 x's	61.15%	107.31%	107.91%	172.45%	229.31%
"Divi-X" Rtrn 80 x's	47.17%	83.26%	85.67%	135.27%	179.16%
154 MultiPick over 80	13.98%	24.05%	22.24%	37.18%	50.15%
Without "Divi-X"	38.43%	68.10%	71.40%	111.40%	146.86%
All returns are accumulated, not averaged.					

GS	Goldman Sachs Group, Inc.	Purchase @ $146.74 share	Yield: 0.95%

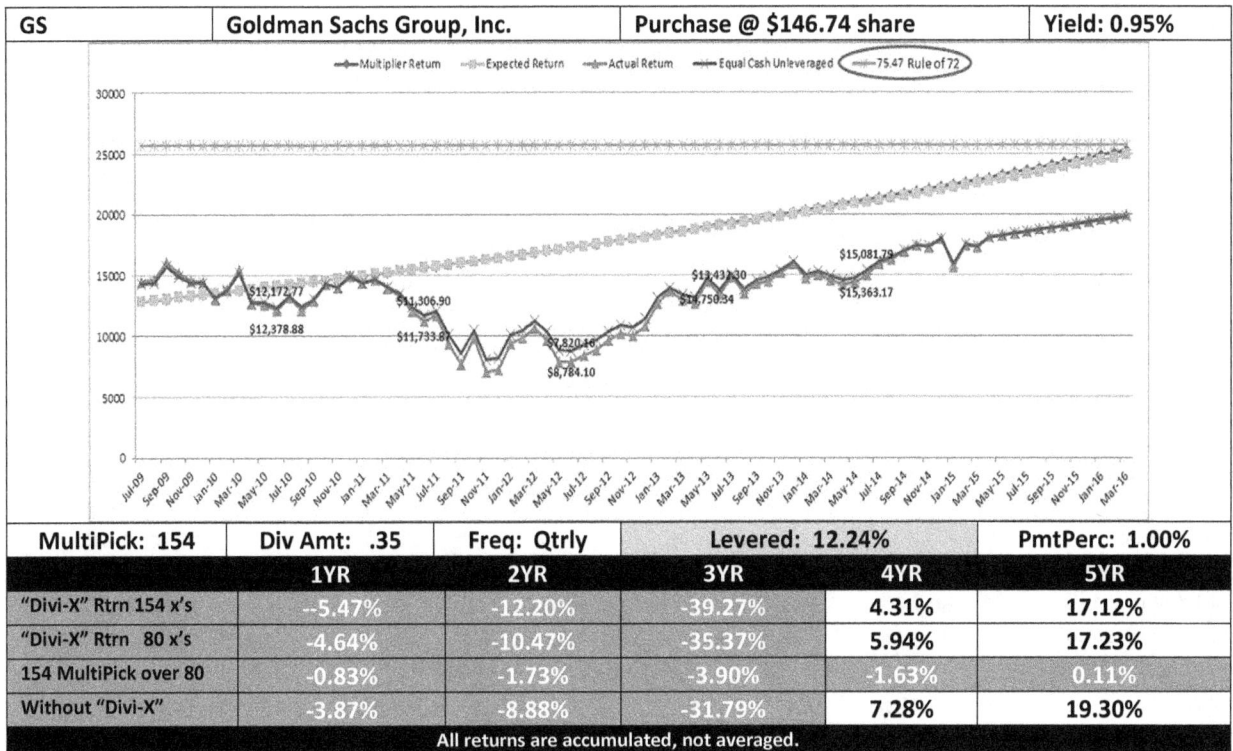

MultiPick: 154	Div Amt: .35	Freq: Qtrly	Levered: 12.24%		PmtPerc: 1.00%
	1YR	2YR	3YR	4YR	5YR
"Divi-X" Rtrn 154 x's	--5.47%	-12.20%	-39.27%	4.31%	17.12%
"Divi-X" Rtrn 80 x's	-4.64%	-10.47%	-35.37%	5.94%	17.23%
154 MultiPick over 80	-0.83%	-1.73%	-3.90%	-1.63%	0.11%
Without "Divi-X"	-3.87%	-8.88%	-31.79%	7.28%	19.30%
All returns are accumulated, not averaged.					

HD	Home Depot	Purchase @ $23.61 share	Yield: 3.81%

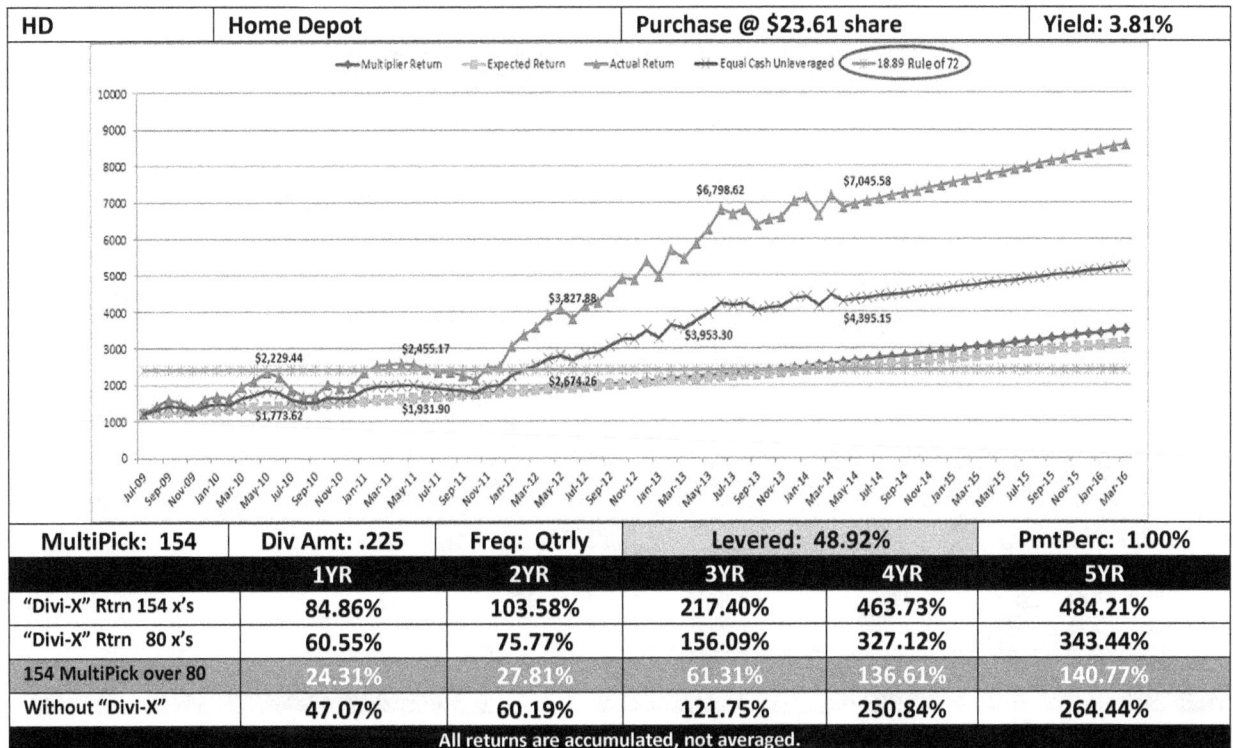

MultiPick: 154	Div Amt: .225	Freq: Qtrly	Levered: 48.92%		PmtPerc: 1.00%
	1YR	2YR	3YR	4YR	5YR
"Divi-X" Rtrn 154 x's	84.86%	103.58%	217.40%	463.73%	484.21%
"Divi-X" Rtrn 80 x's	60.55%	75.77%	156.09%	327.12%	343.44%
154 MultiPick over 80	24.31%	27.81%	61.31%	136.61%	140.77%
Without "Divi-X"	47.07%	60.19%	121.75%	250.84%	264.44%
All returns are accumulated, not averaged.					

MMM	3M Co		Purchase @ $59.37share		Yield: 3.44%

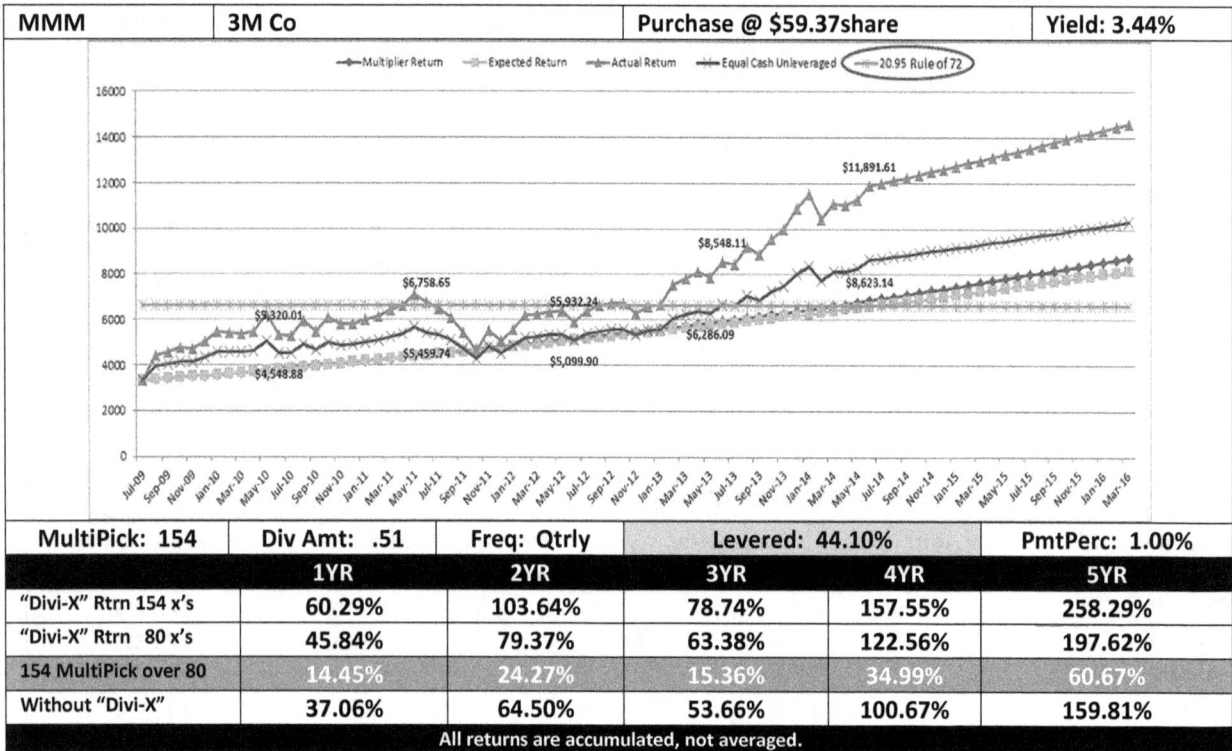

MultiPick: 154	Div Amt: .51	Freq: Qtrly	Levered: 44.10%		PmtPerc: 1.00%
	1YR	2YR	3YR	4YR	5YR
"Divi-X" Rtrn 154 x's	60.29%	103.64%	78.74%	157.55%	258.29%
"Divi-X" Rtrn 80 x's	45.84%	79.37%	63.38%	122.56%	197.62%
154 MultiPick over 80	14.45%	24.27%	15.36%	34.99%	60.67%
Without "Divi-X"	37.06%	64.50%	53.66%	100.67%	159.81%
All returns are accumulated, not averaged.					

T	AT&T		Purchase @ $24.04 share		Yield: 6.82%

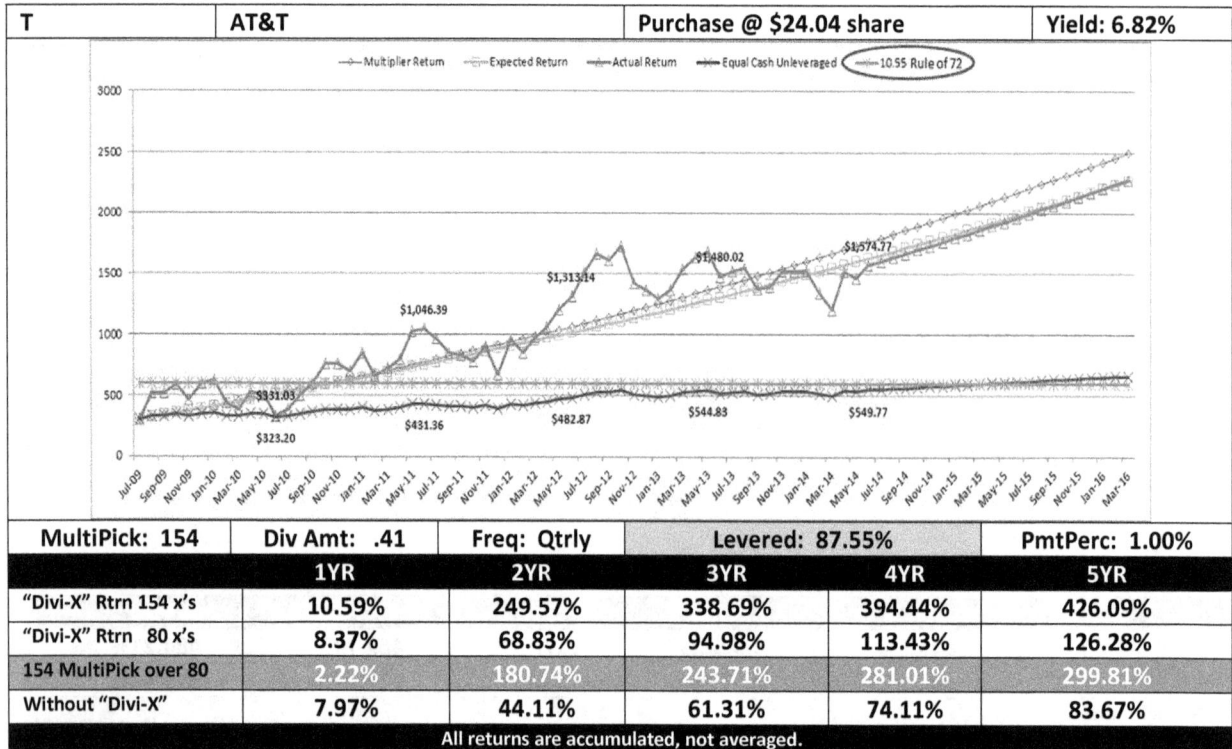

MultiPick: 154	Div Amt: .41	Freq: Qtrly	Levered: 87.55%		PmtPerc: 1.00%
	1YR	2YR	3YR	4YR	5YR
"Divi-X" Rtrn 154 x's	10.59%	249.57%	338.69%	394.44%	426.09%
"Divi-X" Rtrn 80 x's	8.37%	68.83%	94.98%	113.43%	126.28%
154 MultiPick over 80	2.22%	180.74%	243.71%	281.01%	299.81%
Without "Divi-X"	7.97%	44.11%	61.31%	74.11%	83.67%
All returns are accumulated, not averaged.					

INTC	Intel Corporation	Purchase @ $32.08 share	Yield: 1.96%

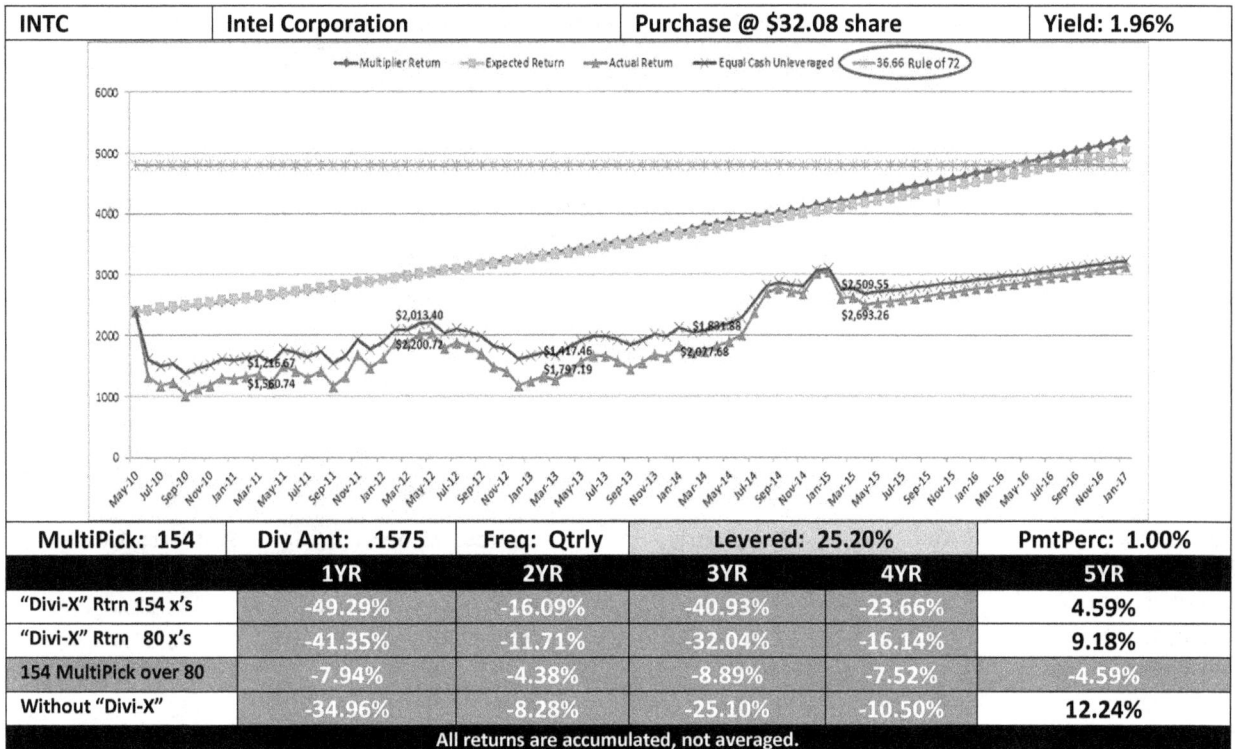

Multiplier Return · Expected Return · Actual Return · Equal Cash Unleveraged · 36.66 Rule of 72

Values shown on chart: $1,216.67, $1,560.74, $2,200.72, $2,013.40, $1,417.46, $1,797.19, $2,027.68, $1,831.88, $2,509.55, $2,693.26

MultiPick: 154	Div Amt: .1575	Freq: Qtrly	Levered: 25.20%		PmtPerc: 1.00%
	1YR	2YR	3YR	4YR	5YR
"Divi-X" Rtrn 154 x's	-49.29%	-16.09%	-40.93%	-23.66%	4.59%
"Divi-X" Rtrn 80 x's	-41.35%	-11.71%	-32.04%	-16.14%	9.18%
154 MultiPick over 80	-7.94%	-4.38%	-8.89%	-7.52%	-4.59%
Without "Divi-X"	-34.96%	-8.28%	-25.10%	-10.50%	12.24%
All returns are accumulated, not averaged.					

XOM	Exxon Mobile Corporation	Purchase @ $71.05 share	Yield: 2.36%

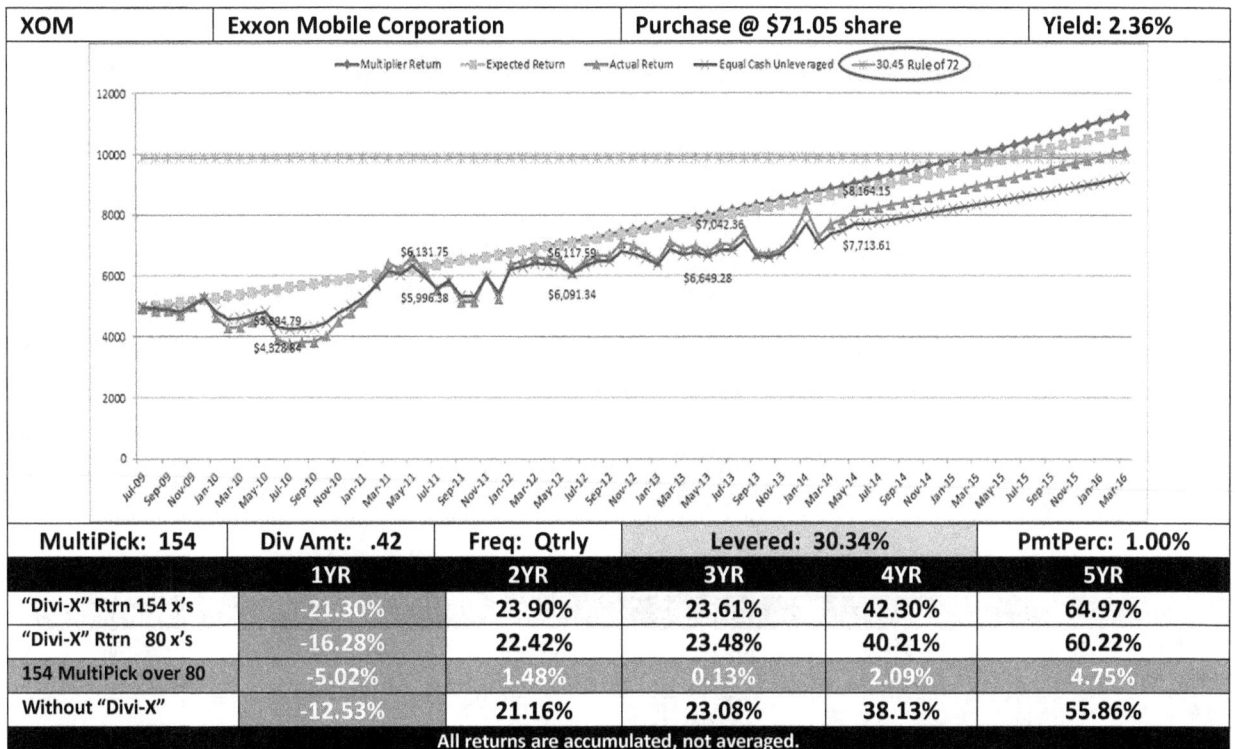

Multiplier Return · Expected Return · Actual Return · Equal Cash Unleveraged · 30.45 Rule of 72

Values shown on chart: $5,084.79, $4,328.64, $5,996.38, $6,131.75, $6,117.59, $6,091.34, $6,649.28, $7,042.36, $8,164.15, $7,713.61

MultiPick: 154	Div Amt: .42	Freq: Qtrly	Levered: 30.34%		PmtPerc: 1.00%
	1YR	2YR	3YR	4YR	5YR
"Divi-X" Rtrn 154 x's	-21.30%	23.90%	23.61%	42.30%	64.97%
"Divi-X" Rtrn 80 x's	-16.28%	22.42%	23.48%	40.21%	60.22%
154 MultiPick over 80	-5.02%	1.48%	0.13%	2.09%	4.75%
Without "Divi-X"	-12.53%	21.16%	23.08%	38.13%	55.86%
All returns are accumulated, not averaged.					

IBM	International Business Machines	Purchase @ $129.99 share	Yield: 2.00%

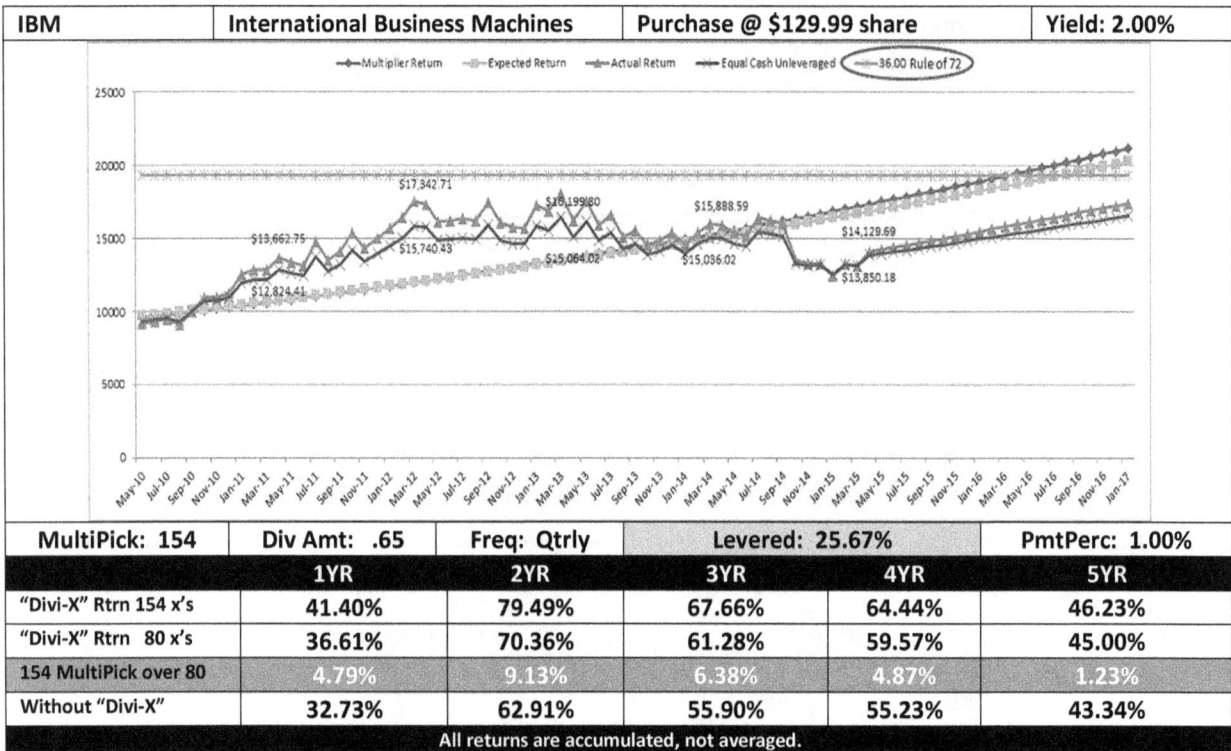

MultiPick: 154	Div Amt: .65	Freq: Qtrly	Levered: 25.67%		PmtPerc: 1.00%
	1YR	**2YR**	**3YR**	**4YR**	**5YR**
"Divi-X" Rtrn 154 x's	41.40%	79.49%	67.66%	64.44%	46.23%
"Divi-X" Rtrn 80 x's	36.61%	70.36%	61.28%	59.57%	45.00%
154 MultiPick over 80	4.79%	9.13%	6.38%	4.87%	1.23%
Without "Divi-X"	32.73%	62.91%	55.90%	55.23%	43.34%
All returns are accumulated, not averaged.					

JNJ	Johnson & Johnson	Purchase @ $64.30 share	Yield: 3.36%

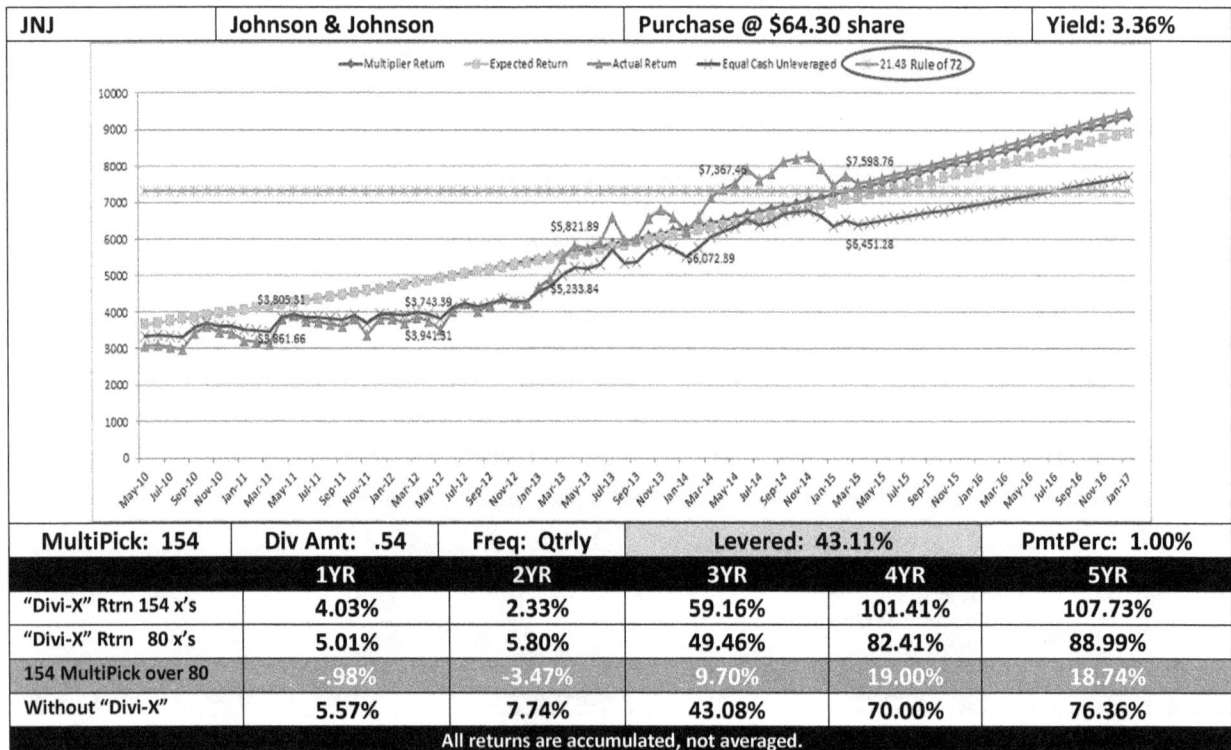

MultiPick: 154	Div Amt: .54	Freq: Qtrly	Levered: 43.11%		PmtPerc: 1.00%
	1YR	**2YR**	**3YR**	**4YR**	**5YR**
"Divi-X" Rtrn 154 x's	4.03%	2.33%	59.16%	101.41%	107.73%
"Divi-X" Rtrn 80 x's	5.01%	5.80%	49.46%	82.41%	88.99%
154 MultiPick over 80	-.98%	-3.47%	9.70%	19.00%	18.74%
Without "Divi-X"	5.57%	7.74%	43.08%	70.00%	76.36%
All returns are accumulated, not averaged.					

JPM	JPMorgan Chase & Co.	Purchase @ $44.94 share	Yield: 0.45%

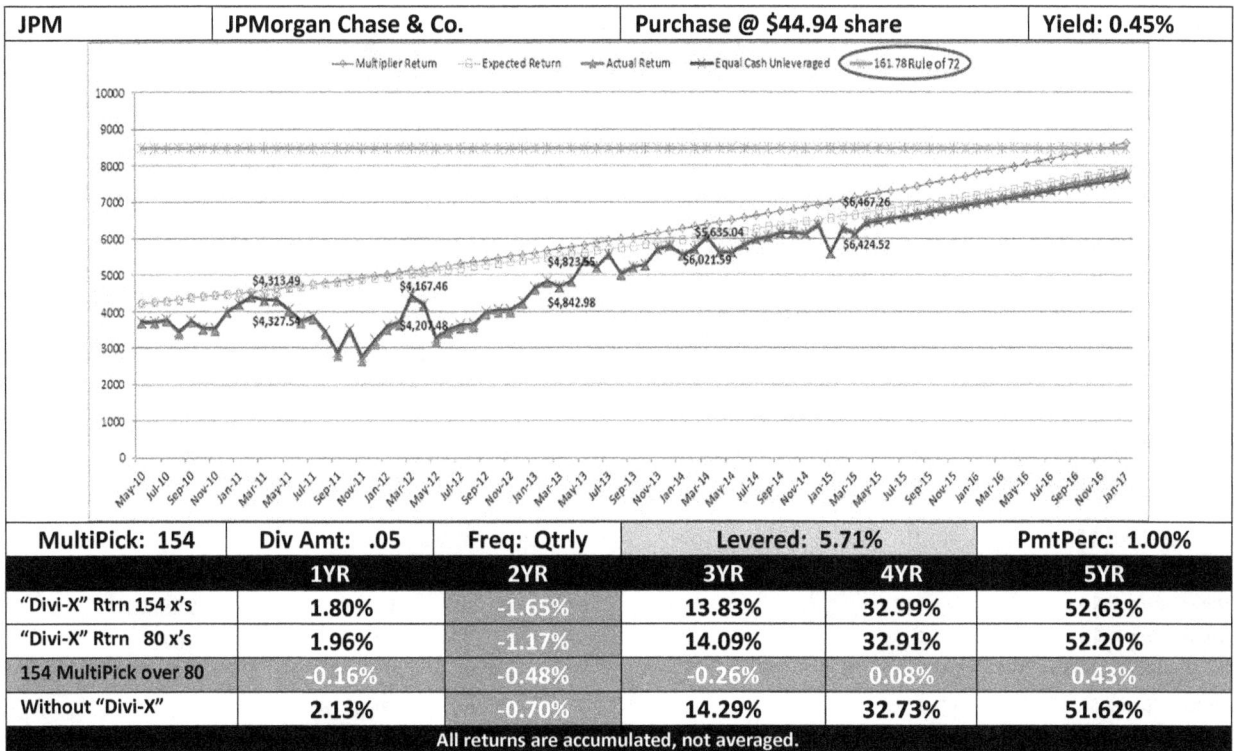

MultiPick: 154	Div Amt: .05	Freq: Qtrly	Levered: 5.71%		PmtPerc: 1.00%
	1YR	**2YR**	**3YR**	**4YR**	**5YR**
"Divi-X" Rtrn 154 x's	1.80%	-1.65%	13.83%	32.99%	52.63%
"Divi-X" Rtrn 80 x's	1.96%	-1.17%	14.09%	32.91%	52.20%
154 MultiPick over 80	-0.16%	-0.48%	-0.26%	0.08%	0.43%
Without "Divi-X"	2.13%	-0.70%	14.29%	32.73%	51.62%
All returns are accumulated, not averaged.					

MCD	McDonald's Corporation	Purchase @ $70.59 share	Yield: 3.12%

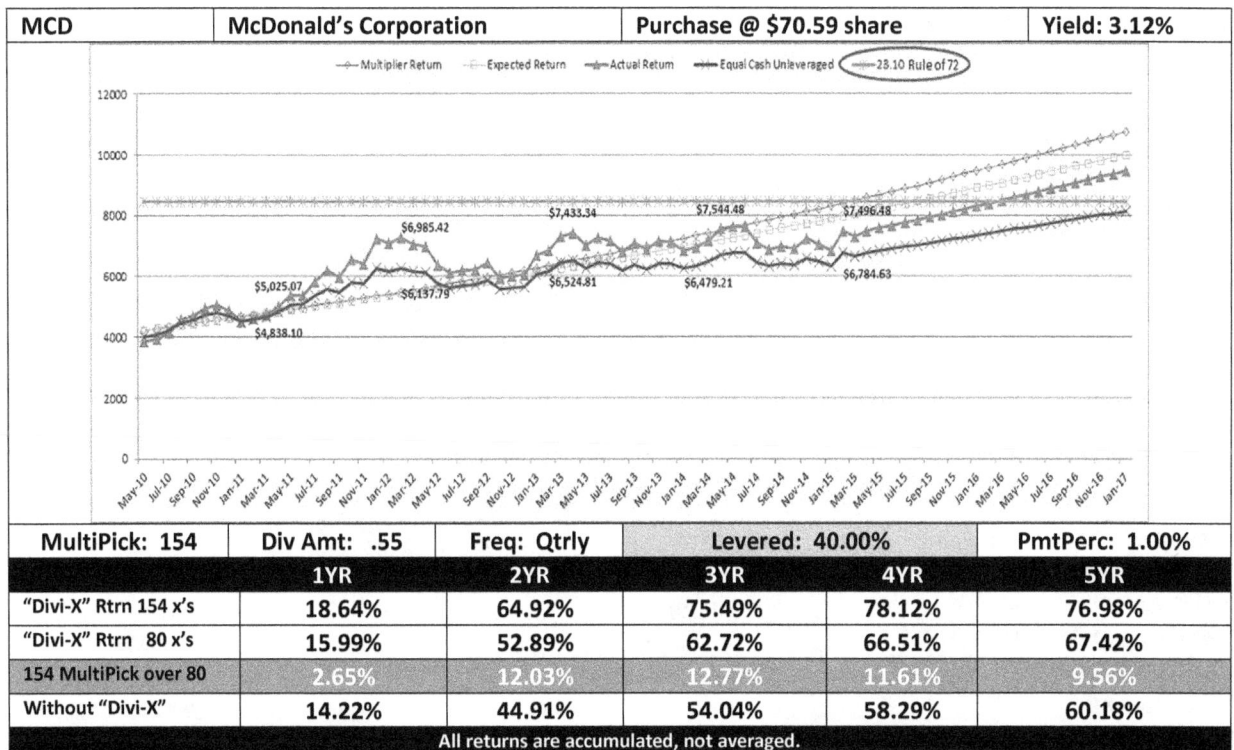

MultiPick: 154	Div Amt: .55	Freq: Qtrly	Levered: 40.00%		PmtPerc: 1.00%
	1YR	**2YR**	**3YR**	**4YR**	**5YR**
"Divi-X" Rtrn 154 x's	18.64%	64.92%	75.49%	78.12%	76.98%
"Divi-X" Rtrn 80 x's	15.99%	52.89%	62.72%	66.51%	67.42%
154 MultiPick over 80	2.65%	12.03%	12.77%	11.61%	9.56%
Without "Divi-X"	14.22%	44.91%	54.04%	58.29%	60.18%
All returns are accumulated, not averaged.					

MRK	Merck & Co Inc	Purchase @ $35.46 share	Yield: 4.29%

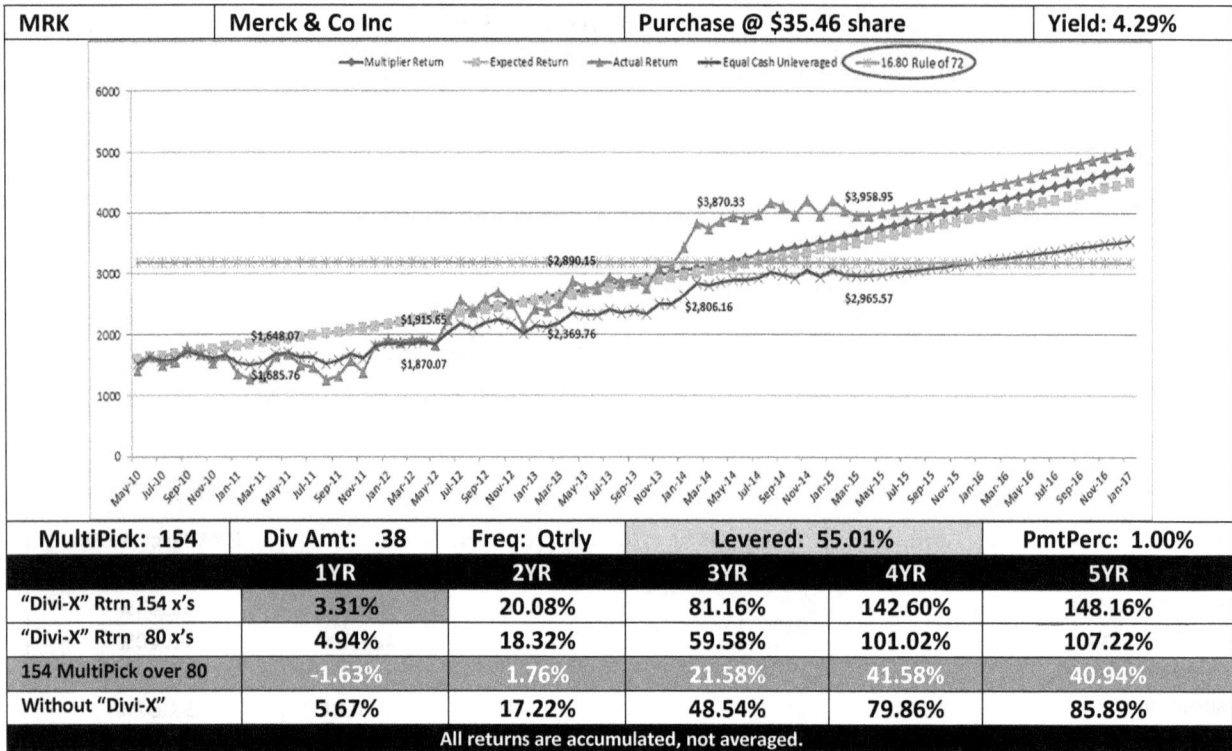

Multiplier Return — Expected Return — Actual Return — Equal Cash Unleveraged — 16.80 Rule of 72

MultiPick: 154	Div Amt: .38	Freq: Qtrly	Levered: 55.01%		PmtPerc: 1.00%
	1YR	2YR	3YR	4YR	5YR
"Divi-X" Rtrn 154 x's	3.31%	20.08%	81.16%	142.60%	148.16%
"Divi-X" Rtrn 80 x's	4.94%	18.32%	59.58%	101.02%	107.22%
154 MultiPick over 80	-1.63%	1.76%	21.58%	41.58%	40.94%
Without "Divi-X"	5.67%	17.22%	48.54%	79.86%	85.89%
All returns are accumulated, not averaged.					

MSFT	Microsoft Corporation	Purchase @ $30.96 share	Yield 1.68%

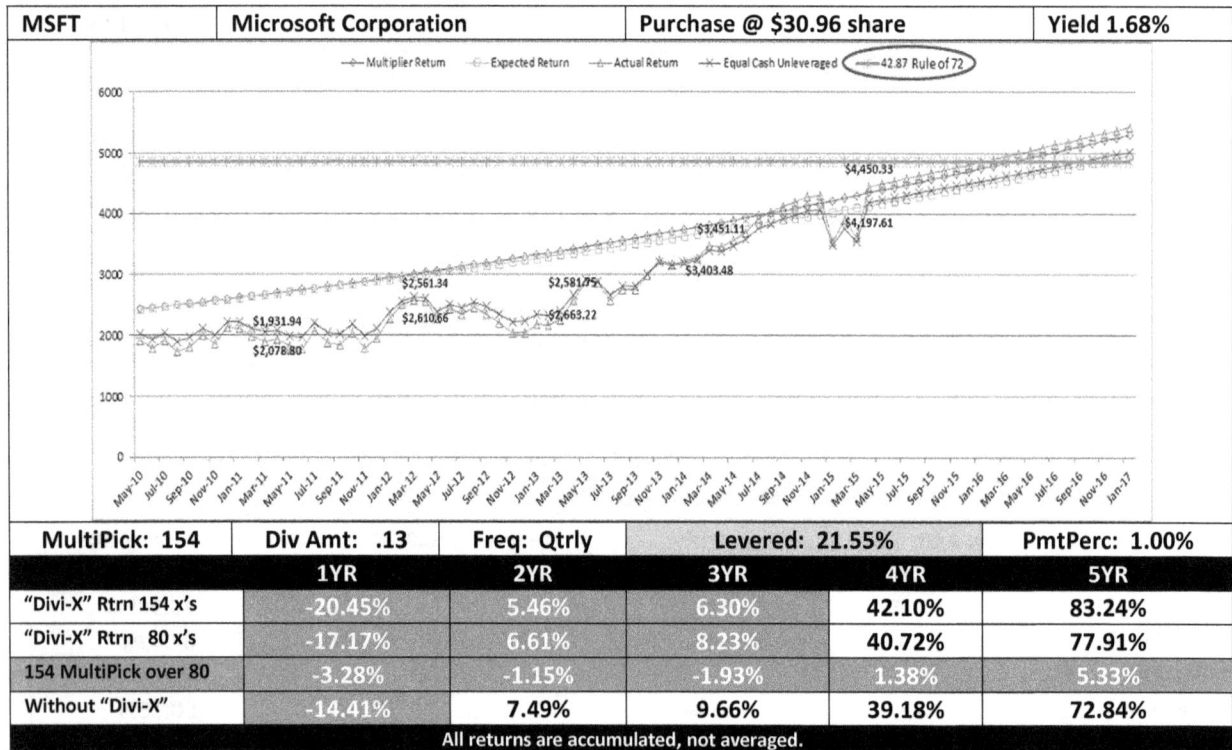

Multiplier Return — Expected Return — Actual Return — Equal Cash Unleveraged — 42.87 Rule of 72

MultiPick: 154	Div Amt: .13	Freq: Qtrly	Levered: 21.55%		PmtPerc: 1.00%
	1YR	2YR	3YR	4YR	5YR
"Divi-X" Rtrn 154 x's	-20.45%	5.46%	6.30%	42.10%	83.24%
"Divi-X" Rtrn 80 x's	-17.17%	6.61%	8.23%	40.72%	77.91%
154 MultiPick over 80	-3.28%	-1.15%	-1.93%	1.38%	5.33%
Without "Divi-X"	-14.41%	7.49%	9.66%	39.18%	72.84%
All returns are accumulated, not averaged.					

NKE		Nike Inc		Purchase @ $38.95 share		Yield: 1.39%

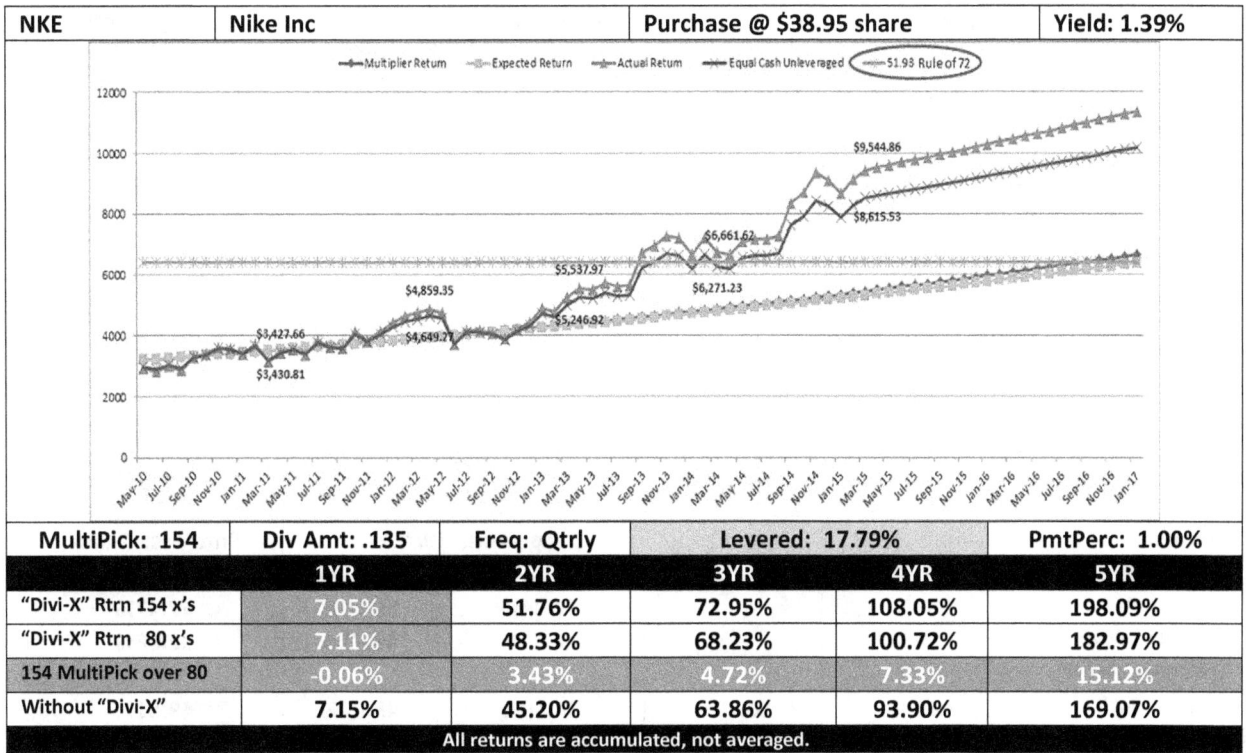

Legend: Multiplier Return — Expected Return — Actual Return — Equal Cash Unleveraged — 51.98 Rule of 72

Data labels: $3,427.66, $3,430.81, $4,859.35, $4,649.27, $5,537.97, $5,246.92, $6,661.62, $6,271.23, $9,544.86, $8,615.53

MultiPick: 154	Div Amt: .135	Freq: Qtrly	Levered: 17.79%		PmtPerc: 1.00%
	1YR	**2YR**	**3YR**	**4YR**	**5YR**
"Divi-X" Rtrn 154 x's	7.05%	51.76%	72.95%	108.05%	198.09%
"Divi-X" Rtrn 80 x's	7.11%	48.33%	68.23%	100.72%	182.97%
154 MultiPick over 80	-0.06%	3.43%	4.72%	7.33%	15.12%
Without "Divi-X"	7.15%	45.20%	63.86%	93.90%	169.07%
All returns are accumulated, not averaged.					

PFE		Pfizer Inc		Purchase @ $16.72 share		Yield: 4.31%

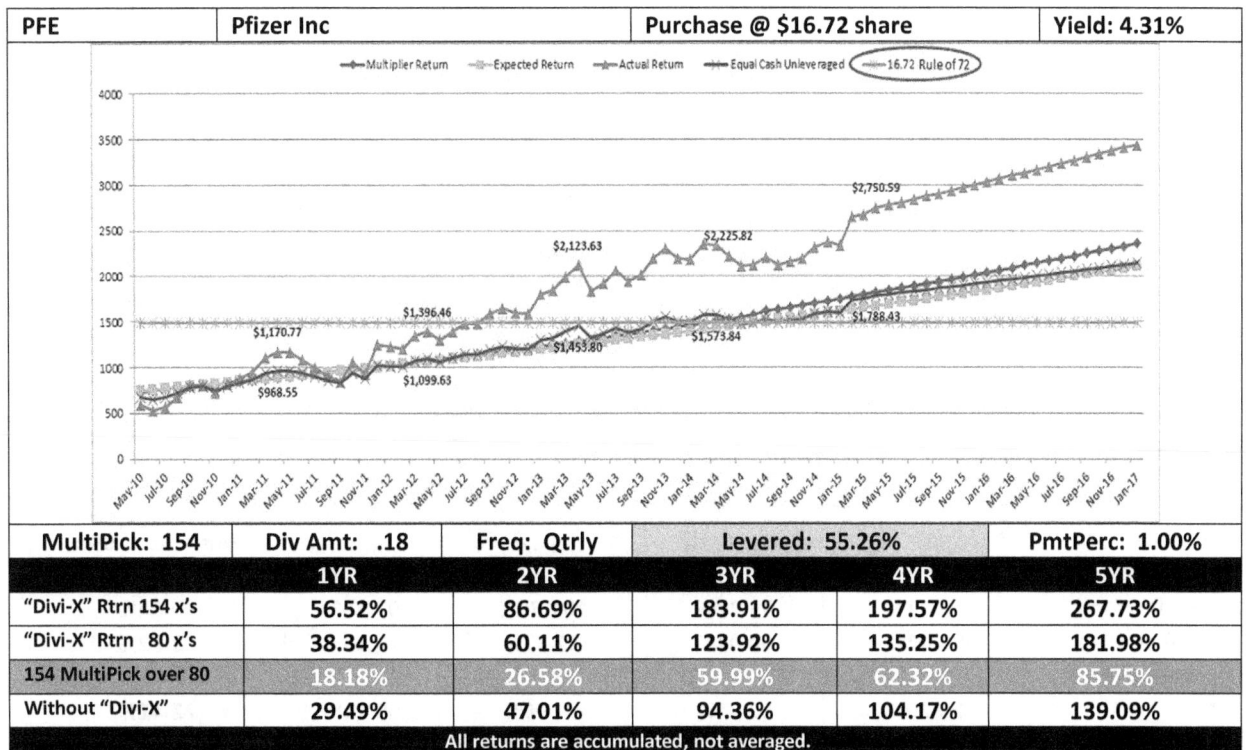

Legend: Multiplier Return — Expected Return — Actual Return — Equal Cash Unleveraged — 16.72 Rule of 72

Data labels: $1,170.77, $968.55, $1,099.63, $1,396.46, $1,453.80, $2,123.63, $1,573.84, $2,225.82, $1,788.43, $2,750.59

MultiPick: 154	Div Amt: .18	Freq: Qtrly	Levered: 55.26%		PmtPerc: 1.00%
	1YR	**2YR**	**3YR**	**4YR**	**5YR**
"Divi-X" Rtrn 154 x's	56.52%	86.69%	183.91%	197.57%	267.73%
"Divi-X" Rtrn 80 x's	38.34%	60.11%	123.92%	135.25%	181.98%
154 MultiPick over 80	18.18%	26.58%	59.99%	62.32%	85.75%
Without "Divi-X"	29.49%	47.01%	94.36%	104.17%	139.09%
All returns are accumulated, not averaged.					

PG	Proctor & Gamble & Co	Purchase @ $62.16 share	Yield: 3.10%

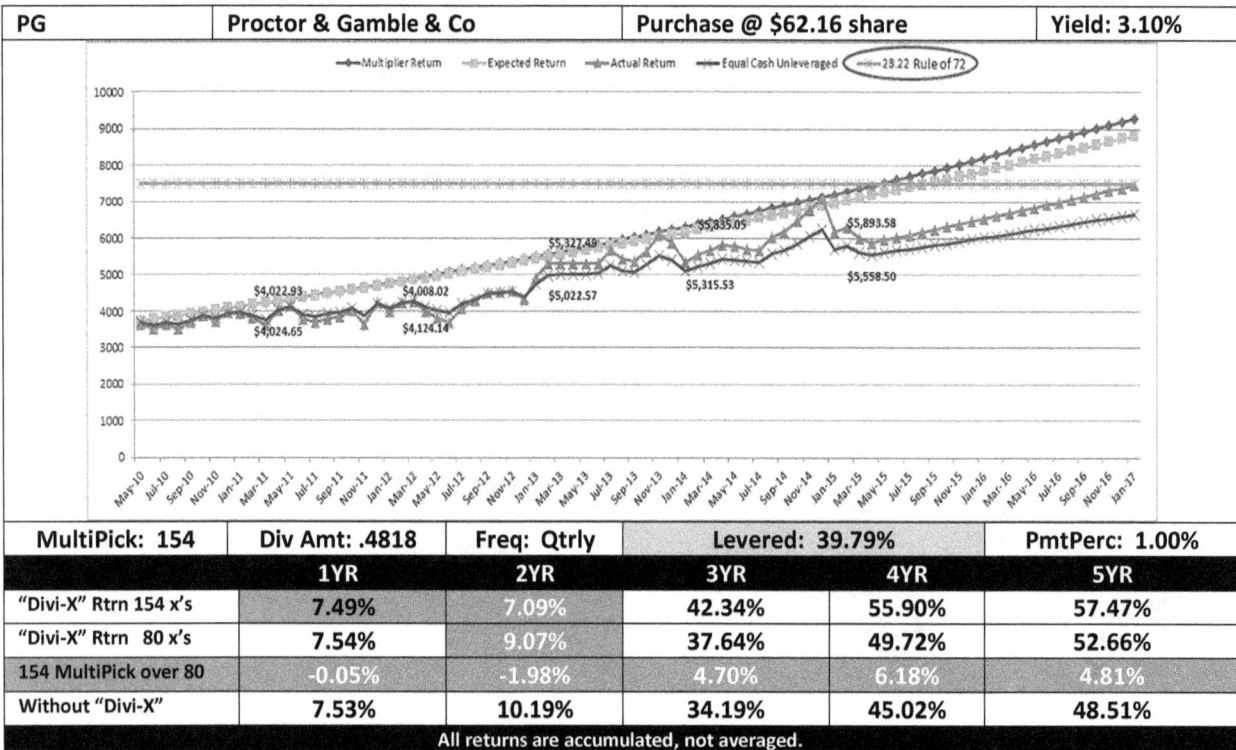

Chart legend: Multiplier Return, Expected Return, Actual Return, Equal Cash Unleveraged, 28.22 Rule of 72

Data labels on chart: $4,022.93, $4,024.65, $4,008.02, $4,124.14, $5,022.57, $5,327.48, $5,835.05, $5,315.53, $5,558.50, $5,893.58

MultiPick: 154	Div Amt: .4818	Freq: Qtrly	Levered: 39.79%		PmtPerc: 1.00%
	1YR	**2YR**	**3YR**	**4YR**	**5YR**
"Divi-X" Rtrn 154 x's	7.49%	7.09%	42.34%	55.90%	57.47%
"Divi-X" Rtrn 80 x's	7.54%	9.07%	37.64%	49.72%	52.66%
154 MultiPick over 80	-0.05%	-1.98%	4.70%	6.18%	4.81%
Without "Divi-X"	7.53%	10.19%	34.19%	45.02%	48.51%
All returns are accumulated, not averaged.					

KO	The Coca-Cola Co	Purchase @ $26.72 share	Yield: 3.29%

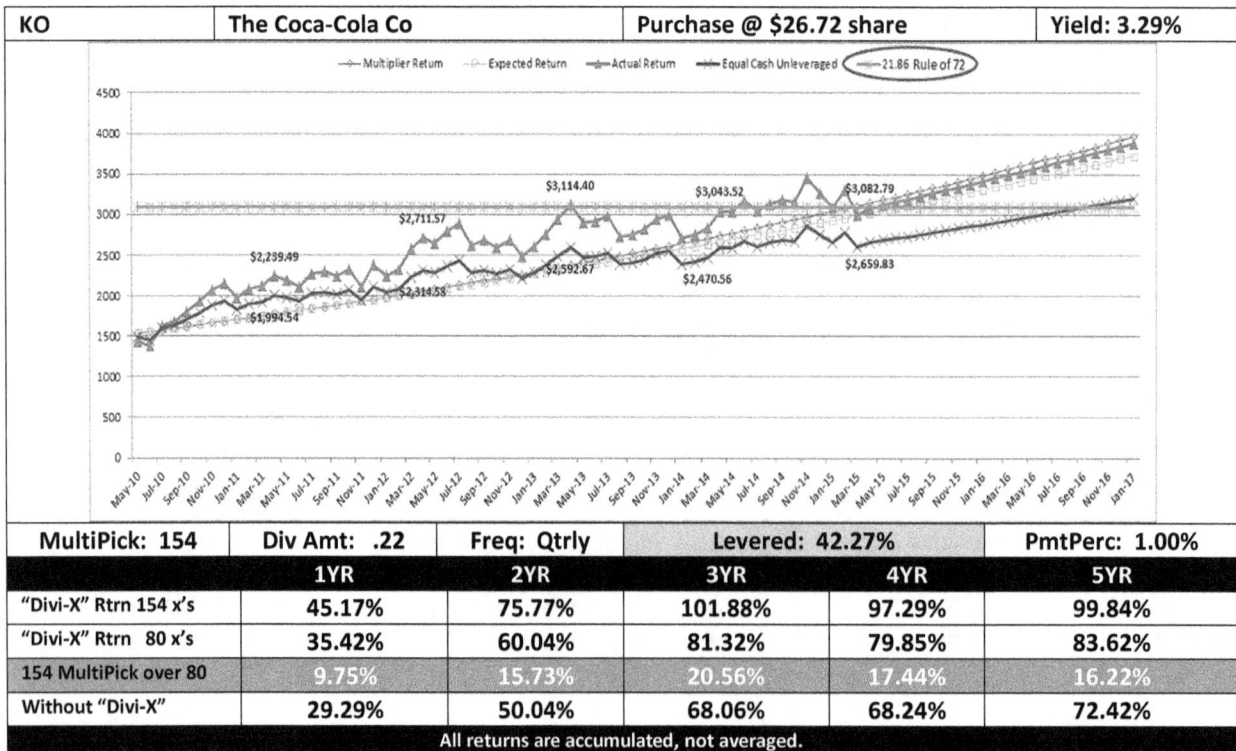

Chart legend: Multiplier Return, Expected Return, Actual Return, Equal Cash Unleveraged, 21.86 Rule of 72

Data labels on chart: $1,994.54, $2,239.49, $2,314.58, $2,711.57, $2,592.67, $3,114.40, $2,470.56, $3,043.52, $2,659.83, $3,082.79

MultiPick: 154	Div Amt: .22	Freq: Qtrly	Levered: 42.27%		PmtPerc: 1.00%
	1YR	**2YR**	**3YR**	**4YR**	**5YR**
"Divi-X" Rtrn 154 x's	45.17%	75.77%	101.88%	97.29%	99.84%
"Divi-X" Rtrn 80 x's	35.42%	60.04%	81.32%	79.85%	83.62%
154 MultiPick over 80	9.75%	15.73%	20.56%	17.44%	16.22%
Without "Divi-X"	29.29%	50.04%	68.06%	68.24%	72.42%
All returns are accumulated, not averaged.					

TRV	Travelers Companies Inc	Purchase @ $50.74share	Yield: 2.84%

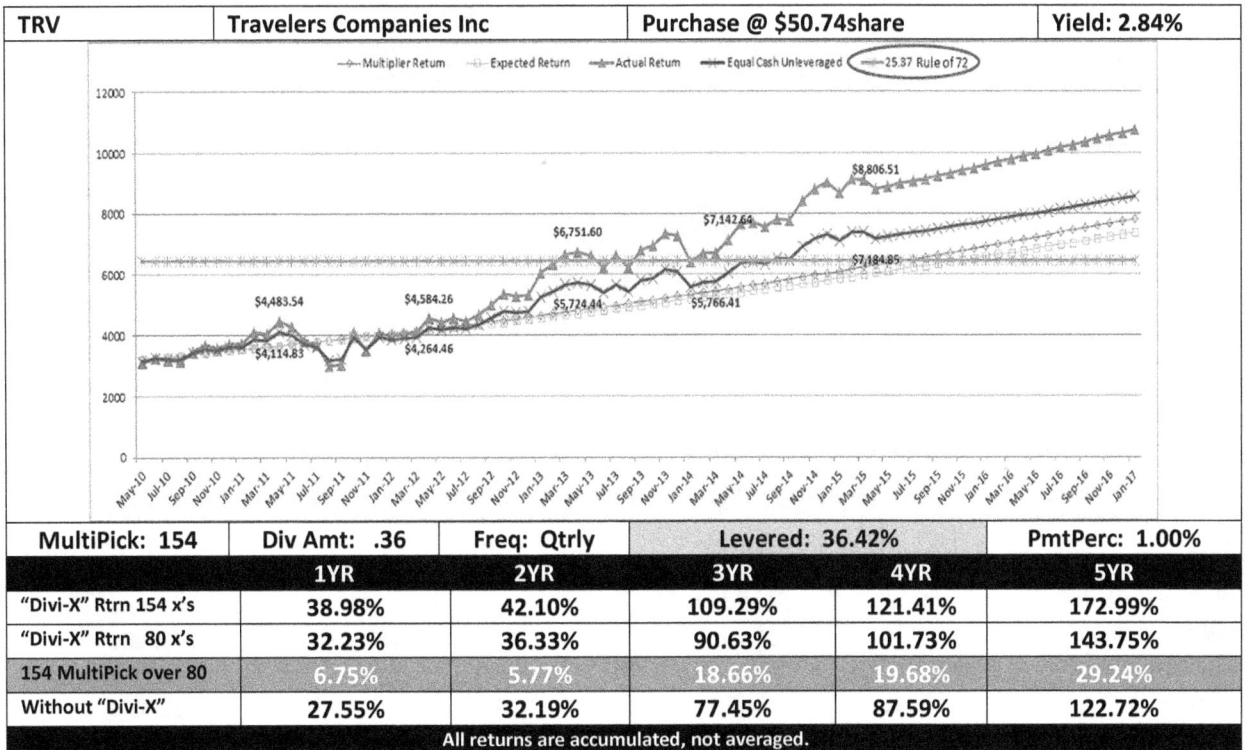

Multiplier Return — Expected Return — Actual Return — Equal Cash Unleveraged — 25.37 Rule of 72

$4,483.54 $4,584.26 $6,751.60 $7,142.64 $8,806.51
$4,114.83 $4,264.46 $5,724.44 $5,766.41 $7,184.85

MultiPick: 154	Div Amt: .36	Freq: Qtrly	Levered: 36.42%		PmtPerc: 1.00%
	1YR	2YR	3YR	4YR	5YR
"Divi-X" Rtrn 154 x's	38.98%	42.10%	109.29%	121.41%	172.99%
"Divi-X" Rtrn 80 x's	32.23%	36.33%	90.63%	101.73%	143.75%
154 MultiPick over 80	6.75%	5.77%	18.66%	19.68%	29.24%
Without "Divi-X"	27.55%	32.19%	77.45%	87.59%	122.72%
All returns are accumulated, not averaged.					

UTX	United Technologies Corp	Purchase @ $74.95 share	Yield: 2.27%

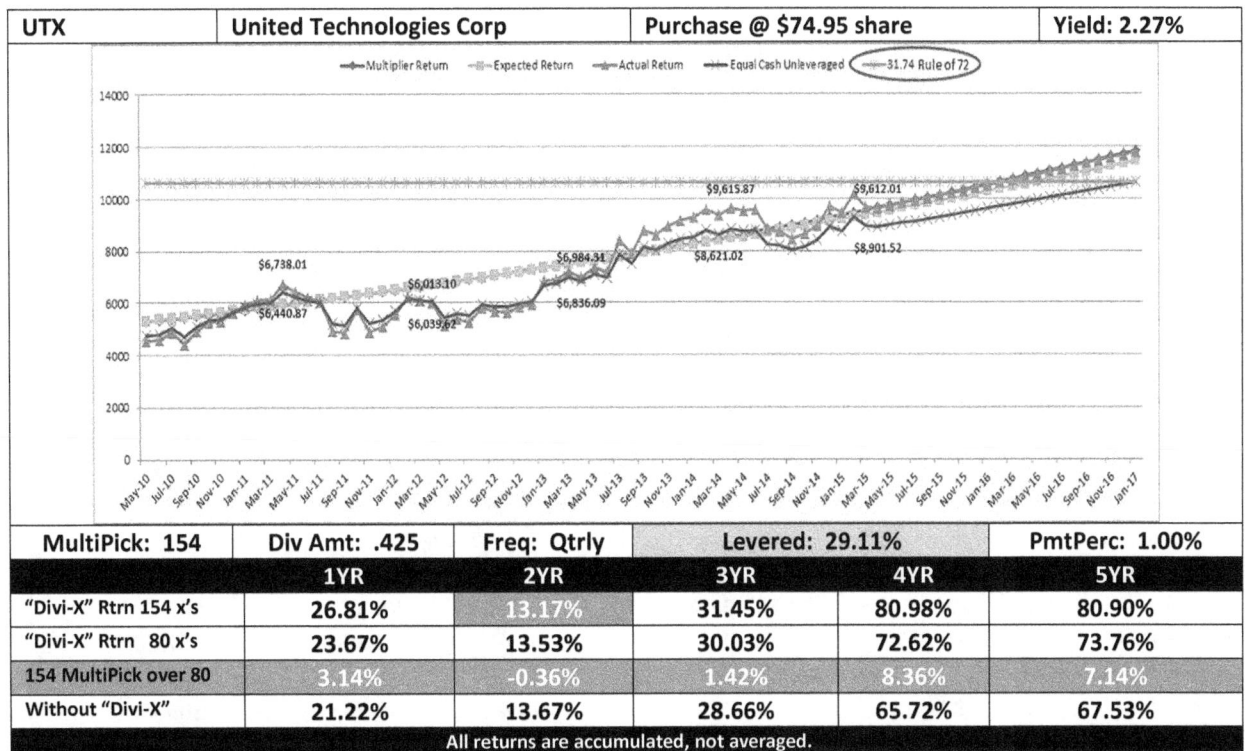

Multiplier Return — Expected Return — Actual Return — Equal Cash Unleveraged — 31.74 Rule of 72

$6,738.01 $6,013.10 $6,984.31 $9,615.87 $9,612.01
$6,440.87 $6,039.62 $6,836.09 $8,621.02 $8,901.52

MultiPick: 154	Div Amt: .425	Freq: Qtrly	Levered: 29.11%		PmtPerc: 1.00%
	1YR	2YR	3YR	4YR	5YR
"Divi-X" Rtrn 154 x's	26.81%	13.17%	31.45%	80.98%	80.90%
"Divi-X" Rtrn 80 x's	23.67%	13.53%	30.03%	72.62%	73.76%
154 MultiPick over 80	3.14%	-0.36%	1.42%	8.36%	7.14%
Without "Divi-X"	21.22%	13.67%	28.66%	65.72%	67.53%
All returns are accumulated, not averaged.					

UNH	UnitedHealth Group Inc	Purchase @ $30.31 share	Yield: 1.65%

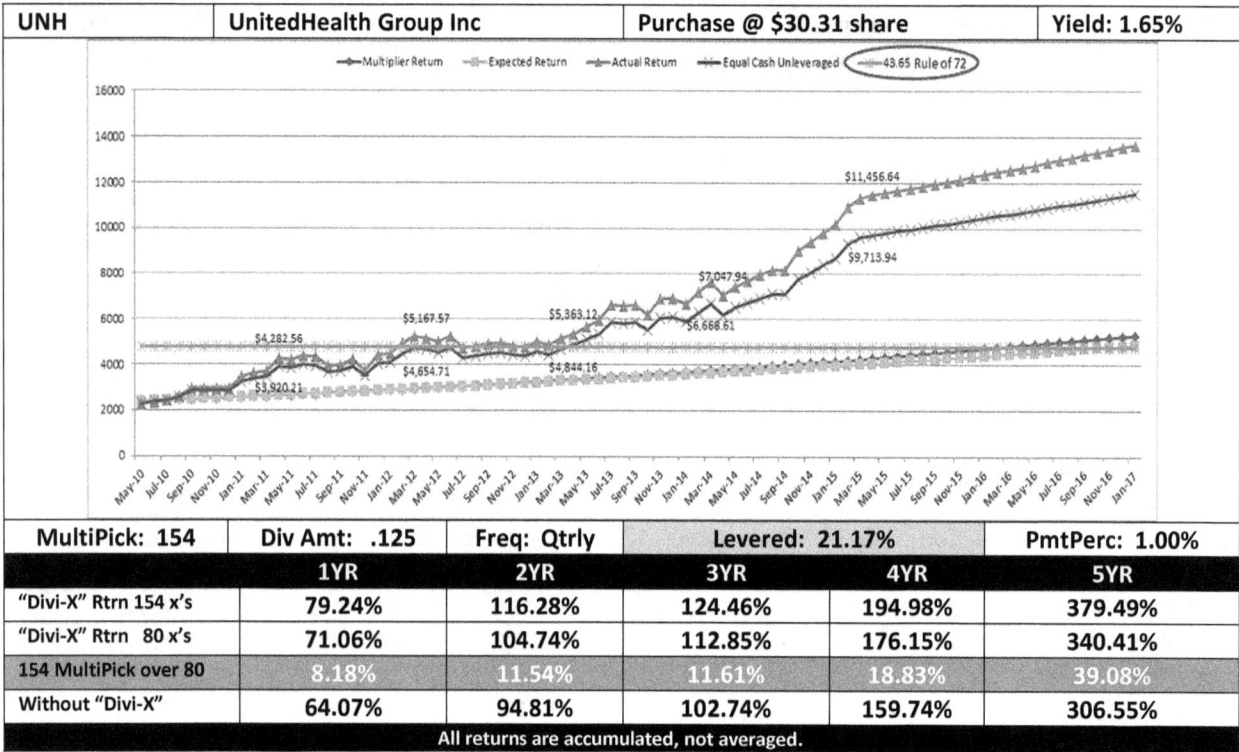

Multiplier Return — Expected Return — Actual Return — Equal Cash Unleveraged — 43.65 Rule of 72

$11,456.64 $9,713.94 $7,047.94 $6,668.61 $5,363.12 $5,167.57 $4,844.16 $4,654.71 $4,282.56 $3,920.21

MultiPick: 154	Div Amt: .125	Freq: Qtrly	Levered: 21.17%		PmtPerc: 1.00%
	1YR	2YR	3YR	4YR	5YR
"Divi-X" Rtrn 154 x's	79.24%	116.28%	124.46%	194.98%	379.49%
"Divi-X" Rtrn 80 x's	71.06%	104.74%	112.85%	176.15%	340.41%
154 MultiPick over 80	8.18%	11.54%	11.61%	18.83%	39.08%
Without "Divi-X"	64.07%	94.81%	102.74%	159.74%	306.55%
All returns are accumulated, not averaged.					

VZ	Verizon Communications Inc	Purchase @ $28.90 share	Yield: 6.57%

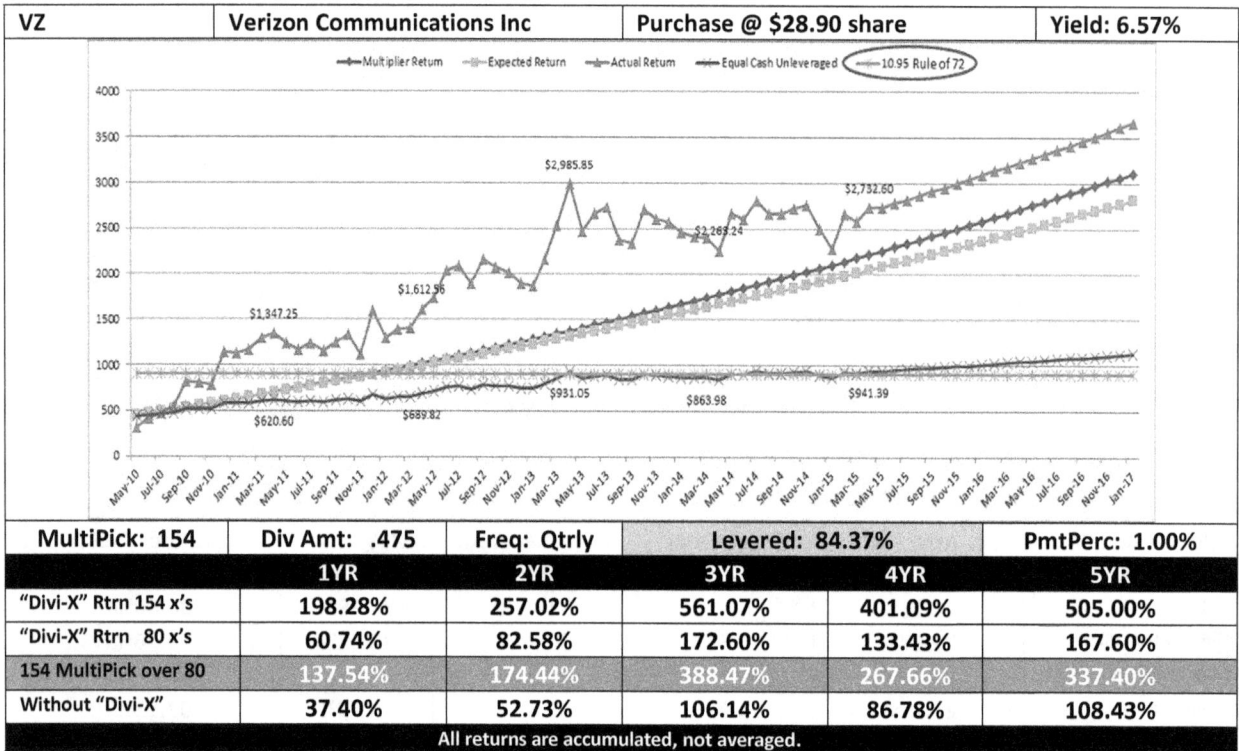

Multiplier Return — Expected Return — Actual Return — Equal Cash Unleveraged — 10.95 Rule of 72

$2,985.85 $2,732.60 $2,265.24 $1,612.56 $1,347.25 $931.05 $941.39 $863.98 $689.82 $620.60

MultiPick: 154	Div Amt: .475	Freq: Qtrly	Levered: 84.37%		PmtPerc: 1.00%
	1YR	2YR	3YR	4YR	5YR
"Divi-X" Rtrn 154 x's	198.28%	257.02%	561.07%	401.09%	505.00%
"Divi-X" Rtrn 80 x's	60.74%	82.58%	172.60%	133.43%	167.60%
154 MultiPick over 80	137.54%	174.44%	388.47%	267.66%	337.40%
Without "Divi-X"	37.40%	52.73%	106.14%	86.78%	108.43%
All returns are accumulated, not averaged.					

V	Visa	Purchase @ $22.558 share	Yield: 0.56%

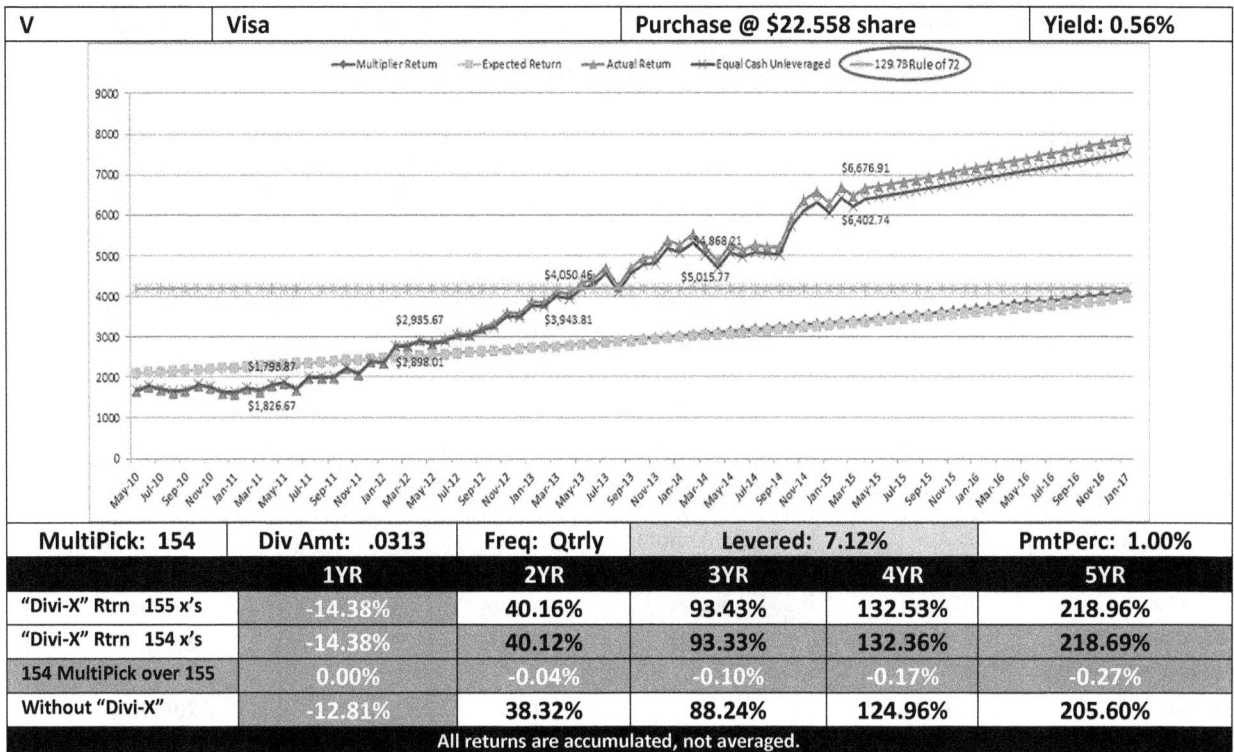

Multiplier Return — Expected Return — Actual Return — Equal Cash Unleveraged — 129.73 Rule of 72

$6,676.91
$6,402.74
$4,868.01
$4,050.46
$5,015.77
$2,935.67
$3,943.81
$1,793.87
$2,898.01
$1,826.67

MultiPick: 154	Div Amt: .0313	Freq: Qtrly	Levered: 7.12%		PmtPerc: 1.00%
	1YR	2YR	3YR	4YR	5YR
"Divi-X" Rtrn 155 x's	-14.38%	40.16%	93.43%	132.53%	218.96%
"Divi-X" Rtrn 154 x's	-14.38%	40.12%	93.33%	132.36%	218.69%
154 MultiPick over 155	0.00%	-0.04%	-0.10%	-0.17%	-0.27%
Without "Divi-X"	-12.81%	38.32%	88.24%	124.96%	205.60%
All returns are accumulated, not averaged.					

WMT	Wal-Mart Stores Inc	Purchase @ $54.53 share	Yield: 2.22%

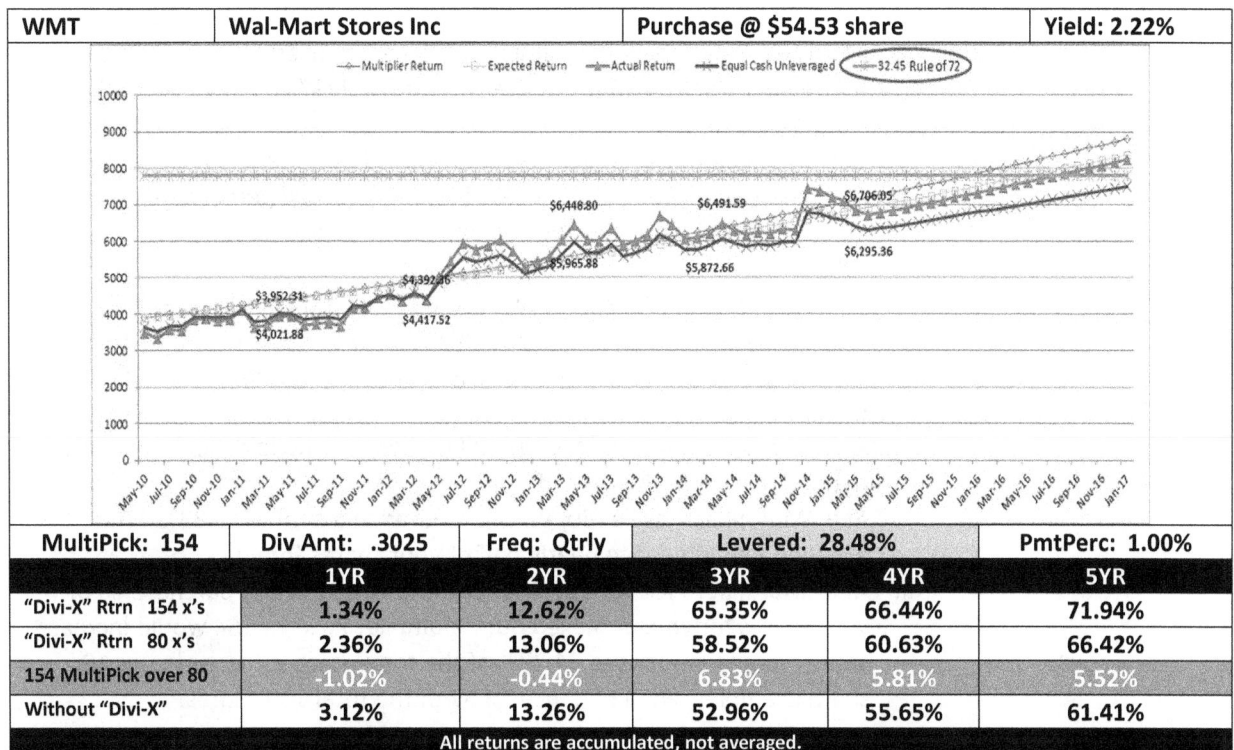

Multiplier Return — Expected Return — Actual Return — Equal Cash Unleveraged — 32.45 Rule of 72

$6,448.80
$6,491.59
$6,706.05
$5,965.88
$5,872.66
$6,295.36
$3,952.31
$4,392.36
$4,021.88
$4,417.52

MultiPick: 154	Div Amt: .3025	Freq: Qtrly	Levered: 28.48%		PmtPerc: 1.00%
	1YR	2YR	3YR	4YR	5YR
"Divi-X" Rtrn 154 x's	1.34%	12.62%	65.35%	66.44%	71.94%
"Divi-X" Rtrn 80 x's	2.36%	13.06%	58.52%	60.63%	66.42%
154 MultiPick over 80	-1.02%	-0.44%	6.83%	5.81%	5.52%
Without "Divi-X"	3.12%	13.26%	52.96%	55.65%	61.41%
All returns are accumulated, not averaged.					

DIS	Walt Disney Co	Purchase @ $36.84 share	Yield: 1.09%

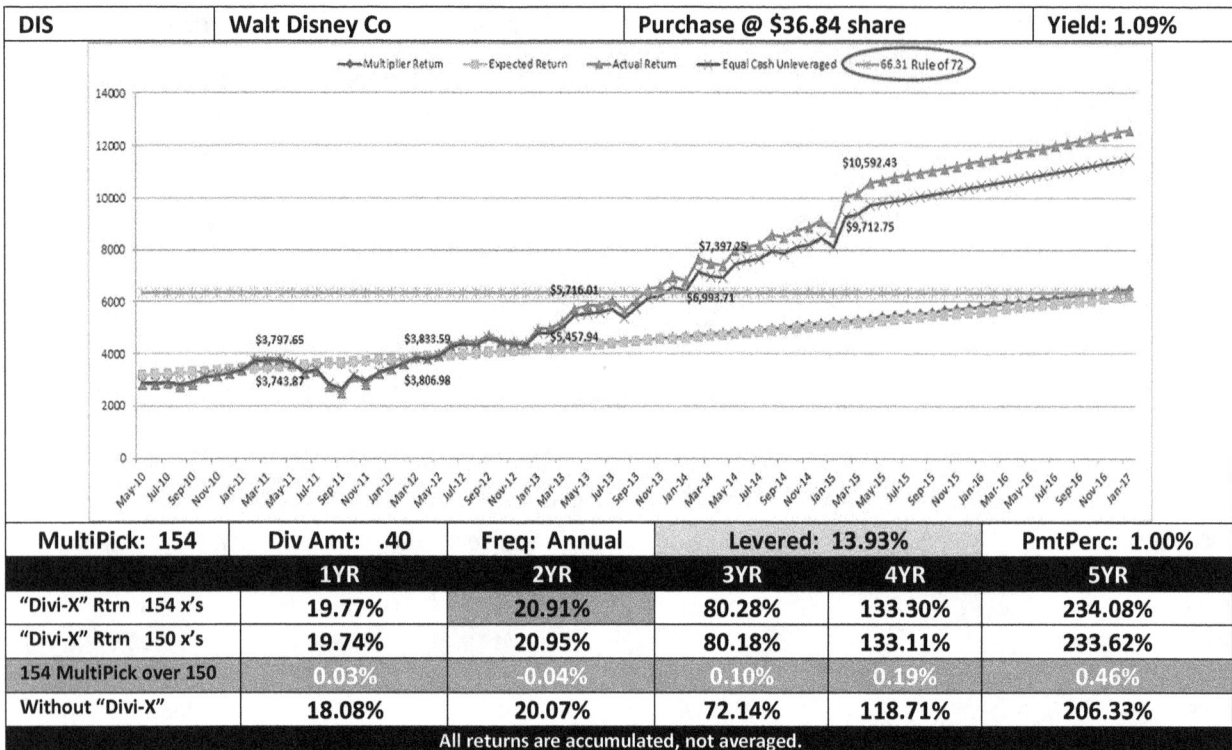

MultiPick: 154	Div Amt: .40	Freq: Annual	Levered: 13.93%		PmtPerc: 1.00%
	1YR	**2YR**	**3YR**	**4YR**	**5YR**
"Divi-X" Rtrn 154 x's	19.77%	20.91%	80.28%	133.30%	234.08%
"Divi-X" Rtrn 150 x's	19.74%	20.95%	80.18%	133.11%	233.62%
154 MultiPick over 150	0.03%	-0.04%	0.10%	0.19%	0.46%
Without "Divi-X"	18.08%	20.07%	72.14%	118.71%	206.33%
All returns are accumulated, not averaged.					

A Few Notes about These Charts

1. The higher the "Multiplier Pick," the higher amount of leverage used.
   a. On a very low yield stock, maxing out the "Multiplier Pick" can have very little effect as in the case of Visa.
      i. At a "Multiplier Pick" of 80, Visa was levered at around just 3.5%.
      ii. At a "Multiplier Pick" of nearly double, the leverage percentage nearly doubled, but you would have still only been levered at just over, a very conservative, 7%.
      iii. This conservative number would also be reflected in your returns as well. After five years it would have added a total of 18.09% to your returns, or an average of 3.62% extra a year. Not a lot to brag about, but it's better than nothing.
   b. On the flip side, maxing out the "Multiplier Pick" on a high-yield stock can have a very dramatic effect, as in the case of VZ.
      i. At a "Multiplier Pick" of 80, VZ was levered at a sizable 43.83%. This dividend would finance nearly half of your shares for you.
      ii. At a "Multiplier Pick" of 154, the dividend would nearly purchase all of your shares for you. A maxed out "Multiplier Pick" of 154 would increase your leverage amount to 84.37% of the total share value, or in our 100 share examples, would finance 84.37 of the total 100 shares.

iii. Go back and look at the chart of VZ in this chapter. Look at what a mind-blowing difference this would have had on your investment. Increasing your "Multiplier Pick" from 80 to 154 would have added 337.40% to your total return after five years totaling 505%, or an average of an additional; not total, an additional, 67.48% a year for five years. Had you not used the "Divi-X" system at all, you would have missed out on an additional 396.57% of returns, for an average missed opportunity of 79.31% a year.

iv. The dividend picture would look incredibly seductive for VZ as well. You'll notice that the actual 'Cash Yield' (the middle bar) had already surpassed the 'Stock Yield' (the left bar) after year three, pulling in a 10.06% yield over the stocks stated yield of 7.04%. After year five, it more than doubles. That number would continue to rise until your dividends completely paid off the margin loan associated with this purchase and if there were no dividend cuts.

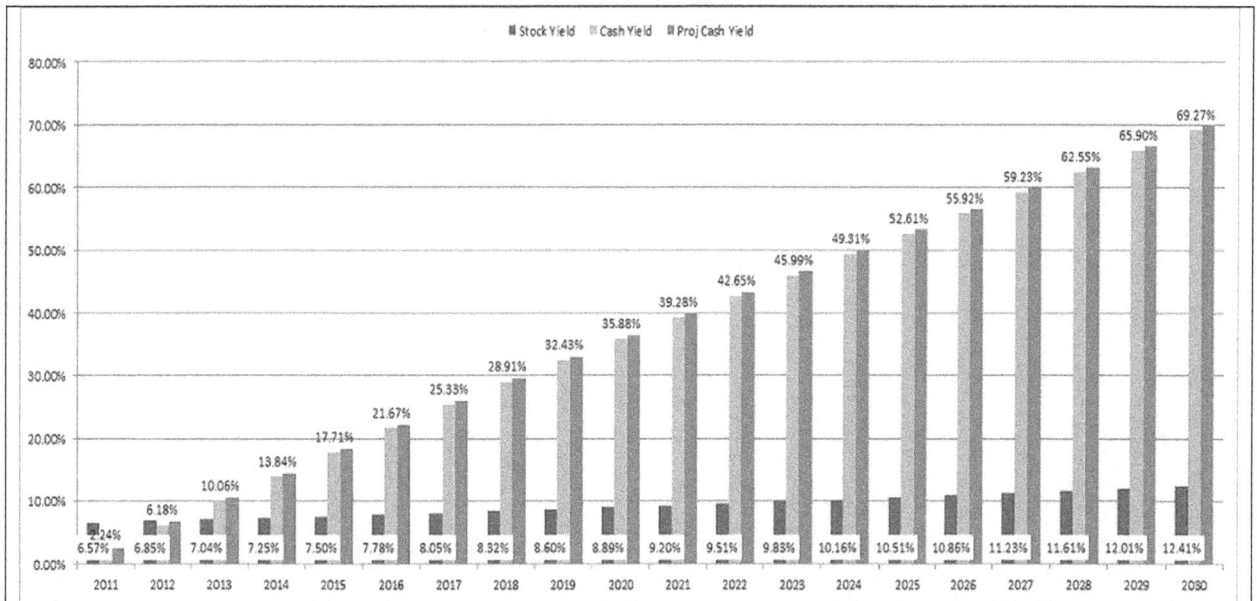

Fig. 10.1

v. A little perspective: As phenomenal as the chart in **Fig. 10.1** is, bear in mind that this is a stock leveraged at 84.37%. In other words, on a $100,000 purchase, $84,370 would be borrowed funds and that awesome yield would only be on $15,630 of your invested cash.

vi. It cannot be stressed enough. VZ would have made you look like Midas, but these situations do not always play out this well. AT&T, Caterpillar, and E I Dupont De Nemours and Co also had very similar gains, but this is not the norm. Just as these handful of companies did unbelievably well, the flip side would have been something entirely different, dark, and dismal if you did not exit your positions in time or if the market crashed, which it has done from time to time.

2. It is hoped that these charts, not just in this chapter but throughout this book, will prove to be an invaluable reference to give you an idea of how different situations could play out over time. Refer to them often.

3. The timeline of results shown in these charts took place after the market selloff in 2008. Had I expanded my timeline to six or seven years, the results shown may not have been as impressive or even more impressive.

4. Showing you the results of "Divi-X" to the Max is not an endorsement to use it "to the Max." I hope I have pointed out clearly, throughout this book, that responsibility for your results are yours.

Chapter 11
Reinvesting Dividends Using the "Divi-X" System

Reinvested Dividends

This is unlike the D.R.I.P.'s I spoke of in an earlier chapter. In this chapter, I'm going to go over the power of reinvested dividends using the "Divi-X" system. Throughout the whole process of creating the "The Dividend Times," or the "Divi-X" system, the system has managed to evolve with some very surprising results. Truthfully, I thought that once I put these methods to work, I feared that I would be in for a huge letdown. I hoped for the best, but after each new calculation or technique, I worried that I would be met with less than impressive results. As it turns out, the "Divi-X" system has far exceeded my expectations and has taught me a lot along the way.

Just through the power of this very chapter, my attitude towards using the "Divi-X" system along with 'dividend reinvestment' has taken on a new light but only in certain circumstances. When I first started this project, it was always in the back of my mind that adding a 'dividend reinvestment' feature would be a "nice to have" feature, much like, the "Rule of 72." It was never intended to be used in conjunction with the "Divi-X" system. I did, on more than one occasion, sit myself down and start to lay out how to incorporate 'dividend reinvestment' into the "Divi-X" system but eventually concluded it was too much work and better left for "Divi-X" v2.0. Then one day (yesterday, actually), it occurred to me that with the thousands of calculated fields already in the "Divi-X" system workbook, surely I already have everything I need to incorporate 'dividend reinvestment' into the program and I was right! After mapping this field with that field, multiplying this, dividing that, and adding the macros to make it all as simple as a mouse click, I pulled it off! Now, with great pleasure, I am thrilled to present to you, "The Power of Reinvested Dividends Using "The "Divi-X" System."

How We Got Our Results

In every example that follows, we use the following criteria:
1. We use a "Multiplier Pick" of 80.
2. We use a "PmtPerc" of 1.25%
3. All remaining dividends were reinvested 'after' the associated margin loan payment was made.
4. The information will be broken down into dividends reinvested after the associated margin loan was serviced using one of the following methods:
   a. No DIV Reinvestment

b. All DIV's - All Dividends Paid towards the margin loan (no dividends to reinvest).
c. "PmtPerc" and
d. Interest Only

Presenting, Yet Once Again and For the Last Time... The Dow 30 (but no charts)

	No DIV Reinvestment Without "Divi-X"	DIV Reinvestment Without "Divi-X"	No DIV Reinvestment "PmtPerc"	DIV Reinvestment All DIV's	DIV Reinvestment "PmtPerc"	DIV Reinvestment Interest Only
AXP	287.79%	308.32%	348.77%	349.28%	353.34%	360.65%
BA	198.11%	221.68%	247.89%	248.48%	253.16%	261.58%
CAT	233.05%	259.85%	332.43%	333.82%	341.83%	351.40%
CVX	104.67%	121.18%	130.85%	132.10%	136.51%	141.10%
DD	211.43%	249.46%	350.73%	352.17%	360.91%	379.36%
XOM	55.86%	62.31%	60.22%	60.84%	62.20%	63.33%
GE	146.86%	168.81%	179.16%	181.02%	190.29%	195.41%
GS	19.30%	20.29%	18.40%	18.58%	18.67%	18.56%
HD	264.44%	297.50%	343.44%	344.59%	354.22%	365.95%
MMM	159.81%	179.35%	189.39%	190.89%	198.07%	202.81%
T	83.67%	104.79%	126.28%	128.18%	132.74%	140.75%
INTC	12.41%	13.53%	9.37%	10.02%	9.65%	9.15%
IBM	43.51%	47.07%	45.19%	45.72%	46.40%	46.61%
JNJ	76.36%	87.87%	88.99%	89.83%	92.16%	95.12%
JPM	51.62%	57.14%	52.20%	56.27%	56.91%	57.11%
MCD	60.18%	68.58%	67.42%	68.69%	70.73%	72.04%
MRK	85.89%	101.39%	107.22%	108.25%	111.28%	115.99%
MSFT	72.84%	82.03%	77.91%	78.97%	82.47%	84.03%
NKE	169.07%	180.01%	182.97%	183.53%	187.08%	189.68%
PFE	139.45%	165.77%	182.49%	184.29%	193.45%	201.57%
PG	48.51%	55.16%	52.66%	53.53%	54.66%	55.63%
KO	72.69%	82.12%	83.98%	84.93%	87.03%	88.93%
TRV	122.72%	137.70%	143.75%	144.69%	148.85%	152.84%
UTX	67.72%	74.42%	73.98%	74.34%	75.57%	77.00%
UNH	306.55%	328.11%	340.41%	342.13%	351.16%	355.91%
VZ	108.43%	133.02%	167.60%	169.50%	175.34%	185.20%
V	205.60%	213.39%	212.25%	214.14%	216.56%	217.89%
WMT	61.41%	68.27%	66.42%	67.34%	69.06%	70.17%
DIS	206.33%	218.04%	219.89%	220.43%	224.90%	227.53%
Avg. Rtrn	126.77%	141.63%	155.25%	156.43%	160.52%	164.94%

Fig. 11.1

A Few Things about the Table in Fig. 11.1

'No DIV Reinvestment "PmtPerc"' vs **'No DIV Reinvestment Without "Divi-X"'** – This is the comparison we have been making throughout the entire book.

1. "Divi-X" outperformed 'Without "Divi-X"' twenty-seven times out of the twenty-nine Dow components, or 93% of the time. CSCO paid no dividends and were not included.
2. "Divi-X" outperformed 'Without "Divi-X"' by an average return of 28.48% over the five year period, or 5.7% a year.
3. Of the two stocks that did not outperform using the "Divi-X" system, (GS) and (INTC), they were the poorest performers in the Dow; averaging 4.1% for (GS) and only 2.7% for (INTC).

'DIV Reinvestment "PmtPerc"' vs **'DIV Reinvestment Without "Divi-X"'** – Compares dividend reinvestment using the "Divi-X" system with the "PmtPerc" and dividend reinvestment without using the "Divi-X" system.

1. "Divi-X" outperformed 'Without "Divi-X" twenty-three times out of the twenty-nine Dow components, or 79% of the time.
2. "Divi-X" outperformed 'Without "Divi-X" by an average return of 18.89% over the five year period, or 3.8% a year.
3. Of the six stocks that did not outperform using the "Divi-X" system, (XOM), (IBM), (GS), (INTC), (JPM), and (PG); all failed to meet our initial goal of a 9% expected rate of return without dividend reinvestment and were the bottom six performers in the DOW 30 over the five year period.

'No DIV Reinvestment "PmtPerc"' and **'DIV Reinvestment All DIV's'** essentially performed the same because **'DIV Reinvestment All DIV's'** applied all of its dividends to principal payments and had nothing left over to reinvest. It performed slightly better than **'No DIV Reinvestment "PmtPerc"'** because of lower interest expense from the accelerated principal payments.

'DIV Reinvestment Interest Only' pulled in the highest average returns overall but still could not outperform **'DIV Reinvestment Without "Divi-X"'** in four instances and if you guessed that it was because of the four worst performers, (GS), (INTC), (IBM), and (JPM); you would be right.

I saved the very best for last. Of course I probably gave it away with all the circles I added to **Fig. 11.1**. Keep in mind that I had no intention of adding a 'dividend reinvestment' function to the "Divi-X" system initially. Imagine my incredulous surprise, after I compiled all the data in Fig. **11.1**, to find that ___the "Divi-X" system WITHOUT dividend reinvestment, in sixty-two percent of the time, outperformed dividend reinvestment without the use of "Divi-X!"___ To me, I find this a fascinating discovery. And out of the remaining thirty-eight percent that the "Divi-X" system didn't surpass, twenty-one percent came within one to two percentage points. Only five stocks, (XOM), (INTC), (JPM), (PG), and to add a new twist, (MSFT), had a difference of greater than two percent. Also, if you look at the overall average of the Dow 30 (Cisco didn't pay dividends, remember), the "Divi-X" system WITHOUT 'dividend reinvestment' outperformed 'dividend reinvestment' WITHOUT the "Divi-X" system by 13.62%, or 2.7% a year.

The returns in the last three columns in **Fig. 11.1** continue to add to your overall performance using "Divi-X" with dividend reinvestment.

The Ugly Ducklings

If you will recall, earlier in the book, we posed the question on whether the "Divi-X" system would still work if the share price went lower than our purchase price. In Chapter 3 we took a quick look at **American Capital Mortgage Investment Crp (MTGE)** using the "Divi-X" system without the consideration of 'dividend reinvestment.' Here is a summary of the results for years one thru five:

	1YR	2YR	3YR	4YR	5YR
"Divi-X" Rtrn	63.93%	52.18%	73.59%	68.14%	93.61%*
Without "Divi-X"	47.77%	41.38%	58.51%	56.29%	76.02%*

*5YR numbers are projected
Fig. 11.2

In this section, we will briefly revisit **(MTGE)** to show how 'dividend reinvestment' would have changed the outcome, with and without the "Divi-X" system. Also, in this section, I would like to showcase three companies that had their share price deteriorate over a five year period to the extent it would be lower than your purchase price five years prior, however, because of 'dividend reinvestment' and using the "Divi-X" system, they still managed to turn in respectable returns. I call these 'Ugly Ducklings' because when you look at their five year share price history, it certainly isn't pretty but in the end (with a little help from "Divi-X") even though they may not grow into beautiful swans, they're certainly worth looking at.

But first, a new look at **American Capital Mortgage Investment Crp (MTGE)**. On its IPO in August 2011, it had a closing price of $18.63. **(MTGE)** didn't quite have a five year trading history, so we used what was available as of the time of this writing and since then **(MTGE)** had its share price decline -6.3% to $17.47. As reviewed in Chapter 3, and without 'dividend reinvestment,' **(MTGE)** still managed to pull a positive return despite its decline in share price. That return was further enhanced when using the "Divi-X" system as highlighted in **Fig. 11.2**.

I'm pretty sure you already know that if **(MTGE)** managed to pull an overall positive return without 'dividend reinvestment, then the use of 'dividend reinvestment' would only enhance those returns. Let's just see how much. Actual results are for year 4 using the "Divi-X" system and keep in mind, net of margin interest expense.

(MTGE) After 4 Years	Reinvestment Without "Divi-X"	No DIV Reinvestment "PmtPerc"	DIV Reinvestment All DIV's	DIV Reinvestment "PmtPerc"	DIV Reinvestment Interest Only
Ttl Returns	71.49%%	68.05%	79.70%	83.80%	84.65%
4YR AVG*	17.87%	17.01%	19.93%	20.95%	21.16%
Ann Yield	19.73%	14.88%	21.47%	22.64%	23.04%

*Only 4 years of data available
Fig. 11.3

The last row shows your cash on cash DIV Yield less margin interest expense on your initial cash investment. "Divi-X" with 'dividend reinvestment' outperforms here as well.

The next 'ugly duckling' we are going to look at is **Pimco Corporate & Income Strategy Fund (PCN).** On July 10, 2010, **(PCN)** had a closing price of $15.50. After five years, **(PCN)** witnessed its share price decline -11.13% to $13.73. That share price decline is almost twice as much as (MTGE)! Can it still muster a positive gain as well? Let's do the numbers and find out.

(PCN) After 5 Years	Reinvestment Without "Divi-X"	No DIV Reinvestment "PmtPerc"	DIV Reinvestment All DIV's	DIV Reinvestment "PmtPerc"	DIV Reinvestment Interest Only
Ttl Returns	54.96%	61.26%	70.46%	67.22%	66.37%
5YR Avg	10.99%	12.25%	14.09%	13.44%	13.27%
Ann Yield	17.61%	17.59%	21.54%	23.00%	24.11%

Fig. 11.4

(PCN) didn't perform quite as well as (MTGE) on the annual average returns but it's still very reasonable. I would like to quickly draw your attention to the **"ANN Yield"** row for **(PCN)** and **(MTGE)**. These are the yields on your actual cash investment after margin interest, when applicable, not the total share value. I include reinvested dividends in that number simply because it is financial compensation to you and you have the choice on whether or not to reinvest them or not. It does not include share price appreciation/depreciation. Those numbers are accounted for in the **"Ttl Returns."** With that being said, LOOK AT THE SIZE OF THOSE YIELDS AFTER 5 YEARS!!!

Moving on to our next example, let's take a look at **Allianzgi Convertible & Income Fund II (NCZ),** a closed-end fund traded on the NYSE. On July 19, 2010, **(NCZ)** had a closing price of $9.01 a share. After five years, the closing price reached a low of $7.49 for a loss of -16.87% of its share value. That's a drop of almost three times as much as **(MTGE)**.

(NCZ) After 5 Years	Reinvestment Without "Divi-X"	No DIV Reinvestment "PmtPerc"	DIV Reinvestment All DIV's	DIV Reinvestment "PmtPerc"	DIV Reinvestment Interest Only
Ttl Returns	46.34%	61.73%	66.93%	62.41%	55.78%
5YR Avg	9.30%	12.35 %	13.39%	12.48%	11.16%
Ann Yield	18.87%	28.91%	31.49%	32.98%	37.19%

Fig. 11.5

This one also managed to pull in a pretty decent return even though its share price took a bigger hit over the five year period than **Pimco Corporate & Income Strategy Fund (PCN)** and look; EVEN BIGGER YIELDS AFTER 5 YEARS!!!

Our next 'ugly duckling' is **Prospect Capital Corporation (PSEC).** This security suffered a -24.1% decline in its share price over the five year period. I personally own this security as of this writing and I just recently read a headline stating that (PSEC) is the most hated stock on Wall Street. More than a slight exaggeration, I'm sure, but you kind of get an idea of the sentiment surrounding this stock and even though it's not in favor right now, neither is any other stock in the same sector. Personally, I like the stock and I am currently riding out an industry trend. Anyway, let's open her up and take a look.

(PSEC) After 5 Years	Reinvestment Without "Divi-X"	No DIV Reinvestment "PmtPerc"	DIV Reinvestment All DIV's	DIV Reinvestment "PmtPerc"	DIV Reinvestment Interest Only
Ttl Returns	42.96%	73.73%	84.30%	71.23%	53.77%
5YR Avg	8.59%	14.75%	16.86%	14.25%	10.75%
Ann Yield	20.40%*	41.95%*	47.27%*	49.95%*	56.01%*

*dividend cut seven months into the fifth year
Fig. 11.6

Folks, I don't know what to say. Even after losing over 24% of its share value, (PSEC) managed to outperform the impressive returns of (NCZ). The annual yields are just unheard of! Even with the dividend cut in year five, if nothing changed, the dividend would still be in excess of a jaw-dropping 40%+ in the sixth year.

Honestly folks, when I prepared for this segment on 'Ugly Ducklings,' I preselected a handful of staggered share price decliners and the only thought I had was that I would post the security with the smallest share price loss first and escalate it to the highest. I had no idea what the results would be, but I suspected that as the share price losses got larger, the overall returns would surely get smaller. This is astounding! I am sincerely in awe of not just (PSEC)'s results, but all of these ugly ducklings.

What Do these Ugly Ducklings Have in Common?

The most obvious thing is that their share price ended lower than when it started. I was quite surprised to find that as the loss in share price got bigger in some cases, the returns got even bigger. If we weren't educated people, one could falsely draw the wrong conclusion that the more a stock falls the better the returns! Boy, wouldn't that be a happy place to live?

Another thing that all of these 'Ugly Ducklings' have in common, is that they are all high yield. **American Capital Mortgage Investment Crp (MTGE)** didn't start out that way, so that will have to be excluded from my next point. But, because all of the others started out as high yield plays at the start, using the "Multiplier Pick" of 80 (which, by now you know, is the most often used in this book) allowed us to buy a lot more stock with a lot less of our own cash (which is a huge reason for the very large "Ann Yields").

When we purchased **Pimco Corporate & Income Strategy Fund (PCN),** our 'Stock Yield' was 8.22%. This yield allowed us to finance 54.81% of our shares. **Allianzgi Convertible & Income Fund II (NCZ)?** That yielded a huge 11.32%, financing 75.47% of our shares. And lastly, **Prospect Capital Corporation (PSEC)** with a yield of 12.36%, paid for 82.39% or our shares (in the interest of full disclosure, I did not use a "Multiplier Pick" of 80 when I purchased this stock, I used something reasonably lower).

Higher Yield = Higher Leverage = Higher Risk and does not necessarily = Higher Returns

Now if you decide not to believe me and start to indiscriminately buy securities just because they have a high yield, I'm going to show you one more example to dissuade you because I do not want to have to talk you off of that ledge when you lose everything. These 'Ugly Ducklings' may paint a different story, but don't ever assume high yield is safe.

I personally like, and own, this stock (mostly because I didn't pay the same price used in this example. I am not recommending it. Do your own due diligence). It is **Navios Maritime Partners L.P. (NMM),** a shipping company that has been punished lately because of an oversupply of ships in the Dry Bulk (iron ore, coal, grain, etc.) sector. As of now, this company pays a ginormous dividend yield of 17.51% with a share price of $10.70. But were going to go back five years before it lost -41.12% of its share value and when the yield was a mere 9.25% and trading at $18.17 a share.

(NMM) After 5 Years	Reinvestment Without "Divi-X"	No DIV Reinvestment "PmtPerc"	DIV Reinvestment All DIV's	DIV Reinvestment "PmtPerc"	DIV Reinvestment Interest Only
Ttl Returns	(-8.04%)	(-33.71%)	(-30.06%)	(-42.90%)	(-63.72%)
5YR Avg	(-1.61%)	(-6.74%)	(-6.01%)	(-8.58%)	(-12.74%)
Ann Yield	15.90%	16.39%	18.15%	19.15%	21.04%

Fig. 11.7

This is clearly one instance where using "Divi-X" would have bit you in the butt. I have been highlighting higher yields using the "Divi-X" system throughout this book, but if you find yourself in a situation where you're earning an awesome 21.04% yield on a security that has devastatingly lost over 63% of its value since you purchased it, it might be time for a sanity check-up. I mean, who would continue to hold something like this?

Now, I know if anyone has any interest in this topic, they are probably long-term investors and may have been confronted with the dilemma of having to consider selling a stock they have been reinvesting in for years when the bottom suddenly falls out. But would it be the best choice in the long-term, at this time? I don't know what the answer to that is, but before you answer it, let me give you a little history on this company.

Navios Maritime Partners L.P. (NMM) started trading in November 2007 at $18.75 a share and immediately started paying a generous 7.5% yield. One year later, the economy bombed and (NMM) saw its shares plummet to $3.36 (a gut-wrenching -82.1% decline) causing its yield to explode to an understandably unsustainable yield of 45.8%. I'm sure you can guess what happened next. That's right! They raised the dividend! What? Oh, you thought they were going to cut it? Anyway, about two and a half years later, (NMM) climbed to an all new high of $21.30 a share. Then it pulled back for a while, and after three years, made it back over $20 a share again. They're not aggressive dividend growers but they have raised their dividend eight times in the eight years they have traded. Okay, so here we are, five years later and the stock has plummeted again but not nearly as bad. What do you think? Should you sell?

Running Leverage Rate

As I was doing my segment on the 'Ugly Ducklings,' one thought kept coming up. What is the 'Running Leverage Rate'? There might be a more technical term for this but that's what I'm calling it, and my definition of the 'Running Leverage Rate' is the outstanding margin loan balance as a percentage of the total share value. The 'Running Leverage Rate' should always be a concern when using margin. This is an additional feature (that you can easily calculate on your own) that I built into 'The "Divi-X" System Workbook.' The formula is simply the outstanding margin loan balance divided into the total share value at that particular time and viewed as a percentage.

Outstanding Margin Balance ÷ Total Share Value

Why this is important. I mention the Running Leverage Rate now because all of the stocks in the 'Ugly Duckling' category are highly leveraged because of their large dividend payouts. Those amazing yields you could be collecting won't mean a thing if at the end of the day, you wind up owing more on your shares than you collected on the dividends (as would be the case if you sold (NMM)), which may already be spent or reinvested elsewhere.

But also, remember when you set up your 'Leverage Projection Worksheet' you had in mind the acceptable level of risk you were willing to take on. That level of risk was the "% Levered" you decided on when you chose the "Multiplier Pick" and "PmtPerc" of your choice. If your loan balance were to continually become a larger portion of the market value of your securities, you would need to give serious consideration to other options and selling might not be the best one.

There is a tremendous amount of flexibility built into the "Divi-X" system and as such, can offer you a few alternatives other than selling. For example, if you were making 'Interest Only' payments, you could modify your situation by then applying principal payments from your dividends to start paying down the balance quicker. If you were already making principal payments using the "PmtPerc" option, you could modify your situation to have all dividends go toward the principal or increase the "PmtPerc" variable so that a higher percentage of your dividends would go towards the loan until you get your margin balance back into an acceptable comfort level.

This is one of the luxuries afforded to you when you use the "Divi-X" system, and having the ability to micro manage your individual holdings even though the decisions you are making are not 'seemingly' reflected on your brokerage statement, has a long-term benefit on the overall health of your portfolio. Just remember to always treat your transactions as if you were borrowing outside money.

Remember, you can modify the amount of leverage you expose yourself to by simply adjusting the "Multiplier Pick" when you initially set up a new 'Leverage Projection Worksheet' but once you settle on a "Multiplier Pick" it cannot be changed. Several other things can be changed, but this cannot. Think of it like going to a bank and asking for a loan. Once you cash their check, you have to pay it back. If you want less leverage (lower risk), then lower the "Multiplier Pick." If you want more leverage (higher risk), then you can raise the "Multiplier Pick." Again, always exercise extreme caution when getting aggressive with high yields.

How to Use the Running Leverage Rate

Since you are already familiar with our 'Ugly Ducklings,' and you're probably burnt out on the Dow 30 by now, we're going to use **Pimco Corporate & Income Strategy Fund (PCN)** as our case study for this segment. And, as I often do, we are going to use the results from a "PmtPerc" of 1.25% and a "Multiplier Pick" of 80, the same that were used in the 'Ugly Duckling' results earlier.

Pimco Corporate & Income Strategy Fund (PCN)

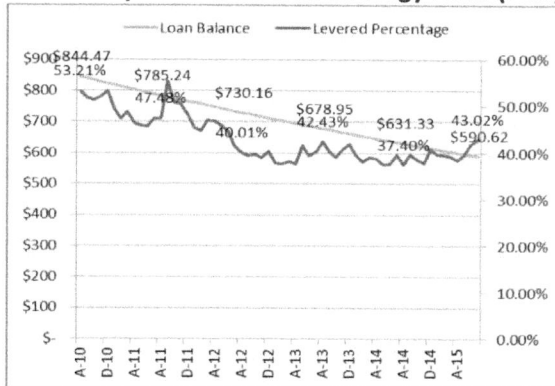

"No DIV Reinvestment"

Fig. 11.8

Option: "PmtPerc"

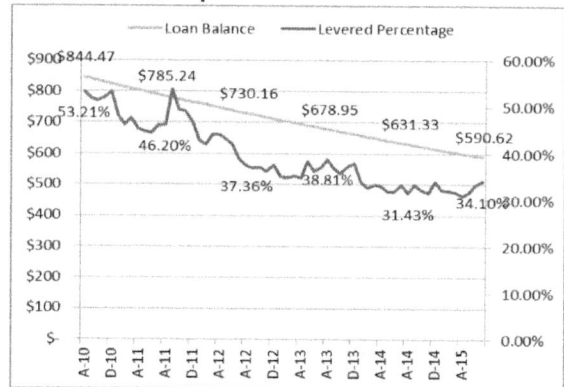

"Div Reinvestment"

In a perfect world, you would want to see the '**Levered Percentage**' also known as the '**Running Leverage Rate**,' drop sharply in relation to the '**Loan Balance.**' This would mean that your stocks are progressing extremely well. It is not a concern if the '**Levered Percentage**' line goes above the '**Loan Balance**' line. The '**Levered Percentage**' line is on a secondary axis and not related to price on the primary axis that the '**Loan Balance**' is on. It would, however, start to become a concern if at any point, the current '**Levered Percentage**' were to exceed the original '**Levered Percentage**.' For example in **Fig. 11.8**, if the '**Levered Percentage**' were to drift, or shoot past the original 53.21% mark, it would not be necessary to panic at this point depending on how far and above and how fast the '**Levered Percentage**' goes above the original '**Levered Percentage**' rate. At this point, you might want to consider alternatives such as some of the ones offered in the previous section, "**Running Leverage Rate.**"

Let's get back to **Pimco Corporate & Income Strategy Fund (PCN)** specifically. We already know the share price is in decline, there is nothing we can do about that, but are you going to have to hock the family jewels to pay back the loan? If you look at the side by side comparison of the two charts in **Fig. 11.8,** you can see a very similar pattern between the two. But the similarities end when you look at the '**Running Leverage Rate**' throughout the five year period. The "**No DIV Reinvestment**" and the "**DIV Reinvestment**" both declined over the five year period but the "**DIV Reinvestment**" side declined much more aggressively to 34.10% vs the "**NO DIV Reinvestment**" of 43.02%. The reason is because as you purchased more shares through reinvestment, you added to your position, weighting it more with equity to offset the leverage.

However, in both cases, because you used the "**PmtPerc**" option, your dividends were continually paying down the outstanding balance on the loan. Since the '**Running Leverage Rate**' continued to decline over the five year period, it would be obvious that your debt payments were outpacing the decline rate in the stocks share price.

Just to be clear, in both the "**No Div Reinvestment**" and the "**DIV Reinvestment**" scenarios, and because you used the "**PmtPerc**" option, both declined at an equal rate of 10.19% (53.21% - 43.02%) because the debt payments from dividends paid down the associated margin loan faster than the rate of decline in the share price. With "**DIV Reinvestment**" on the right of **Fig. 11.8**, the '**Running Leverage Rate**' declined an additional 8.92% (43.02% - 34.10%) because you added weight to your equity position by purchasing more shares through 'dividend reinvestment.'

If you were to choose the "**Interest Only**" option, here is what that would've looked like.

Pimco Corporate & Income Strategy Fund (PCN)

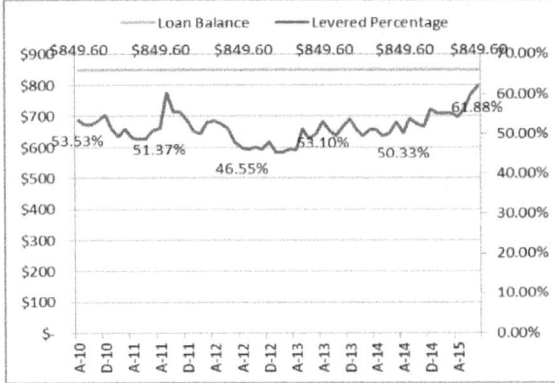

"No DIV Reinvestment"

Fig. 11.9

Option: "Interest Only"

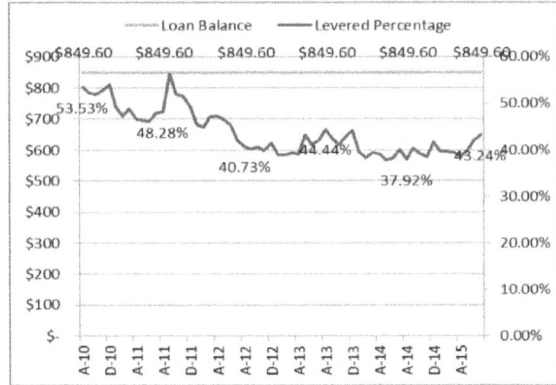

"Div Reinvestment"

Using "**No DIV Reinvestment**" with the "**Interest Only**" option would have caused your '**Running Leverage Rate**' to exceed your initial leverage ratio by 8.35% (61.88% - 53.53%). Now, the share value still exceeds the outstanding loan but because you are not reducing your loan amount, debt is becoming a bigger percentage of your holding. The opposite is true on the right. Because of 'dividend reinvestment, and only because of 'dividend reinvestment', you would've managed to decrease your **'Running Leverage Rate'** by 10.29% (53.53% - 43.24%) by adding equity faster than the decline rate in the share price with share purchases through dividend reinvestment.

Teachable Moment

I want to show you what your brokerage statement would be telling you in comparison to your actual results. For simplification, we're not going to look at 'dividend reinvestment' results.

(PCN) After 5 Years	Cost Basis	Current Value	% Gain/Loss	Est. Ann. Income	Margin Expense
5 Years	1550.00	1373.00	(-11.42%)	135.60*	**

*Does not reflect special dividend paid every year
**Lumped with every other security purchased with leverage so impact can't be accurately accounted for
Fig. 11.10

Now actual results using the "Divi-X" system:

(PCN) After 5 Years		No DIV Reinvestment "PmtPerc"
Ttl Returns		27.68%
"Divi-X"		61.26%
5YR Avg		12.25%
Ann Yield		17.59%
Without "Divi-X"		45.54%

Fig. 11.11

Both results are for the same stock. Which one would you sell and which one would you keep? You held onto this thing for five whole years. You're actually earning a yield of 17.59% on your initial cash investment! Would you sell that income stream? The share price took a big hit and you're still making a decent overall 12.25% annual average return. Are you ready to knowingly give that up? You might when you look at your brokerage statement.

Before we move on, I'm going to show you the charts for **Navios Maritime Partners L.P. (NMM)**. Keep in mind, the **'Running Leverage Rate'** is meant for reference. It is up to you to make judgement calls on whether the debt levels are acceptable to you or not, and don't forget, it is not cause for alarm if the 'Levered Percentage' line goes above the 'Loan Balance' line.

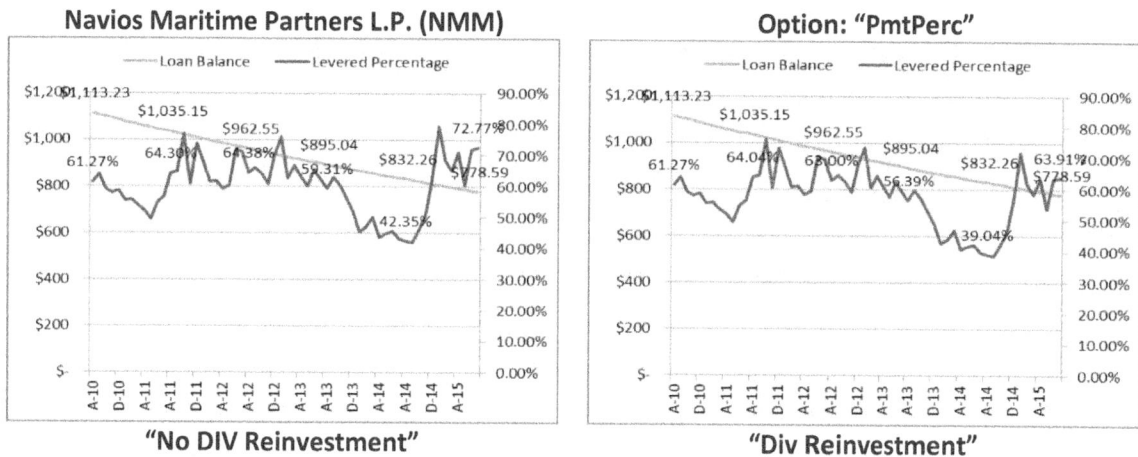

Fig. 11.12

No explanations here, I just wanted to throw one more example in to help you familiarize yourself with the concept of **"Running Leverage Rate."**

If I Choose 'Dividend Reinvestment' With "Divi-X," How Would That Work?

This is actually quite complicated and I would seriously recommend using 'The "Divi-X" System Workbook.' Unlike the usual method where you simply receive dividends and make "margin loan payments," there really is no precise way to reinvest dividends "after" you make your margin loan payments.

First off, your brokerage/margin account would have to allow you the option of 'dividend reinvestment' in the first place. My broker allows it and even allows me the flexibility of allocating what percentage of dividends I would like to allocate to 'dividend reinvestment.' My broker even allows me to allocate a percentage of any dividends from any securities and apply them, all or a percentage, to just one security or many securities."

Since the percentage of "dividends less margin interest" would change every month, you simply can't allocate a certain percentage of dividends to be reinvested. Let us also remember that even though we convert everything to monthly terms in the "Divi-X" system, the actual dividend payout will most likely not be monthly unless you're invested in "MoPays" (see Chapter 4). That being the case, we're going to ultimately have to estimate a percentage of dividends to reinvest that would still allow us to cover the monthly margin payment. Here are the steps that I would recommend but feel free to experiment with it on your own. Heck, if you find a better way, please let me know about it.

1. Choose an option
   a. The table examples in this chapter gave you a choice between **'DIV Reinvestment All DIV's,' 'DIV Reinvestment "PmtPerc",' and 'DIV Reinvestment Interest Only.'** In 'The "Divi-X" System Workbook,' you also have an additional option of **'Fixed Pmt."**
2. Go to the 'Amortization' table (available in '"Divi-X" Lite' and 'The "Divi-X" System Workbook') and calculate the total annual interest payments for the current year. Then divide that by the total annual dividends you expect to receive for the current year. For example:

   We'll use actual data from **Merck (MRK).** The actual numbers behind Year 1, using **'DIV Reinvestment "PmtPerc",** broke down like this:

Total 1st Year Interest:	$ 75.98
Total 1st Year Dividends:	$152.06

   Interest of $75.98 ÷ Dividends of $152.06 = 49.97%

   So that would leave us roughly 50.03% (100% less 49.97% interest), rounded down in this case to simply 50%, of dividends to reinvest. In year two you would simply repeat the process for that current year.

In the event something should change during the year, such as, an increase in interest rates or the dividend should change, recalculate the new numbers for the remainder of the year and do the same after year two, then year three, and so on. If your broker allows you the 'dividend reinvestment' option, as well as the percentage allocation feature, it is very likely that they will also allow you the option to change your allocation percentage anytime you want to by going to your account online.

Final note, you can use 'The "Divi-X" System Workbook" for dividend reinvestment. It would be most useful for projections, but in the case of keeping accurate record of your returns, it would require a little more effort than if you didn't do 'dividend reinvestment.' But, all in all, you could still find it a very useful tool.

Final Thoughts

This concludes your introduction to "The Dividend Times" aka 'The "Divi-X" System.' My only recommended prerequisite for purchasing this book was that a person felt comfortable in their own skin when it came to making their own investing decisions. I have no idea of your familiarity on the topics I discussed in this book but I sincerely hope you learned something new and valuable as well as seeing the potential offered to you through the "Divi-X" system.

A reminder, once again, that the use of leverage is a very risky endeavor. You shouldn't let fear of it exclude you from the use of it. It's just too advantageous a concept to ignore. The "Divi-X" system provides you with a way to ease yourself into it until you become more familiar with it. But no matter how confident you get, always, always, ALWAYS exercise sound judgement.

I had a lot of fun (and frustration) creating this system, as well as 'The "Divi-X" System Workbook.' In the future, I hope to see it evolve into something more, possibly with your help. I'm available for questions, comments and suggestions at wentkerl@divi-x.com. And if it hasn't happened already, I hope to set up a community on my web site @ www.TheDividendTimes.com where anyone can come and witness accounts of success had by users of the "Divi-X" system. You might also want to subscribe to The Dividend Times. It's free and with it, I hope to provide free offers, such as a free exporting summary worksheet where you can have all of your "Divi-X" securities summarized in one sheet with even more analytical tools (release date unknown), system updates, and eventually, potential security selections that will be screened by another Workbook program that I have in the works.

I wish you the very best of success in your investment endeavors and I hope the "Divi-X" system can play a part in that success. Good luck and thank you for purchasing "The Dividend Times."

Continue to Next Page for a Special Offer

The "Divi-X" System Workbook: Keeps track of actual 'cash on cash' yields compared to a company's actual stock yield and even projects them out as far as twenty years.

Special Offer

**All offers can be downloaded securely
@ www.TheDividendTimes.com
or
www.divi-x.com**
(use promo code: ibuydivix)

Free "Divi-X" Lite Worksheet

**$5 off 'The "Divi-X" System Workbook'
Digital Download Only
(List Price $9.95)
Yours for only $4.95
Hardcopy on DVD
(List Price $14.95)
Yours for only $9.95**

**Purchase the digital bundle for $14.90 (List $19.90)
(Book and Workbook Download)**

**Order the hard copy
(Book and Workbook on DVD)
$24.90
(List $29.90)**

Continue on to the "Divi-X" User Form (pg. 170)

Appendix

Five Year Cash on Cash (ConC) Averages @ Various "Multiplier Picks"

	ConC w/o "Divi-X"	"Divi-X" x 25	"Divi-X" x 50	"Divi-X" x 75	"Divi-X" x 100
AXP	57.42%	60.72%	64.48%	68.97%	73.81%
BA	39.62%	42.20%	45.21%	48.78%	53.08%
CAT	46.53%	51.17%	57.03%	64.67%	75.03%
CVX	20.93%	22.24%	23.81%	25.73%	28.13%
CSCO	Did not pay dividends at start of test window				
DD	42.27%	47.96%	55.76%	67.19%	85.53%
XOM	11.17%	11.41%	11.68%	11.98%	12.31%
GE	29.37%	31.06%	33.02%	35.32%	38.06%
GS	3.86%	3.81%	3.75%	3.69%	3.63%
HD	52.89%	56.89%	61.64%	67.39%	74.48%
MMM	31.96%	33.92%	36.21%	38.92%	42.17%
T	16.73%	18.43%	20.79%	24.33%	30.19%
INTC	2.45%	2.34%	2.07%	1.88%	1.65%
IBM	8.67%	8.76%	8.86%	8.98%	9.10%
JNJ	15.27%	15.93%	16.70%	17.60%	18.68%
JPM	10.32%	10.36%	10.40%	10.43%	10.47%
MCD	12.04%	12.42%	12.86%	13.37%	13.97%
MRK	17.18%	18.22%	19.50%	21.08%	23.10%
MSFT	14.57%	14.86%	15.17%	15.51%	15.88%
NKE	33.81%	34.63%	35.49%	36.40%	37.38%
PFE	27.82%	29.92%	32.48%	35.66%	39.74%
PG	9.70%	10.81%	9.92%	10.18%	10.47%
KO	14.48%	15.07%	15.75%	16.55%	17.50%
TRV	24.54%	25.68%	26.96%	28.43%	30.13%
UTX	13.51%	13.85%	14.24%	14.66%	15.14%
UNH	61.31%	63.26%	65.36%	67.61%	63.77%
VZ	21.69%	24.09%	27.41%	32.26%	40.06%
V	41.12%	41.53%	41.94%	42.36%	42.80%
WMT	12.28%	12.56%	12.87%	13.21%	13.59%
DIS	41.27%	42.07%	42.91%	43.80%	44.72%
Rtrn Avg.	25.34%	26.76%	28.42%	30.58%	33.26%

Five Year Cash on Cash (ConC) Averages @ Varying "PmtPerc" and "Multiplier Pick"

	"PmtPerc" 5.0% "Multiplier Pick" 20	"PmtPerc" 4.0% "Multiplier Pick" 25	"PmtPerc" 3.0% "Multiplier Pick" 30	"PmtPerc" 2.0% "Multiplier Pick" 50	"PmtPerc" 1.0% "Multiplier Pick" 100
AXP	60.36%	60.93%	61.62%	64.64%	73.65%
BA	42.05%	42.45%	42.97%	45.41%	52.87%
CAT	50.75%	51.52%	52.57%	57.35%	74.69%
CVX	22.43%	22.53%	22.80%	24.05%	27.90%
CSCO	Did not pay dividends at start of test window				
DD	47.48%	48.46%	49.77%	56.21%	84.96%
XOM	11.63%	11.58%	11.61%	11.81%	12.20%
GE	31.08%	31.30%	31.64%	33.21%	37.88%
GS	3.92%	3.87%	3.85%	3.80%	3.59%
HD	56.48%	57.16%	58.02%	61.87%	74.25%
MMM	33.90%	34.17%	34.57%	36.41%	41.98%
T	18.88%	18.95%	19.32%	21.26%	29.57%
INTC	2.53%	2.41%	2.36%	2.19%	1.56%
IBM	8.97%	8.90%	8.91%	8.97%	9.00%
JNJ	16.18%	16.17%	16.29%	16.89%	18.49%
JPM	10.38%	10.39%	10.39%	10.42%	10.45%
MCD	12.70%	12.64%	12.70%	13.04%	13.80%
MRK	18.50%	18.53%	18.74%	19.75%	22.84%
MSFT	14.99%	14.97%	15.02%	15.26%	15.80%
NKE	34.61%	34.72%	34.88%	35.56%	37.32%
PFE	29.97%	30.23%	30.77%	32.74%	39.48%
PG	10.23%	10.14%	10.17%	10.35%	10.65%
KO	15.32%	15.30%	15.41%	15.94%	17.32%
TRV	25.76%	25.87%	26.10%	27.12%	29.98%
UTX	14.04%	14.01%	14.07%	14.36%	15.02%
UNH	63.04%	63.37%	63.77%	65.44%	69.97%
VZ	24.35%	24.59%	25.13%	27.86%	39.49%
V	41.50%	41.56%	41.64%	41.97%	42.78%
WMT	12.75%	12.72%	12.76%	12.99%	13.48%
DIS	42.03%	42.14%	42.30%	42.97%	44.68%
Rtrn Avg.	26.79%	26.95%	27.25%	28.62%	33.30%

The results in the table above are from the highest allowable "Multiplier Pick" allowed by the "PmtPerc" that covers a minimum of a full interest and principal payment.

Leverage Security User Form (please fill out with pencil)

a) Ticker

b) Purchase Date

c) Stock Price

d) Number of Share Purchased

e) Total Value of Shares Purchased

f) Annual Margin Rate

g) "PmtPerc" or Payment Percentage

h) Return Rate – Your expected rate of return. This is your decision.

i) "Multiplier Pick" – The number times the monthly dividend total that determines your borrowing/margin amount

j) Dividend –The amount paid per share

k) The number of dividends paid per year

l) Annual Dividend Payment – The total amount paid on one share annually.

m) Annual Dividend Total- The total of all dividends received annually.

n) Dividend Yield – The stated dividend yield when you purchased the security.

o) Total Monthly Dividends – Annual Dividend Total (m) divided by twelve months.

p) Amount of Leverage – This figure is the result of the Total Monthly Dividends (o) x "Multiplier Pick" (i).

q) Cash Paid – This is the Total Value of Shares Purchased (e) less the Amount of Leverage (p)

r) Percentage Levered – This is the Amount of Leverage (p) divided into the Total Value of Shares Purchased (e).

s) Statement Date

t) Share Price on Statement

u) Balance Forward – After the first month the new balance carried over to the following month

v) Minimum Monthly Payment – The result of Balance Forward(u) times "PmtPerc" (g)

w) Monthly Interest Rate – The Annual Margin Rate (f) divided by twelve months

x) Monthly Interest Amount – Balance Forward (u) times Monthly Interest Rate (w)

y) Principal Paid – Minimum Monthly Payment (v) less Monthly Interest Amount (x)

z) Net Monthly Dividends – Total Monthly Dividends (o) less Monthly Interest Amount (x)

aa) Unrealized Gain/Loss – Current Share Value (t x d) less Total Value of Shares Purchased (e)

bb) "Divi-X" Share Price Percentage Return – Unrealized Gain/Loss (aa) divided by Cash Paid (q)

cc) Total Share Value Percentage Return – Unrealized Gain/Loss (aa) divided by Total Value of Shares Purchased (e)

dd) Actual "Divi-X" Dividend Yield – Net Monthly Dividends (z) divided by Cash Paid (q)

ee) Total "Divi-X" Percentage Return – Unrealized Gain/Loss (aa) plus Net Monthly Dividends (z) divided by Cash Paid (q).

ff) Total Return – Unrealized Gain/Loss (aa) plus Net Monthly Dividends (z) divided by Total Value of Shares Purchased (e)

a	b	c	d	e (c x d)	f	g	h	i
ABC	1/1/15	$5.00	100	$500.00	7.50%	1.25%	9.0%	80

j	k	l (j + k)	m (l x d)	n	o (m ÷ 12)	p (o x i)	q (e - p)	r (p ÷ e)
$.12	4	$.48	$48.00	9.6%	$4.00	$320.00	$180.00	64.00%

This next part would be a pain to do by hand. If you haven't purchased 'The "Divi-X" System Workbook,' I encourage you to at least take advantage of the Free "Divi-X" Lite Worksheet. It can be downloaded for free at TheDividendTimes.Com.

s	t	u	o	v (u x g)	w (f ÷ 12)	x (u x w)	y (v – x)	z (o – x)*
2/1/15	$5.03	$320.00	$4.00	$4.00	.625%	$2.00	$2.00	$2.00
3/1/15	$5.12	$318.00	$4.00	$3.98	.625%	$1.99	$1.99	$2.01
4/1/15	$5.06	$316.01	$4.00	$3.95	.625%	$1.98	$1.98	$2.02
5/1/15	$5.08	$314.04	$4.00	$3.93	.625%	$1.96	$1.96	$2.04
6/1/15	$4.99	$312.07	$4.00	$3.90	.625%	$1.95	$1.95	$2.05
7/1/15	$4.86	$310.12	$4.00	$3.88	.625%	$1.94	$1.94	$2.06
8/1/15	$4.88	$308.19	$4.00	$3.85	.625%	$1.93	$1.93	$2.07
9/1/15	$5.02	$306.26	$4.00	$3.83	.625%	$1.91	$1.91	$2.09
10/1/15	$5.09	$304.35	$4.00	$3.80	.625%	$1.90	$1.90	$2.10
11/1/15	$5.13	$302.44	$4.00	$3.78	.625%	$1.89	$1.89	$2.11
12/1/15	$5.11	$300.55	$4.00	$3.76	.625%	$1.88	$1.88	$2.12
1/1/16	$5.14	$298.67	$4.00	$3.73	.625%	$1.87	$1.87	$2.13
Totals			$48.00	$46.38		$23.19	$23.19	$24.80

	z	aa (t x d – e)	bb (aa ÷ q)	cc (aa ÷ e)	dd (z ÷ q)	n	ee (aa + z ÷ q)	ff (aa + z ÷ e)
Returns	$24.80	$14.00	7.7%	2.8%	13.8%	9.6%	21.6%	7.8%

* Remember, principal paid toward your margin loan makes that principal available for use again right away.

"Divi-X" Leverage Security User From (please make copy and use pencil)

a	b	c	d	e (c x d)	f	g	h	i

j	k	l (j + k)	m (l x d)	n	o (m ÷ 12)	p (o x i)	q (e - p)	r (p ÷ e)

s	t	u	o	v (u x g)	w (f ÷ 12)	x (u x w)	y (v − x)	z (o − x)*
Totals								

	z	aa (t x d − e)	bb (aa ÷ q)	cc (aa ÷ e)	dd (z ÷ q)	n	ee (aa + z ÷ q)	ff (aa + z ÷ e)
Returns								

* Remember, principal paid toward your margin loan makes that principal available for use again right away.

Continue to next page for a look at the downloadable 'Free "Divi-X" Lite' worksheet

How to Use the Free "Divi-X" Lite Worksheet

This is a sample screenshot of the Free "Divi-X" Lite Worksheet. It is a much simpler version of the full "Divi-X" System Workbook but, believe it or not, the full version is just as simple to use. Here we are going to introduce you to everything you need to know to use the Free "Divi-X" Lite Worksheet, which will also serve as a crash course on what you need to know to use the full version should you decide to upgrade.

Ticker	Stock Price	No. Shares	Purch Date	Margin Rate	DIV Pmt	DIV Yld	Cash Paid
ABC	$ 6.4100	100	06/26/15	7.50%	$ 0.1200	7.49%	$ 369.00

Rtrn Rate?	Multiplier Pick	DIV Per/Year	Monthly DIV	Pmt Perc	Mth DIV Ttl	Leverage %	Leveraged
10.00%	68	4	$ 0.0400	1.25%	$ 4.00	42.43%	$272.00

	Year 1		Year 2		Year 3		Year 4		Year 5	
	"Divi-X"	Without	"Divi-X"	Without	"Divi-X"	Without	"Divi-X"	Without	"Divi-X"	Without
	25.86%	8.57%	54.00%	17.90%	84.61%	28.04%	117.88%	39.07%	154.03%	51.04%
	Annual Average		Annual Average		Annual Average		Annual Average		Annual Average	
	25.86%	8.57%	27.00%	8.95%	28.20%	9.35%	29.47%	9.77%	30.81%	10.21%
	Difference		Difference		Difference		Difference		Difference	
	17.29%		36.11%		56.57%		78.82%		102.99%	

Date	Share Price	Sh Ttl Val	DIV Ttl	DIV Yld	Min Pmt	Interest	Net DIV*	Ttl Unreal Gain/Loss	Ttl DIVs	Ttl Int	DIV's Less Int	Net Unreal Gain/Loss	Net Unreal Gain/Loss %	"Divi-X"	Without "Divi-X"
6/30/2015	$ 6.46	$ 646.34	$ 4.00	7.43%	$3.40	$1.70	$ 2.30	$ 5.34	$ 4.00	$1.70	$ 2.30	$ 7.64	1.19%	2.07%	0.69%
7/31/2015	$ 6.52	$ 651.73	$ 4.00	7.37%	$3.38	$1.69	$ 2.31	$ 10.73	$ 8.00	$3.39	$ 4.61	$ 15.34	2.39%	4.16%	1.38%
8/31/2015	$ 6.57	$ 657.16	$ 4.00	7.30%	$3.36	$1.68	$ 2.32	$ 16.16	$ 12.00	$5.07	$ 6.93	$ 23.09	3.60%	6.26%	2.07%
9/30/2015	$ 6.63	$ 662.64	$ 4.00	7.24%	$3.34	$1.67	$ 2.33	$ 21.64	$ 16.00	$6.74	$ 9.26	$ 30.90	4.82%	8.37%	2.77%
10/31/2015	$ 6.68	$ 668.16	$ 4.00	7.18%	$3.32	$1.66	$ 2.34	$ 27.16	$ 20.00	$8.39	$ 11.61	$ 38.76	6.05%	10.50%	3.48%
11/30/2015	$ 6.74	$ 673.73	$ 4.00	7.12%	$3.30	$1.65	$ 2.35	$ 32.73	$ 24.00	$10.04	$ 13.96	$ 46.68	7.28%	12.65%	4.19%
12/31/2015	$ 6.79	$ 679.34	$ 4.00	7.07%	$3.27	$1.64	$ 2.36	$ 38.34	$ 28.00	$11.68	$ 16.32	$ 54.66	8.53%	14.81%	4.91%
1/31/2016	$ 6.85	$ 685.00	$ 4.00	7.01%	$3.25	$1.63	$ 2.37	$ 44.00	$ 32.00	$13.31	$ 18.69	$ 62.69	9.78%	16.99%	5.63%
2/29/2016	$ 6.91	$ 690.71	$ 4.00	6.95%	$3.23	$1.62	$ 2.38	$ 49.71	$ 36.00	$14.92	$ 21.08	$ 70.79	11.04%	19.18%	6.36%
3/31/2016	$ 6.96	$ 696.46	$ 4.00	6.89%	$3.21	$1.61	$ 2.39	$ 55.46	$ 40.00	$16.53	$ 23.47	$ 78.94	12.31%	21.39%	7.09%
4/30/2016	$ 7.02	$ 702.27	$ 4.00	6.83%	$3.19	$1.60	$ 2.40	$ 61.27	$ 44.00	$18.13	$ 25.87	$ 87.14	13.59%	23.62%	7.83%
5/31/2016	$ 7.08	$ 708.12	$ 4.00	6.78%	$3.17	$1.59	$ 2.41	$ 67.12	$ 48.00	$19.71	$ 28.29	$ 95.41	14.88%	25.86%	8.57%

The screenshot only goes as far as the end of year one, but the actual worksheet goes five years deep. Once I tell you that the light gray shaded areas with black print are user fields to be filled out by you, I'm sure you can already figure out how to use the worksheet on your own. Nonetheless, we're going to do a quick walkthrough.

User Fields

Starting at the very top of the screenshot is the basic security information you would fill out. Again, these are the light shaded gray fields with black print.

1. Ticker
2. Stock/Share Price
3. No. Shares – Total number of shares you wish to purchase.
4. Purch Date or Purchase Date
5. Margin Rate – Annual
6. DIV Pmt – Dividend Payment or payout. This is the actual dividend paid out at the interval the company pays it out. Remember, the "Divi-X" System breaks dividend payments down monthly. In the above example, you'll observe that the **"DIV Pmt"** is $ 0.12 (or twelve cents). This dividend is paid out quarterly, but notice in the unshaded "Monthly DIV" field the amount is only $ 0.04 (or four cents).

7. Rtrn Rate? – This is the annualized return rate you hope to achieve with this security. In the Lite version its, more or less, for reference. In the full version, "Divi-X" uses this field to keep you aware of how well your investment is doing in comparison.

8. Multiplier Pick – This is the number of times the unshaded field "Mth DIV Ttl" is multiplied to give you the total amount of leverage/margin you will borrow against in your margin account. In the full version, "Divi-X" lays out sixteen different projections for sixteen different "Multiplier Picks" at once for you to choose from. Having this feature allows you to look at sixteen scenarios; that quickly gives you an idea of the leverage commitment you might be willing to make by showing you such a broad spectrum of possibilities. In the Lite version, it's still remarkably easy but you have to enter each scenario one by one. When I say one by one, I do not mean you have to go in sequential order. For example, in the screenshot, the "Multiplier Pick" is 80. If 80 seems too high for your comfort level, you don't have to go down to 79, then 78, then 77, and so on until you reach 25 which might look more comfortable to you. If the "Multiplier Pick" seems high or too low, you can change the "Multiplier Pick" in any increment you want to save time (ex., 5, 10, 15 or 100, 85, 50).

9. DIV Per/Year – The number of times in a year the company actually pays out a dividend.

10. PmtPerc – or Payment Percentage. This is the monthly payment amount that you decide to pay. The payment percentage is whatever percentage you choose times the outstanding balance remaining on your margin loan associated with the particular security.

11. Share Price – This field is filled out by you every month. The share price will be the closing share price on your brokerage statement. You'll notice that the share price escalates every month. The increase in share price is based on the "Rtrn Rate?" you entered earlier. You will replace it with the actual share price from your brokerage statement every month.

12. DIV Ttl – This field is automatically filled in with the info in field "Mth DIV Ttl." You do not have to enter this figure unless there is a dividend change. In the case of a special dividend, just add it to the current dividend in the month in which it applies.

Warning: Do not change data in the non-shaded fields. If you do, quickly hit undo before saving and/or closing the file.

The "Divi-X" System Workbook
A Closer Look

All of the data compiled in this book was taken from 'The "Divi-X" System Workbook.' Just to give you a little context, if I had done by hand what 'The "Divi-X" System Workbook did for me in compiling all of this information, it would have most likely become a life endeavor to publish the material you have before you now.

I thought I would present to you some of the many features that would enhance the "Divi-X" system experience for you (i.e. make your life a bit or a lot easier, depending on the frequency of your security purchases).

After you have read all the material in this book you should have a good understanding of how the "Divi-X" system works, so the brief walkthrough I'm presenting to you now should already seem familiar with very little explanation.

The "Divi-X" System Workbook: The following screenshots from the workbook will likely look different at the time of purchase. I am constantly tweaking to make the workbook more user-friendly.

What Can You Do With the "Divi-X" System Workbook?

The following pages will present some screenshots to give you an idea of how useful "The "Divi-X" System Workbook" really is.

Continue to the next few pages for a look at 'The "Divi-X" System' Workbook

Home Page – This is Where it All Begins

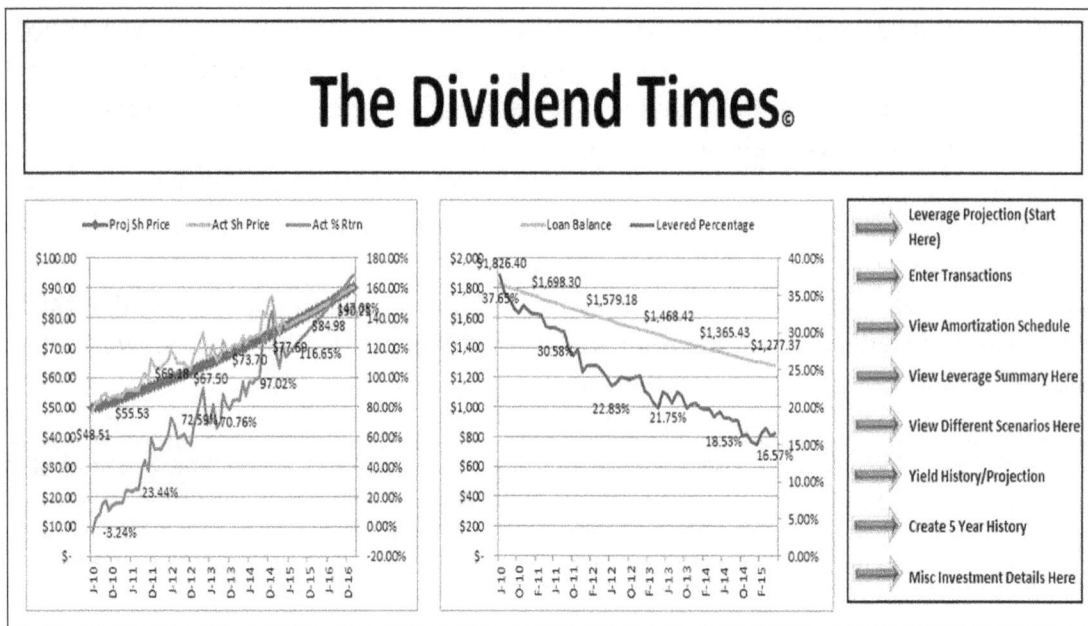

The Dividend Times©

Right-side legend (navigation arrows):
- Leverage Projection (Start Here)
- Enter Transactions
- View Amortization Schedule
- View Leverage Summary Here
- View Different Scenarios Here
- Yield History/Projection
- Create 5 Year History
- Misc Investment Details Here

Calculate Several Scenarios in Seconds with Just a Few Field Entries

"The "Divi-X" System Workbook" allows you to quickly view sixteen different projections at once using the "Leverage Projection Worksheet."

Ticker	Stock Price	No. Shares	Purch Date	End Date	DIV Pmt	Multiplier Start	Rtrn Rate?	% Levered
ABC	$ 48.4400	100	06/19/09	J-09	$ 0.4200	20	9.00%	23.12%

								Rule 72
Multiplier Pick	DIV Per/Year	Monthly DIV	Pmt Perc	Margin Rate	Multiplier Step	Mth DIV Ttl	Based on DIV	20.76
80	4	$ 0.1400	1.25%	7.75%	5	$ 14.00	On Est Rtrn	5.37
							On Act Rtrn	5.37

DIV Multiplier	Cash Out Of Pocket	Leverage Amt	Ttl Share Value	#Shares Purch by Leverage	DIV Yield	Min Pmt	Principal	Margin Interest	Net DIV Cash	Monthly Net Div Cash (1yr)	Monthly Net Div Cash (5yr)	Yield Less Margin Int	Yield Less Marg Int (1YR)	Yield Less Marg Int (5YR)	Leverage Ratio
20	$ 4,564.00	$ 280.00	$ 4,844.00	5.78	3.47%	$ 3.50	$ 1.69	$ 1.81	$ 10.50	$ 10.74	$ 11.84	2.76%	2.82%	3.11%	5.78%
25	$ 4,494.00	$ 350.00	$ 4,844.00	7.23	3.47%	$ 4.38	$ 2.11	$ 2.26	$ 9.63	$ 9.92	$ 11.23	2.57%	2.65%	3.00%	7.23%
30	$ 4,424.00	$ 420.00	$ 4,844.00	8.67	3.47%	$ 5.25	$ 2.54	$ 2.71	$ 8.75	$ 9.10	$ 10.62	2.37%	2.47%	2.88%	8.67%
35	$ 4,354.00	$ 490.00	$ 4,844.00	10.12	3.47%	$ 6.13	$ 2.96	$ 3.16	$ 7.88	$ 8.28	$ 10.01	2.17%	2.28%	2.76%	10.12%
40	$ 4,284.00	$ 560.00	$ 4,844.00	11.56	3.47%	$ 7.00	$ 3.38	$ 3.62	$ 7.00	$ 7.46	$ 9.40	1.96%	2.09%	2.63%	11.56%
45	$ 4,214.00	$ 630.00	$ 4,844.00	13.01	3.47%	$ 7.88	$ 3.81	$ 4.07	$ 6.13	$ 6.65	$ 8.79	1.74%	1.89%	2.50%	13.01%
50	$ 4,144.00	$ 700.00	$ 4,844.00	14.45	3.47%	$ 8.75	$ 4.23	$ 4.52	$ 5.25	$ 5.83	$ 8.17	1.52%	1.69%	2.37%	14.45%
55	$ 4,074.00	$ 770.00	$ 4,844.00	15.90	3.47%	$ 9.63	$ 4.65	$ 4.97	$ 4.38	$ 5.01	$ 7.56	1.29%	1.48%	2.23%	15.90%
60	$ 4,004.00	$ 840.00	$ 4,844.00	17.34	3.47%	$ 10.50	$ 5.08	$ 5.43	$ 3.50	$ 4.19	$ 6.95	1.05%	1.26%	2.08%	17.34%
65	$ 3,934.00	$ 910.00	$ 4,844.00	18.79	3.47%	$ 11.38	$ 5.50	$ 5.88	$ 2.63	$ 3.37	$ 6.34	0.80%	1.03%	1.93%	18.79%
70	$ 3,864.00	$ 980.00	$ 4,844.00	20.23	3.47%	$ 12.25	$ 5.92	$ 6.33	$ 1.75	$ 2.55	$ 5.73	0.54%	0.79%	1.78%	20.23%
75	$ 3,794.00	$ 1,050.00	$ 4,844.00	21.68	3.47%	$ 13.13	$ 6.34	$ 6.78	$ 0.88	$ 1.73	$ 5.11	0.28%	0.55%	1.62%	21.68%
80	$ 3,724.00	$ 1,120.00	$ 4,844.00	23.12	3.47%	$ 14.00	$ 6.77	$ 7.23	$ -	$ 0.92	$ 4.50	0.00%	0.29%	1.45%	23.12%
85	$ 3,654.00	$ 1,190.00	$ 4,844.00	24.57	3.47%	$ 14.88	$ 7.19	$ 7.69	$ (0.88)	$ 0.10	$ 3.89	-0.29%	0.03%	1.28%	24.57%
90	$ 3,584.00	$ 1,260.00	$ 4,844.00	26.01	3.47%	$ 15.75	$ 7.61	$ 8.14	$ (1.75)	$ (0.72)	$ 3.28	-0.59%	-0.24%	1.10%	26.01%
95	$ 3,514.00	$ 1,330.00	$ 4,844.00	27.46	3.47%	$ 16.63	$ 8.04	$ 8.59	$ (2.63)	$ (1.54)	$ 2.67	-0.90%	-0.53%	0.91%	27.46%
100	$ 3,444.00	$ 1,400.00	$ 4,844.00	28.90	3.47%	$ 17.50	$ 8.46	$ 9.04	$ (3.50)	$ (2.36)	$ 2.05	-1.22%	-0.82%	0.72%	28.90%

Simple Transaction Entry

Year 1				Year 2				Year 3				Year 4				Year 5		
	DIV's	Payments	Sh Price		DIV's	Payments	Sh Price		DIV's	Payments	Sh Price		DIV's	Payments	Sh Price		DIV's	Payments	Sh Price
7/31/2009	$14.00	$14.00	$48.44	7/31/2010	$14.00	$13.02	$52.98	7/31/2011	$14.00	$12.10	$57.95	7/31/2012	$14.00	$11.26	$63.39	7/31/2013	$14.00	$10.47	$69.34
8/31/2009	$14.00	$13.92	$48.80	8/31/2010	$14.00	$12.94	$53.38	8/31/2011	$14.00	$12.03	$58.39	8/31/2012	$14.00	$11.19	$63.87	8/31/2013	$14.00	$10.40	$69.86
9/30/2009	$14.00	$13.83	$49.17	9/30/2010	$14.00	$12.86	$53.78	9/30/2011	$14.00	$11.96	$58.83	9/30/2012	$14.00	$11.12	$64.35	9/30/2013	$14.00	$10.34	$70.38
10/31/2009	$14.00	$13.75	$49.54	10/31/2010	$14.00	$12.78	$54.19	10/31/2011	$14.00	$11.89	$59.27	10/31/2012	$14.00	$11.05	$64.83	10/31/2013	$14.00	$10.28	$70.91
11/30/2009	$14.00	$13.66	$49.91	11/30/2010	$14.00	$12.71	$54.59	11/30/2011	$14.00	$11.82	$59.71	11/30/2012	$14.00	$10.99	$65.31	11/30/2013	$14.00	$10.22	$71.44
12/31/2009	$14.00	$13.58	$50.28	12/31/2010	$14.00	$12.63	$55.00	12/31/2011	$14.00	$11.74	$60.16	12/31/2012	$14.00	$10.92	$65.80	12/31/2013	$14.00	$10.15	$71.98
1/31/2010	$14.00	$13.50	$50.66	1/31/2011	$14.00	$12.55	$55.41	1/31/2012	$14.00	$11.67	$60.61	1/31/2013	$14.00	$10.85	$66.30	1/31/2014	$14.00	$10.09	$72.52
2/28/2010	$14.00	$13.42	$51.04	2/28/2011	$14.00	$12.48	$55.83	2/29/2012	$14.00	$11.60	$61.07	2/28/2013	$14.00	$10.79	$66.79	2/28/2014	$14.00	$10.03	$73.06
3/31/2010	$14.00	$13.34	$51.42	3/31/2011	$14.00	$12.40	$56.25	3/31/2012	$14.00	$11.53	$61.52	3/31/2013	$14.00	$10.72	$67.30	3/31/2014	$14.00	$9.97	$73.61
4/30/2010	$14.00	$13.26	$51.81	4/30/2011	$14.00	$12.33	$56.67	4/30/2012	$14.00	$11.46	$61.99	4/30/2013	$14.00	$10.66	$67.80	4/30/2014	$14.00	$9.91	$74.16
5/31/2010	$14.00	$13.18	$52.20	5/31/2011	$14.00	$12.25	$57.09	5/31/2012	$14.00	$11.39	$62.45	5/31/2013	$14.00	$10.59	$68.31	5/31/2014	$14.00	$9.85	$74.72
6/30/2010	$14.00	$13.10	$52.59	6/30/2011	$14.00	$12.18	$57.52	6/30/2012	$14.00	$11.32	$62.92	6/30/2013	$14.00	$10.53	$68.82	6/30/2014	$14.00	$9.79	$75.28

$499.41	$1,086.16	$1,730.86	$2,440.27	$3,221.27
13.41%	29.17%	46.48%	65.53%	86.50%

Everything is already pre-filled. Aside from the share price, there are no more entries to make unless the dividend changes, the margin rate changes, or if you opt to make your own changes.

Amortize Using "PmtPerc", All DIV's, Fixed Payment, Interest Only, or Additional Principal Payments

ABC   Leveraged Amt $1,837.50   Amortization & Margin Replenish Table

Date	Loan Balance	DIV Pmt	MIN Pmt	Act Pmt	Margin Rate	Interest	Cumulative Interest	New Balance	Avail Margin	Cumulative Avail Margin	Net Cash	Full DIV Margin Accum.	Current Market Value
6/30/2010	$1,837.50	$24.50	$22.97	$22.97	7.75%	$11.87	$11.87	$1,826.40	$11.10	$11.10	$12.63	1.53	$4,851.00
7/31/2010	$1,826.40	$ -	$22.83	$22.83	7.75%	$11.80	$23.66	$1,815.36	$11.03	$22.14	$(11.80)	$(21.30)	$5,130.00
8/31/2010	$1,815.36	$24.50	$22.69	$22.69	7.75%	$11.72	$35.39	$1,804.40	$10.97	$33.10	$12.78	(19.49)	$5,208.00
9/30/2010	$1,804.40	$24.50	$22.55	$22.55	7.75%	$11.65	$47.04	$1,793.49	$10.90	$44.01	$12.85	(17.55)	$5,397.00
10/31/2010	$1,793.49	$24.50	$22.42	$22.42	7.75%	$11.58	$58.62	$1,782.66	$10.84	$54.84	$12.92	(15.46)	$5,463.00
11/30/2010	$1,782.66	$24.50	$22.28	$22.28	7.75%	$11.51	$70.14	$1,771.89	$10.77	$65.61	$12.99	(13.25)	$5,256.00
12/31/2010	$1,771.89	$24.50	$22.15	$22.15	7.75%	$11.44	$81.58	$1,761.18	$10.71	$76.32	$13.06	(10.90)	$5,343.00
1/31/2011	$1,761.18	$24.50	$22.01	$22.01	7.75%	$11.37	$92.95	$1,750.54	$10.64	$86.96	$13.13	(8.41)	$5,388.00
2/28/2011	$1,750.54	$24.50	$21.88	$21.88	7.75%	$11.31	$104.26	$1,739.97	$10.58	$97.53	$13.19	(5.79)	$5,361.00
3/31/2011	$1,739.97	$24.50	$21.75	$21.75	7.75%	$11.24	$115.50	$1,729.45	$10.51	$108.05	$13.26	(3.04)	$5,346.00
4/30/2011	$1,729.45	$24.50	$21.62	$21.62	7.75%	$11.17	$126.67	$1,719.01	$10.45	$118.49	$13.33	(0.16)	$5,595.00
5/31/2011	$1,719.01	$24.50	$21.49	$21.49	7.75%	$11.10	$137.77	$1,708.62	$10.39	$128.88	$13.40	2.85	$5,586.00
6/30/2011	$1,708.62	$24.50	$21.36	$21.36	7.75%	$11.03	$148.80	$1,698.30	$10.32	$139.20	$13.47	5.99	$5,553.00
7/31/2011	$1,698.30	$24.50	$21.23	$21.23	7.75%	$10.97	$159.77	$1,688.04	$10.26	$149.46	$13.53	9.27	$5,580.00
8/31/2011	$1,688.04	$25.00	$21.10	$21.10	7.75%	$10.90	$170.67	$1,677.84	$10.20	$159.66	$14.10	13.16	$5,568.00
9/30/2011	$1,677.84	$25.00	$20.97	$20.97	7.75%	$10.84	$181.51	$1,667.70	$10.14	$169.80	$14.16	17.19	$5,997.00
10/31/2011	$1,667.70	$25.00	$20.85	$20.85	7.75%	$10.77	$192.28	$1,657.63	$10.08	$179.87	$14.23	21.35	$6,138.00
11/30/2011	$1,657.63	$25.00	$20.72	$20.72	7.75%	$10.71	$202.99	$1,647.61	$10.01	$189.89	$14.29	25.63	$5,937.00
12/31/2011	$1,647.61	$25.00	$20.60	$20.60	7.75%	$10.64	$213.63	$1,637.66	$9.95	$199.84	$14.36	30.03	$6,600.00
1/31/2012	$1,637.66	$25.00	$20.47	$20.47	7.75%	$10.58	$224.20	$1,627.76	$9.89	$209.74	$14.42	34.56	$6,354.00
2/29/2012	$1,627.76	$25.00	$20.35	$20.35	7.75%	$10.51	$234.72	$1,617.93	$9.83	$219.57	$14.49	39.21	$6,330.00

Change Terms Midstream and Have Its Impact Reflected and Projected Immediately
Compare Your Projections to Actual Performance Data to Keep Track of Your Goals Constantly

Projected Total Returns	1YR	2YR	3YR	4YR	5YR	Projected Returns on Leverage	1YR Lever	2YR Lever	3YR Lever	4YR Lever	5YR Lever
$ Rtrn	$ 557.06	$1,233.60	$1,896.06	$2,701.26	$ 3,576.98		$ 119.38	$ 289.07	$ 459.20	$ 687.43	$ 946.65
"Divi-X" Rtrn	17.81%	39.44%	60.63%	86.37%	114.37%		3.82%	9.24%	14.68%	21.98%	30.27%
Levered Rtrn							6.50%	15.73%	24.99%	37.41%	51.52%
Ttl Rtrn	11.22%	24.85%	38.19%	54.41%	72.04%		2.40%	5.82%	9.25%	13.85%	19.07%

Buttons: All DIV's | Fixed Pmt | "PmtPerc" | Interest Only | DIV's Reinvest | No DIV's Reinvest

"PmtPerc"
No DIV's Reinvest

Actual Total Returns	1YR	2YR	3YR	4YR	5YR	Actual Returns on Leverage	1YR	2YR	3YR	4YR	5YR
$ Rtrn	$ 752.73	$1,925.63	$2,140.01	$2,755.24	$ 3,572.24		$ 191.80	$ 545.18	$ 549.49	$ 707.41	$ 944.89
"Divi-X" Rtrn	24.07%	61.57%	68.43%	88.10%	114.22%		6.13%	17.43%	17.57%	22.62%	30.21%
Levered Rtrn							10.44%	29.67%	29.90%	38.50%	51.42%
Ttl Rtrn	15.16%	38.78%	43.10%	55.49%	71.95%		3.86%	10.98%	11.07%	14.25%	19.03%

Actual Without The "Divi-X" System				
$ 560.93	$1,380.45	$1,590.52	$ 2,047.84	$ 2,627.35
17.94%	44.14%	50.86%	65.48%	84.01%
These are the actual returns on the unleveraged portion of your investment.				

Projected/Actual Total Difference	1YR	2YR	3YR	4YR	5YR	Proj/Act Difference on Levered Returns	1YR	2YR	3YR	4YR	5YR
$ Rtrn	$ 195.68	$ 692.03	$ 243.94	$ 53.98	$ (4.74)		$ 72.42	$ 256.11	$ 90.28	$ 19.98	$ (1.75)
"Divi-X" Rtrn	6.26%	22.13%	7.80%	1.73%	-0.15%		2.32%	8.19%	2.89%	0.64%	-0.06%
Levered Rtrn							3.94%	13.94%	4.91%	1.09%	-0.10%
Ttl Rtrn	3.94%	13.94%	4.91%	1.09%	-0.10%		1.46%	5.16%	1.82%	0.40%	-0.04%

Stock/Cash/Actual Yields on Cash Invested Per Annum				
1YR	2YR	3YR	4YR	5YR
5.92%	6.02%	4.60%	6.26%	6.38%
$ 131.73	$ 170.89	$ 109.38	$ 200.23	$ 214.00
4.21%	5.46%	3.50%	6.40%	6.84%

Returns on Leverage are actual returns/losses on your margin loan. Do not let a negative number discourage you if your Actual "Divi-X" returns are out pacing the returns shown in the 'Actual Without The "Divi-X" System' returns box.

Ticker	ABC	Dividend	$ 0.74
Stock Price	$ 49.65	Multi Pick	75
Purch Date	5/7/2010	Pmt Perc	1.25%

Project Cash on Cash Yields Up to Twenty Years Out

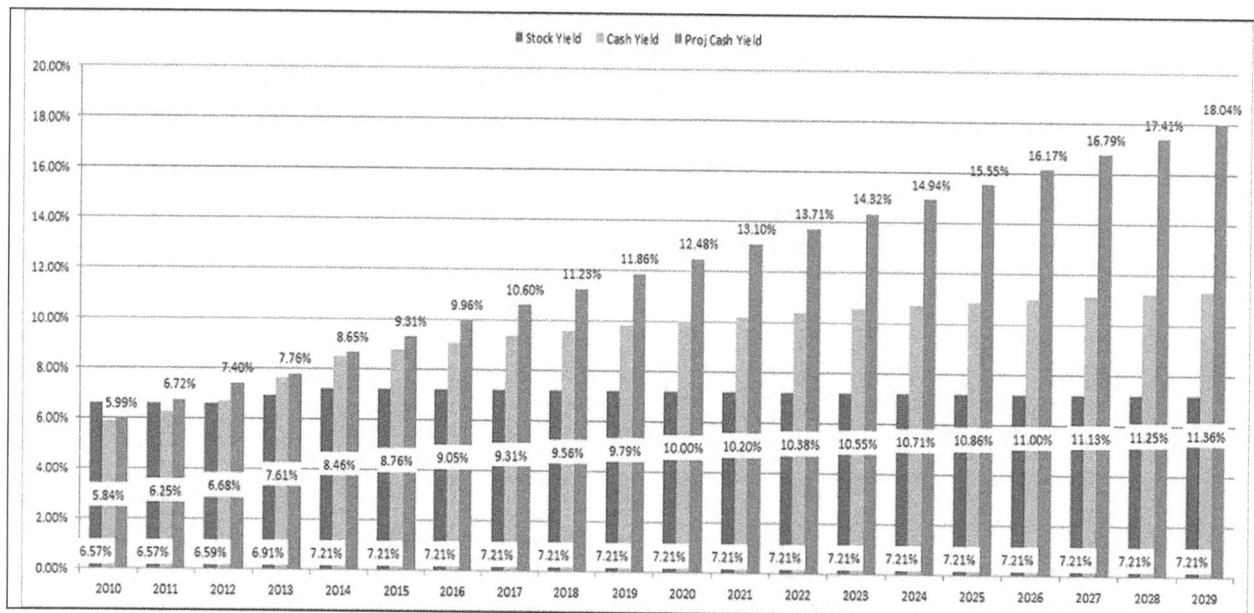

Legend: ■ Stock Yield ■ Cash Yield ■ Proj Cash Yield

Year	Stock Yield	Cash Yield	Proj Cash Yield
2010	6.57%	5.84%	5.99%
2011	6.57%	6.25%	6.72%
2012	6.59%	6.68%	7.40%
2013	6.91%	7.61%	7.76%
2014	7.21%	8.46%	8.65%
2015	7.21%	8.76%	9.31%
2016	7.21%	9.05%	9.96%
2017	7.21%	9.31%	10.60%
2018	7.21%	9.56%	11.23%
2019	7.21%	9.79%	11.86%
2020	7.21%	10.00%	12.48%
2021	7.21%	10.20%	13.10%
2022	7.21%	10.38%	13.71%
2023	7.21%	10.55%	14.32%
2024	7.21%	10.71%	14.94%
2025	7.21%	10.86%	15.55%
2026	7.21%	11.00%	16.17%
2027	7.21%	11.13%	16.79%
2028	7.21%	11.25%	17.41%
2029	7.21%	11.36%	18.04%

Easily View a Securities Five Year History with Simple "Copy and Paste"
Various Return Scenarios in a Single Chart Along with "Rule of 72" and "Break-Even"

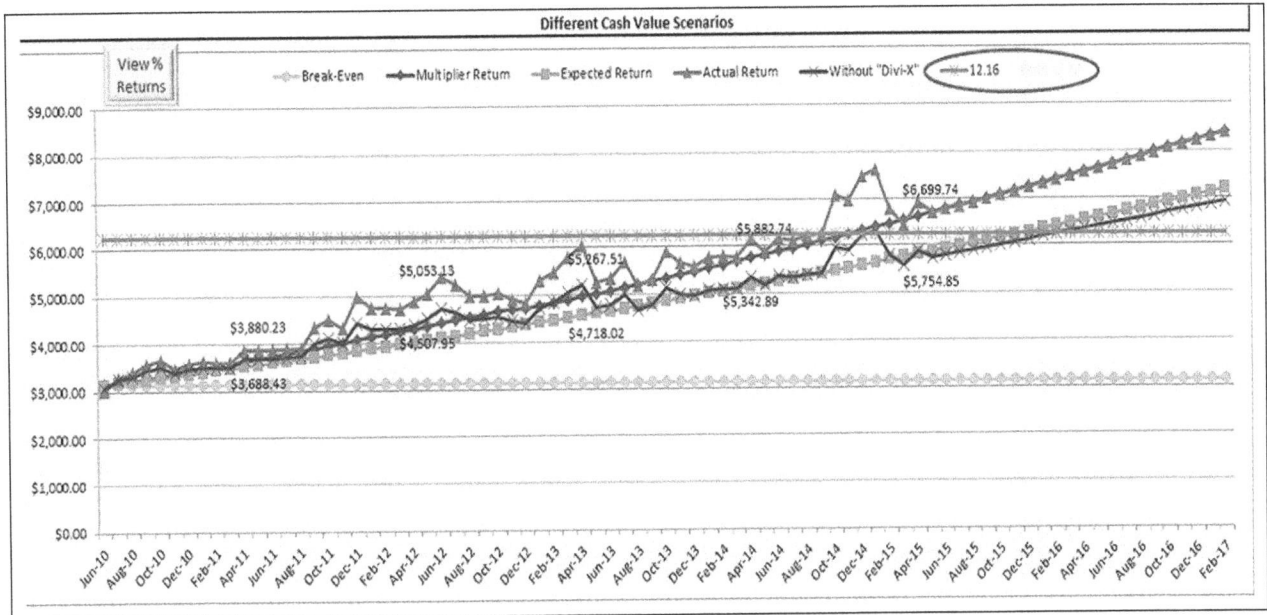

View Percentage Returns at Any Point in Time by Mousing Over any Data Point

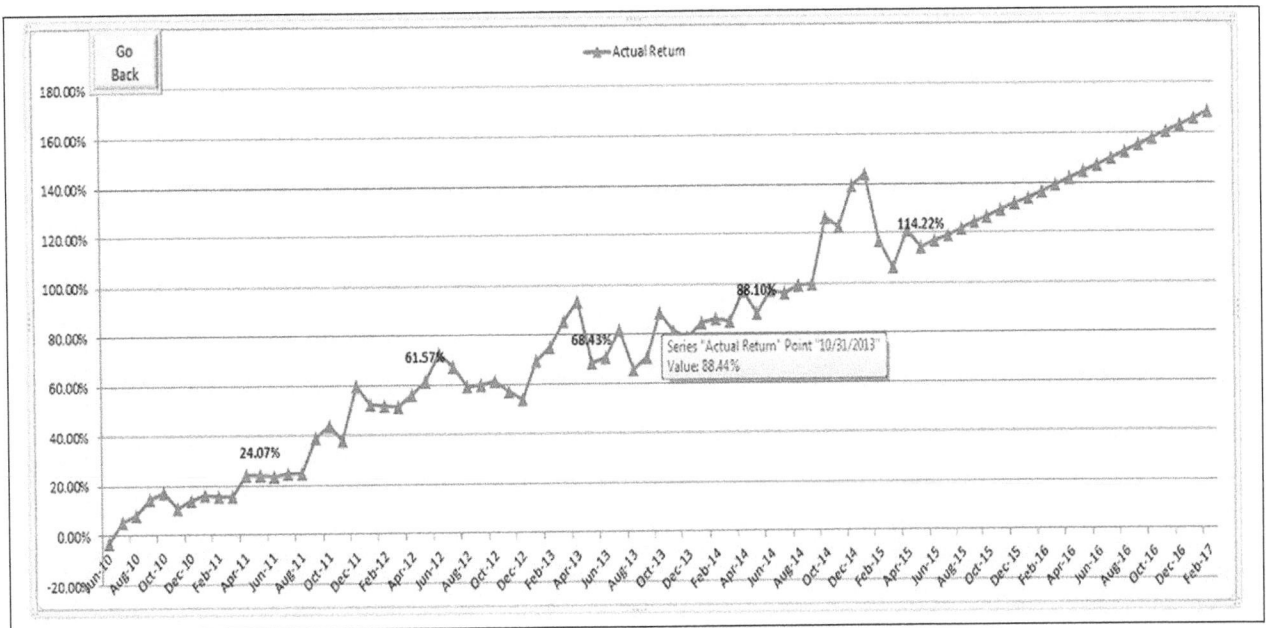

Other Useful Charts as Well

Running Leverage Rate, Share Price History, Life of Loan Stats, and More.